ITALIA
CON GUSTO
E AMORE

A road trip to the roots of Italian cuisine

Annette Canini-Daems

Lannoo

Valle
d'Aosta
268

Trentino-Alto
Adige
304

Friuli-Venezia
Giulia
312

Lombardia
280

Veneto
332

Piemonte
248

Emilia-Romagna
352

Liguria
230

Toscana
210

Le Marche
372

Il mar Adriatico

Umbria
190

Abruzzo
22

Lazio
168

Molise
40

Campania
150

Puglia
48

Basilicata
70

Sardegna
128

Il mar Tirreno

Calabria
88

Il mar Mediterraneo

Sicilia
108

Il mar Ionio

CONTENTS

GUIDE

This book starts by explaining the various **Italian eateries** where people go for a snack, a drink, or a full dining experience. This is followed by a brief explanation of the **European and Italian quality labels** that promote and protect the identity of foodstuffs and wines.

Annette begins her book with an exploration of her personal motivation and interpretation of her *journey of discovery* through a country that has elevated food and drink to an art form.

She starts each chapter with a **regional map** displaying the route she has taken and summarises the region's local *characteristics, products, peasant cooking traditions* and their origins.

Annette interviews inspiring *people* and records fascinating stories and anecdotes related to food and drink. And of course, everything must be tasted... Everything happens 'on the go'.

You will find **authentic recipes** from the countless personalities Annette meets along the way. Together, they make up a unique menu that embodies the heart of Italian *cucina povera.*

Focaccia di Bari

WEIGHTS FOR DRY INGREDIENTS

20g	¾ oz	300g	11oz
25g	1 oz	350g	12oz
40g	1½oz	400g	14oz
50g	2oz	450g	1lb
60g	2½oz	500g	1lb 2oz
75g	3oz	550g	1¼lb
100g	3½oz	600g	1lb 5oz
125g	4oz	650g	1lb 7oz
150g	5oz	700g	1lb 9oz
175g	6oz	750g	1lb 11oz
200g	7oz	800g	1¾lb
225g	8oz	900g	2lb
250g	9oz	1kg	2¼lb

LIQUID MEASURES

METRIC	IMPERIAL	US
25ml	1fl oz	
50ml	2fl oz	¼ cup
75ml	3fl oz	
100ml	3½fl oz	
120ml	4fl oz	½ cup
150ml	5fl oz	
175ml	6fl oz	¾ cup
200ml	7fl oz	
250ml	8fl oz	1 cup
300ml	10fl oz/½ pint	1¼ cups
400ml	14fl oz	
450ml	15fl oz	2 cups/1 pint
600ml	1 pint	2½ cups
750ml	1¼ pints	
900ml	1½ pints	
1 litre	1¾ pints	1 quart

OVEN TEMPERATURES

°C	°F	°C	°F
110	225	180	350
120	250	190	375
140	275	200	400
150	300	220	425
160	325	230	450
		240	475

Annette and Irene make seadas in Olmedo, Sardinia

The **addresses** of the various locations, eateries and producers Annette visits are marked throughout the chapters, such as the Antica Sciamadda on page 230.

A handy **overview of all the recipes** in this book, a **register of place names**, and a **glossary of culinary terms** serve as guidelines to help you find what you are looking for...

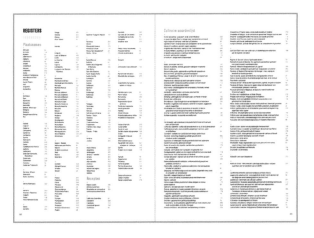

A sciamadda in Genoa

Osteria in Matera

ITALIAN EATERIES

A ristorante or restaurant is an eating establishment where you sit down to be served.

Rosticceria means 'grill'. This is where you order grilled or fried takeaway dishes.

Tavola calda means 'warm table'. This is a takeaway restaurant – often with seating – where you can order warm meals prepared fresh daily.

An osteria is an informal eatery where you can get simple yet delicious regional dishes at an affordable price.

You can also order local dishes at a trattoria, but the menu is slightly more extensive than at an osteria.

A real Italian pizzeria only has pizzas on the menu, but nowadays some of them also serve pasta and other dishes.

A fornaio or panificio is a bakery. Here you can find Italian bread as well as savoury baked goods such as focaccia and pizza.

A pasticceria is a patisserie that sells sweet pastries including, cakes, breakfast sweets and desserts.

A bar is an Italian coffee bar that serves different types of coffee, drinks, and small snacks.

Sandwich with a warm filling from a tavola calda in Rome

Rosticceria in Ascoli Piceno

FUD Bottega Sicula, a Sicilian shop and trendy restaurant in Milan's Navigli district

EUROPEAN AND ITALIAN FOOD QUALITY LABELS

Foodstuffs

DOP

The Denominazione d'Origine Protetta (DOP) or protected designation of origin (PDO) label is the most well-known and most commonly used acronym that is officially recognised and disseminated at a European level. This designation is awarded to foodstuffs and wines that ascribe their characteristic flavour to a specific geographical region. The DOP quality label is only awarded to food specialities in clearly defined regions that are produced and processed according to very specific regulations.

IGP

The Indicazione Geografica Protetta (IGP) or protected geographical indication (PGI) is the second acronym used at the European level. This label applies to foodstuffs and wines that are characteristic of a certain geographical area and are produced and/or processed and/or prepared there. In this case, a product may come from a different region or even from abroad, but the product must be processed in the region using specific techniques. There must be a link with the local terroir for at least one phase of the production, processing, or preparation process. Moreover, the product must enjoy a certain reputation before it is awarded this label.

STG

STG stands for Specialità Tradizionale Garantita, or traditional speciality guaranteed (TSG). This European acronym is the least closely tied to the product's origins. In fact, this label is only used for foodstuffs with traditional and quality characteristics that distinguishes them from other similar products. In Italy, this label only applies to mozzarella and the Neapolitan pizza, which are also produced in countries far beyond Italy but have the same characteristics.

De.Co.

De.Co. stands for Denominazione Comunale or municipal denomination. This certification is managed and awarded by the municipalities. De.Co. recognises the territoriality of a product and formalises its identifying characteristics.

PAT

PAT stands for Prodotto Agroalimentare Tradizionale, or traditional food product, and is a designation exclusively used in Italy to distinguish traditional and niche products. This quality label is awarded by the individual

Parmigiano Reggiano DOP

regions. This increases the value of local specialities that have been processed, stored, and seasoned according to local traditions throughout the region for at least 25 years. These foodstuffs are deeply rooted in the region where they're produced. A PAT designation does not have any regulatory function. Producers do not have to follow any particular regulations to mark their products with the PAT label.

Wine denominations

With changes in European legislation, the acronyms for food products have gradually begun to replace the DOC and IGT denominations for wines; however, sometimes they are still used. Currently, DOP, IGP and STG are used to distinguish high-quality wines.

DOC

This is the historical acronym for Denominazione di Origine Controllata or controlled designation of origin. It is the traditional quality label for high-quality wines produced in small or medium-sized geographical regions, with distinctive characteristics related to the grape variety, surroundings, and production methods. The first wines were awarded this designation in 1966, but this label has not been awarded since 2010. The label now falls under the DOP acronym, but its use as a specific traditional appellation is still permitted.

DOCG

Denominazione di Origine Controllata e Garantita or controlled and guaranteed designation of origin refers to DOC wines that have been recognised as such for at least five years, are of exceptional quality and are nationally and internationally renowned. Examples include: Aglianico del Vulture Superiore, Barbaresco, and Brunello di Montalcino. These wines are subject to stricter regulations. This quality label is now a part of the larger DOP family along with the DOC acronym.

IGT

IGT stands for Indicazione Geografica Tipica or typical geographical indication, the third acronym that was used in the winegrowing industry until 2010. This acronym has now been incorporated into the IGP label. The wines must contain at least 85 per cent grapes from the assigned geographical area to be eligible for the quality label.

Porchetta di Ariccia IGP

Altamura bread DOP

Grapes for the production of Sagrantino Montefalco DOCG

AN ITALIAN LOVE STORY

We were introduced to Annette by a mutual friend, and our connection was immediate. Our shared love for Italy, cuisine, and exploration solidified this bond. When Annette asked us to write an introduction to her book, we were deeply touched and enthusiastically accepted.

At first glance, our connection to Italy might seem elusive. Vanessa, born and raised in America, while Dries, a Belgian national, has lived in the United States for more than thirteen years. Our careers as a technology entrepreneur and an event planning consultant have given us a well-traveled life, experiencing diverse cultures, and offering us a global perspective. These opportunities ignited our wanderlust. No matter where our travels take us, Vanessa, a passionate food enthusiast, is intrigued by the local cuisines and enjoys bringing these flavors into our kitchen. Dries, an amateur photographer, captures Vanessa's cooking and our world travels with his camera, preserving these memories not only for us, but also our friends and family.

Currently, we find ourselves navigating life between two continents, yet our hearts often wander to the dream of retiring in Italy. Our love affair with Italy began many years ago and only grows with each trip. When visiting this beautiful country, we seek out unique destinations, veering off the beaten path to campsites, bed and breakfasts, agriturismo hotels, and occasionally, 5-star resorts. Our shared goal of living and eating like locals further emphasizes our commitment to understanding and embracing the culture of the places we explore. Asking for recommendations from locals adds to our travels, creating opportunities for meaningful connections and discoveries beyond what typical tourist experiences may offer.

Falling head over heels for Italy is easy thanks to its breathtaking landscapes—ranging from impressive mountain ranges to charming seaside villages with pastel-colored buildings that look like they're from a postcard. If Italy's natural beauty doesn't win your heart, then its delicious food definitely will. Here pizza, pasta, and gelato take center stage. However, the true magic lies in all of the recipes blending tradition, fresh ingredients, and culinary artistry. Every village tells a story not just through its food, but through a profound commitment to customs, culture, and upbringing—a balance we find deeply inspiring.

The Italian way of life feels refreshingly simple, exquisitely beautiful, and passionately romantic. It revolves around the art of slowing down. It's a lifestyle that encourages us to open our minds, open our senses and open our hearts to everyday moments in our lives and enjoy them fully. Through our experiences, we've come to understand that this, indeed, is the authentic Italian way. In the US, life moves at such a rapid pace, and many of us find ourselves constantly racing to meet the demands of each day. There's a prevailing notion that to live well, we must continually add more—more possessions, more activities, more noise, more entertainment, and so forth. However, this pursuit often leaves us feeling stressed and exhausted. The Italians, on the other hand, have a deep understanding of the value of slowing down. Tradition dictates that work pauses to allow for leisurely lunches with family and friends.

Choosing our wedding location became a fairytale decision for us when we set our hearts on Tuscany. Nestled in central Italy, Tuscany's allure lies in its perfect landscapes—rolling hills covered with vineyards and olive groves, creating a picturesque backdrop for our celebration of love. Beyond its scenic charm, Tuscany is a culinary haven. From the delicious homemade pastas with wild boar ragù to the iconic steak Florentine and the sweet finale of cantucci paired with vin santo, every bite is a celebration of tradition and flavor.

When in Italy, culinary adventures are high on our list. Authentic Italian cooking, to us, is a celebration of simplicity, wholesomeness, and true nourishment. Italians give priority to the finest seasonal ingredients sourced meticulously from fresh markets. This commitment results in dishes that are refined yet maintain a beautiful simplicity, allowing the quality of the ingredients

to shine through. The Italians also take immense pride in producing quality products, and openly share their craft with anyone interested. We've had the pleasure of encountering Italians from various walks of life—cheesemakers, leather artisans, olive oil and balsamic vinegar producers, wine producers and vignerons. We have been welcomed into their homes to enjoy a meal with them, to explore their workshops, and to touch the grapes in their vineyards. They have shared their stories with us, whether it be a family-owned business being passed down to them by generations before, or forging their own path for a more balanced life.

To truly understand the Italian lifestyle, the joy of slowing down and their traditions, we suggest going beyond the usual touristy spots. When visiting Italy, don't limit yourself to just the big cities, even though they are amazing on their own. Instead, venture into the countryside and discover the charm of its many small towns. It's these experiences that are etched in our memories. Back home in the US or Belgium, infusing the Italian lifestyle into our daily routine is a personal pursuit. Vanessa attempts to recreate cherished dishes from our travels, while Dries perfects his espresso-making skills and crafts Italian cocktails for our aperitivo moments. Beyond these culinary pursuits, we've embraced the deeper lessons Italy imparts: living well entails approaching life with enthusiasm and passion. It's about recognizing and appreciating the beauty of everyday life, turning ordinary moments into extraordinary adventures.

Annette's love for Italy resonates with us. In her travel book, she captures the essence of Italy beautifully, including authentic recipes handed down through generations to the cultural heritage of twenty regions in Italy. Allow yourself to daydream and wonder where your next adventure will take you!

Vanessa & Dries Buytaert

TOURING A COUNTRY WHERE FOOD AND DRINK ARE A WAY OF LIFE

Why did I decide to venture out on this odyssey? Because I'm curious by nature. Because I wanted to draw up a map of culinary Italy. Because I wanted to venture off the beaten path, taste all those amazing products, and immerse myself in their wondrous world and the stories behind them. *Italia con gusto e amore* is an account of my travels through twenty regions and encounters with people obsessed by their culinary heritage. Over the course of seven months, I travelled 23,000 kilometres in search of authentic, underappreciated local fare that you find on the streets and in homes around the country. Along the way, I recorded the countless stories of passionate Italians whose lives revolve around honest, delicious food!

Breathtaking coastlines, sun-drenched countryside, UNESCO World Heritage sites and cities serve as a stunning backdrop for my encounters. What a country! I was blown away by the rich mosaic of remote hillside towns, winding mountain roads, castles, cliffs, seas, and beaches. A different landscape awaited me every hundred kilometres. The journey from region to region was a joy in itself. The soil, the climate and the people changed, as did the panoramic views. Italy really does have it all! Or almost, because the Italians themselves think their politicians are corrupt, their democracy is vulnerable, and their economy and football team is constantly yo-yoing... But their cuisine is first-rate, and nothing can change that!

Food as an art form

There is no other place in the world where food gets taken this seriously. The Italians elevate food and drink to an art form; they are masters at creating irresistible gourmet feasts. Whether it's in family circles, in the local village or town, or during a celebration; there is always an occasion for enjoying traditional cuisine. What used to be considered *cucina povera*, or peasant cooking, is now a celebrated form of cultural heritage. The street food delicacies I sampled taught me much about a city or region's character and history. The recipes and the craftsmanship have been preserved and handed down from generation to generation. 'Con gusto e tanto amore!' or 'with flavour and lots of love!', the many heroes and heroines I met along the way would say with conviction.

Each region has its own history. Italian cuisine has been influenced by the many cultures that have passed through or ruled the regions over the centuries. The Greeks, Romans, Arabs, Byzantines, and Spaniards are only a few of the many cultures that contributed to a gastronomy that has held fast for centuries. Italy as a country didn't exist until the second half of the nineteenth century. Before unification, Italy was one giant puppet show of city-states, constantly at each other's throats. This diver-

Ciambotta from Basilicata

sity is reflected in the region's gastronomic landscape. Meals or dishes were sold and eaten out on the streets long before restaurants made their appearance. The local food culture was shaped by what was offered on the streets, and continues to be so today, from Milan to Palermo. But why is Italian food so delicious? Italians have excellent, sun-kissed ingredients at their disposal, but they also strictly adhere to rules that have been around for centuries. Wasting food is a crime, and you don't mess about with traditional local recipes. Entire generations as well as driven young entrepreneurs safeguard their traditional food culture. I didn't have to go looking for the *nonna* or grandmother because it's the son or granddaughter that is writing family history today.

Nothing goes to waste

Italians know how to transform trash into treasure. 'Non si butta via niente': 'We don't throw anything away!' This practice was born of poverty, yet also brought forth iconic dishes. Regional delicacies are still being made from leftover bread, pasta, meat, and vegetables. I collected recipes for dishes such as *acquacotta, panzanella, caviale dei poveri, pallotte cace e ove, sardine ripiene, panzerotto, zuppa crapiata, pane frattau, tarallo, frittata di maccheroni, polpette, canederli, malfatti* and *salsa al tartufo*.

Food is not wasted. The deep-rooted use of the *quinto quarto* or fifth quarter of the pig or cow is a prime example of this practice. This refers to everything that belongs to the animal but doesn't fall under the four main cuts of meat; the innards, legs and other edible leftover parts. Examples include iconic and relatively little-known regional street food dishes such as *lampredotto, crostino nero, pani 'cà meusa, piedino di maiale, stigghiola, frittola, morzello, 'o per e 'o muss* ...

Dishes with a story

Many unique traditional dishes are linked to a terroir. They are usually accompanied by fascinating stories shaped by events, family relationships or legends, told with great relish and the necessary gesturing. Read about *supplì, pinsa, piadina, sarde in saor, mondighili, zuppa pavese, chichetti, tegamaccio, focaccia barese, sformatino di zucca, 'o bror 'e purp, babà, bagna cauda, scripelle mbusse, caponata, ciambotta, arancini, gelato tartufo* and much more.

It was a joy to discover the countless regional differences and to find my way among the many dialects and exceptional foods.
Travel with me through a country where food is not a product; it's a way of life. Discover Marche, Abruzzo, Molise, Apulia, Basilicata, Calabria, Sicily, Sardinia, Campania, Lazio, Umbria, Tuscany, Liguria, Piedmont, the Aosta Valley, Lombardy, Trentino-Alto Adige, Friuli-Venezia Giulia, Veneto and Emilia-Romagna.

Prepare to be delighted and discover the vast richness of Italy's culinary landscape. Italy is so much more than just pasta!

Annette

Castelmuzio in Tuscany

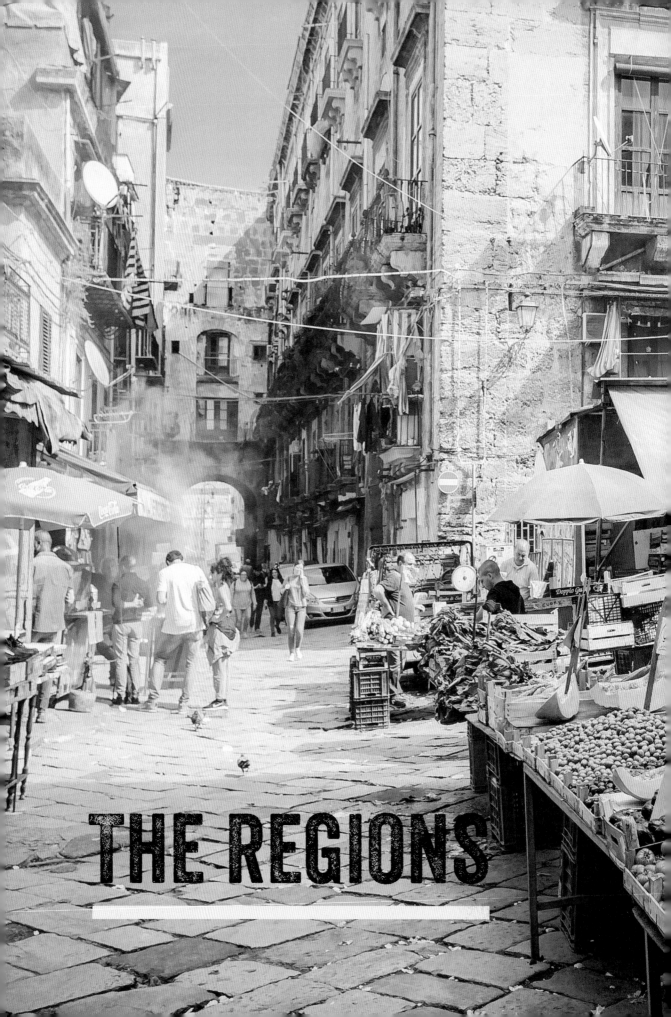

THE REGIONS

Markt in Palermo

ABRUZZO

Abruzzo is located in central Italy and it stretches from the heart of the Apennines to the Adriatic Sea. The border is marked by the Marche region to the north, Lazio to the west, and Molise to the south. The regional capital is L'Aquila. The landscape in this greenest part of Italy is mostly mountainous and rugged. You will find ski and winter sports resorts dotted around the pristine mountain peaks in places such as Pescasseroli, Rivisondoli, Pescocostanzo and Roccaraso.

The route linking the Gran Sasso to the seashore passes through areas that are not only rich in history and culture, but breathtaking in their natural splendour as well. The journey takes you through narrow valleys and down impressive hiking trails that meander through the mountains and hills. The Aterno Valley in the province of L'Aquila is home to many beautiful traditional villages. Equally impressive are the Parco Nazionale nature reserves, which protect the local plant and animal species that thrive in the region, including golden eagles, wolves, and brown bears.

The Adriatic coast boasts a stunning shoreline with wide, sandy beaches in the north and pebble beaches in the south, including Spiaggia del Turchino, Spiaggia di Pescara, Spiaggia di Cologna and Roseto degli Abruzzi.

Man on the beach at Pescara

Teramo **1**

Tordino

Vomano

Lago di
Campotosto

Pescara **2**

3
Costa dei
Trabocchi

l'Aquila

Aterno

Pescara

Navelli **4**

Sangro

Parco Nazionale
del Gran Sasso, Abruzzo

Pescocostanzo **5**

Sangro

La Cantina di Porta Romana

TERAMO ①

My search for Abruzzo's culinary traditions begins in Teramo. I visit Marcello Schillaci from La Cantina di Porta Romana in the town centre. It is a type of *cantina* or wine cellar where food and drink is served all day, every day; a tradition that the owner has continued. In the past, the food that was cooked here included products brought in by people passing through the town. They were the shepherds, hunters, travellers, and farmers on their way to the market square 150 metres down the road. That's where the goods were exchanged. The cellar has been used in this way since the beginning of the previous century. The building itself dates from the year 500. Teramo was the first stop for shepherds during the *transumanza*: the migration of shepherds and their sheep from the mountains of Abruzzo to the Apulian Plain and back.

THE SMELLS, SENSATIONS, AND TASTES OF ABRUZZO

'Of all the Italian regions, Abruzzo is probably the region that has made the most effort to keep its culinary traditions alive,' explains Lidia Sabato, my hostess and owner of the Le Torri hotel in Pescocostanzo. 'This region has best preserved its characteristic products, traditions, rituals and magic.' Lidia has seen and experienced much of Italy during her career. She is convinced that the country's ancient soul resonates most clearly in this region. 'This is the result of the rugged mountains that cut the land off from the outside world. Even the construction of highways and improved communications couldn't drag the region out of its culinary isolation. The dishes in Abruzzo are based on cheap ingredients. For centuries, the region was barely able to make ends meet in economic terms. Neither the farmers in the high Apennines, nor the shepherds and their livestock, provided prosperity. There were no large family estates, no castles with sumptuous banquets, no courtly traditions. So, it comes as no surprise that books about Italian cuisine seldom dwell on Abruzzo's contribution. 'This is also true of the Molise region,' Lidia explains.

Transumanza

These migrations were reintroduced in 1447 when Alfonso of Aragon professionalised shepherding in Foggia (Apulia), thus establishing a livestock industry based on wool. The entire mountain pass was reserved for shepherds. The Duke of Aragon commissioned an extensive network of sheep paths, some of which were no fewer than sixty Neapolitan steps, or 111 metres, wide. The cyclical migration of herders and their sheep started in the autumn with a symbolic ritual on 29 September during the Feast of Saint Michael and All Angels, Saint Michael being the patron saint of the shepherds. Their return to the mountains of Abruzzo aligned with the beginning of the summer.

The harsh winters in the mountains of Abruzzo and the scorching summers on the plains forced the shepherds to migrate with the seasons from Abruzzo via Molise to Apulia. Sheep were always led to the most suitable places to graze so they could produce plenty of high-quality wool, milk, and meat. The shepherds travelled over the sheep paths for 15 to 20 days before reaching their destination. They led a life of sacrifice because they were separated from their families during the long winters and the summer months. Sadly, the traditional transumanza no longer exists today. The sheep are now transported to Apulia by truck over the course of a day.

Scrippelle 'mbusse

I ask Marcello to make me scrippelle 'mbusse, a type of crêpes dipped in broth. Marcello: 'As soon as the weather starts to turn cold, you'll find this dish in every home in Teramo. Crêpes dipped in broth are part of Teramo's culinary tradition. The *crespelle* (the standard Italian word for crêpes) are made from water, flour, and eggs, filled with grated cheese, and then rolled up and served in hot meat broth. And that last step is where the magic happens! The broth soaks into the crêpes, softening them and melting the cheese, so you end up with a really tasty treat. The ideal broth for scrippelle 'mbusse is chicken broth.'

⭐ Stroke of luck

'According to legend, this dish originated in the early part of the twentieth century following a rather clumsy and ordinary mistake,' Marcello continues. 'Enrico Castorani, assistant cook at the French officer's mess in Teramo, made crêpes instead of bread. One night, Enrico was just about to serve dinner when he accidentally dropped the crêpes into a steaming kettle of broth. To cover up for his mistake, Castorani decided to serve the soggy crêpes as a first course. Mistake or not, it has been an excellent Teramo culinary tradition for over a century.'

Marcello serves a deep plate filled with scrippelle and spoons a ladleful of hot broth over the top. As I take a bite of the scrippelle, Marcello tells me that preparing delicious, quality food takes time and hard work. 'That's why our grandparents started in the morning. Long cooking times and plenty of fresh herbs are the secret to good cooking. That also applies to working with offal; the alchemy of cooking organ meats slowly and over low heat transforms unsavoury smells into pleasant flavours and aromas. The ingredients soften in the pot and balance each other out. That's slow food.'

And he is absolutely right: the scrippelle taste surprisingly refined, and the broth makes a perfect accompaniment. Delicious!

La Cantina di Porta Romana
Corso Porta Romana 105, Teramo

MARCELLO'S RECIPE
Scrippelle 'mbusse

FOR THE BROTH
1 chicken
2 stalks celery
1 onion
1 carrot
1 potato
a sprig of parsley
salt and pepper

FOR THE CREPES
4 eggs
8 tablespoons flour
4 eggshells of water
salt
grated Parmesan
or pecorino cheese

BROTH Put the chicken in its entirety or in pieces in a large pot and add the celery, carrots, onion, and peeled potato. Submerge everything in cold water. Simmer the mixture for about an hour over low heat. Strain the broth until you only have the liquid left. Check and make sure the broth is properly seasoned with salt and pepper.

CREPES Combine the eggs, the flour and the salt in a bowl and add four eggshells of water (the recipe calls for one egg per person + two tablespoons flour + an eggshell of water + salt). Combine the ingredients thoroughly with a whisk to prevent lumps from forming. Season with salt to taste and leave the batter to rest for about 30 minutes. Stir the batter one more time. Heat a non-stick pan, grease the pan with a bit of oil or fat and spoon half a soup ladle of batter into the pan; swirl the pan around immediately to evenly spread out the crêpe batter. As soon as the batter no longer sticks to the pan, carefully turn the crepe over and cook the other side. Repeat this with the other crepes until you run out of batter. Arrange the crêpes on a plate. Sprinkle a bit of grated cheese on each crêpe and roll them up tightly. Arrange the rolled-up scrippelle on plates and pour a ladleful of hot broth over them just before serving. Serve everything warm.

Scripelle 'mbusse

PESCARA ②

From Teramo, I drive 65 km to the city of Pescara. The city is located where the Pescara River meets the Adriatic Sea. Pescara's history is marked by plenty of fighting, and much of the city was destroyed during the Second World War. Pescara is now a seaside resort and popular tourist destination. The unbroken expanse of its fine, sandy beaches extends for over 20 kilometres along the coastline.

Arrosticini

Along the road that runs parallel to the beach, I meet Alessandro Zaccharo at a roadside stand named Cuccitella. His food truck is located close to the fish market, or *mercato ittico*, but I haven't come to see him about fish. It's mutton I'm interested in. Because throughout Abruzzo, *arrosticini* is the one dish that you should serve when you have guests coming to visit. It's the embodiment of Abruzzo's heritage that you encounter everywhere, from the mountains to the seaside.

Meat for the shepherds

This mutton on a stick owes its origins to two provinces: Pescara and Teramo. It is believed that the shepherds who migrated between the mountains and the valleys invented arrosticini. Today, you will find arrosticini being served throughout the region, including in the provinces of Chieti and L'Aquila. Traditionally, only mutton from castrated rams, or wethers, was used for arrosticini. Wethers were only used for wool, and those *castrati* that died along the way were eaten, for both practical reasons and to keep the hunger at bay during the long journey. The mutton was chopped up into tiny pieces and skewered on a stick. What makes *arrosticini Abruzzese* unique is that in addition to the meat, pieces of fat are also put onto the skewers. And it's that fat which gives this dish the special, unique flavour that has become famous across the globe.

Searing over the embers

For Alessandro, there is only one possible method for preparing arrosticini: on the barbecue. 'Solo sulla fornacella!' or only on the barbecue. 'Preparing this in a pan is just wrong. That's like drinking expensive wine from a paper cup,' he says sharply.

We're standing next to a long, narrow barbecue. He shows me how he sears the meat over the glowing embers of charcoal and wood. The crackling of fat on the embers and the smell of cooking meat makes my mouth water in anticipation. He turns the skewers once more. The meat is now a lovely golden brown. Alessandro tells me that you don't add salt until the very end as he liberally salts the meat on the skewers.

 Nostalgia on a stick

'Arrosticini are served like a bouquet of flowers,' he continues. 'They should strictly be eaten with your hands, pulling the meat from the skewer with your teeth. In Abruzzo, this is the only way to serve them, as arrosticini bouquets wrapped in a sheet of paper or placed in special containers in the centre of the table.

Arrosticini

They should be served for dinner, not lunch. We eat the meat in its purest form, accompanied by nothing more than toasted bread and olive oil. Nowadays, it doesn't matter whether the mutton comes from male or female sheep; we eat everything.'

'And we also get some of our mutton from France these days,' Alessandro confesses. 'In Abruzzo, we eat more mutton than anywhere else in Europe, because we use the meat to make arrosticini.'

I can taste for myself why arrosticini are such a favourite. I sit down at a wooden table next to his food truck with an arrosticini bouquet and a plate with toasted bread and olive oil. And as I eat this, I imagine the context that Alessandro has so eloquently described to me. 'You're sitting somewhere in a quiet field in the hills of Abruzzo. You hear a babbling brook in the distance, and your faithful dog is by your side. You eat the freshly roasted meat while some of the skewers are still crackling away on an improvised barbecue. You smell the fresh air and the scent of roasted meat. That's how the shepherds used to eat their arrosticini, and that's the best way,' Alessandro says wistfully. He had the privilege of experiencing this scenario as a child.

I actually don't like mutton, and I certainly don't like the idea of fat on a stick. But this tastes divine. Caught in the moment... or perhaps not?

SHOP
At Claudio's

I have arranged to meet Claudio Minicucci at Alla Chitarra Antica in Pescara's city centre. The shop features fantastic local ingredients, typical Abruzzo dishes, but also homemade pastries that you can eat there or take away. But just as memorable is meeting the flamboyant owner, Claudio. Everyone who enters his shop, regulars and passers-by alike, are treated like family. I sit on the patio outside the shop and watch Claudio walk in and out. He talks to everyone who walks past the shop. I am instantly fascinated by his generous good humour and his expressive gestures. Starting an interview with this passionate man who can't sit still is proving to be harder than I thought. But then, I pluck at his heart strings with my mention of the word 'family'. 'That's right, we're a family business. Just like the mafia, eh?' It's the first answer I've been able to get out of him during the interview.

Newspaper article about Claudio's parents and Alla Chitarra Antica

Remembering his roots

'My parents, Pina d'Alonzo and Giovanni Minicucci, met each other in Belgium at the Boch ceramics factory in Walloon province, where they both worked. They had emigrated with their respective families to Belgium, but their dream was to one day return to Abruzzo. In 1966, my mother first set foot in this delicatessen, which she took over shortly thereafter with my father. And that's how the family business started. My parents have fuelled my passion. They taught me to hold on to traditions and respect the products from my region and country. It's a challenge to make traditional products interesting for the younger generations. That's why we experiment every day. Traditional recipes are preserved here, such as the *fiadoni*, hearty pastries filled with cheese; or lemon ravioli; or *pasta alla chitarra*; or *timballo alla teramana*, a pie made from scrippelle, the well-known local crepes, with layers of meat ragout, spinach, eggs, and cheese. And then we have the famous *pallotte cace e ove*.'

And as Claudio tells me about his many dishes, plates with tiny morsels of food pile up in front of me. I must see and try everything. Claudio constantly walks back and forth between the shop and my table. When he notices that I can't keep up, he has everything packed up so I can take it home with me. Thank god. Meanwhile, the *capo della polizia*, or the chief of the Abruzzo police, comes to stand at our table. 'He is a very important person and that's why he's my friend,' Claudio jokes. They start up a conversation about Belgian beer and Trappist beer. Claudio tells us how the beer always grabs him by the throat whenever he drinks it: 'So strong!' He promises the chief of police a couple of bottles of Trappist beer when his family comes to visit from Belgium.

Pallotte cace e ove

This is an immensely popular dish in Abruzzo and Molise. Today it is one of the most popular snacks served during celebrations and events. Pallotte cace e ove are ball-shaped croquettes made from pecorino cheese, eggs, and bread, smothered in a tasty tomato sauce.

⭐ A monument to farmhouse cooking

It was during the Second World War, when houses and farms in the countryside were often plundered, that the locals started to hide cheese, eggs and bread under their floorboards or behind brick walls. With these ingredients, they made a true delicacy, and they continued to do so after the war. Not to survive, but because people's needs suddenly changed: farmers and workers needed a quick, hearty, and tasty meal as a pick-me-up during or after a hard day's work.

Pasta alla chitarra

'Let's move on to a quintessential Abruzzese dish, spaghetti alla chitarra,' Claudio continues. 'The name is derived from the tool traditionally used to make spaghetti, the *chitarra* or *maccarunare* in the Abruzzese dialect, which gives the spaghetti its unmistakable form and texture. This tool is made up of a rectangular wooden frame strung with steel wires reminiscent of the strings on a guitar. By laying the dough on top of this frame and rolling a rolling pin over it, you end up with a coarse, square spaghetti. My mamma was famous for her spaghetti alla chitarra, a tradition we started.' He proudly shows me the authentic frame with which the business started out. 'You'll find that many families in Abruzzo have a similar chitarra frame,' Claudio says.

Spaghetti alla chitarra is traditionally served in the region with a hearty sauce based on mutton, beef or pork or with meatballs: the pasta's porosity is perfect for soaking up the rich, hearty sauces. In less traditional recipes, sauces based on game such as hare or boar meat are used.

Alla Chitarra Antica
Via Sulmona 2, Pescara

THE SUN MAKES PEOPLE BEAUTIFUL

Before I leave, Claudio asks me what my next destination will be, and I answer that I'm heading south. 'The further south you go, the happier the people become. The sun makes the people beautiful.' And with those wise words, I take my leave of Claudio. I leave with a giant bag stuffed with food in my hands. What a fine man, what a delightful shop, and such incredibly delicious food here in Abruzzo!

Claudio in front of his shop in Pescara

Pallotte cace e ove

SERVES 4 PEOPLE

200 g herbed pecorino cheese
150 g homemade breadcrumbs
 or leftover pieces of bread
2 eggs
1 tablespoon chopped parsley
500 g ripe tomatoes
1 small onion – salt to taste
1 bunch basil
1 clove garlic
oil to taste
extra breadcrumbs, optional

FOR THE SAUCE

Finely chop the onion and sauté in a couple of tablespoonfuls of olive oil. Add the washed, peeled and diced tomatoes and a couple of basil leaves. Season to taste with salt and simmer for 20 minutes. If the sauce gets too thick, add a couple of tablespoons of hot water.

FOR THE CROQUETTES OR PALLOTTE

Combine the eggs, the grated cheese, the leftover bread that has been soaked in water and pressed dry (make sure the bread is dry), the garlic and the finely chopped parsley. Knead the mixture to thoroughly combine the ingredients and shape into balls in whatever size you want. You can always add more breadcrumbs to the mixture if it is too soft to shape into balls. Heat a generous layer of frying oil in a pan or saucepan with raised sides and, once the oil has reached a temperature of 170 degrees Celsius, fry the croquettes until they are nice and golden brown. Drain the croquettes on kitchen paper and set aside to let them rest.

Place the warm cheese croquettes in a deep dish and pour the tomato sauce over them.

COSTA DEI TRABOCCHI ③

I drive 50 kilometres south from Pescara to the Trabocchi Coast, or Costa dei Trabocchi. I park my car in San Vito Chietino and continue my journey by bike. This stretch of coastline with hidden pebble beaches, rocky shores and steep cliffs is ideally suited for bike exploration. The famous Costa dei Trabocchi stretches from Francavilla to San Salvo and boasts 32 *trabocchi* (a type of traditional fishing platform) spread out over eight municipalities. And on about 15 of them, you can eat fresh fish on the platform. Bicycle rental facilities are available at various locations along the cycling route.

My cycling journey starts a little further down the route at San Vito Chietino, where I immediately spot the impressive trabocchi. You will come across one every 500 metres or so along the path. I cycle along the coast, enjoying this unique panorama and manoeuvring through several tunnels. After five kilometres, I reach Rinaldo Verì's Trabocco Punta Tufano in Rocca San Giovanni. I cross a wooden walkway over the sea and enter one of the most beautiful trabocchi I have seen so far. The freshly caught fish here goes straight from the sea to your plate. And they organise tours for tourists wishing to learn more.

Colossal spiders

Since childhood, Rinaldo has been fascinated with these 'colossal spiders', as the Italian poet and writer Gabriele D'Annunzio called them. 'Trabocchi are strange, complex fishing machines on wooden poles supported by a web of cables and planks,' he continues. 'They stand perched on primitive piers driven into the sea floor or the rocks. They are connected to the nearby coast by narrow walkways. The fish are caught using nets guided from the platforms through a system of pulleys and ropes.'

FLOATING BEYOND THE ROCKY SHORES

I notice that the trabocchi largely owe their charm to their location. Rinaldo explains that in most cases, the trabocchi are attached to rocky outcroppings where the coastline juts into the sea. 'The water is deep at these points and allows us to fish in the currents that flow past the rocky coastline.'

'The technique used for fishing is similarly fascinating,' he continues. 'We lower the large nets into the sea using a pulley system attached to the centre of the platform. From time to time, we raise the nets slightly above sea level. We catch flathead grey mullet, seabass, Atlantic wolffish, and blue fish species. The fish remain caught in the sturdy net until we draw them onto the platform. We serve the freshly caught fish directly to our restaurant's guests.'

Costa dei Trabocchi

Trabocco Punta Tufano

Brodetto

BIKE TO COAST

After a period of neglect and infrequent use, the trabocchi are back in the spotlight. A touristic cycle route named 'Bike to Coast' was established along Abruzzo's coast. It starts in Francavilla al Mare (Chieti) and continues southwards. This Via Verde della Costa dei Trabocchi, or Green Road along the Trabocchi Coast, has been in use since 2017.

www.costadeitrabocchi.net

⭐ Monumental wooden arms

'The earliest documented records on the existence of trabocchi date from the eighteenth century,' Rinaldo continues. 'Abruzzese fishermen were looking for a fishing technique that wasn't susceptible to changing weather conditions and the capricious sea. The trabocchi made fishing possible without having to go out to sea. We lower the nets into the sea using a system of monumental wooden arms. It has proven to be a wonderfully ingenious system.'

Trabocco Punta Tufano
16 Adriatica, km 483, Rocca San Giovanni

MARINA DI SAN VITO

I cycle all the way back to San Vito Chietino, where I am expected at Trabocco San Giacomo at the end of the pier. I take the wooden stairs up to a platform where the sea surrounds me on all sides. I have to say it's a unique experience. This trabocco is owned by Wilma Mancini. The interior is cosy with a maritime ambience; fish is the only thing on the menu. Wilma serves me an 'aperfish' (a concept she came up with herself that is a combination of 'aperitivo' and 'fish'): a glass of white wine and fish with oil and vinegar. The aperfish is followed by a brodetto (fish stew) with seabass, fresh datterini tomatoes, Taggiasca olives, capers, basil, and other fresh herbs.

⭐ Divine dessert

Wilma also serves me a selection of typical Abruzzese desserts. There are *Tarallucci Abruzzesi al vino*, homemade biscuits filled with a paste made from *Trebbiano d'Abruzzo*, a white wine, or *Montepulciano d'Abruzzo*, a red wine. She has also prepared *bocconnotto*, shortcrust pastries filled with almonds, chocolate, cinnamon, and nutmeg.

And to accompany these divine pastries, I am served a *caffè del marinaio* or sailor's coffee. Sailors used this drink to keep them warm and get them through the night while fishing. The coffee contains *anisetta*, or anise-flavoured liqueur, rum and Borghetti coffee liqueur. The coffee is strong, not too sweet, and the blend of all these flavours gives it a heady kick. Another discovery to add to my list!

Trabocco San Giacomo
Marina di San Vito Chietino

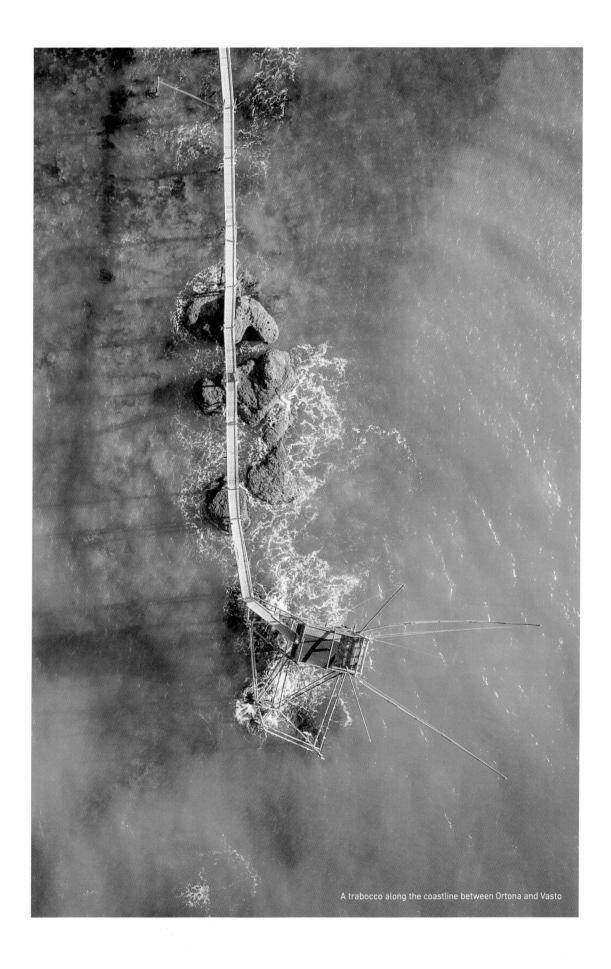

A trabocco along the coastline between Ortona and Vasto

NAVELLI – L'AQUILA ④

My journey continues from the seashore into the mountains, towards L'Aquila. I detour along the Gran Sasso massif, home to one of Italy's most beautiful panoramic routes. This picturesque route is surrounded by breathtaking natural scenery. The higher the elevation, the vaster and more endless the landscape becomes. This trip – literally and figuratively – lasts until I reach the Navelli Plateau. I see the occasional village or town clinging to the hills along the way. As I approach the city of L'Aquila, I see more and more construction cranes towering above the villages, visual reminders of the 2009 earthquake.

Red gold

I have driven out here because I want to learn more about a unique spice that is only produced here, on the Navelli Plateau in the Province of L'Aquila. This saffron has been dubbed 'red gold' and comes from purple flowers with six petals and three long, deep-red stigmas. I have arranged to meet with Dina Paoletti in Navelli. Dina is the niece of the owner of the 'Lo Zafferano dell'Aquila DOP'

cooperative. DOP stands for *Denominazione d'Origine Protetta* meaning only products from a designated place of origin are allowed to bear the label. She is responsible for the consortium's sales and administration of Navelli saffron.

FLOWER BULBS IN A WALKING STICK

'The saffron actually originated from the island of Crete and was introduced to Italy via Spain in the thirteenth century by a monk, Santucci of Navelli, who secretly brought a few of the flower bulbs with him upon his return from Toledo,' Dina says. 'He thought the flowers were so beautiful that he hid a couple of bulbs in his hollow walking stick. And that's how the flowers came to be grown here. The production soon spread throughout the area because the bulbs had found the perfect conditions to grow and flourish. Two winds prevail and cross here on the plateau: one from the Gran Sasso massif and the other from the Maiella massif. These winds are necessary for our saffron production,' Dina explains.

Zafferano dell'Aquila

Charlatans

From the 1960s onwards, saffron began to be imported in large quantities from countries such as Morocco, Spain and Tunisia. As a result, local saffron producers were no longer getting a fair price from their wholesalers. Dina: 'My uncle decided to go to Milan personally to sell his product there. But it wasn't an immediate success. In Milan, they were used to yellow saffron, while the saffron from Aquila has a deep red colour. They didn't want our saffron, and my uncle was treated like a charlatan because they believed he was selling a lower-quality product. He then came up with a plan to make a risotto using his saffron at a local Milanese restaurant and have the most important buyers taste the risotto. Only then did the Milanese realise that our saffron was in a class of its own, and from that moment onwards, my uncle was able to sell his saffron at three times the value of the yellow saffron. Upon his return, the producers joined forces to form a cooperative. They would market their product together and share the profits.'

'The difference in quality when compared to other saffron types is significant,' Dina says. 'They also produce saffron in regions like Sardinia, Tuscany, and Lombardy, but L'Aquila saffron is unique. Not only because of its burgundy-red colour, but our saffron is less sweet, almost bitter. Navelli saffron gained national fame in 2005 when it was awarded DOP status.'

Saffron harvesting

'The flower bulbs need to be replanted in new ground every year,' Dina continues. 'That's why the bulbs are dug up every August and replanted on a different section of land. The characteristic purple flowers appear in the autumn. The saffron is harvested during the flowering season between late October and early November. Different flowers open on different days, never at the same time. The open flowers are picked at dawn and placed in reed baskets. The *sfioratura* involves separating the stigmas, the red filaments that form the saffron, from the stamen and the flower. They are then dried in a sieve over charcoal. It is very precise and labour-intensive work,' Dina explains.

www.zafferanoaltopianonavelli.it

Zafferano dell'Aquila flowers

The stigmas are removed from the flowers

DISHES

There are countless dishes in which this delicacy can be incorporated. Dishes such as *risotto allo zafferano* (saffron risotto), *penne alla mimosa* (penne pasta with vegetables and saffron), and *crocchette gialle* (potato croquettes with Parmesan cheese and saffron). Bread with a tiny bit of saffron incorporated into the dough is also baked here.

Saffron is also a delicious addition to a mousse made from fresh sheep's milk ricotta and coated with a sprinkling of confectioner's sugar and garnished with a couple of saffron threads.

PESCOCOSTANZO ⑤

My idyllic journey through the hills and mountains of L'Aquila continues some 120 kilometres southwards, all the way to Pescocostanzo. This village is a popular point of departure for excursions, including trips on horseback. In the winter, it's the perfect destination for winter sports enthusiasts.

I have been invited here by Lidia Sabato from the Le Torri Hotel to meet her one-of-a-kind chef, Antonio Perna, who runs the Il Gallo di Pietra restaurant at the hotel.

⭐ Chef to the stars

Antonio and I sit in one of the several distinctive dining halls that grace the historic former home of an Italian noble family, the *Antica casa del Barone Grilli.* 'I have been working here for about eight years,' Antonio starts our interview. 'In my previous job, I always had to be available to cook for the major stars that would visit the island of Capri. I have cooked for celebrities such as Whitney Houston, Mariah Carey, Billy Joel, Beyoncé, Justin Timberlake, Lady Gaga and Arabian princes and sheikhs. I was dubbed *lo chef delle celebrità*, or chef to the stars.'

The scent of cooking

'In traditional Abruzzese cuisine, you work with ingredients from the mountains. I have a passion for herbs, scents, and flowers. I cook with my nose; it's how I like to create unique dishes. For me, it has something melancholic and nostalgic. It brings me back to those days long ago when my mother used to cook for us. I could smell her cooking outside from far away because those moments were unique. We were very poor back then. So whenever my mother used to say: *"Farò un buon ragù "*, or I'll make a delicious meat sauce, that was cause for celebration!'

'I haven't only chosen this profession because of my passion,' Antonio continues, 'but also because I was often hungry during my childhood. I was the third eldest of ten children and started working at a very young age. I was allowed to take leftovers from the restaurant home with me for my brothers and sisters. I didn't start studying to become a chef until after my first few jobs.' In other words, from poverty to the wealthiest stars on Earth, I conclude.

Aglio rosso di Sulmona

We start with a plateful of bruschetta drizzled with olive oil that Antonio has scented with *Aglio Rosso di Sulmona.* I immediately smell the flavourful aroma. And when I take a bite of the crunchy bruschetta, I notice a pleasant, refined, garlicky flavour that has perfectly infused into the olive oil. It tastes exceptional.

'This is the only garlic in the world with an IGP or *indicazione geografica protetta* (protected geographical indication) designation, and it's red,' Antonio explains. 'The garlic is solely produced in Sulmona in the province of L'Aquila. I leave the garlic to steep overnight or longer in extra virgin olive oil in a sealed jar. I use the resulting perfumed oil to coat my bruschetta and as a base for my tomato sauces. This garlic also has medicinal properties to alleviate backache and infections. People grow old here in the mountains. As an outsider, you tend to notice these things. I thought: the life and the food here must be very good,' he says with a wink.

Aglio rosso di Sulmona

Golden risotto

Antonio serves a risotto *allo zafferano di Navelli* as a primo, or first
course, introducing me to this unique saffron variety. The first thing
I notice when he places the risotto
in front of me is the colour. This risotto has a golden hue. A beautiful
and unique sight. And the flavour
is indeed different: more robust
and slightly more bitter, but with a
very light sweet aftertaste.

Salsiccia

'Salsiccia is a typical dish of the
region,' Antonio tells me. 'The sausage is a traditional product that
you find throughout central Italy
and which stems from artisanal
farming traditions. In Umbria,
they add garlic; in Tuscany, they
use fennel. Here, the minced meat
is seasoned with just salt and
pepper. The salsiccia in Abruzzo
is very simple but is often used
in combination with scamorza
cheese. The sausage is cut lengthways, and at the end of the grilling
process, slices of scamorza are
draped over the meat and melted. Scamorza is a local, semi-soft
cheese in the shape of a pear. It
is similar to mozzarella, but with
much more flavour.'

Hotel Le Torri
Ristorante Il Gallo di Pietra
Via del Vallone 4, Pescocostanzo

Pescocostanzo

MOLISE

Molise is a mountainous region in southern Italy with a coastline that borders the Adriatic Sea. The area used to be a part of Abruzzo until 1963. However, the separation wasn't official until 1970, making Molise the youngest region in Italy. It's also probably the least well-known region. Molise residents sometimes scoff: 'Molise non esiste,' or Molise doesn't exist. Unknown means unloved. But you'll be surprised how much beauty you find along the way. This mysterious region harbours countless treasures with its natural surroundings, history, centuries-old traditions and delicious food.

Colli Al Volturno

Agnone

Verrino ❶

Volturno

Vandra

Chiaro

Cavaliere

❷ Isernia

S. Bartolomeo

Volturno

Lorda

Trigono

Rio

Calderari

Quirino

Tammaro

Sinorca

Biferno

Lago di
Guardialfiera

Cigno

Sapestra

Tona

Sacione

Cigno

Biferno

Campobasso

Tappino

Fortore

Lago di
Occhito

Fortore

Isernia's old town

Beer with the striking label 'Il Molise non esiste'

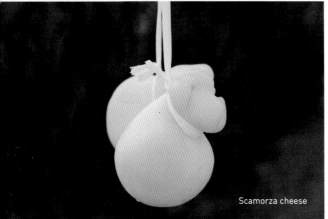
Scamorza cheese

Region of the green highways

This sounds exactly like my kind of trip, a trek past mostly mountainous and hilly landscapes. The impressive Abruzzo National Park continues south into both Molise and Lazio. Along the way, I come across monasteries, towns and castles. Molise is home to the historic paths connecting Abruzzo with Apulia, along which shepherds and their sheep once travelled during the seasonal migration, or *transumanza*. Molise was literally and figuratively the hinge upon which the historical transumanza developed. There were four main *tratturi* or green highways in Molise that sheep and their shepherds, often accompanied by horses, followed during their migration: from L'Aquila to Foggia, Celano to Foggia, Castel di Sangro to Lucera, and Pescasseroli to Candela. Along these wide pastoral roads, you will still find the shelters, cabins, villages and chapels that sprung up along these routes as a result of this historical migration.

The lower part of Molise is called Basso Molise and comprises the shore and hills further inland. The old port of Termoli is the only town on the Molise coast. Interestingly enough, there is an island group in the Adriatic Sea that belongs to the Puglia region, but that can best be reached via Termoli. This island group is called the Tremiti Islands, which includes San Nicola and San Domino, known for the beauty of the clear, cobalt-blue sea surrounding them.

Daily life

The economy is driven mainly by agriculture, which consists mostly of wine, grains, olive oil, vegetables, fruit, and dairy products that are cultivated and processed by small family farms. The tourist sector is small but growing.

★ Molise esiste – Molise exists

The Molise region is gaining a reputation as a destination for harvesting truffles and so becoming increasingly popular among truffle hunters and enthusiasts. It's a trend that hasn't yet run its course and, over the long run, may overshadow the better-known truffle mecca of Alba in Piedmont. Today, forty per cent of Italy's truffle harvesting takes place in Molise. This has tremendous economic potential because such a rich harvest is possible in only a few other regions. Moreover, Molise is situated far away from any type of industrial pollution.

AUTHENTIC CUISINE

In Molise, the locals are proud of their identity and very attached to tradition. The same applies to their cuisine. Its strength lies in its simplicity in terms of preparation and the authentic ingredients. Still, there is a difference between the dishes prepared in the mountains and on the coast. The mountain-based dishes mainly comprise homemade pasta and pork- and mutton-based dishes. Dairy products include *scamorza* cheese, *caciocavallo* (pear-shaped cheese made with unpasteurised cow's milk) and *stracciata* (very fresh curd cheese, like mozzarella but formed into a braid). The region also boasts various exquisite types of salami. On the other hand, the coast boasts a rich maritime tradition and flavourful fish, home to simple yet intense fish dishes similar to those from Abruzzo.

AGNONE ①

Bread in Molise used to be made from various types of local flour, including those made from maize, potatoes and even chickpeas. 'We still add potato flour to our bread,' says Antonino Patriarca from the Panificio Antichi Sapori Patriarca, the Patriarca family bakery in Agnone is located in the upper Molise region and is my first stop. 'Agnone has plenty to offer with its historical town centre, thousand-year-old clocks and countless beautiful churches. People are still devoutly Catholic here,' Antonino explains.

Traditional bread

I find myself in the workplace of fourth-generation bakers dedicated to the art of processing flour in a variety of forms. The business exudes passion and professionalism. Antonino's son, Stefano, helps to serve the customers while Antonino's wife works in the bakery's atelier.

Antonino: 'We Agnonesi are spoilt by the pure flavours of our local products that continue to be made according to artisanal traditions. For instance, we only use flour from grain that comes from Molise or Abruzzo. Moreover, we add potatoes to the flour with natural yeast to give the bread a softer texture. The potatoes make the bread tender. It has always been this way in Agnone. *Io non ho modificato nulla*!' I haven't changed a thing, Antonino says firmly.

Focaccia that we call 'pizza'

I point to a focaccia on the rack behind him and tell him that this looks particularly tasty. Antonino: 'This is a type of focaccia that we call pizza. This focaccia is also made with potato flour, by the way, and is garnished with extra-virgin olive oil, sea salt, and oregano. It is made from the same dough as the bread here.'

Castagne

Antonino leads me to the workbench where his wife, Arianna, makes *castagne*, Agnone's distinctive pastry. 'The castagne is sometimes also called *loffe di Sant'Antonio,* after the church across from here. Our bakery is known as the "panificio di Sant'Antonio". Nearly every street here has its own church,' he continues.

Adriana: 'They are called castagne, or chestnuts, because of their colour and shape. Apart from that, they have

Antonino with Agnone's signature bread

nothing to do with chestnuts. The dough is more or less similar to the dough used for fritters or beignets. It mainly consists of eggs, flour, and a tiny bit of olive oil. No sugar and no butter. The pastry gets most of its flavour from the thick chocolate coating. There is not much fat in the dough, so it's a very light pastry.

We roll the dough into sausages, then cut them into pieces and place them upright. The mounds are then briefly baked in the oven at a very high temperature. The intense heat causes them to rise without yeast, giving them their specific shape.'

Castagne

Chocolate bath

'This is the basic product, which we then submerge in a chocolate bath,' Antonino continues. Adriana: 'We make the chocolate sauce with water, sugar and cocoa, then melt dark chocolate into the sauce. We combine everything until the sauce is thick enough.'

Adriana shows me as she picks up a fritter on a spoon and dips it into the sauce, turns it over to coat the other side and then places the fritter on a rack to dry. 'We dip the fritters one by one.'

Ndocciata

Antonino: 'This pastry is a tradition among the people of this town and its surroundings. It will always have its place here amongst the other pastries. Not a wedding, communion, family occasion or birthday goes by without castagne. And whenever we have a celebration within our community, you will always find castagne from Sant'Antonio, especially during *Ndocciata*.'

I frown as I hear the unfamiliar term.

'Ndocciata is the festival of fire,' Adriana explains. 'Then we hold a great parade with torches several metres high, singers and people playing the bagpipes. The torch carriers are dressed in a traditional costume and represent a 'river of fire'. This ritual brings light to the longest night in honour of the sun god.' It clearly brings back fond memories as Antonino and Adriana tell the story with big smiles and sparkling eyes.

⭐ Interplay of flavours

Antonino invites me to try the castagne. 'Otherwise, you won't know what I'm talking about,' he says.

It's not a particularly sweet pastry. I also taste a hint of saltiness on the inside. Adriana: 'That's the eggs. The dough contains a lot of eggs.' It's a unique interplay of flavours. 'The combination of the hint of sweetness with the saltiness from the eggs and the bitterness of the 72 per cent dark chocolate makes this pastry unique.' My search for the champions of baking has brought me to Agnone, and this castagne takes the crown. I also meet a champion in an entirely different discipline during my visit. The handsome young man standing next to Antonino is his son Stefano Patriarca. Stefano plays volleyball in the Serie A. He also happens to be good friends with the Belgian top athlete Pieter Verhees from when they played at Latina together. 'We still regularly stay in touch,' Stefano says. Papa Patriarca proudly tells me how his son will take over the family business after his sporting career. I'm glad to hear that!

Antichi Sapori di Patriarca
Via Cavour 35, Agnone

Isernia

Pescolanciano

ISERNIA ②

From Agnone, I drive 50 km south to Isernia, capital of the province of the same name. I pass green hills as I leave the National Park behind me. The route is breathtaking. In terms of population, Isernia is the third-largest town in Molise, after Campobasso and Termoli. The historical centre is a collection of beautiful buildings, including various churches and opulent palaces, the town hall and the thirteenth-century Fontana Fraterna, built to commemorate Pope Celestine V.

Street food with a rustic sauce

But, I'm not stopping in the city centre. I drive on into the modern part of town to find Garage Street Food, owned by Mattia Rotolo and Gianluca Cortese Tempesta. I wanted to discover how contemporary food concepts could flourish in conventional, traditional Molise.

'It's very simple,' Mattia explains. 'We make hamburgers based on local, traditional ingredients. We only use the finest quality products from our rich local surroundings: hamburger from Isernia, bread from Montaquila, mozzarella from Bojano, mushrooms and truffles from Cantalupo, vegetables from local farmers and beers from Filignano. The burgers take you on an authentic gastronomic journey through Molise. It's also turned out to be a huge success!'

Scottona burger

As I look at the menu, the first thing that springs to mind is that some burgers are made from *scottona*. Mattia: 'This is very lean meat from a young animal. A scottona burger's tenderness is unsurpassed. Scottona is not the name of the actual meat. A 'scottona' is a female cow, from 18 to 24 months old, that has never given birth and is destined for the slaughter. You will find their meat at supermarkets and butchers under the *supercarni*, or top-quality meat' section. You recognise the meat from the thin lines of fat running through the muscle tissue, like tiny veins. This fat melts during cooking, giving the meat its tenderness and intense flavour,' Mattia explains.

A tartufo hamburger

Terroir on a bun

'A *tartufo* hamburger is a must on the menu in this truffle-rich region,' Mattia continues. 'Sandwiched between the bread, you will find black-truffle carpaccio, caciocavallo cheese, local porcini mushrooms, a scottona burger, and a fried egg. Whenever we use vegetables such as onions, lettuce, courgette, and tomatoes, they must be locally produced. Did you know that each year, we hold a celebration in Isernia to honour the products that come from the soil? Our cuisine is rich in vegetables. On the feast of Saints Peter and Paul, this old city is transformed into a picturesque paradise. This feast is very ancient, and it's generally believed that the onions bought during the feast have strong medicinal qualities.' He winks when he says this last part, I suspect to help me draw my own conclusions about whether I should believe it.

★ Molise non esiste

Having this conversation in a burger bar with young men dressed in the style of American bikers as mopeds race past with deliveries feels surreal. They have taken the region's culinary riches to heart and made it their business's core and trump card. Even their choice of beer surprises me. 'Local beers only, of course,' Mattia explains. The beer labelled *Molise non esiste* – Molise doesn't exist – is particularly unique. But whatever the beer says, Molise certainly exists here. Bravo!

Garage Moto Kafè
C.so Giuseppe Garibaldi 211, Isernia

PUGLIA

Apulia – Puglia to the Italians – in southeastern Italy forms the heel of Italy's 'boot', with the Salento peninsula at its southernmost tip. Apulia borders the Adriatic Sea to the east, while the inside of the heel looks out over the Ionian Sea to the west. Its neighbours are Campania, Basilicata and Molise. Bari is the region's capital.

I am staying in Baia Sangiorgio, just 10 kilometres from Bari, where owner Veneziani proudly tells me about his little slice of heaven. 'We live in a beautiful country that reveals new fascinations every day. The Apulian landscape is unique. The beautiful coastal cities are enchanting with their Roman and Baroque cathedrals, impressive castles and regal palaces. A visit to towns such as Lecce, Bari, Brindisi, Ostuni and Trani are just a few of the many joys the region offers.'

The more than 800-kilometre Apulian coastline is high and jagged at the northernmost Gargano promontory. Further south, the lower-lying sandy shore runs straight down to Brindisi. The coast from Salento onwards is rugged and varied. The Tremiti archipelago, with its three islands, including San Domino, is also part of the region. Pristine landscapes riddled with gorges and caves heighten the islands' magic. The seawater there is crystal clear.

The Grotta Sfondata in Otranto

N'Dèrre a la lanze: Bari's old port

Lago di
Lèsina

Lago di
Varano

Fortore

Candelaro

Cervaro

Carapelle

Ofanto

Santo
Spirito

3

1 Bari

Altamura

2

Gravina

Carovigno

4 **5**

Martina
Franca

Canale Reale

Lecce

6

Marina di
Andrano **7**

Rich history

'Countless peoples have crossed the Apulian region in the past 2000 years,' Veneziani tells me. 'Greeks, Romans, Byzantines, Lombards, Norsemen, Swabians, Angevins, Aragonese, Venetians and Spaniards have all raised their banners here and conquered lands only to lose them later. The most important figure in Apulian history is emperor Frederick II, who ruled from 1197 to 1250. He was a Roman German from the Swabian House of Hohenstaufen. His contemporaries called him *stupor mundi,* the 'Marvel of the World'. Unfortunately, his death was followed by a long period of decline as subsequent generations of foreign rulers neglected our region.' In 1860, Apulia became part of the Kingdom of Italy.

APULIAN TERROIR

Apulia is home to many regional products, from olive oil to Altamura bread, as well as truly delicious vegetables and cheese varieties. The *burrata* is undoubtedly the best-known cheese. This fresh cheese was first produced in Andria in 900 AD. The outside looks like mozzarella but is actually a casing filled with *stracciatella.* Stracciatella are strands or strings of mozzarella in fresh cream. The creamy burrata filling is also sold separately as 'stracciatella'.

The wines are also certainly worth a detour. The popular Salice Salentino and Primitivo are full-bodied red wines.

Apulia is flat, dry and hot; but, with its many fruit trees, olive groves and grapevines, it hardly looks arid. The olive trees have been crucial to the region's agriculture and culture for thousands of years. The many, centuries-old, olive groves give the landscape a magical touch. Stately and often twisted tree trunks crowned with silver-green foliage rise from the russet soil. Apulia is home to the largest number of thousand-year-old olive trees. The olive oil from this region is subtly sweet or bitter with an aftertaste that carries just a hint of pepper.

Trulli in San Giorgio

The port of Bari

Sea urchin

BARI ①

My first stop is the beautiful port town of Bari along the Adriatic coast. The various peoples inhabiting the city over the centuries have given it its rich culture and authentic, vibrant character. Traditions spanning thousands of years add colour to daily life. During the day, the scent of line-dried laundry, freshly baked focaccia, and handmade pasta permeates the old town.

N-DÈRRE A LA LANZE

Avoid the passenger port where the ferries for Greece, Albania, Croatia and beyond depart. Visit the old port instead, where life carries on as it has for centuries. *N-dèrre a la lanze* is quintessential Bari. I walk from the covered Molo San Nicola pier to the fishing boats. That's where I meet the local fishermen. They bring in the catch of the day to sell in town. Some stand on the jetty, pounding white, translucent baby octopuses with a stick. 'We beat the octopus to stretch the hard fibres and make the meat tender,' Domenico Detullio explains after a night of fishing. Others are repairing their nets and banter with each other in some undecipherable dialect. This is the real Bari.

The small pier is one giant open-air restaurant, and the menu is just fresh, raw fish. Some fishermen offer pre-packaged plastic plates with a baffling range of seafood, shellfish, and crustaceans accompanied by a piece of bread and lemon. One fisherman hands me a plate with octopus, plaice, Venus clams, light-coloured and black mussels, and sea urchins. 'This smells like the sea,' I tell him. Domenico joins me with a couple of bottles of Peroni beer. Domenico: 'This is what we call a real breakfast in Bari: raw fish and Peroni. Nothing more, nothing less.' Domenico points to the El Chiringuito bar halfway down the pier, where the fishermen are gathered in a circle. They eat raw fish and quench their thirst with beer. It's nine o'clock in the morning and already quite warm. It's been a long night for the fishermen. Yet they look more content than tired. They're clearly in an exuberant mood.

Sushi from Bari

I sit down on the pier with my plate and beer, feet dangling over the water, and taste the raw seafood. The crunchy octopus tentacles with their bitter-sweet aftertaste, the fresh mussels, and the sea urchin with its bitter-salty orange-red liquid are treasures from the sea. Still, I can't help but notice that the taste of the briny water dominates. One tip: only purchase small octopuses if you want to eat them raw.

I enjoy the disarming atmosphere and soak up this precious moment and the view over the Apulian capital city's skyline. In front of me lies the shore and the seafront promenade, or *lungomare*, of Araldi di Crollalanza. This impressive sea wall was constructed during Mussolini's reign. The bars, restaurants, street food kiosks and cafés along the promenade bring this Bari centrepiece to life. The longest promenade in Italy has been in use since 1927. I see buildings from the late Art Nouveau and the Fascist periods as I stroll along the seawall. Behind me, to the right, I see the wall surrounding Bari's old town. What an eclectic city!

Raw fish at N-dèrre a la lanze
Molo S. Nicola 6, Bari

Breakfast in Bari

An industrious fisherman prepares octopus at the Molo San Nicola wharf

ORECCHIETTE

The handmade *orecchiette* are Apulia's pride. In almost every household, you will find the traditional wooden plank upon which kilos of fresh pasta are made. The name *orecchietta* in the singular refers to the pasta's shape: a 'little ear'. Walking down the streets of old Bari, I pass women selling handmade orecchiette on their doorstep. They make grateful use of tables, planks and rolling pins. Via dell'Arco Basso, better known as Via delle Orecchiette, is the place to be for fresh homemade pasta in the afternoons and early evenings. I walk from the bar across from the N-dèrre a la lanze towards the old town, and after some 700 metres, I reach Via dell'Arco Basso with its rich folklore, colours, women and orecchiette.

Angela Lastella nimbly cuts the pasta into balls and presses them into an ear shapes. Angela: 'I have been doing this my entire life. I make the ears from semolina, water and salt. I leave the pasta to dry on our balcony, next to our jogging bottoms, T-shirts and bath towels.' One of the locals buys a kilo of pasta. Angela checks the weight on an ancient scale. 'Everything's always fresh here,' she says. Through the kitchen window, I spy sauce pots simmering away next to large sacks of semolina flour. An Italian TV show blares in the background.

This street is no tourist trap; this is where the locals come to buy their fresh pasta. This tradition is sacred. You will find pasta in all flavours, shapes and sizes, but Bari's true soul can be found in the orecchiette. These women drew masses of cruise ship passengers and turned Bari into one of Lonely Planet's European highlights. They were also the inspiration for one of Dolce & Gabbana's cosmetics advertisements. In 'Pasta, Amore e Emotioneyes', Sylvester Stallone's grown-up daughters parade in black negligees down 'Orecchiette Street' while the grandmas laugh, dance and make pasta.

Orecchiette in Arco Basso
1/25, Bari

Angela at work in her streetside kitchen

Which sauce should you serve with orecchiette?

The most traditional sauce is made with broccoli rabe, or *cime di rapa*. This is an Italian vegetable with thick stems and flat green leaves, both used in Italian cuisine. In Bari, they're also called *rapini* or *broccoletti*. This slightly bitter green vegetable tastes divine in olive oil. The stems need to cook a little longer than the leaves and florets. You briefly fry them in a saucepan with garlic and olive oil, then add a pinch of salt before serving. According to the Apulians, orecchiette and cime di rapa belong together. A sauce made from tomatoes and basil, sometimes with small meatballs thrown in, is also very popular. They are simple dishes born from poverty, but the first-class ingredients produce rich, pure flavours.

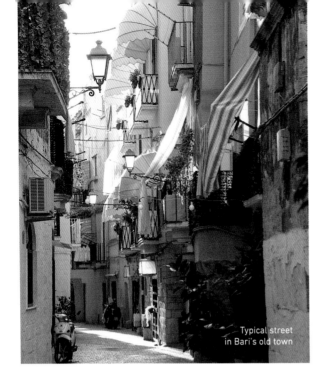
Typical street
in Bari's old town

Sgagliozze

Making *sgagliozze* is another time-honoured tradition
in the narrow streets of Bari. In the old days, homemakers made *polenta* year-round in large pots of oil
out on the street. You now find them on street corners
at the Piazza del Ferrarese, Piazza Mercantile and Piazza Prefettura. This Bari delicacy has taken the rest of
Apulia by storm. Still, polenta is not a typically southern product and it's certainly not native to a seaside
town like Bari. Sgagliozze, or fried polenta, dates back
to the city's origins. Every 6th December, people would
purchase sgagliozze after mass outside the Basilica of
Saint Nicholas to honour the town's patron saint. One
of the region's many foreign rulers probably brought
this dish to Bari.

Sgagliozze, focaccia, *popizze* and *panzerotto* are all
part of Bari's street-food culture. Maria makes and
sells pieces of warm, salty, rectangular fried polenta
or polenta chips on the Piazza del Ferranese. Her table
boasts one cash box with change, a deep fryer, a stack
of greaseproof paper sheets, a salt shaker full of salt,
a bowl of dough for the popizze and the sliced polenta.
I order both. Popizzo are deep-fried fritters made from
a flour-based dough. Maria spoons the dough into the
oil and leaves it to cook for about three minutes. She
places the browned popizze on the greaseproof paper.
My sgagliozze is next. She fries the polenta slices in the
same oil for a few minutes before wrapping them in an
greaseproof paper cone. She generously sprinkles salt
over the hot sgagliozze. It's just what I need after a long
day of walking and meeting people. On the way to the
car, I buy a bottle of water to wash down the salt.

Focaccia di Bari

You will find potatoes in the region's soups and pasta
dishes, and commonly, also in the focaccia. Focaccia is
Bari's snack of choice. The smell of flatbread permeates the city from the early morning. *Focaccia di Bari* is
a suitable alternative for breakfast, lunch or dinner. His
Royal Highness *focaccia barese* is inextricably linked
with the Apulian capital. The focaccia is topped with
ripe tomatoes, olive oil, oregano and olives.

HISTORIC BAKERY

You can eat delicious focaccia at almost every bakery
in town, each one more famous than the other. Fiore
has one of the oldest focaccia ovens in old Bari. I meet
Domenico, the baker, at his shop in the Strada Palazzo di Città behind the basilica. Panificio Fiore (1912)
is situated in a former Byzantine church from 1208.
'La focaccia barese is the most famous in all of Italy,'
Domenico assures me. 'Over the centuries, each Italian
town developed its own recipe. The focaccia in Genoa
is generally thick, soft and elongated. They eat a lot of
focaccia there, usually plain, sometimes topped with
cured meats, often as an alternative to bread. In Bari,
on the other hand, the focaccia is round, often made
with potatoes, and covered with toppings.

Panis Focacius

Domenico: 'My grandfather was a passionate focaccia baker. His life and the lives of his family revolved
around this flatbread. He told us that the focaccia's origins date from the second century BC in what is now
called Lebanon. The Phoenicians who lived there at the
time combined barley and millet with water and salt,
and then baked the focaccia on stones with lots of fat.
When the bread made its way across the Roman Empire, it was called *panis focacius*.'

BAKERY
The eternal flame

I follow Domenico through a beaded curtain to the
atelier at the back of the shop. There's a large workbench, and rows of focaccia are left to proof on wooden
shelves on both sides of the room. An oven door is nestled into the white wall at the back. Domenico: 'My oven
holds 20 focaccia at a time. We move the flatbreads
closer to or further away from the fire using a five-
metre-long stick made from olive wood. This oven has

already fed millions of hungry mouths!' To the right of the oven door, another door leads to the woodpile. The wood is pulled in from the side of the oven to fuel the fire. Domenico: 'Our fire is always burning, and the bakery is never closed. My grandfather and the oven have survived both wars. The fire is not allowed to go out and will burn to all eternity. It just takes too long to heat the wood oven up to 280°C again. You need a lot of wood, and it takes an entire day. So, we just keep baking bread the whole time.'

⭐ The best focaccia in Italy

Domenico points to a trophy prominently displayed in the shop. Meanwhile, I try a piece of focaccia. 'In 2019, we won the title of *La focaccia più buona d'Italia*, or "the best focaccia in Italy." We even beat Genoa at Eataly World in Bologna.' When I ask Domenico what their secret is, he replies: 'Focaccia needs to be juicy and crunchy, and that calls for skilled hands and a lot of practice.' He confides that the tomatoes and olives that serve as toppings make the difference. Domenico: 'We can't do without our elongated, sun-ripened grape tomatoes. We chop them fine to create a cold mass of unpeeled tomatoes or raw tomato sauce. We don't add anything; no salt, no oil... These juicy, full-bodied, bright red tomatoes give the focaccia plenty of flavour and make them irresistible. The extra virgin olive oil coating the bottom of the baking tray and the bread creates a crispy crust. And just to be clear: our family recipe does not need potatoes.' I'll admit, this focaccia is really – and I mean really – good! And yes, the tomato topping makes the flatbread juicy and gives it that sublime flavour.

Fiore
Str. Palazzo di Città 38, Bari

Domenico and his sous-chef bake the best focaccia in Italy

FIORE'S RECIPE
Focaccia barese

DOUGH FOR 2 FOCACCIAS
375 ml lukewarm water
20 g fresh yeast
15 g salt
10 g sugar
500 g flour (or 150 g 00 flour and 350 g semolina)

FOR THE TOP LAYER
extra-virgin olive oil
400 g grape tomatoes
10 pitted green olives
salt
oregano

Heap the flour into a small mound on your work surface and create a well in the middle. Crumble the yeast into the well. Sprinkle sugar and salt over the top. Now, gradually add the lukewarm water and combine the flour step by step with the liquid, working from the outside inwards. Once the ingredients are well combined, knead for another 10 minutes by hand or use a kitchen mixer. Place a towel or cling film over the dough ball and let the dough proof for 2 hours somewhere warm around the house. Divide the dough into two pieces and knead each ball separately once more. Cover and let the dough balls proof for another 45 minutes.

Take two large round, flat baking trays (32 cm in diameter). Coat the base of the trays with olive oil. Spread the oil with a brush to coat the tray thoroughly. Press the dough down firmly into the tray using wet fingers. Make sure that the entire base of the tray is covered with a layer of dough. Use your fingers and thumbs to press the characteristic dents into the dough. Drizzle olive oil over the bread and rub it over the surface. Also, arrange the crushed tomatoes (or the pulp of fresh chopped tomatoes with the skin), the olives, the salt and the oregano over the top.

Let both focaccias rest on the baking tray for another 30 minutes. After 30 minutes, bake the focaccia in an electric oven preheated to 200°C for 20 to 30 minutes. First, check to make sure the dough is cooked through at the bottom. If the bottom is light brown, the focaccia is ready!

Young baker in front of the di Gesù oven from 1892

ALTAMURA ②

I drive 45 kilometres inland to Altamura in the province of Bari. This town, home of Bari's focaccia and Altamura bread, also boasts a cathedral and archaeological museum. I am familiar with Altamura from the 2009 comedy film *Focaccia Blues*. The film is a parody based on a true story: McDonald's in Altamura had to cash in its chips because it couldn't compete with the delicious focaccia from the local bakery, Di Gesù. The story of the fast-food giant's downfall made world headlines. *The New York Times* and the French newspaper *Libération* turned Altamura and Di Gesù into the champions of local, authentic cuisine. It also made for wonderful movie material; *Focaccia Blues* premiered a few years later.

Beppe di Gesù and Annette holding Altamura bread

Panificio di Gesù

Beppe di Gesù waits for me at a bar about 100 metres from his world-famous *panificio*. He embodies the fifth generation of a bread and baked goods empire. Beppe beams when I ask him about the battle between the humble bakery and the fast food behemoth 20 years ago. 'We didn't come to blows,' Beppe smiles. 'When McDonald's opened in 2001, we were happy with the 25 new jobs it created. But the residents were appalled when a larger-than-life bright neon 'M' appeared on a post near the old town centre.

Beppe: 'Soon after, our baker family opened a second shop next to McDonald's. We wanted to take advantage of the hype surrounding the new location. To our amazement, residents and tourists went for our thick slices of focaccia straight from the oven instead.'

No McDonald's in the city of bread

'Which makes sense. Altamura is the city of bread, after all,' Beppe continues. 'Our bread is of the finest quality and always freshly made. On the other hand, McDonald's buns are not fresh and certainly not crispy. The residents scoffed at this bread. People went to McDonald's for an ice cream, a milkshake, or fries – but for bread, they went to Di Gesù. Focaccia is a tradition. It's a way of life. There was apparently no room for McDonald's in the city of bread.' In December 2002, less than two years later, McDonald's closed its doors.

'Just to be clear: we didn't beat McDonald's,' Beppe reiterates. 'Our strong culinary culture beat McDonald's.

My dream is to make peace with McDonald's. We never intended to cause harm. And if the opportunity presents itself, we'd happily work with them. McDonald's hamburgers on an Altamura bun, why not?'

Pane di Altamura, or Altamura bread

As I continue my drive, vast oceans of wheat fields sway softly in the breeze. This picturesque view hints at the main ingredient of the best bread in the world. As I drive into Altamura, the first thing that strikes me is that bread is the hero in this town. A sign by the roadside reads *Benvenuti nella Città del Pane*, or 'Welcome to the City of Bread'. The oldest bakery in Altamura is located near the Piazza del Duomo. The wood-fired oven (1423) from the historic bakery Anticuus Fornus Sancta Clara was built to provide bread for the nunnery of Santa Chiara. Baker Vito still bakes bread here in the traditional Altamura form, including *taralli* and focaccia. Beppe di Gesù has lost his heart to this food for the people. He is vice-chairman of the DOP Pane di Altamura Foundation. We now find ourselves in his bakery in front of a large wood-fired oven built in 1842.

Beppe: 'Altamura bread is the only bread in Europe with a protected designation of origin (POD) status, which it has had since 2003. That means our bread is highly regulated. If a baker wishes to use the Pane di Altamura DOP label, they may only do so under very stringent conditions. For example, the production method must be consistent, and the crust must be over 3 mm thick. Pane di Altamura contains 100 per cent durum wheat flour from the province of Bari.'

Beppe points out a shelf in the atelier where there are a dozen loaves of bread. They are sturdy round loaves with a thick crust and an unusual shape called *u skuanète*, meaning 'overlapped bread' in dialect. It looks like a giant traditional hat.

Antico Forno Santa Chiara
Via Luca Martucci 10, Altamura

SEMOLA DI GRANO DURO OR DURUM-WHEAT SEMOLINA

What distinguishes Altamura bread from other types of bread? 'There are two types of wheat: *grano tenero* and *grano duro*, or soft and hard wheat,' Beppe explains. 'The hard wheat is yellow, sometimes called *semola di grano duro*, or durum wheat semolina. Around the world, people make bread with grano tenero, or white flour. We only use grano duro, or yellow flour, from the wheat harvested here. We make both bread and pasta using this flour year-round. Yellow flour has very different characteristics. For instance, Altamura bread retains its moisture longer. Bread grows stale as it loses moisture, but you can store our bread for up to five days after purchase. The thick crust keeps the inside soft. The larger the bread, the longer it will keep.'

Altamura bread's thick crust keeps the crumb tender for longer

Taralli

You will also find *tarallo* (singular), another Apulian speciality, on Beppe's shelves. The origins of this name remain a mystery. What Beppe does know is that *taralli* has been prepared in the region ever since the 15th century. Beppe: 'The recipe was born of necessity because there was nothing else to eat. A woman found some leftover flour, olive oil, salt and white wine in her pantry. She combined everything to make a dough, which she flattened and divided into thin strips. She rolled the strips into rings and then baked them in the oven. Taralli kept people fed in times when food was scarce. Many homemakers then started to prepare and bake taralli in the town's communal ovens. In no time, this emergency ration became a mass-produced product that today carries the PAT (*Prodotto agroalimentare tradizionale*) label.'

⭐ Farming tradition

I take a tarallo and taste it. This baked ring comes in both sweet and savoury varieties. Beppe quotes the expression *finire a taralli e vino,* or 'finish with taralli and wine.' People here offer guests taralli and wine as a sign of friendship. I am immediately offered a glass of white wine (fiano).

'We now have taralli in different flavours,' Beppe continues. My eyes are drawn to the vast selection: *cipolla* (onion), *cacio e pepe* (cheese and pepper), *cime di rapa* (broccoli rabe), *mortadella* (mortadella ham), *pepe* (pepper), *peperoncino* (spicy red pepper), *finocchio* (fennel seeds), *olio oliva* (plain with olive oil), *dolce* (sweet), and finally *vino rosso* (sweet red wine).

The tarallo is crumbly and crunchy. Truly delicious! I smell the olive oil as I take my first bite. Simple, yet bursting with flavour. The refreshing Fiano wine is the perfect accompaniment.

Panificio Di Gesù
Via Pimental Eleonora Fonseca 19, Altamura

Pecora in pignata

On the bench in front of the large oven at Di Gesù stand several large terra cotta pots covered with aluminium foil. Beppe tells me that these pots contain *pecora in pignata,* which translates to 'sheep in a terra cotta pot'. Neighbours and locals bring these pots filled with mutton, vegetables and herbs to stew in the wood-fired oven. This age-old tradition continues to this day. Di Gesù's wood-fired oven is still a communal oven.

Taralli

I walk 300 metres further down the road to the *macellaria,* or local butcher, La Fiorentina. Giovanni Segreto, Maria Sciannanteno and butcher Irene Spinelli explain how the mutton is prepared.

Giovanni: *'Pecora in pignata,* or *Pecora in Rizzola,* is the quintessential Alta Murgia dish. This Apulian subregion encompasses the provinces of Barletta-Andria-Trani, Bari and part of Taranto. It is a stunning nature reserve with mountain ridges and gorges. You will find everything you need for a traditional stew there. The main ingredient is mutton, and this dish originates from the *transumanza,* the seasonal migration of local shepherds and their flocks.'

'Pecora alla Rizzola is prepared inside a wood-fired oven nowadays. But it was originally cooked over a campfire,' Giovanni reveals as he chops the mutton for the pignata into pieces with a cleaver. 'Almost all parts of the sheep can be thrown into the pot.' In the old days, shepherds from the region cooked this dish outdoors during the transumanza. They would put the mutton and seasonal vegetables in a pot of water, place the pot over the open fire, and leave the meat to stew for hours until it was ready.

'The wood-fired ovens led to the biggest change over the centuries. The stew found its way from the pastures of Alta Murgia to the pignata,' Maria continues. She shows me an earthenware pot in the shape of a pitcher. Maria: 'At night, bread, focaccia, taralli, and biscuits are baked in the baker's wood-fired oven. The fire gradually dies down afterwards, but there is still enough heat left for other uses. We stew dishes such as pecora in pignata or *cavallo* (horse) *in pignata* in the still-hot oven. We leave them to stew for hours in the earthenware pots.'

⭐ Summer dish

'*Pecora alla Rizzola* is a typical summer dish,' Giovanni says. 'That's when the sheep eat fresh grass, making their meat sweeter, more tender, and tastier. In the winter, they eat hay or dried grass, and their meat tastes bitter. That's why we prefer to use lamb in the winter.'

Irene quotes a local proverb: '*Da ottobre si lascia la mamma e si prende il figlio*' or 'when October comes, leave the mother alone and take the child'. The idea sounds harsh to my ears, but thankfully, Irene quickly continues by going through the other ingredients: 'We combine the meat with seasonal vegetables such as fennel, potatoes, tomatoes, celery, chicory, beetroot, onions, endive, courgettes, beans, carrots and sweet peppers. The vegetables are first combined in a tub with fresh herbs, such as fennel fronds, peppers and salt. We place the pieces of meat in the terra cotta pot together with the vegetables and herbs. We pour white wine over the vegetables and top it off with cheese. The melted cheese, herbs and wine give the dish its distinctive flavour.'
Giovanni: 'We cover the pot with aluminium foil. In the olden days, we used to cover the pignata with a piece of dough, which then turned into bread in the oven. The meat is braised at low temperatures, making it tender and juicy.'

Macelleria La Fiorentina
Via IV Novembre 50D, Altamura

RESTAURANT
Tre Archi

Beppe accompanies me to Mina and Peppino's Tre Archi, a restaurant in the heart of Altamura's old town, to try their pecora in pignata. The meat in this mutton stew is exceptionally tender and mild in flavour.
Mina: 'The strong mutton flavour is tamed in pecora in pignata, not just because of the wine, but also by the bitter essences from vegetables such as chicory and wild fennel. The long, slow cooking process in the terra cotta pot tones down the flavour.'
Not only the exceptionally delicious food but also the interior design created by local artist Vito Maiullari is striking. The interior is a nod to the transumanza, and Maiullari's sheep seat is an Apulian icon!

Tre Archi
Via S. Michele 28, Altamura

Pecora in Pignata

SANTO SPIRITO ③

With Bari being one of the capital cities of Italian street food, I decide to remain in the area. You will find countless varieties of *panzerotto* throughout Italy these days, but the panzerotto in Bari remains the ambassador. I drive to the seaside resort of Santo Spirito di Bari, some seven kilometres from the airport. I head to the Christopher Columbus promenade behind the beaches along the Adriatic coast. Michele Florio, owner of the *panzerotto/rosticceria* Qui si gode, is my guide. His business name roughly translates to: 'Find enjoyment here.' Michele: 'People come here specifically for our panzerotti. The beautiful view over the Adriatic Sea is an extra.'

Panzerotti

Michele: 'Panzerotti are half-moon-shaped turnovers stuffed with mozzarella and tomato. They have evolved into a gastronomic speciality in recent decades. We have 27 different fillings for this unfinished taste symphony. In addition to the traditional panzerotto with tomato and mozzarella, we also have: *cacio e pepe* (cheese and pepper), *tonno e caperi* (tuna and capers), *provolone e mortadella* (provolone cheese and mortadella), *mozzarella e cime di rapa* (mozzarella and broccoli rabe), mozzarella, *caperi e acciughe* (mozzarella, anchovies and capers), *mozzarella e fungo cardoncello* (mozzarella and king oyster mushrooms)...'

Half moons in sizzling lard

Is the panzerotto unique to the province of Bari? 'Different cities lay claim to the recipe,' Michele replies. 'But according to gastronomic historians, the panzerotto originates in Bari. When tomatoes suddenly appeared in the seventeenth century, the classic panzerotto filled with tomato and cheese was born. Homemakers made these small, sealed pizzas to avoid wasting dough scraps. Poor people ate similar half-moon turnovers deep-fried in boiling-hot lard. Today, it's an Apulian speciality.'

⭐ What's in a name?

Michele: 'These anonymous housewives came up with the brilliant idea of sealing the dough filling and deep-frying the turnover in oil. The name panzerotto refers to its swollen shape, reminiscent of a bloated belly. *Panza* means belly or tummy in our dialect, and

rotto is like *rotondo,* a round belly. Naples has a similar dish called the *pizza fritta*. The dough and preparation are the same – water, flour, oil, salt, and yeast – but the filling and shape vary. In Bari, the panzerotto is a half-moon of thin, crispy dough; in Naples, the turnover is larger and thicker. But bear in mind that in Naples, they also refer to a potato croquette as a panzerotto.'

In Sicily, the panzerotto goes under the name *pitone* or *pidone*. Their version of panzerotto is a sweet variety.

THE BEST PANZEROTTO LOCATIONS IN BARI ACCORDING TO *LA REPUBLICA* NEWSPAPER IN 2019:

Qui si gode Lungo Mare Colombo Cristoforo 172A, Bari

Pizzeria Di Cosimo Via Giovanni Modugno 1, Bari

Barill Fornaccio Via Francesco Crispi 87, Bari

Cibò Piazza Mercantile 29, Bari

Panificio Dirello Via Napoli 95, Bari

Pizzorante Arlecchino Via Carpaccio 14, Triggiano

Panificio Montecristo Strada Detta della Marina 96, San Giorgio, Bari

The panzerotti from Panificio Montecristo

Panzerotti

FOR THE DOUGH

500 g flour

300 ml lukewarm water

3 g dried brewer's yeast
   or 10 g fresh yeast

1 tablespoon extra-virgin olive oil

6 g sugar (1 teaspoon)

10 g salt (1 teaspoon)

FOR THE FILLING

300 g diced mozzarella

200 g tomato passata

salt and pepper to taste

oregano to taste

rapeseed oil
   or peanut oil for frying

Sprinkle the flour into a bowl, add the yeast and sugar to activate the yeast. Combine everything with your hands. Pour the lukewarm water into a separate bowl, add the salt and extra-virgin olive oil, and mix it with your hands. Add the flour bit by bit and knead until you have a smooth, homogenous, elastic dough. Place the dough on your work surface, knead with your hands, or knead it for 10 minutes in a mixer.

Once the dough is ready, place it in a bowl, score it with a classic cross-cut, and cover it with cling film. Let the dough proof for 2 hours in a warm spot until it has doubled in volume. Once the dough has risen, place it on a lightly floured surface, knead lightly with your hands and shape into a loaf. Now shape into twelve balls of around 80 grams each. Place the dough on a baking tray lined with parchment paper and leave the dough to proof for 20 minutes in a warm spot.

Meanwhile, make the filling. Put all the ingredients in a bowl: the diced mozzarella, the tomato passata, salt, pepper and oregano to taste. Combine the ingredients with a spoon and set aside.

After 20 minutes, place the balls of dough on your work surface. Roll the dough out with a rolling pin; make sure the dough is not too thin. If the dough is still sticky, dust your work surface underneath the dough with flour. Place the filling in the middle of the dough circle, moisten the edges with a bit of water and fold the dough over to seal the turnover. This is how you end up with the classic half-moon shape. Press the edges down with a fork. Heat the oil in a deep-fryer or frying pan. The ideal temperature for deep-frying is 170 °C.

TIP If you don't have a thermometer, do the toothpick test: dip a plain wooden toothpick in the oil. If bubbles start forming outside, the oil is ready to use.

Fry the panzerotti for about four minutes until golden brown on both sides. As soon as the panzerotti are golden brown and cooked through, drain them on paper towels to remove the excess oil. Eat the panzerotti while they're still hot!

The cathedral at Martina Franca

MARTINA FRANCA ④

From Santo Spirito di Bari, I drive 80 km southwards to the region's heart. Valle d'Itria is the most famous valley in Apulia. The valley owes its fame to the enchanting *trulli*, or white huts with conical roofs. Some five thousand trulli exist in this part of Apulia, particularly around Alberobello. The oldest houses are some three hundred years old. They have been listed as a UNESCO Heritage site since 1996. The fairy-tale-like conical roofs appear everywhere along state highway SS172, also known as *Strada Statale 172 'Dei Trulli'* . A premonition of what's to come?

I leave the car on the outskirts of Martina Franca and walk towards the town centre. Martina Franca is one of the most beautiful white towns in the region, surpassed only by *la città bianca*, Ostuni. I wander through a tangle of narrow streets between gorgeous Baroque and rococo buildings, with cast-iron balconies decorated with geraniums. Even in this sweltering summer heat, the temperature in the shaded narrow streets feels comfortable. On the impressive, vast Piazza Plebiscito, I witness a fairy-tale-like wedding celebration. A just-married couple or *sposi* kiss each other on the steps of the gorgeous Basilica di San Martino in front of family and friends as balloons rise into the air. What a spectacle!

Bombette

Capocollo is Martina Franca's cold-cut speciality. Capocollo is the Southern Italian version of the dry-salted and often gossamer-thin pork *coppa* from northern Italy. The neck and shoulder muscles from pigs roaming the Murgia hills surrounding the Valle d'Itria are processed into capocollo. The butchers in Martina Franca, Cisternino and Locorondo mainly make capocollo.

Bombette are meat rolls made from raw (unprocessed) capocollo. A slice of pancetta, *caciocavallo* cheese and finely chopped flat-leaf parsley are placed on a thin slice of pork. They are then rolled into 5 to 6-cm balls and stuck on a skewer. This street food has been gaining in popularity since the 1960s. Various butchers in towns in Valle d'Istria also sell them warm. Grilled and served with a glass of local red wine, it's the perfect snack for meat lovers. Countless such butcher-slash-restaurants are situated in Martina Franca, Alberobello and Cisternino. Bombetta literally means 'little bomb' because the combination of melted cheese and salted ham is a taste explosion in your mouth. You will find bombette everywhere at village festivals and annual fairs throughout Apulia.

The photogenic white town of Ostuni

SALENTO

Salento is the southernmost part of Italy's heel. This is where the land flattens into an elongated peninsula, with the Adriatic Sea to the east and the Ionian Sea to the west. Salento is the home of coastal gems such as Gallipoli and Otranto and the charming region of Leuca with its white buildings and sapphire-blue seas on the southernmost tip of the peninsula.

CAROVIGNO ⑤

My next stop, Carovigno, lies 40 kilometres southeast of Martina Franca. This charming village in the province of Brindisi is just a few kilometres from the seashore. I lose myself in the white-stuccoed streets of the old town centre. The impressive Castello Dentice di Frasso stands watch over the city as it did under Norman rule. The town boasts another eleven towers in addition to the castle tower; that's why Carovigno is also known as *Terra di Torri*, or the 'Land of Towers'. The wind soothes the sun on my skin. I follow the scent of freshly baked bread. Through a very narrow street, I reach the historical bakery, Lu Scattusu. This is where bread, *taralli, frise* and focaccia bread have been baked daily for four generations. Sounds like the perfect excuse for a tasty snack!

BAKERY
Panificio Lu Scattusu

I meet Carmela Spano, who has just finished loading frise, or *friselle,* into an enormous wood-fired oven. We find ourselves in the castle annexe, where the largest wood-fired oven in Italy spans a massive six metres wide by six metres long. 'This oven has been in my family for 130 years,' Carmela tells me. 'Lu Scattuso was the nickname given to my great-grandfather. I grew up in this bakery.'

Carmela opens the tiny oven door, where I can see frise laid out on iron trays as far as the eye can see. Ashes from burnt wood are piled up the oven's sides. 'We hoist the iron trays in and out of the oven using a large stick,' Carmela explains.

The facade of Panificio Lu Scattusu

The oven at Panificio Lu Scattusu

Freshly baked friselle

A shiver runs down my spine when I think of how dangerous these red-hot trays must be. Carmela puts my mind at ease: 'We do this with the utmost care, and no one else is allowed near when we fill or empty the oven.'

Frise

Carmela: 'Friselle are made from durum wheat, wholemeal or spelt flour. The method is always the same. They are baked twice to remove moisture from the dough. The dough is then shaped into a doughnut and baked for a few minutes at high temperatures in the wood-fired oven. The still-warm bread is then cut into two slices with a thin wire to form two rough, uneven surfaces. The slices are baked again at lower temperatures until they're nice and crispy. And those are the *frise!*'

'But they're too hard to bite into,' I continue. Carmela: 'That's right. First, you need to keep them under running water for a couple of seconds to soften them up. Then, you rub garlic over the surface and season them with extra-virgin olive oil, tomatoes, salt... According to legend, pilgrims and crusaders would take frise with them for the long sea voyages that took them from the port of Salento to the Holy Land. This "bread of the crusaders" kept well on board a ship. During their sea voyages, fishermen would first dip their bread in the briny seawater before adding the toppings. Thanks to the hole in the middle of the doughnut shape, they could be easily attached to the boat by passing a rope through the hole and tying them up.'

Armed with this knowledge and a bag of friselle, I leave the Lu Scattusu bakery. I need to leave, because it's high time to remove another batch of friselle from the oven.

Panificio Lu Scattusu
Via del Prete 12, Carovigno

CARMELA'S RECIPE
Friselle al pomodoro

SERVES 4 PEOPLE

8 friselle measuring 8 to 10 cm
700 g cherry or other small sweet tomatoes
8 fresh basil leaves
2 cloves garlic
extra-virgin olive oil to taste
salt to taste
water to taste

To make the friselle with tomato sauce, peel and rub the garlic over the friselle. If you don't like garlic, skip this step. Then, soak the friselle briefly under running water without letting them get soaked through. Arrange the friselle on a plate, drizzle a bit of oil over the top and leave to soften up for about 10 minutes. Dice the cherry tomatoes, put them in a bowl and combine with extra-virgin olive oil and the finely chopped basil. Add salt to taste. Leave the mixture so the flavours can blend.

Once the friselle is soft and the tomato sauce flavours are well-blended, evenly divide the topping over the frise. Serve immediately!

Tip You can also top the friselle with anchovy fillets, olives and capers.

LECCE ⑥

Lecce is located 80 kilometres south of Carovigno. I park on the outskirts of the town and walk to Via Principe di Savoia next to the majestic Porta Napoli, one of the monumental city gates to Lecce's old town. I explore the historic centre of this cosmopolitan city. The buildings have an unusual, milky hue. I make my way towards the Piazza del Duomo, one of the city's main squares. Davide Rollo waits for me at L'angolo Della Puccia in Via Giuseppe Libertini.

Puccia leccese

I look at the roll that Davide takes in his hands. Davide: 'This may look like just another roll, but the *puccia leccese* has its own distinctive character. Puccia is a takeaway dish, a fast-food delicacy, not a dish for in a restaurant. Farmers used to take this bread with them into the fields. We make puccia from semolina and natural yeast and replace the lard with olive oil. The dough is prepared, baked and then filled. The ingredients are similar to those used for pizza.'
I select a puccia with burrata, olives, tomatoes, rocket and a slice of cooked ham. Once the toppings are selected, the roll briefly returns to the oven.

I calmly nibble at the creamy, crispy, golden-brown roll while elegantly-clad couples walk past me, hand in hand. Children chase each other in circles on the other side of the square, with the *duomo* in the background. A group of friends happily chat over drinks at a table behind me. A slice of quality time in a gorgeous city!

L'angolo Della Puccia
Via Giuseppe Libertini, Piazza de Duomo 78, Lecce

RESTAURANT
Povero

The city once more becomes magical at dusk, when the setting sun bathes the typical white-yellow stones, or *pietra leccese*, in a pinkish-red hue. The city is teeming with life. People flock to the shopping streets full of boutiques, restaurants and outdoor patios. Restaurant Povero is located at one of the more popular locations in the historical centre, near the Piazza Sant'Oronzo and the famous Basilica di Santa Croce. Povero literally means 'poor', which is quite appropriate once you learn that Salento's cuisine was borne out of poverty. People had to get by with the few ingredients that were available. And I am curious to discover what 'poor man's' dishes Angela's kitchen offers.

The characteristic white buildings in Lecce's town centre

Fave e cicoria (above), carne di cavallo alla pignata and verdure

Cucina povera, or 'peasant cuisine'

Angela: 'We never throw anything away in Salento. We've never been hungry because we could always put something on the table, even though we had very few ingredients to hand. Moreover, in every season, you will find wild herbs and vegetables in the countryside. In the olden days, poorer farmers had little meat, so they made meatballs from bread, potatoes and aubergine. Occasionally, a delicious ragu or stew made with horse meat with tomato sauce would appear on the table. La cucina povera, or 'peasant food', is very popular today. Our dishes contain humble ingredients, although ironically enough, some have become quite expensive over the years. This farmhouse fare that was once born of necessity now evokes a sense of nostalgia. These dishes represent authentic cooking.'

I go through some of the delectable cucina-povera dishes displayed at the open counter with Angela, and I notice that Salento's cuisine is anything but poor.

Angela: 'Take ciceri e tria, a fresh homemade chickpea pasta. Carne di cavallo alla pignata is a stew made from horse meat, prepared in earthenware pots typical of the region. Another pignata dish is lu purpu all pignata, or octopus in pignata. The octopus is prepared in an earthenware pot with plenty of herbs and vegetables. Schiacciatine di melanzane, also known as polpette di melanzane, are deep-fried aubergine croquettes, and polpettoncini prosciutto e formaggio are meatballs with ham and cheese.'
I am drawn to a tall earthenware pot containing a yellow, creamy liquid. Next to it is a plate of stewed green leafy vegetables. Angela: 'These are broad beans and chicory, the quintessential poor man's dish from this region!'

Fave e cicoria, or broad beans and chicory

The colours of this dish look so enticing. I want to give it a try. I sit at a table on the patio amongst the cheerful crowd. All the seats are taken in this idyllic spot in the old town. The wait staff busily walk to and fro carrying dishes that all, without exception, look mouthwatering. It is still hot outside, and I order a vino spumante, a refreshing sparkling white wine, to set the mood. Angela starts me off with an antipasto called paolotte. It is an appetizer plate featuring a couple of small frise with tomato, a stewed vegetable caponata, olives and three types of cheese: fresh ricotta, semi-soft pecorino and scamorza cheese.

'Fave e cicoria, or broad bean puree with stewed chicory, is made from two dirt-cheap ingredients,' Angela resumes her explanation as she sets a plate at my table. 'It's a match made in heaven between the bitter, leafy chicory and the relatively sweet pureed broad beans. You can find chicory in the fields around the city, and broad beans are found everywhere. In Apulia, you can go out into the fields to harvest wild chicory, but if you can't find any, you can also use farm-grown chicory.'

Enogastronomia Povero
Via Francesco Rubichi 4, Lecce

HOW DO YOU MAKE IT

'The preparation is simple,' Angela continues. 'The broad beans are soaked for about 12 hours in cold water and then cooked for a long time until they fall apart. We make the beans creamy with a blender and then add salt and pepper for extra flavour. You can blanch or stew the wild chicory with a bit of salt and pepper, which you then serve with a splash of high-quality, extra-virgin olive oil or pine nuts and olives.
I don't wait until my plate cools to taste the rich flavours of this poor man's dish. Angela leaves me to savour this incredible meal in silent contemplation. I can't praise her enough as I leave the restaurant. Fave e cicoria; a timeless dish in a timeless setting!

Porto Miggiano, near Salento, is known for
its pristine nature and breathtaking shoreline

MARINA DI ANDRANO ⑦

My journey continues even further south. From Lecce, I drive 50 kilometres to Marina di Andrano, in the lowest part of Salento in the province of Lecce. I have arranged to meet with Irene Rossi for a day of sun and sea. Irene: 'The landscape in Andrano is pristine and rugged. Tall, jagged cliffs alternate with lower, less jagged rocky outcroppings that let you walk to the shore. The coastline stretches to Santa Maria di Leuca, the southernmost point of this peninsula, and harbours heavenly bathing spots. In recent years, this region has repeatedly been awarded the *Bandiera Blu*, the international Blue Flag quality mark, for our clean, pure waters and magical cliffs,' Irene proudly tells me.

We lay down our towels on a rock and dive from a ledge into the water. Here, at the southernmost tip of Italy's heel, we are surrounded by the Adriatic and Ionian Seas. While swimming, I feel the occasional warm glow beneath me. Irene explains that this coast harbours countless natural springs. Back on land, we rinse off the briny water in the ice-cold water of a natural spring rising between the rocks, one that is deep enough for me to submerge my head.

Caffè alla Salentina

Feeling refreshed, we head to the beach bar for a time-honoured tradition, iced coffee. Irene: 'Our characteristic iced coffee with almond milk originated in Lecce in the heart of Salento. It is easy to make. Put some ice cubes and almond milk in a glass and add coffee. You don't need to add sugar because the almond milk is already sweet. Authentic Salento coffee is prepared with a *Moka*, a cast aluminium espresso coffee maker made to work on a gas hob . Every family in Italy owns one of these,' Irene says.

Coffee is sacred to Italians; they need several shots of espresso throughout the day. I can see why a warm drink isn't always the best option when you want to cool off in the summer. This is a fabulous way to freshen up while savouring your favourite cuppa.

Irene and I sip the iced coffee. The flavour of coffee and almonds go well together. This perky caffeine shot with the sweet almond aftertaste provides refreshment under the sweltering Mediterranean sun. I'm ready for another dive into the water.

Ristobar Malibù
Viale Europa 19-23, Marina di Andrano

IRENE'S RECIPE
Caffè alla Salentina

FOR 1 MUG OR GLASS

3 ice cubes
2 tablespoons sweetened almond milk
1 small cup boiling hot espresso
1 rum or whiskey glass for the iced coffee

First, put the ice cubes in the glass, followed by the almond milk. Pour the hot espresso over the top and stir for a couple of seconds.

BASILICATA

Basilicata is situated in southern Italy, just north of Calabria and nestled between Campania and Apulia. This idyllic oasis is far removed from the outside world. Lucania, as the region was called in ancient times, boasts a surprisingly rich history and stunning landscapes. People here live according to the laws of nature, in close harmony with their surroundings. Tranquillity reigns in the streets and towns. Matera and the regional capital of Potenza are the only large cities. Life here is simple, with a down-to-earth atmosphere. The Appennino Lucano dominates the mountainous west. While travelling across mountains and through forests, I discover villages that come straight out of a picture postcard, sometimes at elevations of over 1000 metres. The practically pristine *Laghi di Monticchio* or Monticchio Lakes work their magic with breathtaking natural splendour. The oldest tree in Europa, Heldreich's pine, flourishes in the *Parco Nazionale del Pollino* or Pollino National Park. The natural forests stretch out as far as neighbouring Calabria. Another natural phenomenon awaits to the north: Monte Vulture, an extinct volcano rising like a beacon out of the landscape. Vulture is the birthplace of Basilicata's Aglianico del Vulture red wine. Every year, the Aglianico wine festival takes place in and around castles in the Vulture-Melfese region. Low hills and broad valleys colour the region's eastern part, while narrow coastal plains hide behind sand and clay hills along the shores of the Ionian Sea.

At the farm where the Peperone di Senise IGP is processed

Tuff landscape near Matera

Laghi di
Monticchio

Lago di Serra del Corvo

Avigliano
4

Matera
1

Gravina

Potenza

Basento   Lago di S. Giuliano

Bradano

Lago del
Pertusillo

Agri

Agri

Diga di
Monte Cotugno

Sinni

Senise **2**

Sinni

Sinni

Terranova di Pollino **3**

Matera, one of the oldest cities in the world

MATERA ①

Matera is the region's crown jewel. The city was Basilicata's capital until 1806. Matera is one of the oldest cities in the world; the earliest residents date from the third century before Christ. The city is situated in the beautiful Parco della Murgia Materana. People settled here in ancient times for protection from numerous threats. Matera stretches over two karst rocks: the Sasso Barisano and the Sasso Caveoso. The Sassi, which translates to 'stones', are prehistoric cave dwellings. People carved homes – and sometimes even churches – from the soft tuff stone of the Sassi di Matera to give this city its unique shape. The city's decline started in the nineteenth century. Living conditions were atrocious in this rocky city. The resulting ghost town later served as a source of inspiration for film-makers. The tide turned when Hollywood discovered Matera's magic and produced mega-productions such as *King David*, starring Richard Gere, and *The Passion of Christ* with Mel Gibson. Matera was suddenly in business again, and a new law in 1986 allowed people to inhabit the Sassi once more. The government pumped money into the city, and since 1993, Matera has maintained a spot on the UNESCO World Heritage List. The cave dwellings were transformed into inns, restaurants, cafés and shops. In 2019, Matera was awarded the title of Europe's Cultural Capital for that year.

Happy people

Many people I talk to in Basilicata have a family member or acquaintance who went abroad to seek fame and fortune. To the people who live in the South, historically self-governance has been a vague concept but never a reality. Greeks, Romans, Saracens, Byzantines, Lombards, Swabians, Aragonese, Bourbons... They all came and went, and they all left their mark. In 1861, the Kingdom of Naples made way for the Kingdom of Italy, but not much changed for the people who lived there. The region remained poor and was treated like a red-headed stepchild. Still, this did nothing to diminish the remarkable friendliness and helpfulness of those left behind. And that's because this little slice of heaven has everything you need to be happy. You don't need to tell American director Francis Ford Coppola twice. His grandparents emigrated from Basilicata. They lived in the town of Bernalda before moving to the United States. Coppola became a household name with films such as his *The Godfather* trilogy, with stellar roles for Al Pacino and Marlon Brando. The famous director has always had a soft spot for his beloved *Bernalda bella* or 'beautiful Bernalda'. It is said that his artistic roots stem from the region. In 2014, Coppola bought the Margherita luxury hotel in Bernalda, located in a palazzo dating from 1892.

TERROIR

This small, thinly populated region has proudly maintained its pastoral traditions and surroundings. It's a mecca for regional specialities. Wheat, rye, beans, grapes and olives are the main crops. Animal husbandry involves sheep, goats, pigs and bovines. There is hardly any industry except for the production of the popular red wine, Aglianico del Vulture DOCG, the Olio Oliva IGP Lucano olive oil, and flour.

Fagiolo di Sarconi IGP are beans that can be fresh or dried. The town of Sarconi is known for its first-class beans. The unique climate ensures that the starches in the beans are converted into sugars, giving them a pleasant, sweet flavour.

The *melanzana rossa di Rotonda DOP*, or Rotonda red aubergine, is a unique agricultural product. The fruit looks like a tomato but retains the spongy texture of an aubergine. It tastes slightly spicy and bitter. Red aubergine from Rotonda is used in a variety of ways in Basilicata's cuisine. You can coat them with batter and fry them, grill them as a side dish, or incorporate them into vegetarian sauces. Its shape is perfect to hold highly creative fillings for oven-baked, stuffed aubergine. The aubergine is grown and harvested in the Pollino National Park valleys in the Castelluccio, Rotonda and Viaggianello municipalities.

And then there's also the small, pointed, hook-shaped *peperone di Senise IGP*. This sweet, elongated pepper is used to make *cruschi*, or crisps.

Food is sacred

Basilicata's inhabitants, also known as Lucanians, enjoy a fresh supply of first-class vegetables year-round and make optimal use of delicious ingredients such as tomatoes, artichokes and leafy vegetables. Their food culture is founded on traditional principles. Lamb and mutton take centre stage. Fish is relegated to a supporting role because of the region's limited coastline. The fabled Matera bread lays the foundation. This durum wheat bread has been a favourite of townspeople and farmers alike for thousands of years. The *Caciocavallo Podolico* is a cheese variety also found in Calabria and Apulia. Another winner on the cheese front is *Canestrato* from Moliterno. The region also has its own brand of Lucanica pork sausages seasoned with fennel seeds.

CITTÀ DEI SASSI

My culinary roots journey through Basilicata starts in Matera. I park the car on the city's outskirts and stroll through the old part of town along the main street, Via del Corso, to my destination: a small inner courtyard on the right. Here I find the La Fedda Rossa restaurant, where I have arranged to meet the owner, Annalisa de Bellis. I sit at a table under the watchful eye of Saint Eligius, whose statue guards the square. The seventeenth-century church next to the square also bears

his name. Dusk is settling in, and the tables on the patio gradually start to fill up. I have come just in time for Annalisa to tell me about Matera's characteristic dishes before all the tables are occupied. We go through the menu, and I settle on the *bruschette* and *zuppa crapiata*.

La Fedda Rossa

Annalisa: *'Fedda rossa*, or "red slice", is dialect for bruschetta topped with fresh red tomatoes. This typical peasant's dish reflects our restaurant's philosophy: simplicity and quality.' Meanwhile, I sip the glass of *vino della nostra zona,* or local wine, Annalisa has recommended. It's a red Anglianico, of course.

I ask Annalisa what makes the bruschette here so popular. 'The bread for the bruschette is made from the durum wheat that has been grown here for centuries,' she replies. 'This bread used to be baked just once a week, but it would keep for the entire week. People would eat this in the morning, afternoon, and evenings. The bread slices were grilled over a coal or wood fire and then seasoned. It was the perfect accompaniment to grilled meat or other delicacies. Bruschette grilled on top of the wood-burning stove were often eaten as the evening meal. Families would gather around the fire in the evenings to warm themselves and catch up on their day. This ritual survived until the 1950s.

Matera

Today, bruschette are incredibly popular among the tourists in Matera. It is a very simple dish that highlights our delicious Matera bread and the tomatoes that grow and flourish in the sun. A peasant *(contadina)* version of the bruschetta is topped with caciocavallo cheese, followed by bacon or pancetta and grilled potatoes. We use a large piece of bread for the bruschette, and the toppings are usually hearty. It's a meal in itself.'

Contadina bruschetta

ANNALISA'S RECIPE

Contadina bruschetta from Matera

MAKES 4 BRUSCHETTE
4 large, thick slices of (Matera) bread
1 clove garlic
4 slices caciocavallo cheese
12 slices round pancetta
extra-virgin olive oil
dried oregano
12 slices cooked potato

Take a thick slice of bread and coat it with extra-virgin olive oil. Place a slice of caciocavallo cheese (or *caciotta, scamorza* or semi-soft pecorino cheese) over the top so it covers the entire slice. Arrange the pancetta slices over the cheese and sprinkle oregano over the bruschetta. Garnish with three slices of cooked potato. Bake the slices of bread in an oven at 200 °C for six to ten minutes. Serve warm.

ANNALISA'S RECIPE

Fedda rossa bruschetta

MAKES 4 BRUSCHETTE
4 large, thick slices of (Matera) bread
1 clove garlic
12 g cherry or other small sweet tomatoes
extra-virgin olive oil
dried oregano
salt
basil (optional)

Toast the bread however you wish: on the grill, in an oven or using a toaster (oven). Peel the clove of garlic and rub the clove over the bread, preferably while the bread is still warm. Wash and halve the cherry tomatoes. Take one of the tomato halves and place it cut side down on top of the bread. Rub the tomato over the bread until you're left with just the skin. The coarse bread will soak up the tomato pulp and juices and turn red. Repeat this until the entire surface of the bread is covered in red tomato pulp. Some people leave the crushed tomato on top because they love the tomato skins and texture. Others remove the tomato skins and simply eat the soaked bread. It's entirely up to you which you prefer. Season to taste with salt and lots of extra-virgin olive oil. For a real fedda rossa, your bread should be drenched in oil. Sprinkle a pinch of dried oregano and finely chopped basil, if desired, over the top.

Crapiata materana

Annalisa: 'Matera started its year as the Cultural Capital in 2019 with this dish. Crapiata is a vegetable soup that's highly characteristic of this town. It's actually more of a ritual. *Crapiata* reflects the close bond between the farmers in the fields around Matera and the Sassi cave dwellers. Everyone would bring a handful of pulses for the soup to contribute to this quintessential communal dish, the crapiata materana. All these different pulses were cooked in one giant pan on the street for the entire neighbourhood. That is how we celebrate the harvest on the first of August each year. In the olden days, only the potatoes in the crapiata were fresh. People used the leftover pulses from the previous harvest for the soup. Everyone looked forward to the celebration, and the excellent red wine flowed freely to accompany the soup.'

Crapiata is a very healthy and nutritious hearty meal made with dried peas, broad beans, chickpeas, wheat, spelt, lentils, beans, potatoes, cherry tomatoes, celery, onion and carrot. The soup is seasoned with a splash of olive oil, bay leaf and a little bit of salt. Its secret lies in the quality of the pre-soaked and slow-cooked ingredients.

⭐ Crepula

I enjoy my bruschetta contadina and my hearty soup. The Aglianico wine is a divine accompaniment. When I ask what *crapiata* actually means, Annalisa comes up with several explanations. Annalisa: 'The name could be derived from *cràpia*. This Calabrian term refers to the tripod on which the huge pot was placed to cook the pulses. A second possible explanation comes from the Greek word *crampa*, or *krambe*, for legumes.' It could also be derived from the Latin word *crepula*, which makes sense. Annalisa: 'Crepula means to rattle or crash, perhaps in a drunken state. During the festivals, everyone drank so much local wine that the soup is possibly named after the exuberant behaviour caused by the alcohol.'

I've been warned. I've finished my soup – and with it, my second glass of Anglianico. I say goodbye to the friendly Annalisa and stroll back to my car. The sounds of this lively city reverberate from the centuries-old Sassi cave dwellings. I hear the strains of Dean Martin's version of that timeless classic, *Volare,* from a patio. I sing along to the music. Uh-oh. Crepula? Whatever it is, this is an experience I won't easily forget.

La Fedda Rossa
Via del Corso 90, Matera

RECIPE
Zuppa crapiata materana

SERVES 4 PEOPLE

- 100 g unhulled broad beans
- 100 g spelt
- 100 g chickpeas
- 100 g peas
- 100 g white beans
- 100 g black or red beans
- 100 g lentils
- 100 g hard wheat berries
- 1 carrot
- 1 stalk celery
- 1 onion
- extra-virgin olive oil
- 2 bay leaves
- 100 g cherry tomatoes
- water
- salt and pepper to taste

Soak the dried pulses in water for about 24 hours and then rinse them before preparing the soup. Clean the potatoes. Leave the skin on if you're using new potatoes.

Put all the pulses, the bay leaves and the diced potato in a pot and submerge the ingredients in water. Add enough water so the water level measures a generous three fingers above the vegetables. Simmer over low heat for about 45 minutes.

Add the remaining ingredients and a pinch of salt. Dice the carrots, celery and onion. Add the whole cherry tomatoes. Check regularly to ensure the pulses at the bottom don't stick to the pan, and add more water if needed. Cook for another 45 minutes over low heat.

Turn off the heat and add a splash of extra-virgin olive oil. Check to see if enough salt has been added. Serve warm.

A plateful of hearty zuppa crapiata materana

SENISE ②

From Matera, I drive about 100 km to Senise. The city is surrounded by the magical and rugged natural landscapes of the protected wilds of Pollino National Park. Senise is situated close to Europe's largest artificial lake, a beloved destination for water sports enthusiasts. This breathtaking setting serves as a backdrop for the Masseria Agricola Buongiorno, home to a very unusual pepper. Enrico Fanelli, the owner and chairman of the consortium for the protection of the IGP Peperone di Senise, welcomes me to his farm in the hills.

From the Antilles to Basilicata

Enrico: 'Peperone di Senise is the king of Lucanian gastronomy! In the 17th century, the *capsicum annumpaprika* made its way from the Antilles to Europe and found the perfect soil and climate conditions around Senise. Today, the pepper grows abundantly in these fields, where it flourishes to its full potential and dries to perfection. Peperoni di Senise are 15 centimetres long. They are harvested from July to late September. The harvest is labour-intensive because we harvest the peppers by hand. Processing the peppers is also an artisanal process.'

Cruschi

The famous chilli pepper shape is symbolic of Senise's beauty. The bundles of fruit suspended on thick cords are an essential part of this beautiful region.

Enrico and I walk over to a spot where women are sitting on a cloth, drawing a heavy cord through the pointed peppers. The scene looks like a picture postcard with the colourful, smiling women, the mountains of bright-red 'peperoni' spread out on cloths, and the fairy-tale-like hills in the distance. Enrico: 'The peppers are left to dry on the cord for about 20 days. Notice how these are not chilli peppers, but sweet peppers. Once they're dried, they're sold as bunches on a cord or deep-fried. Many restaurants order our fried peperoni, or cruschi.'

Enrico takes me to the workroom on the outskirts of the village, where Isabella and Maria process the peperoni. They welcome me warmly. Maria selects the finest specimens from large tubs containing dried

Farmer at work

Fried peperoni, or cruschi

At work at the Masseria Agricola Buongiorno

peppers and slices them open. 'About half of this tub ends up as leftovers,' she confides in me. The stem and seeds are removed, and the remaining dried pepper pieces are fried. 'This requires a lot of patience,' Maria says. 'Just like at home, but on a much larger scale.'

In the next room, Isabella deep-fries the pepper pieces in an electric deep-fryer, tray by tray. Isabella: 'That's how we make them nice and crispy. We fry them in oil from our own olive grove and then leave them to dry on greaseproof paper. Once they're fried, they're ready to eat, or you can store them in special jars.'

I try a piece of fried pepper. It's delicious; fresh and crispy, like bittersweet crisps.

Enrico: 'Since the end of the 20th century, these pointed peppers have been deep-fried into cruschi, the word for 'crispy' in our dialect. Cruschi influence our local cuisine's flavours. We use them in meat and winter vegetable dishes and grate them as a topping over seafood or pasta dishes. We grind cruschi down with a mortar and pestle. We sprinkle the powder over fried eggs or a classic *spaghetti aglio, olio e peperoncino* (spaghetti with garlic, olive oil and chilli peppers). In recent years, the Peperone Crusco has found its way to countless chefs, who process this ingredient in various gourmet dishes. That's how the product's fame grew both nationally and abroad.'

At Masseria Agricola Buongiorno, they also process the cruschi into other products such as powder, ketchup, and dark chocolate-coated crisps. Many other vegetables are grown and processed in addition to the sweet pepper. The shelves boast numerous vegetables preserved in olive oil, including *melanzana rossa di ro-*

tonda (red aubergine), *melanzana bianca* (white aubergine), *carciofi* (artichokes), *fungo cardoncello* (king oyster mushrooms), *zucchini* (courgettes) and *pomodorini* (mini tomatoes).

⭐ Turn your passion into your career

Enrico: 'I do this work mainly because I strongly believe in the unique riches this region offers. My parents moved from the countryside to Rome, where I studied to work in the financial sector. Not long ago, I took over my grandparents' farm and started this project. I had to invest, develop products, and take care of marketing and communication. It's much more than just farming because you need to be a jack of all trades. But you always win when you can turn your passion into your career. And you need to have the grit to do something like this. Now it's up to the young generations to give new life to farming. Young entrepreneurs need to work together with experienced farmers so they can learn from each other. You need farmers and entrepreneurs. We strive to achieve the highest quality and make no concessions in that respect. It's what our customers expects from us. Today, we're the second largest producer of cruschi, and the number of producers is relatively small. There is a lot of growth potential for the relatively unknown cruschi. We still have a lot of work to do to sell this product beyond Basilicata. But, I'm convinced we'll get there in the end.'

www.masseriagricolabuongiorno.it

TERRANOVA DI POLLINO ③

My next stop, Terranova di Pollino, is located 30 kilometres west of Senise. It doesn't sound like a great distance, but the last 10 kilometres are slow going on the narrow, winding roads. I don't mind, as I get to enjoy the pristine landscape and astounding views. Terranova is one of the gates to the Parco Nazionale del Pollino. The mountain range is part of the southern Apennines, which extend over Basilicata and Calabria. The highest mountain peaks reach 2200 metres above sea level. The nature reserve boasts forests, rocks, cliffs, deep gorges, caves, plateaus and pastures where wolves, deer, foxes, little bitterns, peregrine falcons, Egyptian vultures, and other animals roam freely. Terranova is the place to be for hikes and winter sports and for fans of the traditional Lucanian (Basilicata) cuisine. The location of the Luna Rossa restaurant is far removed from the outside world. Chef Frederico Valicenti has put Lucanian cuisine on the map throughout Italy with his cooking programmes on television. This philosopher disseminates the richness of traditional cuisine with his projects. On the terrace, looking out over his beloved park, he talks passionately about the earth, oxygen, and love in his dishes.

Cibosofia – food philosophy

Federico: 'Cibosofia means telling the story about a region and its culture through the local products and cuisine. I started this restaurant by accident, but it gradually turned into an obsession. The farmers taught me that food is more than just a product; it's a culture that has stood the test of time. Initially, Terranova wasn't the most obvious location for a restaurant, but I'm glad I stayed. Our region is a treasure trove of quality products and a first-class gastronomic destination. I don't believe in the myth of cucina povera, or peasant cuisine, being the result of poor people hardly having anything to eat. These traditional dishes were also served at the tables of the rich. That's why I study the gastronomic tradition of people with a true food culture, inextricably linked to a terroir.'

Parco Nazionale del Pollino

Federico's kitchen

LUCANIAN CUISINE – THE CUISINE OF BASILICATA

'What is characteristic of Basilicata's cuisine?' I ask. 'Above all, it's a robust cuisine that respects the quality of local ingredients,' Frederico replies. 'The region's biodiversity ensures a rich and varied cuisine. We use a lot of natural herbs and vegetables that feature different aromas and flavours than they have in the north. Basilicata has been a crossroads over the centuries. The many people who passed through here left their products and recipes behind. I have collected the history, stories, centuries-old recipes and techniques in my book *Dalla tavola lucana al paradiso:* "From the Lucanian table to paradise" (2019).'

Luna Rossa serves a selection of unique, traditional dishes from Terranova di Pollino on the menu, including:

Lagane dei Jalantuomini

Fresh, egg-free tagliatelle made from a variety of grains and pulses. The pasta is rolled out with a *laganatura*, a rolling pin. The sauce is a cream of caciotta ricotta cheese, finished with tomatoes, walnuts and breadcrumbs.

Ciammotta

A fried aubergine stew with potatoes, tomatoes and sweet peppers. This classic dish is seasoned with peperoni cruschi from Senise, giving the dish a smoky aroma.

Grattonato

Trippa (tripe) seasoned with eggs, pepper and cheese in a meat broth. This was once the traditional first course at peasant weddings.

Ciambotta lucana del contadino

'And don't forget our *ciambotta*,' Federico adds. 'This dish probably made its way to us around 1500 from the Balkans. Ciambotta is a bread stuffed with sweet pepper, tomato, egg and *salsiccia*, or fresh sausage. People used to fill this bread with whatever was available at the time. That's why I call it *panino democratico*, or democratic bread. The bread was simply the packaging for the filling. Farmers, shepherds and donkey drivers would take these stuffed breads with them on the road. The bread carried the filling. The breads were filled the night before, and the juices from the ingredients would soak into the breadcrumbs creating a unique flavour experience. The large piece of bread had a thick crust and was made from grano duro, or hard wheat, and sometimes potato. Our forefathers were familiar with the *transumanza* (sheep migration), just like in Abruzzo and Molise. The famous *ciambotta lucana* made a perfect meal for breakfast, lunch and dinner. Bread was – and still is – a very important and highly nutritious foodstuff. The loaves of bread could weigh anywhere between two and four kilograms. Smaller loaves of bread didn't exist back then. The larger the loaf, the longer it would keep. People used the bread to make bruschette as well as ciambotta. For the former, the bread slices were toasted and then topped with lard and herbs.'

Ciambotta

SERVES 4 PEOPLE

loaf of bread, about 1 kg
2 red sweet peppers
2 green sweet peppers
2 aubergines
1 onion
4 ripe tomatoes
200 g salsiccia (fresh sausage)
3 eggs
extra-virgin olive oil
salt and pepper to taste

Mince and then sauté the onion in plenty of olive oil. Meanwhile, rinse the sweet peppers and slice them into strips. Rinse and dice the aubergines. Add the sliced vegetables to the pan. Cook the vegetables until they're soft.

Chop the sausage and tomatoes and cook them separately in another pan. Once the sausage turns brown on the outside, add the meat and tomatoes to the vegetable stew. Leave everything to simmer over low heat for 15 minutes, stirring occasionally. Add a splash of water if the vegetables start sticking to the bottom of the pan.

Remove the pan from heat. Beat the eggs and add them to the stew. Stir everything together so the eggs can cook using the heat from the other ingredients.

Hollow out the inside of the bread until you are left with a crust about two centimetres thick. Crumble 1/4 of the removed breadcrumbs into the stew. Season to taste with salt and pepper. Fill the bread with the sausage-vegetable mixture and leave to rest overnight. Slice and serve the bread the next day like you would serve a cake.

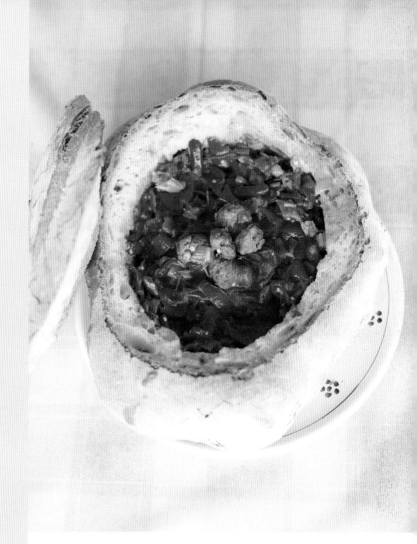

⭐ Slow travel

Frederico and I sit out on the terrace. He invites me to lunch and serves me a slice of stuffed ciambotta. It is a refreshing and hearty meal to go with the warm weather. We talk about this little piece of paradise on earth as we enjoy the view of the impressive mountains and forests. Federico: 'I hope that Basilicata will remain authentic and be spared from mass tourism. Our guests are lyrical about the rich flavours and traditions. I've had offers in New York and opened restaurants in Rome. But I keep coming back to Terranova. Money doesn't count; the life you live does. And for me, I don't mind it being a slow life. Never give up your freedom because nothing is more valuable!'
And with those wise words, I take my leave. I resume my journey to my next destination feeling contented.

Luna Rossa
Via G. Marconi 18, Terranova di Pollino

Avigliano

AVIGLIANO ④

A journey of 170 kilometres northwards towards Avigliano awaits me. Some 25 kilometres before my destination, I pass through Potenza in the heart of the pristine Lucanian Dolomites. This is the highest regional capital in Italy. I stop by the roadside, and in the distance, I see a sober, modernized curtain of buildings fall over the valley. I'm not far away from the city, and yet I feel completely isolated from the outside world. The hills have this mystical quality, and windmills rise up from the fields around the capital city, organically interwoven with the landscape. Along the way, I see fields with vegetables and groves of fruit trees. Sadly, the electricity pylons spoil the panoramic views. Close to Avigliano lies Lagopesole castle, where the Swabian emperor Frederick II often sought refuge. The impressive Vulture region, named after the extinct volcano of the same name, is just a stone's throw away.

Artisanal village

The artisanal village of Avigliano sits high atop a hill amidst a crown of forests. The typical local delicacy here is *baccalà,* dried, salted cod, and the *tarallo aviglianese,* a brittle biscuit covered with a thin layer of sugar frosting. Cod takes centre stage here; every year in August, a baccalà festival is held.

The bread in Avigliano exudes tradition; its delicious scent intoxicates those wandering the village's narrow streets. The *Antico forno di Valvano* in the town centre is the oldest oven currently in use. The owner, Vitantonio Valvano, continues the age-old tradition that was once so characteristic of Avigliano in the sixteenth-century. This is where artisanal practices thrive. The Valvano family has been baking the same type of bread for over 400 years, to Vitantonio's immense pride.

BAKERY
L'antico forno di Valvano

It's early in the morning, and finding the bakery amongst the maze of streets and alleys is proving to be a challenge. The bakery doesn't look like a shop. I walk down a set of stairs into a cellar opening, which gives way to a giant wood-fired oven. In a space measuring about two by two metres, I see the bread loaves stacked on the shelves. Vitantonio uses a large baker's peel to take the loaves of bread out of the oven, one by one, and place them on the shelves. The bread is made with a mixture of hard and soft wheat. I watch in fascination from the stairs. The breads, weighing at least a kilogram each, smell like beech wood. 'We have been using beech wood for ages,' Vitantonio assures me. The baker is busy because all this bread has already been ordered and needs to be brought to the supermarket. Vitantonio also makes *strazzata* and *fucuazza* in his ancient oven. 'The inside of the oven measures 16 square metres,' he tells me. Occasionally, a local villager peeks in through the cellar door and orders something for later in the early afternoon. 'It's better to be on time. Our production is modest and everything is always sold out. And sold out means no more bread,' Vitantonio says. At Avigliano, they know the ropes. The message is clear: get up on time because, by late morning, the shelves will be empty.

Fucuazza

After the bread is baked, Vitantonio makes a type of elongated pizza. The baker frowns at my mention of the word pizza and immediately interrupts: '*Fucuazza* is the fruit of our centuries-old art of baking and an ode to simplicity. You will only find this bread here. In dialect, this is called *Fucuazza cu la prmmarora,* and it's authentic Basilicata street food. The flat, elongated, crispy focaccia is topped with extra-virgin olive oil, oregano and tomato sauce. We prepare a relatively flat dough so the edges turn crunchy on the baking tray. The current fucuazza does differ somewhat from the original because we have been adding tomatoes since the 19th century.'

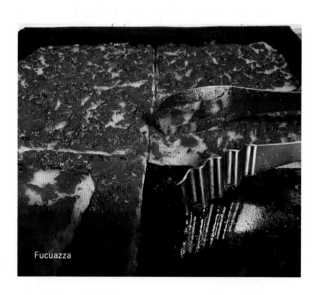

Fucuazza

Vitantonio removes the bread from the large wood-fired oven – L'antico forno di Valvano

Strazzata

Strazzata is another Avigliano speciality. This baked treat looks completely different from the fucuazza. The large doughnut shape and the hole in the middle remind me of the *pitta calabrese* from Catanzaro. Vitantonio: 'We use soft and hard wheat flour, water, yeast and a pinch of salt for the dough. It is the coarsely ground black pepper that makes the difference. The name strazzata is derived from *strazzare* or *straccare*, meaning 'to tear' in our dialect. We tear the large focaccia into pieces to share instead of using a knife. A good strazzata is filled with local cheeses such as *caciocavallo lucano* (a pulled-curd cheese made from cow's milk), *casieddu* (goat cheese) and *canstrato di Moliterno* (a hard, mature cheese made from a combination of sheep and goat's milk), and of course, the lucanica sausage with wild fennel!'

Strazzata

⭐ Matrimonio – a wedding celebration

Claudio, a lawyer from the village, walks into the cellar and joins in the conversation. Claudio: 'Who will replace Vitantonio when he retires? It's very hard work and his daughters won't take over the business. Our 400-year-old oven will be extinct, or rather extinguished. This oven holds a rich history and plays a central role in the folklore. Did you know that strazzata was traditionally served at weddings here? Weddings used to take up two entire days, on Saturday and Sunday. It would start with breakfast at the bride's home. Halfway through Saturday morning, the bridegroom's family would be offered strazzata, richly filled with ham, pecorino, provolone cheese... Meanwhile, the bride's family members would be offered the same treat at the bridegroom's house. People believed that the more well-filled the strazzata,

the brighter the couple's future would be. Both families competed to make the best strazzata. The dough had to be liberally treated with pepper. The more pepper, the thirstier people would get. And that thirst was gladly slaked with regional wines.'

A broad smile appears on Vitantonio's face as Claudio tells his story with relish. He remembers those celebrations. Before I continue on my way, I thank Vitantonio for preserving this wonderful piece of cultural heritage. 'As long as these legs will still carry me, I will continue to work!' he solemnly promises as he presses a freshly baked fucuazza into my hands.

L'antico forno di Valvano
Via forno ai giardini 4, Avigliano

Avigliano

CALABRIA

The 'toe' of the Italian boot speaks to the imagination. Calabria is an irregularly shaped peninsula pinned between the Tyrrhenian and the Ionian Sea. Picturesque traditional villages and magical beaches bathe in sunlight. Rugged cliffs and sandy beaches intertwine to form 800 kilometres of coastline. Calabria's mountainous interior is a fascinating region with beautiful forests and no fewer than three nature reserves. To the north, the Pollino massif links Calabria to the Appennino Lucano in Basilicata. Catanzaro is the regional capital. The largest coastal town, Reggio Calabria, is situated on the Strait of Messina, just a stone's throw from Sicily. Calabria is not a prosperous region; its greatest treasure is its beauty.

Prickly pear cacti with fruit in Calabria

Pristine white beaches grace the waterfront of the town of Pizzo

Diamante ❶

Cosenza ❷

Catanzaro ❺

Golfo di
Taranto

Golfo di
S. Eufemia

Pizzo ❸

Spilinga ❹

Golfo di
Gióia

Stretto di Messina

History

Calabria shares its history with Basilicata and Apulia. In ancient times, the region formed the heart of a powerful and prosperous Greek colony. After the Greeks, the Romans, Byzantines, Lombards, Vikings, Hohenstaufen or Swabians, Angevins and Bourbons all reigned here at some point. Later, the southern region was an Italian republican stronghold until the *Risorgimento*, the unification of Italy. In 1860, Calabria joined the kingdom of Italy under the republican revolutionary, Giuseppe Garibaldi. This general was welcomed as the liberator from Bourbon tyranny. Italians consider Giuseppe Garibaldi a national hero.

Latifundium, large estate

Agriculture is the foundation of this mountainous region's economy. In the olden days, large country estates, or *latifundia*, existed alongside tiny farmsteads. The farms were almost entirely devoted to grains, olives, sheep and goats. Soil erosion and primitive agricultural practices ensured that Calabria remained one of the poorest regions in Italy for a long time. Starting in the 1950s, agricultural reforms and government investments led to newer, more profitable crops. Today, the Calabrians not only earn their living from the agrifood industry; they're proud of it.

⭐ The mafia and emigration

The Calabrian mafia, known as the *'Ndrangheta',* impedes economic growth. The same goes for the rough, mountainous interior, earthquakes and poor infrastructure. The railroads primarily serve the coastal areas, but beyond that, there is hardly any industry. Catanzaro, Reggio di Calabria and Cosenza are the only cities of notable size.

Life in Calabria has always been hard, which explains why many people sought their fortune elsewhere. Speak to any Calabrian, and they'll undoubtedly tell you they have cousins somewhere in America, Australia, or elsewhere in Europe. The Calabrians are masters in the art of living. They like to talk and sing and have hearts as vast as the azure-blue sea.

TERROIR

Calabria pulls out all the stops when it comes to typical, southern Italian, Mediterranean cuisine, including meat dishes (pork, lamb and goat) with plenty of vegetables, especially aubergine, and a little fish. Despite Calabria's vast coastline, there is no significant gastronomical tradition involving fish. The sea is seen more as an enemy than a friend, given that foreign invaders and pirates often came from the sea.

A whole range of products has a protected quality, or IGP label. IGP products include the *cipolla rossa di Tropea*, the red onion from Tropea, potatoes from Sila, and *'nduja* from Spilinga. Examples of DOP products include *sopressata* (cured salami), *caciocavallo* cheese and *bergamotto*, a citrus fruit from Reggio Calabria.

In ancient times, the Greeks called Calabria *Enotria*, 'the land of wine'. Some vineyards' origins date back to the ancient Greek colony. The most famous DOC wines are the *cirò* from the province of Crotone and the *donnici* from the province of Cosenza. The red gaglioppo and white greco are the best-known grape varieties. Calabria has also made a name for itself with its amaro digestives, including the Vecchio Amaro del Capo, which has a complex flavour palate of mint, aniseed, orange, and liquorice.

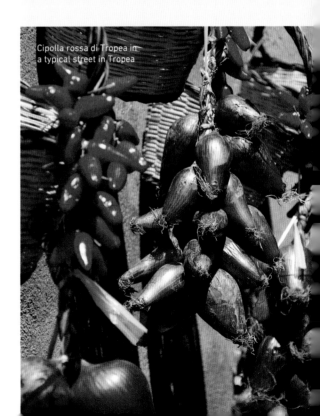
Cipolla rossa di Tropea in a typical street in Tropea

DIAMANTE ①

My Calabria road trip starts at the Riviera dei Cedri on the shores of the Tyrrhenian Sea in the northwest. The region owes its name to the local citrus fruit, *cedro,* a unique variety of giant lemon. This lemon country stretches from Tortora on the northern border to the town of Paola further south along the coast. Diamante is situated halfway. In September, the town holds a week-long festival honouring the region's star product: the *pepperoncino,* or chilli pepper. Diamante, also known for its many murals, is where I meet Enzo Monaco. He's chairman of the Academia Italiana del Peperoncino and a self-professed fan of His Royal Highness, the chilli pepper!

Peperoncino

Enzo: 'The pepperoncino means everything to us, not only in terms of nutrition and gastronomy but also as a cultural symbol. The hot, red spice reflects the Calabrian spirit. Anthropologists ascribe the following characteristics to this fiery red pepper: *duro* (hard), *bastarde* (bastard), *brigante* (bandit), *violente* (violent) and *sensuale* (sensual). This characterisation is not based on science, of course,' Enzo says with a wink.

'Whenever Calabrians travel anywhere,' he continues, 'they always pack some pepperoncino in their suitcase. Today, the chilli pepper is crushed or ground in a mortar and pestle and stored in a small silver container for travel.'

Enzo shows me a small container attached to a keychain that Liz Taylor's goldsmith, Gerardo Sacco, designed for the academy. The dried powder is kept in a tiny holder shaped like a pepperoncino. Enzo: 'The Aztecs, Mayas and Incas cultivated chilli pepper thousands of years ago. Through the centuries, it was considered a holy fruit, a medicine, an aphrodisiac, a preservative and an excellent seasoning. The chilli peppers ended up in Europe after Christopher Columbus discovered America. This plant, which takes root in practically anything, even in a pot, flourishes wonderfully in our poor soil.'

Dried chilli peppers ready for grinding

FROM AXI TO CHILLI PEPPER

A poster on the wall displays peppers of all shapes and sizes with various names. Enzo: 'Axi was the name the indigenous people gave to chilli peppers in the time of Christopher Columbus. In Europe, we called the spice Indian pepper, horned pepper, and *siliquastro.* The term *peperoncino* is the diminutive of *peperone,* the sweet pepper. The peperoncino group includes many different varieties. We do not have a specific variety with a DOP or IGP quality label in Calabria, like they do in Spain or France. Just to give you an idea of the variety of spicy peppers out there: there's habanero (the spiciest variety), *chilli d'Espelette* (French), *piquillo de Lodosa* (Spanish), *tabasco* (Louisiana), *cayenne* (Mexico), *Diavolicchio Diamante* (Calabria), Naga *Morich* (India), *Big Jim* (New Mexico), *chiltepin* (Mexico)...'

⭐ Poor man's spice

The 1891 book, *Pellegrino Artusi La scienza in cucina e l'arte di mangiar bene* (Science in the Kitchen and the Art of Eating Well), does not mention the spice. Enzo explains that the wealthy and the nobility did not like the spice, and according to the church, peperoncino was believed to be 'the root of all evil'.

Enzo: 'During those years, only the poor farmers and labourers used chilli peppers in the south. They ate mainly vegetables that grew in the wild. Peperoncino was used to add flavour and was soon dubbed the 'poor man's spice' in popular speech. It was love at first sight for peasant cooking. Moreover, peperoncino was an excellent preservative and disinfectant back when the refrigerator was nothing more than a dream for many – an important consideration in the hot Calabrian climate. Peperoncino was mixed into everything as a food preservative, and we fell in love with its spicy flavour.'

Academia Italiana del Peperoncino

I ask former Latin and Greek teacher and journalist Enzo what drives him to champion pepperoncino. Enzo: 'I am *Calabrese*. Peperoncino is our daily bread. And yet, 30 years ago, I realised how little we actually knew about this staple. That's why I founded the Academia Italiana del Peperoncino here in Diamante and wrote the book *Peperoncino, amore mio* (Chilli pepper, my love).'

Enzo hands me a copy of this fine book in which he reveals the secrets of his beloved spice with well-founded explanations as well as a nod and a wink. 'At the Academia, we study this fiery spice within a broader framework and monitor its expression in gastronomic circles, film and literature, medicine, cosmetics and biology. We also organise fun events such as the annual Italian chilli pepper eating championship. Moreover, the world's only peperoncino museum is located right here in Diamante, Enzo concludes, beaming with pride.

Academia del Peperoncino
Via Fausto Gullo 1, Diamante

Bomba calabrese

Bomba calabrese, or *piccantino*, is a spicy sauce made from vegetables and chilli pepper. The sauce comes in different versions with varying degrees of spiciness depending on the amount of chilli pepper used.

The sauce serves as a topping for bruschette and as a seasoning for pasta, pizza or meat dishes. You will find this sauce throughout Calabria, packaged in glass jars. But in many families, the sauce is still made at home. Enzo gave me this recipe.

Peperoncino, also known as poor man's spice

Bomba calabrese

MAKES 3 SMALL JARS

250 g aubergines
250 red sweet peppers
75 g hot chilli peppers (between 30 g and 75 g,
    depending on the desired spiciness)
½ carrot
½ stalk celery
2 fresh basil leaves
1 small clove garlic
coarse salt to taste
15–25 g anchovy fillets
    (leave them out for a vegan/vegetarian version)
1 tablespoon wine vinegar
additional extra-virgin olive oil to taste

Rinse the aubergine, carrot and celery and dice into cubes measuring 1/2 cm. Finely chop the chilli peppers after removing the stems and weigh them. This is where you decide how spicy your Calabrian 'bomb' should be.
Layer the diced vegetables together with the peppers in a colander. Sprinkle coarse salt over each layer: first layer = aubergine + salt, second layer = sweet pepper + salt, third layer = chilli pepper + salt, fourth layer = carrot, celery and garlic + salt.

Put the colander in a pot or bowl and cover with a lid or plate. Chill in the refrigerator for 24 hours.

During this period, the vegetables will lose a lot of their water because of the salt.
After 24 hours, press out the remaining moisture with a potato ricer or masher.

Place the pressed vegetables in a bowl and drizzle the white wine vinegar over the top. Leave to soak for three hours. Then, wring the diced vegetables in a kitchen towel to remove all the vinegar moisture. Make sure the vegetables are thoroughly dry. Wrap the vegetables in a clean towel and leave to dry for at least six hours.

After six hours, the vegetables are ready for the oil. Place the vegetables in a bowl and add the coarsely chopped anchovies and basil leaves. Pour extra-virgin olive oil over the top until the mixture is submerged, and leave to rest for a week. Check the sauce and give it a stir every day for a week. If it needs more oil, add more oil. The vegetables should be constantly submerged in oil.
At the end of the week, fill clean, sterilised pots with the sauce. Make sure the vegetables are completely submerged in oil.

Use the *bomba* as a topping for bruschetta or a sandwich. The bomba calabrese is sure to spice up even the most boring sandwiches!

COSENZA ②

The Calabrian capital, Cosenza, is situated at the foot of the Sila mountains about 100 kilometres south of Diamante. The modern part of the town is to the north, and the historic old town perches on a steep hill on the other side of the Busento River. Southern Italy, in all its authentic, self-willed and unpolished glory, comes alive here in romantic, dark, dingy alleyways under rusty balconies laden with laundry flapping in the wind. Bric-a-brac shops contribute to the retro atmosphere. As a tourist, you're an outsider looking in on the street theatre that marks this no-nonsense city.

ROSTICCERIA/RESTAURANT
Polpette

At the foot of the old town, I visit the Antica Rosticceria Polpetteria Sasà. Father Sasà, alias Salvatore, and son Michele Altimari wait for me at their typical *rosticceria* with grilled and fried foods. 'I am the fourth generation in our family business, and my great-grandfather, grandfather, and father have invented and developed every recipe here,' Michele tells me. The counter is filled with freshly baked *panzerotti* and a myriad of different types of *polpette*. A sign by the counter reads: *Le nostre polpette,* or 'our croquettes' come in several varieties: *melanzana* (aubergine), *tonno* (tuna), *carne* (meat), *alici fresche* (fresh anchovies), *riso in bianco* (white rice), *riso scamorza e 'nduja* (rice with scamorza cheese and 'nduja), or *patate* (potato).

Cosenza

Purpetti

'The polpette, *purpetti* in dialect, are a true Calabrian tradition,' Sasà continues. 'We use all sorts of basic and seasonal ingredients that we then process with eggs and flour or breadcrumbs before frying or baking them. You can eat them warm or cold. Purpetti symbolise our simple yet creative cuisine because you can make them in a variety of flavours, and it lets you reuse all kinds of ingredients. Wasting food is unacceptable here, hence all these unique dishes.'

Michele: 'Purpetti are traditionally also prepared in a pan with sauce. They form the basis of the illustrious 'meatballs in tomato sauce'. We had to feed large families, so we needed a lot of croquettes. We would dip them in a tomato sauce with vegetables and peperoncino for extra volume. And that's how a phenomenal, world-famous dish found its origins.'

⭐ Never refuse food from a Calabrian

I take a seat at a table on the patio. Sasà will join me to taste the wine and polpette. 'You cannot refuse,' he says. 'Did you know that sitting at the dinner table is sacred to us? We enjoy the food and the company and stick to the rules. When a Calabrian offers you coffee, wine or food, you may never decline. We are very hospitable, but we also have a very short fuse.'
I obediently eat the proffered polpette, sip from my glass of white cirò and ask whether there are any other rules. Sasà: 'Certainly! We have many rules. Small portions are unacceptable, for example. The more you eat, the more you show how much you enjoy the food and the company. And there are also rules for in the kitchen. We use chilli peppers in all our dishes. Cream, béchamel sauce or other north-Italian ingredients that may mask the flavour are not allowed. And we are generous with the salt. We feel that you need to spice up the good things in life. We Calabrians only use red onions from Tropea; we throw away the rest. And finally, aubergines are sacred in our kitchen!'

Devil's egg

Michel tells me about the aubergine, which wasn't introduced to Italy until the eighth century: 'The Arabs brought the fruit with them from India and called it the

Polpette di melanzane

MAKES ABOUT 15 CROQUETTES

500 g aubergines
2 eggs
100 g bread
50 g pecorino cheese
50 g Parmesan cheese
parsley to taste (or basil)
1 clove garlic
salt to taste
pepper to taste
breadcrumbs (extra)

Soak the stale bread in cold water for an hour. Rinse the aubergines, cut them in half and cook them in plenty of salted boiling water for 10 to 15 minutes until tender. Drain and let cool before pressing them to remove the excess water. This is important because watery aubergines can ruin the dish. You can also use a potato masher to press them, or you can steam the aubergines instead of boiling them, which requires less water. After pressing them, place the aubergines on a cutting board and chop them as finely as possible with a sharp knife.

Put all the ingredients for the aubergine croquettes in a bowl. Start with the cooked aubergines. Make sure they're cool and well-drained.

Also squeeze out any moisture from the bread. Add the bread to the bowl, along with the eggs, minced garlic, finely chopped parsley, black pepper, salt and grated cheeses. Combine everything with your hands. If the mixture is too sticky, add breadcrumbs or flour. Shape the mixture into slightly elongated aubergine croquettes.

Fry the croquettes in plenty of oil in a non-stick pan. You don't have to submerge them. Don't turn them over until they're golden brown on one side. Otherwise, they'll break up when you turn them. Let them brown on both sides. Remove the polpette from the pan and drain off the excess fat on paper towels. Serve warm. Polpette di melanzane are also delicious in tomato sauce.

They're called *purpetti i mulingiana* in the local dialect. The aubergine croquettes from Calabria are delicious and refreshing in terms of flavour, with aromas of garlic and parsley.

"devil's egg". People back then believed that the conquerors had brought the aubergine with them to eliminate Christians. The name *melanzana* (aubergine) is derived from the Latin term *mela insana*, or 'mad, unhealthy apple'. You can't eat them raw as they'll make you ill. Back then, there weren't any good recipes for aubergine. Initially, it was the Arabs and Jews that ate the fruit; they developed the first aubergine dishes.'

'We have more than made up for the damage,' Sasà continues. 'We make the most delicious dishes with aubergine. We eat them fried, grilled, deep-fried, as a first or side course... The aubergine is omnipresent in our cuisine. Typical dishes include *melanzana alla parmigiana* (casserole with aubergines), *peperonata alla calabrese* (a vegetable stew), *melanzane ripiene* (stuffed aubergines), *melanzane sott'olio* (preserved in olive oil) and *polpette di melanzane* (aubergine croquettes). The Ministry of Agricultural Food and Forestry Policies assigned the PAT (Prodotti Agroalimentari Tradizionali) quality mark to these dishes, the label that marks traditional Calabrian foodstuffs.

Antica Rosticceria Polpetteria Sasà
Piazza Dei Valdesi 214, Cosenza

The town of Pizzo

PIZZO ③

From Cosenza, I drive 100 km further south until I reach the seaside resort of Pizzo – or Pizzo Calabro – on the Tyrrhenian Sea. The *Costa degli Dei*, or Coast of the Gods, owes its name to its beautiful coves, white, sandy beaches and azure-blue sea. In addition to Pizzo, the coast is home to Zambrône, Capo Vaticano, and the breathtakingly beautiful Tropea. This Calabrian gem is situated another 50 kilometres further south, where you have fantastic views of the volcanic island of Stromboli.

I take the exit to Pizzo. The village is situated on a steep cliff overlooking the Golfo di Sant'Eufemia with its stunning beaches and crystal-clear sea. This romantic village is teeming with life – and *gelati*, or ice creams. 'It can get pretty hot here in the summer with the warm air streaming in from Africa. Only our delicious ice cream can offer refreshment!' Alessio Di Iorgi from the Ercole ice-cream parlour laughs.

Tartufo di Pizzo

The famous *tartufo* ice cream found its origins in this small fishing town on the west coast. Pizzo is the home of the Italian *gelato*. On summery days, it's always crowded at the Piazza della Repubblica, where Alessio and I sit on a terrace. Alessio: 'We have been making delicious ice cream here for a very long time. Pizzo has been the North Star in the gelato firmament since the tartufo was invented in the 1950s. We follow the traditional recipe and adopt an artisanal preparation method that has been passed down through the generations. The ball is layered with half chocolate and half hazelnut ice cream, with a molten chocolate ganache centre and a coating of bitter cocoa powder. We also make a *smeraldo* version with pistachio, chocolate sauce and chopped almonds, and a *bianco* or 'white ball' with a rum crisp and coffee mousse. On this square, you will find the five top artisanal ice-cream parlours. Gelateria Artigianale Bar Dante, Bar Gelateria Del Centro, Pasticceria Gelateria Raffaele, Gelateria Morino Pizzo dal 1973, and our Bar Gelateria Ercole.'

Ice cream from the palm of your hand

The ice cream preparations for the day are completed, and father Ivan Di Iorgi joins us at the table. Ivan: 'Everything started in 1940 with Sicilian master patissier Dante Veronelli and his Gelateria Dante across from us. After the Second World War, various patisserie shops opened in Pizzo, and cream, crèmes and ricotta cheese took our village by storm. Dante's business was a huge success because the proprietor and Dante's business partner, Giuseppe De Maria alias Don Pippo, made ice cream of the finest quality. De Maria continued to run the business after Veronelli's death. And by a happy coincidence, he came up with the current recipe for truffle ice cream. This was in 1952, to be exact. He had to make a lot of ice cream for a wedding celebration, but he didn't have enough moulds to serve the ice cream for the countless guests. So, Don Pippo made individual ice creams by moulding the ice cream by hand; he placed a portion of hazelnut ice cream in the palm of his hand, covered it with a layer of chocolate ice cream and added the chocolate sauce in the middle. He then wrapped the ball in paper, giving the ice cream its distinctive irregular truffle shape. It was genius. In 1970, *tartufo di Pizzo* became the first ice cream in the world with an IGP label, which refers to its *Indicazione Geografica Protetta* (Protected Geographical Indication) status.'

ICE CREAM PARLOUR
for artisanal ice cream

Alessio adds: 'My grandfather Gaetano worked in the Dante ice-cream parlour in the 1950s and spent 15 years learning the trade from the masters. He went on to become a ship's cook. He didn't start this ice cream parlour until 1975, together with his brother Antonio. Today, my father Ivan, my brother Francesco, and I run the family business. We make everything ourselves, and that's hard work.'

'We continue the artisanal tradition,' Ivan continues. 'People come here for the real tartufo, and we want to keep it that way. And even if the demand increases, we will never make concessions in terms of quality. They want our ice cream in Rome, and countries abroad are looking to import it, which I'm not too thrilled about; we're from Pizzo, and we want to keep our ice cream here. We made a name for ourselves with this artisanal product, and we don't want to lose that.'

'You won't notice the difference until you actually taste the ice cream here.' And with these wise words, Alessio serves me a plate of tartufo di Pizzo. Its shape is anything but round, and chocolate sauce oozes from the centre as I cut into the ice cream. Alessio: That's the difference between the mass-produced tartufo you also find abroad. Our chocolate sauce is always liquid, even at very low temperatures. Look at how creamy that is!'

A vintage advertisement in Pizzo

I taste *dolce e amaro,* the combination of sweet ice cream and bitter cocoa powder. The dark chocolate ice cream flavour dominates but combines wonderfully with the outspoken hazelnut ice cream. The spectacular half-liquid filling gives my ice cream a velvety, shiny look.

Bar Gelateria Ercole
Piazza della Repubblica 18, Pizzo

Growth and distribution

Alessio: 'Various mass-produced tartufo ice cream varieties that have nothing to do with the artisanal IGP label have been inspired by our unique dessert. The artisanal preparation has to make way for industry due to the growing demand for this product. In the olden days, you could only find handmade tartufo gelato here in this central square in Pizzo. Now, you will find our ice cream throughout Italy and beyond. Famous brand names include Tre Marie, Algida/Ola, Sammontana, Antica Gelateria del Corso, Gelateria Callipo and Grandinetti.'

I enjoy spending time at this square, and I meet inspiring figures. And for dessert, I am treated to a spectacular sunset over the Tyrrhenian Sea that lies beyond the end of the Piazza. Gorgeous orange and red hues light up the sky and frame the few ships sailing far in the distance. An unforgettable sight.

ALESSIO'S RECIPE
Tartufo

MAKES 5 TARTUFO BALLS
250 g hazelnut ice cream
250 g chocolate ice cream
cocoa mixture: 50 ml water, 80 g caster sugar,
    40 g cocoa powder, 6 g dextrose
100 g bitter cocoa powder
paper towel/parchment paper
disposable gloves

COCOA MIXTURE OR CHOCOLATE GANACHE Start by preparing the cocoa mixture. Add the water, sugar, dextrose and cocoa powder to a pan and whisk everything together. As soon as the mixture starts to boil, remove the pan from heat and leave it to cool to room temperature. The cool sauce will later be added to the centre of the ice cream ball.

ICECREAM BALLS Tartufo di Pizzo is made of half spheres of 50/70 g chocolate ice cream and 50/70 g hazelnut ice cream layered by hand (hence the gloves) or with a special portioning tool such as a silicone mould or a very large ice cream scoop. First, shape the two half a spheres and then make a small well measuring two to three centimetres in the first ice cream half and fill the well with about 15 to 20 g of the cocoa mixture. After the well is filled with the chocolate mixture, press the two ice cream halves together and wrap them in parchment paper. Store the ice cream balls overnight in the freezer.

PREPARATION WITH SILICONE MOULDS Take a silicone mould and fill the half spheres with a scoop of chocolate ice cream. Spread the ice cream over the mould with a spatula, cover with parchment paper and chill in the freezer for an hour. Take another mould and fill these half spheres with the hazelnut ice cream. Even out the surface and place them in the freezer for an hour as well. Remove the ice cream from the freezer, make a small well in each half and fill the well with the chocolate ganache. Even out the surface, cover them with parchment paper once more and return them to the freezer for another hour. Remove both halves from the silicone moulds and place them on top of each other. Use gloves. Press the halves together with your hands to form a solid ball. Wrap the balls in parchment paper and place them in the freezer for another hour.

COATING WITH COCOA POWDER Take the mould out of the freezer just before serving. Roll the balls through a bowl dusted with cocoa powder. If you prefer a slightly sweeter version, combine the cocoa powder with a layer of caster sugar. Place the coated tartufo ball on a plate and serve.

Deliciously creamy tartufo ice cream on Gelateria Ercole's terrace

VIBO VALENTIA

Just 2 kilometres from the village centre, along the Strada Statale is the *buccacci* warehouse of the late Rosa Fanfulla. I approach a white building with a green metal gate along a busy road by the seaside. Her grandson Giuseppe Sabato is my guide. He will introduce me to the art of preserving Calabrian vegetables *sott'olio* (under olive oil) in the typical *buccacci* or glass mason jars. Homemade preserves are part of the Calabrian cultural heritage. Giuseppe: 'My grandmother, Signora Rossa, made such delicious sauces and preserved vegetables that the whole village asked her to sell them. And that is how *nonna* (grandma) started our Fanfulla Rosa di Sabato Vittorio business some 50 years ago. We process local vegetables, herbs and fish in glass jars the way our forefathers have done for centuries.'

Vegetables grow quickly here, and the Calabrians have been preserving the right balance between not letting anything go to waste and experiencing pure, fresh flavours year-round since ancient times.

Buccacci

Giuseppe: 'Over the last century, buccacci were also produced for export. Mothers and aunts passed the lovingly filled glass jars among family members who had emigrated abroad. Each visit to the home front was accompanied by the pots filled with terroir, which were given as a souvenir to take back home with them. The *buccacci melanzane a filetti* (aubergine fillets), *giardiniera* (garden

vegetable mix), *pomodori secchi* (sundried tomatoes), *carciofi* (artichokes), *peperoncini* (chilli peppers), *piccantino* (spicy sauces), *passata di pomodoro* (tomato passata), *peperoncini ripieni* (stuffed mini peppers) and so on were trophies from our local kitchen. In August and September, we prepare the *buttigli*, the glass jars with vegetables. My grandmother always used to say that you had to harvest the vegetables when the moon was in the right position, otherwise the vegetables would rot in the jars. We preserve the products in the buccacci by pickling them with salt, preserving them in oil and vinegar, marinating them or cooking them.'

Tomato community

The entire village makes tomato sauce and passata at the end of the summer, according to tradition. Giuseppe's story is incredibly nostalgic. Giuseppe: 'So many memories. August summers, the 40-degree weather outside, the large crates brimming with tomatoes, and my grandma's sweet, loud voice: 'Tomorrow, we make the sauces!' Buccacci was not only for spending time with families; neighbours and friends joined in. Everyone helped each other; we would give the neighbours a hand as soon as our stock was ready. And that continued throughout August because not joining in meant breaking with the family and *la merda* (trouble) within the community.'

'Papa or my uncle and our neighbour would bring in a shipment of tomatoes with the Ape (a three-wheeled micro-lorry). Family members, neighbours, friends and acquaintances were there to take the tomatoes. We cleaned them on large, improvised tables as we laughed

Typical materials for preserving tomatoes

Glass jars filled with passata

and bantered back and forth. The tomatoes were cut up, and the gas was ignited underneath a huge cooking pot used to sterilise the empty jars. We made tomato passata by passing the sauce several times through a hand sieve, although we use electric blenders these days. After the sauce was sieved, it was stored in bottles. Another group blanched the whole, peeled tomatoes. We cooked the peeled tomatoes so we could store them in the cooking water in the buccacci. Other tomatoes were cut in half and laid out to dry on mats. Which we then covered with a layer of tulle to dry in the sun. Then they were preserved with capers, anchovies and olive oil.'

⭐ Tomato feast

Giuseppe: 'Each family member and friend had their own task on the "assembly line". One person would dry the glass jars, another would add fresh basil leaves or drizzle olive oil, screw the lid on or wrap the jar in cloth. The last person in the row placed the filled jar in boiling water. After about 20 minutes, the jars were removed from the cooking pot and placed upside-down in crates. And then it was time for the feast, with lots of food, drink and dancing. In the evening, we would place the buccacci in the larder to replenish our stock of fresh, delicious sauce for the entire year. And the following day, we would start all over again and

help the neighbours in exactly the same way, with another feast at the end of the day. It was wonderful! We treasure this valued, fine tradition within our community; learning to share. Our tomato community exists to this day, although it's perhaps more modest than it was back then.

Peperoni ripieni al tonno – Mini sweet peppers filled with tuna

We inspect the glass jars in Rosa Fanfulla's warehouse. I tell Giuseppe that I would like to have the spicy peperoncini filled with tuna. Giuseppe: 'The spicy flavour of the mini pepper is a perfect match for the soft tuna centre. We use a less spicy chilli pepper that resembles a sweet pepper. We preserve the small, rounded, filled peperoncini in oil. The preparation and conservation of these small chilli peppers dates back to the Calabrian farming tradition. You can choose fillings with tuna, soft cheese or olives.

The preparation is very simple. All you need is a handful of ingredients. But cleaning chilli peppers requires a lot of patience.'

Fanfulla Rosa
Via Proviciale per Vibo Valentia Marina

Mini sweet peppers filled with tuna

Tuna in Pizzo

My eye is drawn to the *bottarga di tonno* or 'dried tuna eggs' on the shelves. They are grated and used as a seasoning for pasta dishes. Next to them stands a row of jars containing delicious tuna fillets. Tuna steals the show next to the preserved southern vegetables. Giuseppe: 'Catching tuna is a deep-rooted tradition here in Pizzo. It started in ancient times with the Greeks. For years, Pizzo Calabro was the home port of the largest tuna fishing fleet on the Calabrian coast. It is now a museum. When the harbour closed in 1963, hundreds of fishermen went out of work. Some tried other trades, while others left aboard large merchant ships. A few struggled to continue their fishing livelihood. The tuna processers preserved the tradition. Take Callipo (1913) from founder Giacinto Callipo, one of the larges tuna processing businesses in Italy. Although most tuna nowadays comes from the Atlantic, Pacific and Indian Oceans, this fish has been processed for over 100 years in Calabria.

Museo del Mare
Piazza della Repubblica 1, Pizzo

Peperoncini ripieni al tonno

MAKES 500 GRAMS

250 g round hot peppers or mini sweet peppers
200 g tuna in oil, drained
3 salted anchovy fillets
½ tablespoon capers to taste
extra-virgin olive oil
2 tablespoons vinegar
salt and pepper
oregano
glass jars

PEPERONCINI

Wash the mini hot peppers or peperoncini thoroughly and remove the stems.
With a thin knife, dig into the peppers and remove the seeds and insides. Take a pot of water and add vinegar, salt, pepper and oregano. Bring to a boil. Put the mini peppers in the pot and cook for three to four minutes. Drain the peppers and leave them upside-down on a towel to dry overnight. Drier chilli peppers are better and can be stored longer. Once the peppers are dry, you can make the filling.

FILLING

Finely chop the capers and anchovies with a knife. Put the anchovies, capers and tuna in a blender and mix for a couple of seconds. Make sure the tuna doesn't become too creamy. Pour the mixture into a bowl and fill the peperoncini with a small spoon. Make sure that the filling is divided evenly over the peperoncini.

STORING

Place the filled peppers in a glass jar with the filling facing up.
Fill the jar with extra-virgin olive oil and make sure that the peperoncini ripieni al tonno are fully submerged.

Seal the jars with a lid. The peppers will keep for up to a year when stored in a cool, dark, dry place.

The beach at Pizzo

SPILINGA ④

The town of Spilinga is situated 45 kilometres further south, near Tropea on the flank of the Poro mountain, about 450 metres above the Tyrrhenian Sea and the beautiful beaches of Capo Vaticano. In this humid, windy microclimate, the 'nduja, which owes its distinctive aroma and flavour to the Poro plateau, originated centuries ago. And although you will find original 'nduja across Calabria, Spilinga is the only town to hold the title of *Città della 'nduja*, 'the city of 'nduja'.

'Nduja is the uncrowned queen of Calabrian cuisine, widespread throughout Italy but also beloved abroad, especially among chefs. In Spilinga, I visit the artisanal 'nduja producer San Donato, owned by the Pugliese family. In the 1950s, Antonio Pugliese was already processing meat at various farms that slaughtered pigs. Grandfather Antonio created a name for himself with his skilful hands and excellent 'nduja dishes. He started his own 'nduja atelier with his sons, Pasquale and Armando. Today I get to meet the third generation, Antonio Pugliese and his brother-in-law, Rocco Colaci.

'Nduja

But what is 'nduja exactly? Antonio: "'Nduja is a spicy smoked sausage. It is a typical Calabrian peasant dish that incorporates pork fat trimmings and peperoncino. We have refined the recipe over the years, and the mixture today includes pork cheek, bacon, lard and hot chilli pepper. We mince this into a homogenous whole, which we then leave to rest for a day.
The mixture is then stuffed into a 'blind cap' or *orba* casing. And then the sausages are smoked.'

We walk over to the smokehouse with the smouldering wood-fired stove. Antonio: 'We let the dry sea breeze circulate through this room. We use mountain bushes for the artisanal *fumicatura* (the smoking process). We smoke the meat for three to six months, depending on the sausage size. It is an entirely natural process.
The 'nduja contains a lot of chilli pepper, over one-third of the total mass. Peperoncino has strong antioxidant and antiseptic properties, so no preservatives or other additives are needed to store the sausage.

DOUBLE-EDGED SWORD

'*Nduja di Spilinga*'s huge success also has its downsides,' Antonio continues. 'Twelve years ago, we started the procedure to protect our product with a label, but without success thus far. Together with ten producers from Spilinga, we want to demarcate the production area for 'Nduja di Spilinga with an IGP quality label. But there is some disagreement about the extent of this zone. Today, producers outside our territory promote their products under the name 'Nduja di Spilinga. It's going to be an uphill battle.'
'But we're optimistic,' Rocco says. 'Many delicatessen shops in Calabria try to reproduce our 'nduja. Without success. The real 'nduja comes from Spilinga!'

Market stall with typical Calabrian ingredients

orecchiette with meatballs and 'nduja

SERVES 4 PEOPLE

320 g orecchiette
500 ml tomato passata
1 clove garlic
50 g 'nduja
30 g grated Parmesan cheese
125 g mozzarella
olive oil and salt

FOR THE MEATBALLS

250 g mixed meat mince
1 egg
grated cheese to taste
breadcrumbs to taste
salt and oil for frying

For the meatballs, put the minced meat in a bowl and add the egg, grated cheese, breadcrumbs, and a pinch of salt. Combine all the ingredients. Shape the mixture into balls and fry them in a pan with oil or butter. Drain on paper towels and set aside. Pour a splash of olive oil into a pan and fry the crushed garlic. Add the tomato passata and cook for ten to fifteen minutes. Add salt and the meatballs to the sauce at the end. Cook the orecchiette in salted water. Drain and add to the sauce. Add the diced 'nduja and mozzarella. Combine everything together. Spoon the pasta into four terra cotta bowls, add grated cheese, and bake in the oven at 200 °C for 15 minutes.

'Nduja in the smokehouse

'Nduja in the kitchen

I say goodbye to both cheerful, driven young men and wish them all the best. They hand me a portion of 'nduja, and I immediately ask them for cooking tips. Antonio: 'The fatty 'nduja, with its distinctive flavour, is a great addition to sauces, stir-fries, vegetables and meat and is a perfect accompaniment to cheese. The spicy filling is also popular as a pizza topping.'

**'Nduja San Donato Srl
dei F.lli Pugliese Loc. Lariat – Monte Poro, Spilinga**

CATANZARO ⑤

From Spilinga, I drive another 95 kilometres to Catanzaro via the impressive and controversial Bisantis viaduct (1960) designed by engineer Riccardo Morandi. This construction, measuring 112 metres across, connects the old town to the outside world. There is much to discover in this magical land on three hills, embraced by the sun and wind from two seas. It is always windy here because the province of Catanzaro is wedged between the Ionian and the Tyrrhenian Sea. The churches and monuments dating from different periods with their unique architecture bear witness to a rich history. As I stroll through the narrow streets of the old town some 330 metres above sea level, I am drawn back into the distant past. Gonzalo Borondo's street art on the panoramic terrace in the San Giovanni complex is a real showpiece. Naked women in profile grace Catanzaro's skyline.

Morzeddhu

Some dishes are so inextricably linked with their origins that they develop into a symbol of a town or region. Such an example is the *morzello* or *morzeddhu* from Catanzaro. I head over to the last authentic *putica* in town: Trattoria 2T Talarico. Up until the mid-1970s it was easy to find a putica, or typical *osteria*-style restaurant, in Catanzaro where customers could eat morzello and a few other dishes. Today, Salvatore Talarico's restaurant is a rarity; his daughter, Giusy Talarico, manages it. At the entrance, I read 'morzello'. This is a dish made from a combination of tripe and offal that have been stewed for hours and submerged in a thick, spicy sauce. I take a seat at a table and take in the delicious aroma coming from the sauces simmering on the stoves.

⭐ Pitta

'We eat morzello with a piece of *pitta* bread,' Giusy tells me, and she sets off to get a pitta from the kitchen. I see a loaf of bread in the shape of a giant wheel with a large opening in the middle. Giusy: 'The crumb of this typical Catanzaro bread soaks up even the most savoury spices. We usually cut the pitta into different pieces, four to six pieces per pitta. Each piece is cut lengthways in half. Before we fill the bread, we dip it in the sauce and then fill it with the meat.'
Salvatore beams as he tells us that the best way to eat the sandwich is with your hands. Salvatore: 'The experience of biting into the sandwich and feeling the sauce drip down your cheeks is phenomenal. That is pure enjoyment, and that is how we do it in Catanzaro!'

Legend

Giusy: 'The story behind the origins of this dish is worth telling. A very poor young woman, Chicchina, worked as a servant for a couple of Catanzaro nobles. During the Christmas season, she was ordered to clean the slaughterhouse courtyard, where the feast for the nobles was prepared. Instead of throwing away the meat scraps, she took them home with her. There, she carefully cleaned the meat, cut it into tiny pieces and cooked the scraps with tomatoes, water and aromatic herbs. Everyone at the table loved the dish. News of this exceptional dish travelled fast, and it became a huge success. Since then, even the tiniest scraps of meat have been put to good use, thanks to our hero, Chicchina.'

And although you'll only find morzeddhu at a few places today, the legend lives on. Giusy: 'People traditionally used almost all the innards of the cow. Now, we limit ourselves to the leanest parts of the stomach, heart and lungs. We stew the meat for a very long time and then cut it into tiny pieces. For the sauce, we add water, olive oil, tomato concentrate, oregano, salt and chilli pepper. The more peperoncino in the sauce, the tastier, we always say.'

Trattoria 2T Talarico
Via Alessandro Turco 16, Catanzaro

A pitta bread with morzeddhu and the house wine

SICILIA

Sicily is situated a mere 160 kilometres north-east of Tunisia (Northern Africa). The Strait of Messina separates this island from the mainland. It takes me half an hour to make the eight-kilometre crossing by car ferry.

History, rich traditions and delicious food are the highlights of this island, the largest in Italy and the Mediterranean Sea. It is home to the picturesque, historical and vibrant towns of Taormina, Palermo, Catania, Cefalù and Siracuse. Palermo is Sicily's capital and Mount Etna, the volcano, is the eternally burning heart of this fascinating island. Sicily's necklace of pearls includes other treasures, such as the northern Aeolian Islands near Messina and the Aegadian Islands near Trapani. Lampedusa and Pantelleria are situated further south in the Mediterranean Sea, halfway between Sicily and Tunisia. In Sicily, you can enjoy the sea ten months a year, thanks to its mild climate. The former king of Sicily, Frederick II, Duke of Swabia, summed Sicily up as follows: 'I do not envy God's paradise because I'm well-pleased to live in Sicily.'

Street scene with enoteca in Catania

Trapani

Palermo ①

②

③

A cove near Taormina

Marsala

Taormina

Acireale ⑤ ⑥

④

Catania

History

Over the centuries, Sicily has been a crossroads for peoples as well as a coveted prize because of its strategic central location in the Mediterranean Sea. The Greeks settled in Sicilian towns between the eighth and sixth centuries BC. Three centuries later, the island became the first Roman province. The Byzantines conquered Sicily, after which the island fell victim to Arabs from Northern African until the Norsemen landed in 1060. From the 12th century onwards, the island fell under the rule of the Hohenstaufen dynasty headed by Frederick, Duke of Swabia. What remained on the mainland became a part of the Kingdom of Naples, and the island became the Kingdom of Sicily. Powerful noble houses fought each other for centuries for possession of the island. From the 18th century onwards, this responsibility fell to the House of Bourbon, and Sicily's seat of government moved to Naples. In 1860, Giuseppe Garibaldi liberated Sicily from the Bourbon yoke; one year later, the island became a part of the Kingdom of Italy.

Food fest

Sicily is one giant food fest. The island takes pride in its rich and unique gastronomic heritage, both in terms of street food and traditional preparations. The cuisine is the culmination of thousands of years of cultural cross-contamination. Restaurants, bars, and roadside stalls spare no expense with a myriad of sweet and savoury specialities. Sicily is the perfect destination for a culinary journey of discovery.

CULTURAL CROSSROADS AND SHADOW GOVERNMENT

In light of this, one thing is perfectly clear: Sicily is a melting pot, the result of centuries of exchange with and domination by foreign peoples. The mafia has been a part of this isolated island since the Middle Ages. Organised crime forms a shadow government parallel to the official government. Who doesn't remember Don Corleone from the village of the same name from Francis Ford Coppola's *The Godfather?*

WINE IN SICILY

The best Sicilian wines are based on local grape varieties such as the red *nero d'Avola, nerello Mascalese* and *frappato*. Delicious white wines include *catarratto, grillo, zibibbo secco, inzolia, grecanico, malvasia delle Lipari* and *moscato d'Alessandria*. Many wines from international grape varieties such as chardonnay, syrah, merlot and cabernet sauvignon are also produced here.

PALERMO ①

Palermo is exotic, chaotic, sultry and very much alive. I find myself in the heart of an ancient world on the fringes of Europe. I stroll through bazaars among the Baroque churches, date trees and breathtaking Gothic-style palaces. This city boasts a bustling harbour and modern residential neighbourhoods. But I feel Palermo's heart beating in the many street markets where I completely lose myself in a melting pot of cultures, colours, sounds, smells and flavours among a maze of stalls.

The markets in the old part of town are the social hub of Palermo. In the Albergheria district, I visit Ballarò; in the Loggia district, I explore Vucciria; and in Monte di Pietà, I discover the Capo market.

Via Vittorio Emanuele in Palermo

Lorena and Annette in Ballarò

MERCATO DI BALLARÒ

Ballaró, with its history spanning a thousand years, is one of Palermo's most bustling locations. Its origins date back to a time of Arab rule. The name is derived from the Arabic *Suq Al-Balhara*, the 'market of mirrors'. The distinctive atmosphere of a souk, or bazaar, reigns in these narrow alleyways. Food is spread out on improvised counters called *bancate*. Merchandise is displayed on tables resting on two or more trestles. Fresh fish is kept cool by constantly soaking the wares in fresh water. Cheese and meat are displayed on lettuce leaves. I also notice lots of fruits and vegetables on display in the narrow alleyways. Rickety red umbrellas provide shade from the sun. Powerful lamps arranged haphazardly on tables illuminate the merchandise. The red fabric, warm light, packed stalls, steaming pots of street food and all-encompassing smell of spices... this is Ballarò!

Mercato Ballarò
Via Ballaro, Palermo

Tavola Calda al mercato

Octopus tentacles simmer away in some pots, while elsewhere, market vendors are grilling *stigghiola* or frying *arancini* in deep fryers. Ballarò is the place to be for street food dishes, too numerous to mention. In fact, they're all stands where you can settle down to a ready-made meal, which is the principle of a *tavola calda*. The dishes are served hot or cold.

I stop at Trattoria del Carmine near the Chiesa di Santa Maria del Carmine. The friendly Giuglia Losasso explains which dishes she has on offer. Giuglia: 'These are *puippu vugghiutu* of *polpo bollito* (cooked octopus), *sardine fritte* (fried sardines), *sardine beccafico* or sardines stuffed with breadcrumbs, raisins and orange juice, *pesci fritti* (fried fish), *polpette di melanzane* (aubergine croquettes) and *caponata di melanzane*, a cold vegetable stew with aubergine.' She immediately hands me a small plate with stew.

Vicolo San Giuseppe in Palermo

Caponata di melanzane – cold aubergine stew

Giuglia: 'Caponata with aubergine is very flavourful and refreshing, a must for every visitor. You eat it cold as a first course or as a side dish. Caponata comes in a whole range of varieties. Each province and every family has their own recipe for this sweet-and-sour stewed vegetable dish. We season the aubergine with tomato sauce, celery, onion, olives, capers and a sauce with vinegar and sugar. The most famous recipe comes from Palermo, although Trapani's version is also very popular. Until a couple of decades ago, the recipe also included tuna. The fish has been phased out over the years.'

⭐ Even fruit is street food in Sicily

As I prepare to leave, Giuglia tells me that I have to taste the fresh fruit from the colourful roadside stalls along the way. 'The prickly pear, or *ficurinnia*, is one of Sicily's symbols. If you want to try one, the vendor will slice the fruit for you. Delightfully refreshing watermelon, *muluna russa*, is served in slices or pieces, ready to eat. And the freshly squeezed orange or pomegranate juice and the Sicilian citrus fruit *pipittuna*, served sliced with just a pinch of salt, are an absolute must,' Giuglia concludes.

Trattoria del Carmine
Piazza del Carmine 22, Palermo

GIUGLIA'S RECIPE
Caponata

SERVES 4 PEOPLE

500 g aubergine
200 g white celery
200 g white onion
100 g vine tomatoes
100 g seeded green olives
25 g rinsed salted capers
26 pine nuts
60 g sugar
60 g or ½ cup white wine vinegar
fresh basil to taste
40 g or 2 ½ tablespoons concentrated tomato puree
extra-virgin olive oil to taste
fine salt to taste

Clean and thinly slice the onions. Chop the celery into thin slices. Halve the green olives. Wash and dry the aubergines, dice them into pieces about 2 1/2 cm thick. Do the same with the tomatoes. Roast the pine nuts for a couple of minutes until golden brown.

Pour the olive oil into a heavy-bottomed pan and add the aubergines. Fry for a couple of minutes. As soon as they turn golden brown, take the aubergines out of the pan. Place them on paper towels to drain off the excess oil. Set aside.

Pour a generous splash of olive oil into a pan and fry the onion. Fry until the onion turns light golden brown. Add and brown the celery. Add the capers, olives, roasted pine nuts and tomatoes.

Cover the pan and simmer everything over low heat for 15 to 20 minutes. Meanwhile, make the sweet-and-sour sauce; add the vinegar, tomato puree and sugar in a pan. Combine everything well. Add the sweet-and-sour sauce once the caponata has cooked for 15 to 20 minutes. Turn up the heat and continue to stir until the vinegar smell has evaporated. Turn off the heat and add the fried aubergine. Sprinkle plenty of basil over the top. Combine everything well. Transfer the caponata to a bowl and place the bowl in the refrigerator. This dish must be served cold or at room temperature, and it tastes even better if left overnight.

MERCATO VUCCIRÌA

I walk 900 metres from Ballarò to the Vucciria market. This noisy, lively market is a reflection of Sicilian street food. The oldest market in town is situated in the old Loggia district. The name is reminiscent of *bucceria*, which in turn is derived from the French *boucherie*, or butcher. At this market, cattle were once sold and slaughtered for meat. Later, fish, fruit and vegetables were sold over the counter. The stalls are scattered out in the alleyways around the impressive Piazza Caracciolo. The square was constructed in 1783 by viceroy Caracciolo and boasts a lively market during the day. The atmosphere is authentic, and the traditions here go as far back as about 700 years. Vucciria is recommended for when you're looking for a quick bite to eat. I let myself be intoxicated by the smells and colours of the *arancini, frittola, crocchè, panelle, stigghiola* ... and surrender myself to the joys of street food. I try all this tasty goodness on a rickety stool, surrounded by the smoke of a nearby barbecue. It is dusk, and the streets fill up with young people looking to eat something before perhaps moving on to the pubs and clubs later. Reggae and rap hangs in the air.

Mercato Vuccirìa
Via dei Frangiai 50, Palermo

Pani 'cà meusa

At the market, I meet Giuseppe Basile at his stall with the red sunshade at Piazza Carocciolo. Bread with spleen is one of Palermo's most famous street food dishes. You eat the meat on a large, round, *vastedda* bread with sesame seeds. Giuseppe fills the bread with a mixture of cow spleen, lungs, and trachea, seasoned with salt, lemon and *caciocavallo* cheese. Giuseppe: 'I prepare everything beforehand at home. I cook the innards for at least two hours, leave them overnight in the refrigerator, and cut the meat up the next day into fine pieces. At the market, I fry the meat with a splash of olive oil in this large pot. You eat the warm spleen sandwich wrapped in paper.'

I ask Giuseppe whether he is always around at the market. 'I'm actually retired,' he answers. 'I sometimes come to the market, but often, I have my brother or son take my place. This is our permanent spot. It's part of the tradition. Did you know that Pani 'cà meusa is a peas-

A food stall at the Mercato Vucceria

Giuseppe's stall in Vucciria

Pani 'cà meusa

ant dish that was introduced over a thousand years ago by Jewish butchers? Their religion forbade them from taking money as compensation for their work, and so they kept the innards from cows and calves – the lung, spleen and heart – for themselves as compensation. They thought up a sandwich filled with innards for the Christians. In 1492, the Jews were driven out of Palermo, under the reign of king Ferdinand II of Aragon and the Spanish Inquisition. But by then, the poor Christian residents were attached to the sandwich. They collected the waste products from the slaughter from the nobility. This is my contribution to this part of history, together with my family, here in this spot. After all these years, the Palermitani and many tourists are still addicted to their spleen sandwich. That makes me happy.'

⭐ Blood dessert

I accept a pane 'cà meusa to be polite. I explain that we are not used to eating innards. 'Such a shame,' Giuseppe replies. 'We have been eating this for centuries. And it's a very good habit. I believe that you should use all the parts of a slaughtered animal. Don't throw anything away. Slice the beef heart after cooking into pieces and season it with oil and onion. Did you know that we even make desserts from pig or cow blood? We season the boiled blood with chocolate, egg whites and oranges. Truly delicious! We eat this dessert during the Christmas season.' I'm glad to hear it. Unfortunately, we are not familiar with these practices. I thank Giuseppe for his lovely story and the delicious food. I eat the sandwich carefully, while no one's watching.

GRILL
Stigghiola & frittola

I make my way to the Da Jolly stall at a small piazza hidden under a cloud of smoke. Angelo is frying *stigghiola* on a large grill. Tanino operates the counter in the back. Angelo: 'Stigghiola are the innards of lamb, sheep, or calves that we turn into sausage or stick on a skewer. We season the meat with parsley and onion and then grill them on the barbecue. We serve the dish with salt and lemon on a plastic plate.' Tanino continues: 'We also make *frittola*. We cook the bones and other offal for a long time so the remaining meat around the carcass turns very tender. These scraps of meat are then fried in lard and seasoned with bay leaves, saffron and spices. We serve this wonderful, soft meat mixture on a sandwich. Would you like to try it?'

MERCATO IL CAPO

The Capo, one of the oldest markets in Palermo lies a kilometre away. The market is situated at a crossroads in the heart of the Capo district; its main entrance is Porta Carini next to Palermo's courthouse. The entrance is narrow, and you have to press your way past the many stalls. Historians claim that a secret cult once met in these streets. The Capo district dates back to the Arab period. Back then, it was the home of the *schiavoni*, Arab mercenaries and slave traders. I find myself in an authentic souk. As the sun rises, the stalls and shops come to life. The distinctive, colourful canopies protect the vendors and their merchandise from the sun and occasional rain showers. It is a place for tasting and bargaining. The colourful and creative displays of merchandise include fish, meat, olives, bread, fruit, herbs and spices. The surrounding streets are riddled with bars and restaurants. I meet Filippo Quagliata from Sit & Mancia, a restaurant that immediately draws my attention with its abundance of Sicilian delicacies displayed on long, tall tables with red chequered tablecloths. Filippo beams as I inspect his wares. I can try everything, he says. What will it be? Cooked octopus, grilled fish, swordfish rolls, sardines in batter, *sfincione, panelle, crocchè*, aubergine rolls...?

Mercato del Capo
Via Cappuccinelle, Palermo

Filippo at his stall Sit & Mancia

Crocchè, panelle, sfincione

Filippo: 'Crocchè are potato croquettes with mint. We also call them cazzilli. We make our fried panelle fritters with chickpea flour, water, salt and parsley. Here in Sicily, we eat them like tapas or on a round, soft sesame roll. Sfincione is a small, elongated Palermitan pizza. We top the soft, spongy dough with tomato sauce, salted ricotta, onion, anchovies and sometimes caciocavallo-ragusano cheese. In Palermo, you can buy pizza at one of the roadside stalls or at the market.

I take a seat at a table at Sit & Mancia in Via Carini. The tasty treats are finished in no time. And the refreshing glass of grillo is the perfect accompaniment. I see the chefs in the kitchen pass a constant stream of plates carrying cold and warm snacks over the counter. Caponata, arancini, fried courgette flowers, couscous with raisins and sardines, orange slices with red onion, involtini (rolls) with aubergine, filled sweet peppers, filled courgettes, polpette, filled tomatoes, fried artichokes... All in small portions. The display counter, without any form of heating or cooling, is constantly being replenished. Mouths water as passers-by see all this delicious food. It is irresistible; you can't help but buy something on the go or find a seat at a table. Meanwhile, the fresh food just keeps on coming. It's a joy to see how the food goes straight from the kitchen to the tall tables. I enjoy the smells of Palermo.

Sit & Mancia
Via Porta Carini 63, Palermo

Cannolo

Cannolo

People with a sweet tooth will undoubtedly be familiar with the cannolo. One of the oldest desserts from the Italian patisserie tradition consists of a rolled-up, crispy wafer filled with sweet ricotta mixed with drops of dark chocolate and candied orange peel. This traditional Carnival pastry has become a prime example of Italian flavours. Although ricotta has been around in Sicily for a very long time, it was the Arabs who first mixed sugar into the cheese to create a delicious cream for Italian pastries. The Arab rulers kept countless harems for their emirs. The emir's favourites were responsible for preparing the desserts. The ladies were believed to have developed a dessert that resembles cannolo. One day, they decided to produce a pastry that illustrated the potency of their partner. The pastry was meant to symbolise fertility and ward off evil spirits. It was both a phallic symbol and a talisman. And that is how the cannolo came to be. The name is derived from the cane that was used to wrap the dough to create the characteristic cannoli shape. Later, the arrival of the Norsemen in Sicily ended Arab rule on the island. The harems emptied, and the freed women converted to Christianity and took up residence in convents. Some of them did so of their own free will, while others were forced to do so by the Christians. These women introduced their traditional recipes to the convents. In Palermo, the nuns prepare their own version of this centuries-old cannolo recipe that made its way across the entire island. And so, the cannolo became one of the most famous pastries in the world.

Fedde del cancelliere

The inner courtyard at the Santa Caterina convent is an idyllic spot
to try the sweets from Palermo

A plate of sweets from the convent

For generations, the nuns were the treasurers of Sicilian patisserie traditions. The sale of sweets brought money to the convents. Today, the patisserie at Santa Caterina was revived by a project named '*I segreti del chiostro*', 'The Secrets of the Convent'. Patisserie, biscuits, and sweets are made at the convent using the traditional recipes from nuns from the 21 convents in Palermo. Santa Caterina is situated in the historical heart of the old town. For generations, the scions of the most powerful noble families resided in this 16th-century complex. Until the 1980s, you could buy sweets from Santa Caterina's atelier. Since 2017, there have been no more nuns and preparing pastry is now the work of pâtissiers.

Virgin's breasts

Today, you can buy sweets and desserts from Santa Caterina once more. The shop on the first floor is a celebration of colours and aromas. My senses light up at the sight of all those delicious foods spread out on long tables. I have never seen anything like it. Georgia approaches me from behind her counter to guide me through the shop. Georgia: 'We have the typical *cassata* in all shapes and colours. The traditional round cassata is coated with a layer of pistachio green, pink or light-yellow marzipan. Here, at the top, we have candied fruit. We call this cream puff filled with ricotta *testa di moro* (Moor's head) or *testa di turco* (Turk's head). We also have homemade cookies such as *biscotti papali*, *nucatoli*, *nzuddi* and *erbanetti*. And this is our famous *fedde del cancelliere*, or 'chancellor's buttocks'. The nuns invented these marzipan biscuits shaped like buttocks. It was their peccadillo.' My eye is drawn to a glass cabinet with dozens of round-breasted pastries. Are they another product of the sister's less pure thoughts, I wonder aloud. Georgia laughs. 'Those are the *minne di vergine*, or virgin's breasts. 'They are miniature cassata, biscuits filled with ricotta cream under a layer of glazed marzipan, crowned with a candied red cherry. The shape resembles a breast, *minna* in Sicilian.

The frutta di martorana was actually traditionally hung in trees

Frutta di martorana

Georgia: 'Our *frutta di martorana* is also typical Sicilian. The martorana is an almond sweet in the shape of a fruit, an invention of the nuns at the convent of the same name in Palermo. Legend has it that one October, a king wanted to admire the beautiful and much-talked-about convent gardens. The mother superior and her nuns were on the verge of despair because the trees and rose bushes were bare in the autumn, without flowers or fruits. So, they made fruits from almonds and honey, which they then painted to look like real citrus fruits and hung in the trees. The king was ecstatic about the garden and the delicious fruits. And that is how frutta di martorana originated.'

⭐ Cannoli and a fountain of flavours

Giusi stands behind another counter. She hands out freshly filled *cannoli*. Giusi: 'I fill the cannoli rolls and garnish them with chocolate pieces, pistachios, hazelnuts and different types of candied fruit.' With skilled hands, she fills a pastry for me to enjoy in the convent garden. The convent hallway leads to an open inner courtyard, and I feel the serene atmosphere. It is a magical green oasis with red and orange roses. In the centre stands a large fountain with a statue. I take a seat on a bench on the tiled floor and eat my cannolo in meditative silence. The incredibly crispy crust has a unique taste that reminds me of this building and its rich history, as does the incredibly sweet ricotta, the candied orange peel and the chocolate drops for a truly divine taste experience. Amen.

I Segreti del Chiostro
Piazza Bellini 1, Palermo

Sicilian arancini

Arancino or *arancina* is a textbook example of Sicilian street food. These rice croquettes are usually filled with meat sauce, peas and caciocavallo string cheese. The contrast between the crispy, golden-brown crust and the soft, flavourful centre is striking. You will find these round arancini at roadside stalls, bars, bakeries, and markets. In Palermo and western Sicily, *arancina* is the singular and *arancine* is the plural form. In Catania and eastern Sicily, they're cone-shaped and called *arancino and arancini*, respectively.

Orange origins

The name *arancino* or *arancina* perhaps refers to the orange or *arancia*, with its round shape and colour. The orange suggests a round shape. The cone shape seems to be a relatively recent innovation.

The arancino's origins and history are a source of debate. No one really invented it. The food stems from a folk tradition that has changed significantly over the course of history. It started with the Arabs, who ate rice with saffron. They would place a large platter with saffron rice on the table, roll the rice into balls with their hands and then consume the balls. A few centuries later, the technique of coating the balls with breadcrumbs was developed. The fried golden outer crust turned out to be an excellent preservative for the rice and the filling. Frederick II loved arancini and brought them with him on his long hunts. The arancini were a handy snack for on the road even back then. Street food *avant la lettre*!

From street food to gastronomic highlight

I visit KePalle, a shop entirely dedicated to arancini, in Via Maqueda in the heart of Palermo. The owner, Danilo Li Muli, proudly tells me about his contemporary culinary showpieces. Danilo: 'Arancini are supposed to be crispy on the outside and soft on the inside. Good saffron is essential for the gorgeous yellow colour. The arancini with peas and meat sauce are the most popular. Other combinations include mozzarella with ham or spinach and mozzarella. The *arancini alla catanese* with aubergine is delicious, and the *arancino al pistacchio di Bronte* with pistachios from Bronte is also popular. The possibilities are endless. We fill our rice croquettes with mushrooms, sweet peppers, artichokes, salmon, chicken, swordfish, seafood, and squid. We also have sweet varieties with cocoa and sugar, hazelnut paste or chocolate.'

KePalle
Via Maqueda 270, Palermo

Arancini

TRAPANI ②

From Palermo, I drive 100 kilometres to the province of Trapani on the island's western point. The Mediterranean and Ionian Sea meet at the provincial capital with the same name. Trapani boasts regal palaces, lively piazzas, ancient city gates and a baroque church. Over the years, Trapani's economy has flourished as a result of bluefin tuna fishing, marble exports, and salt extraction.

SALT PANS

Along the way, I meet Rosa Casano at the Salina Genna salt evaporation ponds. Rosa: 'Trapani's world-renowned sea salt carries an IGP quality label. The salt is still produced using a traditional, artisanal process that takes five to six months and ends with the salt being harvested by hand in the summer. The sea salt is extracted by allowing briny seawater to evaporate in large, artificial coastal basins, which are known as *saline* or salt pans. You need seawater, sun, and wind to produce this salt. The sea salt contains more potassium and magnesium and less sodium chloride than your average table salt. We harvest the Trapani salt along the coast between Trapani and Marsala in a beautiful area with windmills, white salt pyramids and pink flamingos.'

www.salinegenna.it

Water, wind, sea and salt

Before I immerse myself in this scenic beauty, I ask Rosa why salt is harvested here, of all places. 'Trapani has a relatively low shoreline and an excellent climate,' she replies. 'These salt pans have been around since the eighth century BC. Since the Middle Ages, windmills have been used to pump the water from the salt pans to the plains beyond. The water evaporates during the long, dry Sicilian summers, leaving behind a layer of salt. In the 17th and 18th centuries, Trapani became one of the most important ports on the Mediterranean and in Europe, thanks in large part to the salt trade. The extraction of salt was a booming business until the 1960s. When increased competition, high transportation costs and floods led to a setback, the sector was thankfully able to bounce back when the state monopoly was abolished in 1973. Today, it is part of our heritage and an artisanal economy in a breathtaking setting.'

⭐ Salt route

The salt route extends some 30 kilometres along the Sicilian shoreline between Trapani and Marsala. The route starts in the centre of Trapani. I drive past old salt processing sites between windmills and white dunes. The sun shines, it's late in the afternoon, and the colours are gorgeous. Salt extraction still takes place here using natural means. My journey takes me past no fewer than 27 different salt pans and two pro-

tected nature reserves. I feel like I'm in a painting in this stunning, authentic setting. My route ends when I reach the Saline dello Stagnone di Marsala. If it had been earlier in the afternoon, I would have been able to take the ferry to the beautiful island of Mozia in the breathtaking Stagnone lagoon. I sit down by the water and savour one of the most beautiful sunsets I have seen during my culinary journey of discovery.

Matarocco sauce, or pesto trapanese

I make my way back to Trapani where I will dine in Michele Bellezza's restaurant, Salamureci. I order a dish made from pesto unique for this town. Michele: 'The origins of *pesto trapanese* stem from our maritime history. Ligurian sailors would drop anchor here after their travels through the Far East. They introduced us to their *pesto alla genovese*, the classic basil pesto. They taught us how to grind the fresh ingredients down to a silky-smooth sauce, to which we later added fresh tomatoes and almonds.' Why *mandorle*, almonds, instead of the pine nuts you find in green pesto? Michele: 'Because Sicilians love almonds. Moreover, you can find them everywhere here. We are also masters in preparing sweets where almonds feature prominently.' I also see a couple of couscous dishes on the menu. Michele: 'You haven't been to Sicily unless you've tried couscous with fish at least once. It is the regional speciality of Trapani and the entire coast from Mazara del Vallo to San Vito Lo Capo. Maghrebi cuisine is a strong presence in this part of our island.' I know exactly what I'll have to end the day in style. As a *primo*, or first course, I choose the *salamureci* (a soup based on *pesto alle trapanese)*, followed by seafood couscous for the main course. I order a Sicilian catarratto wine to go with the meal. 'An excellent choice,' Michele assures me.

Ristorante Salamureci,
Piazza Generale Scio 17, Trapani

Salt pans between Trapani and Marsala

MICHELE'S RECIPE
Pesto alla trapanese

SERVES 6 PEOPLE
250 g ripe cherry tomatoes
50 g fresh basil leaves
1 clove garlic, peeled
50 g peeled almonds
50 g Parmigiano Reggiano DOP or mild pecorino
100 ml mild extra-virgin olive oil
sea salt and black pepper to taste

Add the tomatoes, olive oil, almonds and garlic in a mixer and mix everything together for two minutes. Add the basil, but don't blend the basil too much so that it retains its intense flavour and colour. Remove the mixture from the mixer and fold the grated cheese in to form a creamy, homogenous pesto. Season to taste with salt.

Serve and eat fresh, or store it up for two days in the refrigerator. This pesto is a wonderful dipping sauce and goes extremely well with pasta such as *busiate*, penne or spaghetti.

Note: Do not cook the pesto! The heat will change the flavour and freshness of the ingredients. Simply add the sauce to freshly cooked pasta. You can also prepare the sauce by grinding the ingredients by hand in a mortar.

Marsala's old town

MARSALA ③

In Marsala, I head out in search of the iconic wine that bears the town's name. In the courtyard of the l'Enoteca wine bar in Via XI Maggio, Romano Modi tells me enthusiastically about their showpiece. 'Marsala used to be a very important city because of its strategic location,' he begins. 'The name is derived from the Arabian *marsa Allah*, "the harbour of God". The harbour was a hub in the time of the Phoenicians, who introduced the practice of winegrowing. The Greeks and the Romans also carried on the tradition of Marsala wine. This fortified wine owes its strength to its impressive sugar content. The English merchant John Woodhouse made Marsala wine world famous. He disembarked here during a storm in 1773. And when he tried our wine, it was love at first sip. Woodhouse then shipped a couple of barrels of Marsala wine to England; he 'diluted' it with alcohol to help it keep it longer. It was a brilliant move. Marsala wine then became one of Europe's favourite fortified wines.'

A centuries-old tradition

What makes Marsala wine so special? Romano: 'The barrels containing Marsala wine are never completely emptied. The product from the latest harvest is poured into the same barrels so it naturally blends with the different flavours from previous years. Today, Marsala wine still retains its distinctive character through the skilful blending of wines of different ages. What happens in those barrels is what makes our wine unique. And the sea breeze also influences the way the wine ages.'

Types of Marsala wine

Marsala is not a specific grape variety. The Oro and Ambra are produced with white grape varieties such as *grillo, cataratto, ansonica* and *damaschino. Perricone, nero d'Avola and nerello Mascalese* are used for Marsala Rubino. Both the Oro, Ambra and Rubino types carry a DOP label. Marsala wines come in many different varieties: strong and less strong, sweet, semi-sweet and dry.

L'Enoteca
Via XI Maggio 32, Marsala

Farmers from the area grow the grapes for Marsala wine

Carlo Martinez

RECOMMENDED COMBINATIONS

What do we drink Marsala wine with? Romano: 'The texture, the high alcohol content, and the spicy flavour lend themselves well to combinations with chocolate, spoon desserts, cannoli, candied fruit and pistachios, Tuscan *cantucci, zuppa inglese*, tartufo ice cream, tiramisu, apple pie or crème brûlée. A dry Marsala Fino, on the other hand, goes very well with seafood dishes.'
Italians add Marsala wine to *boccioni al marsala* (stewed beef), *carote al marsala* (stewed carrots), *scaloppine di vitello al marsala* (veal cutlets), *zabaione, confettura al profumo di marsala* (Marsala-wine-flavoured jam) and *coniglio con marsala* (rabbit).

CATANIA ④

The distances between cities in Sicily are not something to be taken lightly. Catania is a 300-kilometre drive from Marsala. The second-largest Sicilian city lies on the shores of the Ionian Sea, overshadowed by the Mount Etna volcano. Mount Etna determined how the city developed. Various volcanic eruptions, particularly those in the 17th century, destroyed the city. In 1669, Catania was flooded with lava, and no fewer than 24 years later, in 1693, the city was struck by an earthquake. The aftermath of this disaster is still visible today. The old part of the city was completely rebuilt. The impressive baroque buildings are made from volcanic stone. The grey city is unique in the world.

Pasta alla Norma

If Sicilian fish dishes are not your style, try the *pasta alla Norma*, Catania's culinary pride and joy. According to insiders, this was Vincenzo Bellini's favourite dish, hence the name. Bellini wrote the opera *Norma*, which premiered in the Massimo Bellini theatre in 1890. This exquisite dish is traditionally prepared with macaroni (or another type of pasta), diced and sautéed aubergine, tomato sauce, fresh basil and a dollop of freshly grated *ricotta salata*, or salted ricotta.

Pasta alla Norma

ACIREALE ⑤

The Sicilian *granita* is a light and refreshing dessert. Granita with brioche is a daily morning ritual for many Sicilians. This world-renowned crushed-ice dish is the next stop on my culinary odyssey. I drive to Aci Castello, about 10 kilometres north of Catania, at the foot of Mount Etna. I savour the fantastic panorama of the Ionian Sea and the volcano from this town in the hills. But, I'm here because Mount Etna and granita are inextricably linked. Peppe Caudullo from Pupi Catania B&B is my guide in my search for granita's origins.

www.pupicatania.com

Origins of the Sicilian granita

Peppe: 'In Sicily, the trade of *nivaroli* has been around since the Middle Ages. These men collected snow on the flanks of Etna, Peloritani, Iblei and Nebrodi. They stored the snow for the remainder of the year in *neviere*. These subterranean pits in mountains and gorges protected the white gold from the summer heat. In the summer, the nivaroli, or ice carriers, transported the stored snow to the coast, and that's how the sorbet originated. In the 16th century, sea salt was mixed into the snow to keep it cold. You will still find the pits in the mountains where snow and ice were once stored. They were ingenious constructions. The pit was filled with a mixture of salt and snow and sealed with a burlap bag. The churning motion of the paddles within prevented large ice crystals from forming. The nivaroli hauled the snow out of the pit with zinc buckets. The snow was then grated and used to prepare popular sorbets. People would add lemon juice to the grated snow for the flavour. From the 19th century onwards, different types of refreshing Etna ice started to appear. Sicilian almonds proved to be an excellent accompaniment. The *rattata* – grating – technique was popular until the beginning of the last century.

Magic and craftsmanship

According to Peppe, the recipe for granita hasn't changed much over the years. 'The snow has been replaced by water, the honey is now sugar, and the storage pit is now an ice machine,' he explains. 'You will find the best granita on the shores from Messina to

Strawberry granita

Catania; nothing can beat that. You need to experience the granita ritual here. The colours of the Tyrrhenian Sea blend with the hues in the sky. This celebration of colours, delicious smells and the local ingredients and masterful flavours make a real granita a joy to the senses.

In Acireale, I try a strawberry granita at Nunzio Napoli's Très Noir. Nunzio: 'Granita indeed requires craftsmanship, but also a respect for tradition and the patience to develop the right consistency without using preservatives, colouring agents or other additives. We offer the classic flavours of pistachio, lemon, coffee, almond, and chocolate year-round. In the summer, you will also find mulberry, strawberry and roasted almonds on the menu. A little further down the road at Loredana Aloisi's ice cream parlour, Rococo, I try a granita with almonds and chocolate. Loredana explains that they first prepare a paste from the raw ingredient (almonds, for example) and then add the ice. You do not make granita with milk or cream. But you can top your granita with whipped cream.

Très Noir
Piazza Inirizzo 12,13,14, Acireale

Rococo
Corso Umberto, 109-111, Acireale

TAORMINA ⑥

The following day, I stop in Taormina for a breakfast of brioche with granita, and I heartily agree with Peppe. An experience like this is unsurpassed, one for my personal bucket list. Taormina is beautifully situated atop a hill on the east coast. The ancient Greek-Roman theatre draws tourists in droves. Pristine sandy beaches lie tucked away between tall cliffs. I visit *pasticceria/ gelateria* Nonna Rosa in the old town.

I order a *granita caffè con panna e brioche,* or coffee-flavoured granita with whipped cream and a brioche. I settle down at a table outside. The theatre and the ice demand love and endorsement. Experience it for yourself, and you'll know what I mean. The glass in front of me, the spoon and the buttery brioche on the plate demand my full attention. The ice heaps just long enough on my spoon, only to melt away in an instant in my mouth. The granita is just perfect; not too icy or grainy, but not entirely smooth either. I now dip my brioche in the glass with the granita and cream as is the custom. The coffee, the cream, the buttery pastry... intense!

I dolci di Nonna Rosa
Via San Pancrazio, Taormina

A granita caffè con panna e brioche

MESSINA ⑦

From Taormino, I drive the last 50 kilometres to the port of Messina, from where I will continue my journey by boat to Sardinia. But first, I go off in search of a typical street food dish: the rustic, half-moon-shaped *pitoni* or *pidoni.* This pastry looks like a fried calzone or folded-over pizza. *Pitoni messinesi* is what this Sicilian town is best known for in terms of street food. You can try arancino on every street corner in Italy, but for pitoni, you have to travel to Messina.

BAKERY
Panificio focacceria rosticceria

La Boutique Del Pane in the heart of the city is my next stop. Salvatore and Tommaso Cannata also run the *panificio focacceria rosticceria* in Milan. Salvatore is a fourth-generation master baker who makes daily use of high-quality, traditional Sicilian grains and ingredients. Signora Chiara takes me on a guided tour through their assortment: 'We bake more than twenty types of bread, including the famous Tumminia bread with Sicilian almonds and black olives. In addition to the many types of bread, we also have *pitoni, arancini messinesi, focaccia,* pizza, biscuits and sweet pastries.'

Gold-coloured, filled soft rolls

I order a *pitone* and ask Chiara what makes this product unique among the many versions of 'pizza' you find on Italian soil. Chiara: 'The pitone is distinctive because of the soft dough, the gold-coloured breadcrumbs, and the rich filling with local ingredients. The *rustico* originated in the peasant kitchen. In Messina, people would bake scraps of bread dough into half-moons filled with pieces of cheese and *escarole,* or endive. The pitoni doesn't have an official recipe or preparation method. The dough doesn't contain any yeast, which is why most recipes use lard or margarine to soften the dough instead. We fry the filled dough in hot oil.'

Cannata – La Boutique Del Pane
Via XXVII Luglio 83/85, Messina

Catania, the second-largest city in Sicily

SARDEGNA

Sardinia is the second-largest island group in the Mediterranean Sea after Sicily. Its location has always been of strategic importance. Historically, this island group has always had close ties with Spain, particularly along the western coast. The capital is Cagliari. Mountains dominate the island, with the highest point being Punta La Marmora (1834 m) in the Gennargentu range. The climate is subtropical and Mediterranean.

Sardinia is a magical island with many natural variations in light and colour. You will find an emerald-blue sea with both small and large bays as well as pure white, sandy beaches. Islands of unsurpassed beauty are situated just off Sardinia's stunning coastline. The La Maddalena archipelago just off the Costa Smeralda is a prime example of this natural splendour.

Cagliari, Sardinia's capital

The La Maddalena archipelago

Alghero
5

Golf dell'
Asinara

Lago del
Coghinas

Tirso

Fonni
4

Cabras
2

Lago
Omodeo

Flumendosa

Cagliari
1

Golf di
Cagliari

Villasimius
3

NATURE AND LEGENDS

The interior is still dominated by a virgin wilderness that is both rugged and charming. Vast expanses remain untouched; its residents include deer, wild horses and large birds of prey. Other regions harbour the remains of settlements inhabited thousands of years ago by the Nuraghi, the shepherd kings, with their *nuraghi*, conical-shaped towers. Also unique are the *domus de janas*, or the homes of the half-fairies, half-witches of Sardinian legend, which are carved out of the rocks. Their small size allowed these mythical creatures to live in these abnormally small houses *(domus)*. Several of them are still scattered around the island. These types of legends and the many tombs hidden among the rocks with their murals and evocative inscriptions have turned Sardinia into the most mysterious island in the Mediterranean.

Unique Sardinian identity and way of life

Different peoples succeeded in controlling Sardinia's excellent strategic position in the Mediterranean in both military and economic terms. Each ruler left their own mark. They came, they conquered, and they were conquered.

From the 19th century onwards, however, many island residents left because of the poor economic conditions. 'But once a Sardinian, always a Sardinian,' Giovanni Francello, author and a professor of Sardinian gastronomy, adds as we sit on a terrace in Alghero. 'We are the children of various rulers. They are all in our blood, and that makes us unique. We are, first and foremost, *Sardi* and, secondly, *Italiani*. Our identity has always had something mythical. For decades, I lived and worked outside of Sardinia. And as much as I love Milan, I came back here. This island won't let you go. Moreover, our island is recognised as one of the five blue zones in the world.

Remains of the Nuraghi culture

Cannonau grapes

CUCINA SARDA

'Food tells a region's story, and that is definitely the case with Sardinia,' Giovanni resumes. 'Here, you will find simple, high-quality ingredients with strong yet delicate flavours. Our peasant cuisine from the coast and the interior, with a history of agricultural and pastoral culture spanning thousands of years, is amazing. The various Mediterranean influences from all the people that once inhabited the island also play a significant role. Our cuisine is still dominated by wild herbs, cheese and meat from the hunt. We have never experienced a *rinasciamento* or Renaissance.'

A blue zone is a geographic area where the population lives significantly longer and is healthier and happier. Our island has the most men over 100 years old. Why do we live so long? It's a combination of factors, including our genetic make-up and our isolated location. But it also has to do with how we live, what we do, and what we eat and drink. In addition to Sardinia, the Japanese island of Okinawa, the Nicoya peninsula in Costa Rica, the Greek island of Ikaria, and Loma Linda in California make up the five blue zones.'

It was no accident that Giovanni ordered a glass of red Cannonau di Sardegna DOC. 'Drink a glass or two of red wine with your friends every day. That is one of our principles,' he continues. 'We moderate our wine intake. One of the most popular grape varieties is the cannonau, or grenache, which is full of antioxidants. The wine contains three times the level of flavonoids as other wines. This antioxidant keeps the arteries clean and may help to prevent disease. Cannonau wine is made from garnet-red grapes.' I sip the wine and taste ripe cherries, spices and just a hint of vanilla. It tastes fabulous, and I ask Giovanni what else the island has in store for me in terms of wine.

Giovanni: 'Sardinia is an island where unique local wine varieties flourish. On this sunny island, we make both full-bodied, sturdy red wines and fresh, savoury white wines. Cannonau, vermentino and carignano are grape varieties that best represent the region's potential. Our wines are not as well-known beyond this island, so we mostly drink them ourselves,' he says as he raises his glass. '*Salute!* And may you live to become 100 years old!' I reply.

Once a Sardinian, always a Sardinian

CAGLIARI ①

From Cagliari, I immerse myself in the world of *bottarga di muggine*. Cagliari is situated on the southern coast and is the capital of the region and province of Sardinia. The city is built on seven hills and is situated in the heart of the beautiful Golfo degli Angeli, or Gulf of the Angels. In Cagliari, I meet Francesco Congiu from Smeralda, a business that processes red mullet roe to produce the world-famous *bottarga*. Francesco: 'The roe pouch is removed from the freshly caught fish before being salted, pressed and pickled. That's why we use the strongest roe pouches from fish such as mullet or tuna that can withstand rough treatment such as rubbing with salt. We leave them to dry for about three months in the sunny outdoor air, which is what transforms them into that priceless Sardinian gold.'

Golden roe pouches

Francesco: 'Connoisseurs consider our mullet to be the finest in the world. The waters around Cabras, Sant'Antioco, Porto Pino, Cagliari and Tortolì are the most important production sites. The strength and trump card of our local bottarga is the unique combination of the seabed, climate and high-quality processing methods. The best roe comes from the Cabras lagoon in western Sardinia. The climate and water in this isolated paradise form the perfect habitat for the *Mugil cephalus*, or flathead grey mullet.

'The breeding season is from July to October. This is when the female fish are full of eggs,' Francesco explains. 'It is then very easy to catch female fish laden with roe. In Sardinia, we do this under strict regulations so we do not endanger the fish population. The process towards the final product is labour-intensive and artisanal. The only ingredient is *sale marino* – sea salt. The drying process removes any moisture so the bottarga keeps well. The roe pouch changes colour and consistency during the process. The roe turns yellow/brown/orange and glitters like gold. The gold/amber-coloured product that remains was historically a useful ingredient for sea voyages on large and small ships because the dried and salted roe pouch kept well. It was also an excellent combination with the long-lasting, tough Sardinian bread. On the island, bottarga was traditionally the meal the fishermen ate while they were out at sea during the day. The fishermen were allowed to keep part of the roe, as well as other fish offal, to process themselves. To think that this was once third-rate food made from fish scraps. Today, it's a gourmet product that is eaten in a variety of ways. Even the great Italian chefs take the plunge with futuristic and complex combinations incorporating our bottarga,' Francesco says with pride.

Beloved salted fish eggs

Francesco: 'The Phoenicians, the Romans, the Carthaginians, the Spaniards; all these Mediterranean peoples loved this amber-coloured delicacy. The market for bottarga is booming, and the demand from countries such as France, Germany, Japan, Spain, and the United States is huge. That means that we had to look beyond Sardinia for our fish roe pouches.

We have two production lines: grey mullet roe pouches exclusively from Sardinia and roe from the rest of the world. Our local fish supply is sadly limited. We buy roe pouches from Australia, Africa, the United States and Brazil. We select and process the raw materials ourselves. We process the fish roe from the frozen fish just the same way we do a freshly caught fish.'

PRODUCER
Bottarga in the kitchen

Francesco and I walk to the warehouse where his wares are proudly displayed. 'We sell bottarga in its entirety or in grated form,' he explains. We use it in countless dishes, such as our famous *spaghetti alla bottarga*. Dried roe can also be grated as a garnish for appetizers or sliced into very thin slices to be eaten on toast. It's a very tasty, protein-rich foodstuff with a slightly bitter flavour. So it's better to use it sparingly in your dishes. The *carciofo*, or *spinoso della Sardegna* artichoke, also has a very distinctive flavour, which pairs perfectly with our bottarga. We also make bottarga from tuna roe. The colour is light to dark pink, and it has an even stronger flavour.

Smeralda
Via del Lavoro, 8, 09122 Cagliari

Bottarga

The lagoon with pink flamingos

LAGOON OF CABRAS ②

From Cagliari, I drive 110 kilometres northwards until I reach the exceptionally beautiful and authentic municipality of Cabras. The region is situated on the western coast near the Sinis peninsula, a 19-kilometre stretch of land with jagged cliffs, beaches, lagoons harbouring turtles, briny lakes and pink flamingos. I end up in a vast landscape filled with ditches and ponds surrounded by reeds. The purple flowers from the wild artichoke plants colour the landscape. I see beaches with phenomenally blue water reminiscent of the Caribbean.

At fishery and restaurant Consorzio, I meet Carlo Sanna. He explains that you can recognise the real *bottarga di Cabras* by its savoury, salty, dry almond flavour and its colour, which varies from golden to amber. Carlo: 'Production of the local product is unfortunately very limited. Bottarga di Cabras is immensely popular in countries like Japan, for instance. And despite its high price, we cannot meet the demand.'

Carlo takes a piece and tells me to watch the silver-coloured sac on the end of the hard roe. Carlo: 'This is the placenta. That grey sac at the end characterises the real bottarga. And you need to be able to see that through the packaging. And to make sure that your bottarga is 100% made in Sardinia, you should always read the label. If the label reads: *Pescato nella laguna di Cabras*, or "Fished in the Cabras lagoon", then you've hit the jackpot!' he says, laughing.
Carlo advises me to explore the region further. He tells me that the waters around Sinis hold shipwrecks from throughout the ages: Roman, Spanish, and 20th-century ships. Snorkelling and scuba diving are permitted at a couple of locations. He also recommends I visit the archaeological site of the Phoenician-Roman town of Tharros, and the Cabras museum. Six kilometres from here lies the village of San Salvatore, which served as a backdrop for countless spaghetti westerns between 1967 and 1999. I thank Carlo and head over to Far West Sardo!

Nuovo Consorzio Cooperative Pontis A.R.L,
Via Dei Mestieri, Zona Artigianale, Càbras

www.consorziopontis.net

CARLO'S RECIPE

Spaghetti with venus clams and bottarga

SERVES 4 PEOPLE
350 g spaghetti
600 g venus clams
40 g bottarga
2 to 3 cloves garlic
15 g pesto
½ glass dry white wine (e.g. vermentino)
4 tablespoons olive oil
salt

Soak the venus calms for about 30 minutes in salted water. Make sure all the sand is removed from the shells. Rinse them under running water. In a large pan, sauté the garlic cloves in olive oil. Add the clams, cover, and lower the heat. Cook gently until the shells open (about 10 minutes).

Add the wine and allow it to evaporate. Turn off the heat. Remove the clams from some of the shells. Remove the skin from the bottarga and grate over a small dish. Finely chop the parsley. Meanwhile, cook the spaghetti al dente and drain, but set aside some of the cooking water for later. Combine the spaghetti with the venus clams over high heat (for about two minutes). Add a little bit of the cooking water if needed. Toss the pesto and the grated bottarga into the spaghetti. Garnish the pasta with a couple of thin slices of bottarga and serve immediately.

The Porto Giunco beach in Villasimius

VILLASIMIUS ③

I leave Cabras for a 160-kilometre drive to the south-eastern side of the island. My journey takes me through Villasimius. This region is a gem of the south. I drive along a scenic road that reveals magical hidden coves and bays at every turn. The colour around me is gorgeous. The sparkling, crystal-clear water and white sands create a scenic contrast with the granite cliffs, green hills and beautiful lagoons. Breathtaking. This is the stuff of dreams. My destination is Ristorante De Barbara di Asuni Lazzaro e C. in Solanas, a hamlet in the province of Sinnai. The restaurant is located close to the picturesque coastal road to Villasimius. On the outside, it looks like just another roadside restaurant, but nothing could be further from the truth.

Asuni Lazzaro, who runs the restaurant together with his brother, sister and all his children, gives me a warm welcome. His mother, Barbara, started the family restaurant in 1955. I sit at one of the tables of this authentic restaurant.

Frégula

'Pasta originated from our need to eat. The ingredients are the same everywhere: water, flour and sometimes egg. However, the form is culturally determined, shaped by its surroundings. And so, it becomes a tradition.' This elegant truth came from Giovanni Francello, an author and professor of Sardinian gastronomy.

During my travels for this book, I haven't written much about pasta because pasta is pretty much the same wherever you go. Frégula in Sardinia, however, is a notable exception.

Lazzaro comes to my table to take my order. But before I place my order, I ask Lazzaro for some background information. 'Frégula, also known as *fregola* or *fregua*, depending on which part of the island you are, Is a traditional pasta made from durum wheat semolina flour. The shape looks like couscous, with its large, round grains. Still, frégula differs from other types of Italian pasta because the grains are roasted in the oven, giving the pasta its unique flavour. The pasta is then cooked like normal pasta. This pasta was traditionally made fresh daily in Sardinian kitchens; it was a culinary ritual. The semolina is placed on a large, deep tray and mixed in with warm, salted water.

Frégula with cocciula

The small, irregular, spherical grains are formed by rubbing pieces of dough firmly between your hands. The grains are then transferred onto a cloth to dry. After roasting them in the oven for about 15 minutes, they gain their characteristic golden colour and unique taste.

Frégula cun cocciula the traditional recipe

I ask Lazzaro what I should eat the pasta with. 'The best-known and common recipe is *cocciula*,' he replies. The pasta is served with cockles or venus clams and mussels sautéed in a pan with olive oil, garlic, parsley and a pinch of breadcrumbs. The dish is garnished with grated bottarga and bottarga shavings. We also make our own bottarga. The industrially produced bottarga lacks flavour, and the artisanal product has become too expensive.'

I haven't tried cockles before, so I ask if they taste very different from venus clams. Lazzaro: 'They're not the same, but there's not much difference in terms of flavour. If you like *spaghetti con le vongole,* you will also like cockles. As far as appearance goes, there is a distinct difference. Venus clams are slightly larger, smoother and flatter than cockles.'

'But there are plenty of other options too,' Lazzaro continues. 'The Sardinian frégula lends itself to numerous preparations, varying from rich such as this version with seafood, to poorer versions such as *frégula incasada,* a first course with simple ingredients such as parsley, tomato, sometimes saffron, and plenty of grated pecorino. We also add frégula to our soups with meat or fish, or we treat it like a risotto. The rough texture and consistency make this pasta perfect for a variety of sauces and preparations, and they vary from region to region on this island. It also makes sense that there should be a lot of different recipes for a pasta that has been around for over a thousand years,' Lazzaro concludes.

The frégula with cocciula, mussels and bottarga I had the pleasure of tasting here at Da Barbara is delicious. The flavour of the frégula and the seafood is excellent. The shape takes some getting used to. I have to admit, I prefer a larger pasta on my plate. The cocciula sauce and the bottarga shavings are phenomenal. The glass of vermentino completes the picture. Thank you for this, Lazzaro.

Da Barbara,
Strada Provinciale per Villasimius, Solanas

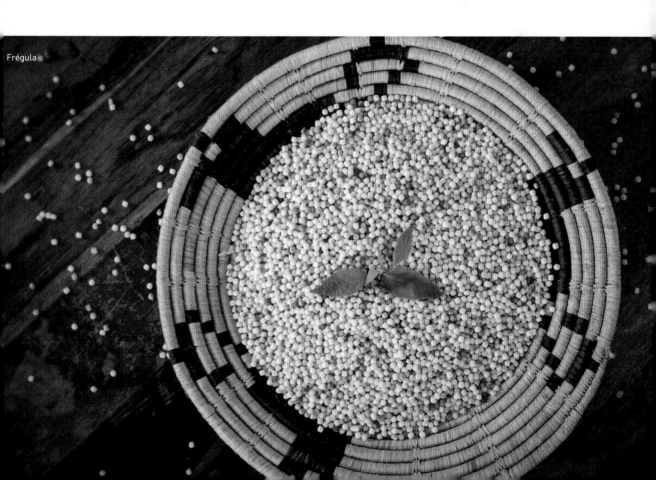
Frégula

BARBAGIA ④

My drive from Solanas continues 150 km northwards through the mountains to Fonni. Fonni is one of Sardinia's highest villages, situated in the Barbagia region on the north face of the Gennargentu mountains. From these mountain tops, you have spectacular, panoramic views of the valleys below. The village is situated some 1000 metres above sea level, and you can go skiing there in the winter. Outside the winter season, the fields and forests offer an abundance of colour with peonies, gentians, briar roses and countless other flowers. Barbagia is also the setting for intense hiking routes through forests, natural springs and bird sanctuaries. In Fonni, you can walk in the footsteps of shepherds at the *Museo della cultura pastorale:* The Museum of Pastoral Culture.

Pane carasau

I want to find out why this crispy flatbread was invented here. 'This was a *transumanza,* or sheep migration area,' Fabrizio explains. 'During the winter, the sheep were guided towards the lower-lying pastures in the region by the shepherds. They would descend from the mountains towards the plains. During the winter, this area is covered with snow, and there is no grass for the animals to graze on. So, the shepherds had to travel far from home and needed food that would keep throughout the journey, such as salami, cheese – and bread. And so, the women in the village baked our flatbread twice. Twice-baked bread keeps longer. The shepherds travelled about 100 to 150 kilometres, and the journey lasted three to four weeks. Keeping the twice-baked bread nice and crispy during the trip was no problem.

Sardinia still has many sheep today. Almost three million. Tending sheep continues to be an important part of the economy. For instance, we make the best Pecorino Romano in all of Italy. Nowadays, the sheep are transported by truck instead of on foot. But the paths on which the shepherds and their animals walked still exist. It's a unique experience to follow these same paths on horseback today. There are various *ippovia* (bridlepath) routes to choose from.'

The Barbagia region is characterised by hills and mountains

Assortment of pane carasau

ANCIENT MODERN BREAD

Pane carasau embodies Sardinia's true essence. This bread was first produced in the Barbagia region. In Fonni, I have arranged to meet Fabrizio from the Urrai family, owners of the traditional oven, *Vecchio Forno Sunalle*. In 1991, Sara and her brother Antioco Urrai, together with their partners Fabrizio di Napoli and Maria Marceddu, decided to take over an existing bakery in Fonni. Over the past 20 years, this family business has grown into an important player in the artisanal production of pane carasau in its region of origin.

'We are carrying on a tradition,' Fabrizio explains. 'The flatbread that families used to make in large quantities and kept in beautiful chests still has a home here. We only make pane carasau and *pane guttiau*. To make this, you need water, semolina, yeast, a touch of tradition and skilled, patient hands. The breads are still circular in shape. In the olden days, they also used to be oval-shaped. A fun fact is that this ancient bread is becoming very modern today,' Fabrizio says proudly.

Carasau routine

Francesco: 'The name carasau comes from the Sardinian verb *carasare*, which means 'to toast'. The *casadura*, the phase in which the bread is baked a second time, removes most of the moisture from the bread, increasing its lifespan by 180 days.'
Francesco and I walk over to the atelier. 'This is where the magic happens,' he continues. I see stacks and stacks of round flatbreads on the shelves and workbenches being processed by the many female hands. In the back of the room, a conveyor belt rotates the puffed rounds of bread that have just come out of the oven to let them cool.

Guglio slices the flatbread in two using a special machine. Women carefully pull the sliced bread apart, one by one, on giant tables. The stacks of individual, thin breads are ready to be baked a second time. The atmosphere is friendly, while many hands nimbly process all this bread. But there is also time for a chat and a laugh in a Sardinian dialect I don't understand. Seeing everyone working with their hands, gathered together around these big, round tables, reminds me of an old Italian film. I see white aprons and caps, grey workbenches, pink blushes on the cheeks of happily flushed ladies and the omnipresent yellowish beige of the countless slices of future pane carasau.

The carasau bread after it's been baked the first time

The carasau breads are pulled apart by hand after being sliced in two

Pane guttiau

Francesco shows me a stack of freshly baked pane guttiau. 'This is actually carasau bread with extra salt and olive oil on top. Back in the olden days, people would hold the bread under the fat drippings of a roast pig. Guttiau is Sardinian for *giocciolare*, or 'to drip'. The pig fat had a salty flavour. We now replace the fat or lard with olive oil and salt. The difference from plain carasau is that this crispy guttiau has more flavour.

Pane frattau

'Pane carasau is also an ingredient in numerous Sardinian dishes,' Francesco resumes. '*Pane frattau*, for example, is one way of recycling the leftover pieces and crumbs from pane carasau. They were soaked in broth and flavoured with whatever people had around the house, such as pecorino cheese, tomatoes, tomato sauce or eggs. Eggs weren't always available, so they were considered a more luxurious version. *Frattare* means to break up; pane frattau translates to broken bread. To this day, we still make frattau lasagne. To make this dish, the carasau bread is very briefly dipped in boiling salted water or broth and then placed on a plate in layers, alternating with tomato sauce or meat sauce and grated pecorino or more soaked bread. And we top it all off with a poached egg.'

I say goodbye to Francesco, his team and this wonderful place. I'm carrying a large bag filled with their bread in a variety of forms. The recipe for pane frattau that I'm given is an extra bonus for a fascinating morning here in the isolated town of Fonni.

Il Vecchio Forno
Via Ogliastra 10, Fonni

Pane carasau

FRANCESCO'S RECIPE

Pane frattau

SERVES 4 PEOPLE

16 sheets carasau bread
500 ml meat broth
   (the traditional recipe calls for mutton broth)
500 g tomato passata
   (or peeled tomatoes)
1/4 onion
1 clove of garlic

To make the sauce, mince the onion and sauté in the oil, together with the peeled and crushed garlic. Add the tomato passata or peeled tomatoes and salt. Cover the pot and leave the mixture to simmer for 15 minutes. Add the finely chopped basil . Keep the sauce warm over very low heat.

Take the pane carasau and break them up, if the sheets are very large, into two or four pieces. We usually use four layers of bread per person. When you make the broth, bear in mind that you need to be able to submerge the carasau sheets in the pot. Take four plates to serve your bread on. Make the bottom layer with a spoonful of tomato sauce.

Once the broth is ready, place your first carasau sheet on a slotted spoon and submerge it for a couple of seconds in the pot. Lift the soaked bread sheet out of the pot and drain well. Place the sheet on the plate. Cover the bread surface with a spoonful of tomato sauce and grated Sardinian pecorino. Repeat this process for all three or four layers.

Now, make the poached egg. Transfer the broth to a smaller pan. Once the broth boils, lower the heat so it doesn't reduce too much. Add a tablespoon of vinegar to the broth and stir to form a whirlpool. Drop the first egg immediately into the centre of the whirlpool. This will cause the egg white to wrap itself around the yolk. Cook the poached egg for three minutes. Drain the egg on a slotted spoon and place it on top of the pane frattau. Do the same with the other three eggs. Cook them one by one and place them on the individual pane frattau servings. Finish with a grinding of freshly ground pepper and a drizzle of extra-virgin olive oil over the top.

Pane frattau is traditionally prepared with mutton broth. You can also use another type of meat or vegetable broth. The frattau can also be prepared with a fried egg or leave the egg off altogether.

ALGHERO ⑤

From Fonni, I drive another 150 kilometres to Alghero. This town and its surroundings are an important tourist hub in Sardinia. The clear waters and sandy sea bottom are idyllic for the countless families and surfers who come here every year. The yellow walls and old houses in the town have Catalan origins. That also goes for the cathedral and churches you find here. The entire town still breathes Spain, specifically Catalonia. The traditional religious rites and folklore during annual celebrations are a testament to this. Alghero is also nicknamed La Barceloneta or 'little Barcelona' because people speak Catalan as well as Italian.

Cucina Algherese

I park my car on the town's outskirts and walk through a labyrinth of alleyways that lead to the bustling squares in Alghero's old town. Eating in Alghero also means trying out the locally caught fish. I have been advised to try *arastoga alla Catalana*, Catalan-style lobster, and *ricci,* or sea urchin. My search for local food brings me to the flamboyant Antonietta Salaris from Mabrouk restaurant in the heart of Alghero. When I ask her whether I can try Catalan lobster or sea urchin at her restaurant, she replies vehemently: 'I will never make sea urchin. It's an endangered species in our waters. And the season for Alghero lobster is over. You will only find lobster in March through August, and even then, in limited quantities. The problem is that everyone was always asking for these dishes, and now we can't supply them. The excessive demand has destroyed our sea. I am a native Algherese, born in this very street. I love our town and the sea. We need to take care of it. Nature does not belong to us; we need to respect it like we respect our family home.'

Aragosta alla Catalana

Even though I won't have the opportunity to try it, I'm nonetheless intrigued by what makes aragosta alla Catalana so special. Antonietta: 'Catalan-style lobster is a dish that is eaten in Sardinia but tastes like Spain. We prepare the lobster by boiling it in salted water for 15 to 20 minutes before draining it and leaving it to cool. We then cut the lobster in half and remove the meat. We chop the meat and combine it with raw onion, cherry tomatoes, olive oil, salt, pepper and lemon juice. We also add a little bit of the cooking water to the mixture. The mixture is left to steep for fifteen minutes, and then we fill the empty lobster shells with the filling. To make Catalan lobster, it's essential that it's made with simple ingredients. We don't use too many herbs and spices, so the dish retains its original flavour. I regularly make a variant of this dish with scampi or jumbo shrimp.'

Alghero

Antonietta makes ravioli with nero di seppia

Nero di seppia

'We remove the sac containing the ink from the *seppia*, or squid, and use this to make the sauce. The seppia ink has a savoury, briny flavour with a hint of iodine. It is a unique colouring agent because whatever you mix it with turns black. In the time of the Romans and Greeks, it was used as an ink for writing and painting. Today, we only use it in the kitchen. It is a highly valued ingredient in Italian and Catalan cuisine, as well as in other countries around the Mediterranean Sea. In the Venetian Lagoon, they use the black ink to season the cut-up squid, but also to make a black sauce for the pasta. *Arroz negro*, a type of black paella with seafood, is still very popular in Catalonia,' Antonietta explains.

⭐ Siamo Sardi di mare

It's clear to me that you don't come to Marbrouk to eat touristy food. There is no menu, and Antonietta and her team prepare whatever she finds fresh at the market that morning. 'The sea is full of delicious fish, and we just let our imagination go wild with it. I cook from the heart and with love for Alghero. *Siamo Sardi di mare*, we are Sardinians of the sea!'

She takes me to her kitchen and shows me the seppia, or squid, she had bought this morning. 'Today, I will have ravioli filled with soft ricotta in a tomato sauce with *ricotta mustia*, smoked, salted ricotta made from sheep's milk. To accompany this, we will serve a small plate with the squid in a sauce with *nero di seppia*, or the black ink from the squid.'

Ravioli with nero di seppia

On my way to Ristorante Mabrouk in the heart of Alghero

Ricotta mustia

In the kitchen, a large pot of tomato sauce for the ravioli is simmering away. I am allowed to taste the sauce and notice that it tastes very savoury. And exceptionally delicious. 'This is a sauce with fresh tomatoes and *mustia*,' Antonietta explains. She shows me this basic ingredient. It is a ricotta made from sheep's milk, white with no crust, with a semi-solid consistency and a lightly smoky aroma. 'The smoked, salted and seasoned ricotta is made from Sardinian sheep's milk and is an excellent seasoning for our dishes. We use it in tomato sauces as well as in vegetable, pasta and meat fillings.'

Ristorante Mabrouk
Via Santa Barbara 4, Alghero

LAS RAMBLAS

It is dusk by the time I walk back down Via Giuseppe Garibaldi to my car, which is parked at the foot of the old town in the Piazzale della Pace car park. The avenue leading up to it has been transformed into the Las Ramblas of Alghero. It is a crowded street filled with bars and the different stands selling typical foods. But my attention is drawn to a stand that belongs to Macelleria Roberto Contini. On the ground next to the stand, I spot an improvised square barbecue measuring a metre and a half fuelled by a wood fire. The fire is flanked by 18 large skewers with pork carcasses and pieces of meat. The smell coming from the grilled meat instantly whets my appetite. Next to the barbecue stands a table with a large cutting board. When the skewer is done, it is removed from the barbecue and the hot, freshly grilled meat is immediately cut into pieces. I take a plastic plate with the meat and somewhat clumsily try to eat it standing up. The warm and friendly Roberto joins me and gives me instructions on how to best eat the meat. The meat is on the bone, so I can easily grab it with my hands and nibble it off the bone. He reacts instantly when I start to talk about *maiale*, or pork. *'No no, questo è porceddu,'* this is suckling pig, he says emphatically.

Porceddu

Roberto: 'The Sardinian porceddu is a typical Sardinian delicacy. We grill the animal vertically on a skewer, as opposed to the horizontally grilled *porchetta* from Lazio and Umbria. Did you know that it's completely wrong to grill suckling pig horizontally? The meat loses all its liquids, taking all the flavour with it. As soon as we place the skewer upright and apply heat to it, the pig starts to lose moisture. We then turn the skewer upside down. This method ensures that the pig doesn't lose its flavour. And we keep turning the skewers over all the time. We grill until all the meat has been cooked through, and we end up with a crispy crust. The great thing about the Sardinian pig is that it doesn't need any herbs, spices or marinades. We don't use any seasoning except for salt. Spices would only dry out the meat. Only once the meat is grilled do we season it with myrtle leaves. And, of course, we also add our unsurpassed passion and skill to these finest-quality ingredients,' Roberto jests.

Roadside grill featuring typical
Sardinian porceddu (top) and innards (below)

Sa Mandra

I drive a short way from Alghero to Sa Mandra. This *agritourismo* is both a family farm and a culinary institute for Sardinia and for any lover of the authentic gastronomy of the Barbagia region. Rita Pirsi and her husband, Mario Murroco, run the farm and the restaurant together with their three children. I have arranged to meet Maria Grazia, Rita and Mario's daughter, in the area where we find the restaurant, the shop and the rooms that are available for holidaymakers. Maria: 'In the restaurant, you will find typical Barbagian dishes made from our own products. Barbagia is the heart of Sardinia. The area encompasses the slopes of the Gennargentu, the mountain range dominating the island's central region. It was here that the Sardinians found their sanctuary when the Romans and Carthaginians attacked the island. Barbagia is famous for its cannonau wines but perhaps even more for its pastoral culture and animal life. We have a fantastic farm with a lot of sheep and pigs. We also produce *grano duro,* or hard wheat, with which we make pasta such as frégula as well as pastries. In our restaurant, you can enjoy dishes such as *culurgiones, pane frattau, perceddu,* lamb with artichoke, *còrdula,* or lamb innards on a spit, *polpettine di agnello,* or lamb meatballs, and so on.'

Artisanal cheeses and cured meats

Maria and I walk to the farm's shop, where their agricultural products are displayed. These include *sa frue, ricotta mustia¬* and different types of pecorino or sheep's milk cheese, but also *guanciale* or pork cheek, *coppa en lardo* or pork fat, *frégula,* pickled artichokes, olives …
Maria: *'Sa frue* is a traditional cheese, or rather cheese rennet, that used to be added to soups. The shepherds here in the region used to make this straight from fresh sheep's milk as soon as it was collected. We also make this cheese using an artisanal process.'

She gives me a piece to try. The cheese is white and has a soft, buttery consistency. There is no crust, and I don't see any holes. The cheese tastes very fresh, and I sense an aroma that tends towards yoghurt or sour cream but with a sweet aftertaste.

Pecorino Sardo

'And this is our island's finest dairy product,' Maria continues. Several different types of homemade sheep cheese are spread out in a chilled display case. Maria: 'The history of pecorino in Sardinia dates back to the

Sheep graze on the Barbagia hills

Casu marzu

'worm' cheese. Nonetheless, the European Union has prohibited its production and sale on health and hygiene grounds.'

The *Piophila casei* fly is not your ordinary house fly, and therefore it is not dangerous to human health. The fly cannot survive in our stomachs; the acidity kills them.

Maria: 'Casu marzu was considered by shepherds to be symbolic of magic and inexplicable supernatural events. The cheese is not for sale. But Sardinians still always manage to procure the cheese directly from the shepherds. You can't just erase a deep-rooted tradition like this. And besides, what the rest of the world doesn't know, won't hurt them, right?'

I had hoped to see and perhaps even try this fabled cheese, but Maria couldn't – or perhaps 'wasn't allowed to' – offer me any. So, I stick to the pecorino and *sa frue* for my goody bag as a souvenir of this exceptional culinary agribusiness.

Azienda Agrituristica Sa Mandra,
Strada Provinciale 44, Alghero

end of the 18th century. This is a product from our shepherds, and today we make them in all sorts of varieties: *semicotto,* or semi-cooked; *affumicato,* smoked; *con latte crudo,* with raw milk; and *maturo,* or aged. We use full-fat sheep's milk from our own animals. The maturing period varies from twenty days to two years.'

In light of its unique character, Pecorino Sardo was awarded a DOP quality label in 1996, with a *dolce* (soft) and a *mature* (ripe) variant. Pecorino Sardo differs from the other sheep's milk cheeses on the island. The Fiore Sardo DOP and Pecorino Romano DOP use the same raw material, but the processing is different.

Casu marzu, or cheese with worms

As far as Sardinia's truly unique cheese products go, Maria says that I must mention *casu marzu.* This cheese made international headlines in 2009 because the *Guinness Book of Records* had called it the most dangerous cheese in the world.

Had I heard of this cheese before? No. Maria: 'It's a creamy cheese that is only produced in Sardinia. Another word for it is worm cheese. After maturation, the cheese is still very soft due to the colonisation of larvae from the cheese fly, the *Piophila casei,* that penetrates the cheese. Casu marzu is produced in the spring and summer months. The wheels of pecorino cheese are eaten by the cheese fly, which subsequently lays its eggs in the cheese. Once the eggs hatch, the enzymes from the tiny larvae turn the pecorino into a soft cream. The maturation process takes three to six months. To this day, no direct causal relationship has been found between any kind of illness or condition and the consumption of this

Casu marzu

Horses on the Fattoria dei Piani grounds

Annette on the shores of a lagoon near Alghero

Seadas

Irene: 'When we talk about the desserts that are typical of our island, there is one which surpasses them all: *seadas*. It is, in fact, a dish straight out of the farmhouse kitchen, using simple and readily available ingredients. It looks like a ravioli made from semolina with a fresh pecorino filling. Seadas are fried in oil and drizzled with honey. The term seadas, or *sebadas*, is always used in the plural, even when referring to a single piece.

The Sardinian seadas come from the rugged, arid Sardinian interior. This sweet was made for special occasions such as Christmas, Easter or when husbands returned home from the *transumanza*, the annual sheep migration. Seadas were initially unsweetened and almost as big as a *calzone* (folded-over pizza). It stilled the hunger of shepherds who had been away from home for a long time. It wasn't until later that they were turned into a dessert by adding honey and making them smaller.

OASIS OF GREEN, HORSES AND PASTA

After a 10-kilometre drive, I arrive at Irene Matacena's Fattoria dei Piani in Olmedo. I have registered for a lesson in homemade pasta. And to be specific, I want to learn to make *seadas*, a typical Sardinian dessert.

I receive a warm welcome as I drive up to the house. It is a breathtaking green estate. I see fruit and olive trees, rose bushes, and plant and vegetable gardens everywhere. Horses graze on part of the grounds in the shade under the trees. We go to her kitchen, which is beautifully furnished in a traditional style. The wooden pasta table is long, and the flour, rolling pins, jugs with water and other tools lie in readiness for our lesson.

Ingredients for seadas at Irene's

Pasta praxis

As we make the dough, Irene explains that preparing the perfect seadas involves two essential elements: the pasta and the cheese filling. The pasta is typical Sardinian, made with durum wheat semolina and lard. We gradually add water to the semolina and lard until we have a smooth, homogenous, elastic mixture. Then, we press and turn the dough with loving care. After more than 10 minutes of kneading, we leave the dough to rest in a covered glass bowl. For the filling, we grate the pecorino cheese that Irene has set aside for us. 'The pecorino needs to be very young, so it still has that slightly sour taste,' she explains. To the grated pecorino, we add some grated lemon peel from a lemon that Irene has picked from the garden. 'Lemon zest gives the dessert a refreshing and distinctive nuance,' she continues. We also add a little bit of cane sugar to the mixture.

After 30 minutes, we roll the dough out into thin sheets and cut it into squares. We place the filling on the squares before covering it with a second sheet of dough. We moisten the edges with water before pressing them shut. Irene: 'It is important to press the edges firmly so they don't pop open during the frying process.'

We fry the seadas in a generous amount of sunflower oil. 'Lard was formerly used to do this as well,' Irene explains. After a couple of minutes of frying, the seadas are removed and drained. We then place them on a plate and drizzle a spoonful of honey over the top. We garnish the dish with a bit of lemon zest.

Time to taste. The flavour palate lies somewhere between savoury and sweet. The dark chestnut honey has a strong, bitter-sweet taste. The lemon zest adds a refreshing touch, and the cheese with cane sugar is salty yet sweet. All unique aromas, scents and flavours. Divine!

Fattoria dei Piani (Irene),
Strada I Piani 13, Olmedo

IRENE'S RECIPE
Seadas

SERVES 4 PEOPLE
300 g semolina
50 g lard or butter
a pinch of salt
150 g water (approximately)

FILLING
300 g young pecorino cheese
grated zest of 1 lemon (organic)
1 tablespoon cane sugar

TOPPING
liquid honey
grated zest of ½ lemon (organic)

Combine the semolina, salt and softened lard or butter. Gradually add the water until you end with a homogenous, elastic dough. Knead the dough with your hands for at least 10 minutes. Shape the dough into a ball, place it in a bowl, and cover it with cling film. Leave the dough to rest for about 30 minutes at room temperature. Roll out the dough (not too thinly). Cut into sheets measuring 10 cm across (square or round). Place the filling on one of the sheets. Moisten the other sheet with water before sealing in the filling, and press the edges down firmly to prevent them from opening up during the frying process.

Fry the seadas in sunflower oil at 180 °C, constantly spooning hot oil over the surface until they puff up; turn them over and fry on the other side to give the seadas their golden colour. Place them on baking parchment and serve with honey drizzled over the top and lemon peel. You can also use confectioner's sugar.

CAMPANIA

The southern Italian region of Campania is situated on the shores of the Tyrrhenian Sea, with Lazio to the north, Basilicata to the south and Molise and Puglia to the east. The Romans called this fertile region 'Campania felix'. Natural springs rise up from the deep, soft soil at different locations. Sunshine, enough rain and the fresh sea breeze ensure a pleasant climate. Its ecosystems are varied; from Mediterranean coastal areas to mountain ridges. Popular destinations include the Amalfi Coast, with its intense colours and gorgeous bays and cliffs, and the islands of Capri, Ischia and Procida. The region also boasts two national parks, nine regional parks and 18 nature and marine reserves. The reserves take up about 27 per cent of the Campania's total surface area; a figure surpassed only by Abruzzo.

The region features no fewer than five UNESCO World Heritage Sites: the historical centre of Napoli, the archaeological sites of Pompeii, Herculaneum and Torre Annunziata, the 18th-century royal palace of Caserta, the Amalfi Coast and the Cliento and Vallo Diano national parks. They exemplify Campania's rich history, cultural heritage and exceptional natural beauty.

Pompeii with the Vesuvius in the background

Via Krupp in Capri, also known as the serpentine path

Napoli
1

Amalfi
2

Via Pura

Calore Irpino

Volturno

Ofanto

Sele

Calore Lucano

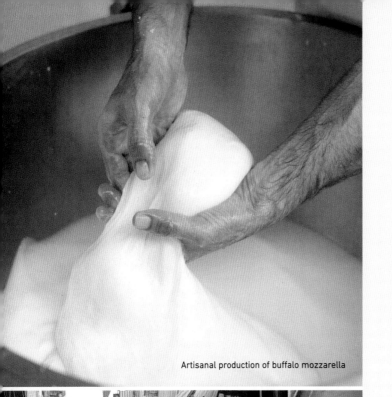
Artisanal production of buffalo mozzarella

INTERNATIONAL CUISINE

The cuisine is characterised by typical Italian dishes and ingredients, including pizza, pasta and tomato. *Mozzarella di buffala DOP*, made from full-fat buffalo milk, is one of Campania's most coveted dairy products. In fact, Neapolitan cuisine has always been largely representative of Italian gastronomy abroad. The international star of Italian cuisine, the pizza, comes in a variety of forms in Naples. And pasta has been elevated to an art here. Skilful hands prepare fresh *cavatelli*, tagliatelle, fusilli, *orecchiette*... These exquisite pasta varieties are topped with sauces such as lamb ragù (a type of bolognese sauce), beans, truffles from Bagno Irpino, delicious seafood, or any of the countless vegetables that grow in the fields.

VOLCANIC WINE

Campania made a name for itself with wines from the province of Avellino. The best-known wines are the whites: Greco di Tufo and Fiano di Avellino, along with the red Taurasi. The white Lacryma Christi del Vesuvio wine is also inextricably linked to the region. The inactive volcanoes in the region are beneficial to the wine industry. Moreover, the vineyards are often positioned on steep flanks, an ideal location for grapes to flourish. The Sorrento-Amalfi-coast, on the other hand, is a well-known name in the production of limoncello.

FISH, MEAT AND DESSERT

The Tyrrhenian Sea is a source of inspiration for Campanian cuisine. Swordfish, gilthead, sea bass, mussels, shrimp, anchovies... they are all prepared on the grill, crusted with salt, or added to *acqua pazza*, fish soup. Moreover, *pesce fritto*, fried fish in a *cuoppo*, or greaseproof paper cone, are highly popular in Naples and seaside resorts. Meat and sausage are more common on menus in the mountainous regions. And the region's best-known dessert is probably the *babà* pastry flavoured with rum. Another delicious local sweet is *sfogliatelle*, a shell-shaped puff pastry filled with ricotta or custard and candied fruit.

Annette in the streets of Naples

San Marzano

The San Marzano tomato owes its name to its place of origin. Francesco Cirio made this meaty, elongated tomato world-famous. In the early 20th century, this pioneer from Piedmont chose the San Marzano from hundreds of tomato varieties to produce the first preserved peeled tomatoes. Large industrial tomato processors such as the Cirio and Elvea (Luigi Vitelli back then) families moved to the region and brought jobs to many generations of Neapolitans and Salernitana natives. New tomato varieties often with similar forms, including the Roma variety, took the market by storm in 1970. The growers wanted tomatoes that they could harvest mechanically. The production area expanded to other regions in the north and south, and the San Marzano tomato was gradually replaced. Today, it's a niche product exclusively picked by hand.

About half the national production of *pelati*, tinned peeled tomatoes, takes place in Campania. Other popular products include peeled and diced tomatoes, tomato passata or paste, tomato concentrate, and countless ready-made tomato-based Italian sauces. The region has as many producers as it has tomato preparations.

Re pomodoro – Tomato is King

The iconic tomato forms the basis for many Italian dishes, from pasta with tomato sauce to pizza. This famous fruit was imported via Spain in the 16th century and has since flourished in Campania. The volcanoes, the ancient, fertile subsoil and the countless natural springs make this area unique in the world. There are four volcanic centres: Roccamonfina, Campi Flegrei, Ischia and Vesuvius. The surrounding plains, mountains, and hills with their microclimates are highly suitable for growing wine grapes, trees, vegetables and, of course, tomatoes.

San Marzano tomatoes

A typical fish stall in Naples

NAPOLI 1

Naples is a beautiful coastal city with a unique histori-cal, cultural, and artistic heritage. The historical centre is the largest in Europe and was listed as a World Her-itage Site by UNESCO in 1995. A maze of picturesque streets harbours countless old churches, museums, and theatres. You can even wander through Naples' history below-ground. Following a catastrophic mud-slide, the Romans rebuilt the new city on top of the old one. The harbour has always been a plentiful source of jobs for the Neapolitans.

The Neapolitans live outside, whether it's for travel, work or pleasure. This has everything to do with the Mediterranean climate, the city's structure, and the lively working-class districts. Sometimes, ten people would live in a *basso* (a single room on the ground floor of a building). The residents ate outside because there simply wasn't enough room indoors.

⭐ Naples makes you fat

There's no getting around it: Naples makes you fat. The no getting around it part is literal because you experience the Neapolitan food culture in all its oily glory on the streets. And yes, Naples is very much alive. Millions of people move through the city streets and they're constantly eating – everywhere! The local food is served from a refrigerated display case, in a small shop, prepared in a doorway or on the pavement from stalls with minimal cooking facilities. A deep fryer, a fridge holding drinks and a tiny cash register or box for the receipts are all you need. I take in the smells and vapours of food prepared next to the impressive walls of extravagant, tumble-down, historical *palazzi*. I walk past food stands and tables, enthralled by the brightly coloured graffiti reflected in the rays of a Med-iterranean sun, which finds its way into every nook and cranny. So incredibly infectious!

Calciomania – football madness

In the working-class district of Quartieri Spagnoli, I notice that Naples reveres not only its saints but also SCC Napoli. The square looks like a place of pilgrimage with its impressive mural, posters, banners, photos, scarves, and candles. Football legend Diego Maradona is revered like a god, or rather, 'the hand of God'. A hundred metres further along in Via Emanuele de Deo, more football heroes are portrayed. The Neapolitan love for their football heroes is unique and authentic. These football players are not just star players. Neapolitans are aware of the city's less-than-stellar reputation and value those who view it with an open mind. If you love Naples, Naples loves you back.

HISTORICAL PIZZERIAS

But the working-class city of Naples is, above all, the city of pizza. A couple of iconic pizzerias here have been around for a very, very long time. The Antica Pizzeria daMichele dates from 1870, and Pizzeria Brandi was believed to be where the *pizza margherita* was invented in 1889. According to the current owner, Paolo Pagnani, the pizza margherita is the most classic of all Neapolitan pizzas. Paolo: 'We top them with the best San Marzano tomatoes, mozzarella from Agerola on the Amalfi Coast, basil from the villages around Mount Vesuvius, and the finest extra-virgin olive oil in Campania.' As to whether the story of this world-famous pizza originating in this small alleyway is true, his reply is non-committal. 'What we can say is that our Neapolitan pride is named after the erstwhile queen of Italy: Margherita di Savoia, or Margaret of Savoy.' Pizzeria Starita is another famous name in the city of pizza because this is where the film *L'oro di Napoli*, starring Sophia Loren, was filmed in 1954. Loren was and continues to be a city icon. You will often find images of this Hollywood diva on the streets or indoors. La Sophia herself loves Naples because the city reminds her of her childhood and youth.

Pizzeria Brandi,
Salita Sant'Anna Di Palazzo 1/2 in Via Chiaia, Napoli

Pizza portafoglio

Naples is the birthplace of pizza, the city where you will find a pizzeria on every street corner. Giovanni Kahn della Corte makes skilful use of this tradition. The creative Neapolitan caterer equipped three-wheeled Apes with fireproof wood-fired ovens under the brand Take Uè. I meet him at one of his Apes in the Corso Vittorio Emanuele. Giovanni: 'In this town, pizza frequently used to be eaten standing up or on the go. That's why they were sometimes made *a portafoglio*, meaning "per portare" or "portable". After baking, a pizza would sometimes be folded into quarters. It was both easier to eat and keep warm. My business is founded on that principle.'

The *pizzaoilo* folds my margherita in half and folds it again into quarters. 'The portafoglio is sometimes called a *libretto*,' Giovanni elaborates, 'and it's a light version of the margherita. You can also order the portafoglio with other fillings.' Johnny Take Uè is the only three-wheeled vehicle equipped with a patented traditional wood-fired oven. This Neapolitan pizza baker is based along the Corso Vittorio Emanuele and in the Edenlandia amusement park but also has outlets in London, Perugia, Milan, Bergamo (Sarnico), Rende and L'Aquila.

Johnny Take Uè
C.so Vittorio Emanuele 84, Napoli

Annette next to an image of Dries Mertens in Quarteri Spagnoli, when he played for Naples

A larger-than-life Sophia Loren is displayed next to trattoria e pizzeria 'o Vesuvio's entrance.

Pizza fritta

After a long walk, I reach my destination: Passione di Sofi on Via Benedetto Croce. A crowd of people stands around the stall, eating a type of calzone wrapped in greaseproof paper. 'This is the most famous type of pizza in Naples, Carmela explains as she hands me the deep-fried pizza. 'The *pizza fritte* is also called the *pizza a otto* because you could eat it straight away and didn't have to pay for it until eight (otto) days later. The fried pizza is a reminder of the difficult years after the war and the Neapolitan creativity. You didn't need a wood-fired oven to make these. The dough was fried in hot oil, causing the pizza to swell up and give it the impression of substance. Today, the fried pizzas are filled with salami, cheese or *friarielli,* a type of broccoli rabe. People used to fill the pizzas with cheap ricotta and *cicccioli,* pieces of lard, or whatever else they could find. Pizza fritta, also known as the *pizza del popolo,* or people's pizza, was a source of extra family income. The women went out to sell the pizzas, fried in the typical cooking pans that are a part of Naples' collective memory.

Passione di Sofi,
Via Toledo 206 and Via B. Croce 42, Napoli

ROSTICCERIA
Donna Sofia

Seven hundred metres further along, in Via Tribunali, I speak to Gaetano Zarelli from pizzeria Donna Sofia. Images of the ravishing diva of the same name abound. It's not hard to guess how this business came up with its name. Gaetano: 'Sophia Loren is, without a doubt, the most famous pizza fritta seller in the world. In the

film *L'oro di Napoli,* she calls out: "Eat today and pay eight days from now." The film is a fine portrayal of daily life in the Neapolitan streets at that time, with pizza as the starring role.

Although Sophia's lovely cleavage features quite prominently in the various scenes as well.' Detail from *L'oro di Napoli* with Sophia Loren.

Pizzeria Donna Sofia
Via dei Tribunali 89/90, Napoli

Montanara

I walk another two and a half kilometres southwest to Pizze e fritte Napolitani Donna Sofia in Via Chiaia. Owner Enzo Zarelli explains to me the ins and outs of typical Neapolitan fried food. In addition to the classic and deep-fried pizzas, the menu features dishes that I'm not familiar with, such as *montanara.*

Enzo: 'Montanara is a deep-fried mini pizza where we add the toppings after frying. It is perhaps the most bizarre and least well-known type of pizza. The traditional toppings are tomato sauce, cheese and a basil leaf, but we also make other variations.

Frittatina

Enzo serves me a mysterious, crispy, steaming, round, croquet-like filled slice of... something. Enzo: 'This is *frittanina,* the modern-day version of the macaroni omelette.

The omelette was invented in Naples a long time ago to reuse pasta leftovers. Any leftover pasta from the evening meal would be fried up the next day with a couple of eggs and some cheese. It was a hearty lunch at work. Today, you will find variations with minced meat or mozzarella, and we have added a crispy crust. It's a popular first course in Neapolitan pizzerias.'

Cuoppo di frittura

'The *cuoppo di frittura* is symbolic of Neapolitan street food,' Enzo explains. 'You can fill this greaseproof paper cone with whatever you want. For instance, *zeppole*, dough made from water, flour, yeast and salt that is left to proof and then fried. Or rice croquettes, seasonal vegetables such as aubergine and courgette flowers in batter, or *scagliozzi* (polenta triangles). Or macaroni *frittanine*, or *crocchè* potato croquettes. As long as the colour of the fried food is light, the breadcrumbs are crispy, and the contents are served hot. The contents of this greaseproof cone are usually determined and fried on the spot, depending on the customer's wishes. There are generally two types of cuoppo on these streets. The *mare* or fish variant contains fried fish, *baccalà* or salted cod, *zeppoline* or fried seaweed balls, breaded calamari and baby octopus. The other variant is the *terra* or land version.

Donna Sofia a Chiaia
Via Chiaia 188, Napoli

O' per e o' muss

Wasting food was considered a capital crime in Naples. Street food such as *o' per e o' muss* and *o bror e purp* has left its mark on the city's history and its residents. Strict hygiene regulations have made both products practically extinct on the streets.

o' per e o' muss literally means 'the foot and the snout'. Initially, this referred to the calf's feet and snout; pork wasn't added until later. Aside from these two parts, many other meat scraps are used as well, including the tongue, skin, udder, uterus, and intestines. The offal is washed, soaked, blanched, stripped and then cooked for four to five hours. Once the meat is tender, it is cut into pieces and seasoned with salt and lemon or mixed into a salad with beans, olives, celery, onion, tomato, fennel, gherkins, or chilli pepper.

Pizza fritta

Frittatine

Enjoying a cuoppo di frittura

O' per e o' muss in the pot, ready for cooking

QUARTIERI SPAGNOLI

I wander through the picturesque Pignasecca market in the Quartieri Spagnoli district. Pignasecca is the oldest market in Naples. You can buy fresh fish, fruits, and vegetables here. I discover a variety of fried foods as well as typical sweets in these streets. In Via Pignasecca, I spy small display counters with ivory-white innards suspended between lemons and bay leaves. I visit *trattoria* and *tripperia* Le Zendraglie, owned by Antonio Moglie. Antonio: 'La Zendraglie is derived from the French *les entrailles*, or entrails. Court servants used to call out "Les entrailles!" before throwing leftovers out the window. And crowds of hungry people would flock to the source of the call. Our business has been here since 1927.' Tripperia Fiorenzano is situated a couple of metres further along. Their sign reads: 'since 1897'.

Le Zendraglie, Via Pignasecca 114, Napoli
Tripperia Fiorenzano, Via Pignasecca 50, Napoli

'O bror e purp

There was a time when, during the winter months, the alleyways would be heated by aromatic, steaming hot pots of octopus broth. In 1884, author and journalist Matilde Serao wrote about the Neapolitan working-class districts and the art of survival among the poor in her chronicle, *Il ventre di Napoli* (The belly of Naples). She writes about *'o bror e purp,* octopus boiled in seawater and seasoned with strong peppers. The women on the street heated a small pot over a small fire. You no longer see them on the streets, but you can still order a cup of hot broth with *ranfetella* (tentacle) in some trattorias.

I make my way over to 'a figlia d'o Marenaro on the Piazza Enrico de Nicola for my meeting with owner Assunta Pacifico. In this quintessential Neapolitan restaurant, you can taste the sea. Thankfully, I don't need to queue in the long line of waiting customers. They don't take reservations on Sundays, so you simply wait in line until a table becomes available. The message is clear: be on time. The staff is dressed in sailor costumes. I wait inside next to an aquarium filled with lobsters and a counter that looks like a painting with all sorts of brightly coloured fish. La signora Assunta comes out to meet me. She is also a part of the spectacle, dressed in a blue suit with trousers that flare out at the bottom like giant fins as if she's just risen from the sea.

A fish stall in Quartieri Spagnoli

A Neapolitan fish vendor in action

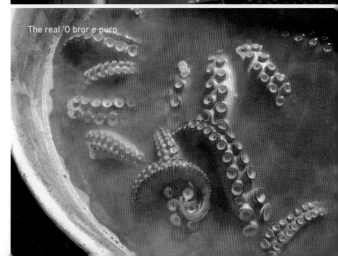
The real 'O bror e purp

Fish is a much-sought-after ingredient in Neapolitan cuisine

⭐ Cooking liquid as the elixir of life

Assunta: 'The poor man's elixir of life has always been *o' bror e purp*, the cooking liquid from the octopus. Our family business started when my father Raffaele, alias "Papucc o' marenaro", sold o' bror e purp by the glass in the districts of Naples. The people loved his special drink. In fact, broth like this is incredibly healthy, especially during the winter. Father Papuccio's soup was a huge success, and he soon opened a shop in Porta Capuana together with his mother, Maria l'Acquaiola. Ever since I was seven years old, I helped my father clean mussels for what later became our signature dish: *zuppa di cozze* or mussel soup. I learned the ropes at a very young age. I now have my own restaurant in Via Fiora, and people call me the queen of the *zuppa a cozzeche*,' she says with her charming Neapolitan accent.

Modern version of Zuppa di Cozze

'Maundy Thursday' soup

Assunta is something else; that much is clear. I feel honoured to be allowed to sit at one of the tables on the patio and taste the fabled mussel soup. Assunta: 'Neapolitans eat mussel soup on Maundy Thursday. This custom dates to the turn of the 19th century. The mussel soup was first prepared by order of Ferdinand I of the house of Bourbon and the Kingdom of Naples. He loved seafood. But the clergy advised him to eat in moderation during the Holy Week. So, he ordered mussel soup to be prepared. The news spread throughout the city, and everyone, poor and rich alike, followed the king's example. Different variations were made. The poor replaced the mussels with *lumache* (snails), and the rich added octopus to their soup. Today, we eat the soup year-round and have developed our own version of this classic.'

A deep dish with steaming hot soup and *freselle*, or hard bread, is placed before me at the table. The ritual has something spiritual and artistic. This piece of Neapolitan history is accompanied by seafood. Mussels, squid, sea slugs and venus clams lie half submerged in the steaming soup, seasoned with a generous splash of *'o russ*, a special oil with chilli peppers. The finishing touch is a *tarallo hzogna e pepe*, unique to Naples.

A Figlia d'o Marimaro
Via Foria, 180/182, 80137 Napoli

Tarallo 'nzogna e pepe e mandorle

The round, braided, crumbly *tarallo* biscuits made with lard, pepper and almonds are the Neapolitans' favourite snack and have become a piece of immaterial cultural heritage. Its composition means that it was considered an important food as early as the 19th century. This savoury biscuit with animal fat or lard is also highly nutritious.

Intrigued by these Neapolitan biscuits, I visit the Taralleria Napoletana in Via San Biagio Dei Librai. Mauro Bruner tells me that the Neapolitan tarallo differs from those from Apulia. Mauro: 'Our tarallo is a cheap meal substitute, appetiser, or tasty snack. People would bake the biscuits enriched with fat and seasoned with pepper to reuse leftover bread scraps. The fat used is *'nzogna,* lard. Later, almonds were also incorporated into the *tarallo,* and the biscuit became a delicacy. The tarallaro wandered through the city streets carrying baskets full of these warm, fragrant rings.'

The tarallaro

'Sadly, the wandering tarallaro is a thing of the past,' Bruno continues. Fortunato Bisaccia was the most famous and favourite of them all. This comical character would brighten the streets with songs, jokes and real Italian sketches. Between 1950 and 1990, you would bump into him in his white uniform on the streets. He was recognizable by his converted pram, which he used to push the bakery's taralli through the streets.

Laboratorium shop

Today, you will only find taralli in bakeries and at kiosks. Taralli have been baked in this house by the Infante family since the 1940s. Leopoldo Infante started one of the most famous bakeries in town. His sons expanded the assortment in the 1970s with traditional Neapolitan patisserie and ice cream products such as sfogliatelle and babà in a variety of forms. Shops carrying the 'Leopoldo dal 1940' and 'Casa Infante' brands pop up all over town.

Their Taralleria Napoletana is a shop with a workshop dedicated to the tarallo. While you wait, the savoury biscuits are prepared in countless flavours and surprising combinations. Displayed on the counter, you will find the classic *'nzogna e pepe-taralli* alongside variations with tomatoes, pesto, and even vegan taralli. A four-man team prepares the taralli entirely by hand. Two separate pieces of dough are thinly rolled out into a sausage shape, placed next to each other, braided, and shaped into a small circle. 'They follow our almost hundred-year-old recipe and the technique our founder Leopoldo used,' Mauro explains.

Neapolitan taralli in a variety of colours and flavours

⭐ Tutti colori – all colours

I sit outside at a table in front of the shop with a glass of fiano and assorted taralli. The tall, blue tables against the rough graffiti-clad walls set a brightly coloured scene. The many-hued taralli are stacked like a tower around a skewer on a stand. The glass of white wine looks extra delicious next to this gold-coloured dish. The people complete this fascinating spectacle. It is crowded in this colourful alleyway. It's all you need to fall madly in love with this amazing city.

Taralleria Napoletana
Via San Biagio Dei Librai 3, Napoli

Babà

Marta from the Antica Pasticceria Armando Scaturchio (1903) in the heart of Naples guides me through the world of the Neapolitan babà. She immediately serves me the pastry and a cup of coffee in her patisserie/coffee bar. 'You don't know what you're talking about until you've tried it first,' Maria laughs. And she's right. One bite, and I'm sold. The soft, airy cake and spicy rum are a delight to the senses. The rum-soaked sponge cake melts in my mouth. 'Just to be clear, the original babà contains rum, not limoncello,' Marta assures me.

The original babà contains rum

'If someone says to you in dialect: "Tu si ṅu babbà," or "you're a babà" they mean that you're sweet,' Marta explains as I continue to enjoy this divine cake. I understand that this is not just about sweetness, and I wait to hear more.

The Neapolitan babà was born in France

Marta: 'The babà journey starts in the late 18th century in Lunéville in the French region of Lorraine. This sweet connects Naples, France, and Poland because it was invented by the Polish king Stanislaus Leszczyński, who was in exile there at the time. He decided to add rum to the *kugelhopf*, or Bundt cake that he felt was far too dry to eat by itself. The Polish royal called his cake *ali babà*, after the popular fairy tale from *One Thousand and One Nights*.

From Versailles to Naples

Ali babà became the latest craze at the Versailles court, in part thanks to the incredibly popular Jamaican rum. In Paris, the babà was shaped like a swelled-up dome. It was a long journey from France to Naples, but the nobility helped things along. Marie Antoinette was the wife of King Louis XVI, and her sister, Maria Carolina of Austria, was married to the king of Naples, Ferdinand IV of the House of Bourbon. She introduced new foods such as *béchamel, gratin and babà* in Naples at the end of the 18th century. Babà soon became a highly popular dessert among the Neapolitan beau monde and later became a typical Neapolitan street food.

⭐ The sound of babà

Did you know that musicality is very important when a Neapolitan argues?' Marta asks. 'The singsong sounds of our conversations are complemented with gestures and facial expressions. That goes for every Italian in the large port towns. It's how we communicated with the many foreigners with whom we traded, by using our hands, facial expressions, and melodic tone of voice. Babà never needed to be said twice. We just sing the first letters of the alphabet twice. How can you ever forget a spicy sweet with a name like that?' She's right: babà. How cool is that!

Antica Pasticceria Armando Scaturchio,
Via Portamedina 4, Napoli

A typical street in the Quartieri Spagnoli district

The route along the Amalfi Coast boasts spectacular views

EPIC ROUTE

From Naples, I set a course for Sorrento. I enjoy the spectacular journey through the region's rich history, and the phenomenal panoramic views are a bonus. From Sorrento, I take the Amalfi Drive SS163, which winds 60 km along the coast until Vietri sul Mare and passes the stunningly beautiful towns of Positano, Praiano, Ravello and Amalfi. Most of the road has been hewed out of impressive cliffs that plunge into the sky-blue sea. Tiny houses seem to cling to the rocks in a pink, yellow and orange mosaic. This stretch of road is definitely going on my bucket list.

AMALFI ②

The Amalfi Coast is named for the town of Amalfi, situated halfway along the Costiera Amalfitana at the foot of Monte Cerreto. I drive past delightfully green hills boasting terraces with lemon and olive groves under an azure-blue sky that just breathes *la dolce vita*. I am now entering the land of lemons. In Amalfi, 87-year-old Luigi and his son Salvatore from the Aceto lemon company are waiting for my arrival. I walk up a steep hill towards their domain past the various terraces with lemon trees; I feel like I'm walking through a green and yellow fairy-tale-like forest. Before I'm halfway up, I come across Luigi and Salvatore, and I immediately congratulate them on their slice of paradise on earth. 'Our region boasts two iconic varieties,' Salvatore says. 'The amalfi and the sorrento lemon. Both are cultivated on hillside terraces, supported by low walls called *macere*. Our fruit trees are surrounded by chestnut wood constructions that support the heavily laden branches. On the Amalfi coast, we grow the lemons in the shelter of their own canopy to protect them from the wind and cold. In Sorrento, they place straw mats or nets instead.'

 Blood doesn't flow through my veins; only lemon juice

Luigi tells me that his family has been growing lemons for six generations. 'I come from a family of thirteen. I have been working with lemon trees since I was six years old. I was allowed to help carry the baskets filled with lemons on the donkey. As a teenager, I raced around the orchard on a Lambretta with a wooden crate filled with harvested fruit. The Lambretta was eventually replaced by three-wheeled Ape trucks, and today, we drive around in golf carts with large tyres. And we use a zipline,' he says proudly. We climb up the hill and Luigi shows me where they operate the zipline. A row of posts runs up the hillside, connected by a sturdy iron cable. Luigi: 'We were the first to transport lemon baskets up and down the hill using a zipline.' This piece of industrial archaeology is cutting-edge technology as far as this man is concerned. Beaming, he tells me how lemons have coloured his whole life. 'Blood doesn't flow through my veins; only lemon juice.'

A source of vitamin C

Salvatore: 'The Arabs introduced the lemon in Spain, Sicily and Campania during their campaigns. But they didn't become truly popular in this region until they discovered that the fruit helped prevent scurvy. This illness is caused due to a lack of vitamin C, and our citrus fruits just so happen to contain an abundance of the stuff. The Amalfi people were seafarers, so they always needed a large supply of lemons during their sea voyages. In 1825, one of my forefathers, Salvatore Aceto, bought a small plot of land in the neighbouring village of Ravello. That's where we started. The business flourished between 1930 and 1938. After the Second World War, our family became the largest lemon grower on the Amalfi Coast, larger than our Calabrian and Sicilian competitors.'

Lemon tour

We walk over to a patio in the centre of the grounds. The chairs and tables are occupied by a group of tourists who have just completed their tour of the lemon grove. The Acetos are busily serving their guests from the bar. Luigi and I sit at a table, and I am served a slice of sponge cake and a glass of lemon juice. The homemade cake soaked in lemon juice tastes delightfully refreshing.

Luigi: 'There was no room left to grow, and so I decided to focus on quality instead with the Sfusato Amalfitano brand. In the 1980s, I started a cooperative, which was a lot of hard work. I visited every farm in the region to acquire the IGP quality label. It took us twelve years, but we were the first to distinguish ourselves with a quality label for lemons and later for limoncello. Our family story is all about our passion and sacrifice to preserve a unique heritage. Large businesses such as ours continue to survive. But a number of lemon growers have ended up quitting because they can't find personnel for this difficult work.'

Lemon grove in Amalfi

Varieties

'The Sfusato Amalfitano lemon with the Limone Costa d'Amalfi IGP label is light yellow in colour, tapers to a point and is medium to large in size,' Luigi explains. 'This IGP lemon may be grown in 13 municipalities along the Amalfi Coast; the lemons can be harvested between February and October. This almost seedless lemon is popular with cooks because of its intense aroma, thick peel and juicy, semi-sweet pulp.

'The region's other star product is the Sorrento lemon, or the *Ovale di Sorrento*,' Salvatore joins in. 'This lemon variety flowers up to five times each year. They're slightly darker and bigger than the Sfusato Amalfitano, but similar in terms of aroma and flavour.'

Limoncello or liquore limone

Luigi and I walk down to the workshop run by his son, Marco Aceto. 'This is where we make liqueur from our lemons,' Marco explains. 'Drinking lemon liqueur or limoncello is a real tradition in Campania, just like coffee. Limoncello is an infusion of lemon peel submerged in pure alcohol. The essential oils from the peel give the liqueur its heady aroma. We filter the infusion once or several times and then add water and sugar. The liqueur is mixed and stored in these stainless-steel containers. Amalfi lemon liqueur has an alcohol content of 25 per cent. This lemon liqueur carries the protected geographical indication of Liquore di Limone Costa d'Amalfi IG. The IG label is applied for spirits instead of the IGP quality label.'

Marco admits that the Sorrento limoncello is far more famous than Amalfi's liqueur. Marco: 'The Sorrento IG lemon liqueur is prepared in the same way but using Ovale di Sorrento lemons. However, its alcohol content is 30 per cent. The recipe originated in the early 20th century. The residents of Sorrento, Amalfi and even Capri still argue over where the recipe originated. Lemons thrive in many other parts of Italy. The limoncello name is not legally protected in any way. In northern Italy, lemon liqueur is referred to as *limoncino*.'

Salvatore Aceto,
Via delle Cartiere 59, Amalfi

LUIGI'S RECIPE

Limoncello Costa d'Amalfi

INGREDIENTS FOR 1 LITRE
6 large, untreated (organic) lemons
500 ml alcohol
500 ml water
400 g sugar

Remove the yellow peel from the lemons and let the peels steep in the alcohol in a sealed barrel for five days. Dissolve the sugar in the water and combine the syrup with the infusion with the peels removed. Leave to rest for another two days. Filter the liquid and pour the liqueur into a bottle that can be sealed properly.

Positano

LAZIO

My journey of discovery brings me to a treasure trove of archaeology and history in a breathtaking landscape with volcanic lakes, a sky-blue sea and luscious nature. Lazio – or Latium – is home to the Eternal City of Rome, a jewel among the Italian cities. The streets exude a grandiose past. Tuscia, Viterbo and Montefiascone delight with their Etruscan sites and tombs.

Castel Sant'Elia, beautifully situated on a clifftop in Lazio

The Piazza Navona, with the similarly named Palazzo,
is the most beautiful and most important square in Rome

Lago di
Bolsena

Flora

6 Montefiascone

5 Viterbo

Marta

Mignone

4 Nepi

Salto

Lago di
Bracciano

Tevere

Turano

Aniene

1 Roma

3 Ariccia

Sacco

Liri

Melfa

Tevere

Liri

Amaseno

2 Gaeta

Campanilista (of the bell tower), yet cosmopolitan

Campanilismo, that's what Italians call feeling strongly loyal to their place or town of birth. The *campanile* refers to the church or bell tower around which every hamlet, village or town is built. Many celebrities from Lazio who have conquered the world have always remained true to their bell tower: emperor Julius Caesar, filmmaker Roberto Rossellini, composer Ennio Morricone, actor Marcello Mastroianni, and many more. Including Bartolomeo Scappi. Back in the 16th century, Scappi wrote a masterful cookbook featuring thousands of recipes. His work became so popular that he was invited to display his culinary skills all over Italy. This renaissance chef became a gastronomic icon, much like Michelangelo in the fine arts. Scappi was the personal chef of various popes in Lazio, but no one knows where he was actually born. Bartolomeo invented breading, the technique of coating dishes with fine breadcrumbs. This technique is often used in street food.

⭐ Cuisine and dialect

In Fabrica di Roma, I meet up with former journalist and culinary programme writer Maurizio Bianchini. He gives me a primer on Lazio's street food, although it's hard to apply a framework to all those countless customs and traditions. 'Our cuisine is like a dialect,' Maurizio believes. 'It differs among regions. In the olden days, you didn't have a culinary culture. Cooking was a necessity that later turned into a habit. We have excellent basic ingredients that we use to create culture today.' Moreover, the gastronomic culture of centrally situated Lazio betrays the influence of Abruzzo, Molise, Umbria, Tuscany, Marche and Campania.

The Santuario della Santissima Annunziata bell tower in Gaeta

TRADITIONAL INGREDIENTS FOR SOPHISTICATED DISHES

Lazio's cuisine is distinctive in its simplicity. Their dairy is a case in point. Every Italian knows *Pecorino Romano* (DOP), the crucial ingredient in *pasta cacio e pepe* and countless other dishes. Ricotta, the characteristic cheese from the Roman countryside, is made here from sheep or mixed milk. And you will find buffalo mozzarella in the provinces of Frosinone and Latina. The cured meats are another example of culinary excellence. *Guanciale,* or pork cheek, is an essential ingredient in *pasta alla carbonara* and *pasta all'amatriciana.* The latter, named after the town of Amatrice in the province of Rieti, is world-famous.

Guanciale

ROMA

Lazio's gastronomic history is alive and well in Rome. Italy's capital is also the capital of Lazio. This bona fide metropole is situated on the banks of the Tiber. The city is too vast and too beautiful to do it justice with a brief description here. The historical centre has rightfully earned a spot on the UNESCO World Heritage list and Vatican City is a country in itself within Rome.

MERCATO COLDIRETTI

My cultural odyssey starts with the picturesque stalls featuring local products in the Mercato Coldiretti, an indoor market. The Azienda Agricola Greco looks extremely enticing with its warm colour palette of cured meats. Rosanna Greco welcomes me warmly. The farmer's market turns out to be an initiative of the Campagna Amica network. Rosanna: 'We keep short supply chains. You will only find raw ingredients and processed products straight from the farm. The ricotta here comes from local producers who tend their own sheep; the flour and baked goods are supplied by farmers who produce their own grain. Our farm is located in Castelli Romani in the Colli Albani near Rome. We have about 200 pigs and a workshop in which we make products such as salami, *guanciale* (pork cheek), *pancetta* (bacon) and *strutto* (lard).' I try the pork cheek and notice that the meat flavour is very intense. 'That's why guanciale is a favourite ingredient in many dishes throughout Lazio and Italy.'

Coppiette

My eye is drawn to an earthenware pot filled with *coppiette,* bright red strips of dried meat. Rosanna: 'This is a snack for on the go or served with a glass of wine or beer, traditionally seasoned with salt, fennel seed and chilli pepper. But a good white wine, rosemary and garlic work equally well.

Preparing the coppiette is simple: slice the meat into strips measuring 15 centimetres long and 2 centimetres wide. Season the meat and bake it in the oven for 30 minutes. Drain off the excess liquid and bake the meat in the oven for another hour. Once the strips are cooked, leave them to dry for half a day. Then, tie them in pairs

Coppiette at the Coldiretti market

FRASCHETTE

'You will find coppiette nowadays in *fraschette*, but also in markets and at the butcher's,' Rosanna explains. 'Fraschette refers to the typical restaurants where wine and beer are served accompanied by savoury snacks. The dried meat is spicy and salty, so you need something to quench your thirst. In the golden years of the taverns in and around Trastevere in the heart of Rome, coppiette were the perfect snack with Castelli Romani wines.' I leave the indoor market with this newfound wisdom and a bag of coppiette in my hands.

to a rope, hence the name "coppiette" or couples. Finally, hang the meat strips to dry for another two months.

A century ago, this food was prepared by the poor with meat from dead animals, particularly horses. Soldiers would take it with them in their satchels, but the farmers, cowboys and shepherds would also eat this handy dried meat as they worked. The coppiette today are mostly made from pork or beef. You will find them in Castelli Romani and throughout Lazio.

Azienda Agricola Greco in Mercato Coldiretti
Via Tiburtina 695, Rome

MERCATO·TESTACCIO

At the Mercato Testaccio

Pinsa romana

MERCATO TESTACCIO

I walk two kilometres through the city to the Mercato Testaccio in the district of the same name. I enter a modern, minimalistic building that is open on all sides. It looks like a lively Roman piazza with all those covered market stalls. Here, I find meat, poultry, fish, cheese, nuts, honey, pickled goods, pastry, ice cream, coffee, wine, household goods, vintage clothing, flowers, and much, much more. Pinsa and panini filled with the finest ingredients from grandmother's kitchen are typical Roman snacks.

Pinsa romana

At Da Teo, I find owner Matteo Strino. Matteo is a passionate *pinsa* maker. This Roman snack holds no secrets for him. Matteo: 'Pinsa in its current form was invented by businessman Corrado Di Marco. He reinvented a traditional recipe and introduced it on the market. Long ago, the farmers beyond the walls of ancient Rome would process unsold grains and coarse flour into the dough of a light and crispy focaccia. And that is how the pinsa we know today was created. The name comes from the dialect word *pinsère,* which means to push and stretch. The dough is stretched into an elongated, oval form without using a rolling pin. We add a variety of toppings, which gives the pinsa the appearance of a pizza.'

Revolution in pizza land

Corrado Di Marco experimented until he had just the right flour mixture for his pinsa. The Roman baker's son added rice flour to pizza dough. No one had ever used a water-absorbent and light alternative such as rice before. Corrado's mixture includes wheat, rice and soy flour, but the exact proportions remain a secret.

Pinsa dough contains much more water, less fat and sugars and less yeast than pizza dough. And the low-calorie pinsa digests easily. Most pinsa bakers in Rome and the surrounding area now use Di Marco's flour mixture and method. In 2001, Corrado single-handedly brought the pinsa back from the dead. The Pinsa Romana association safeguards its authenticity and production guidelines.

MATTEO'S RECIPE

The real Pinsa Romana

1 kg Pinsa Romana mix
6 g fresh yeast
20 g salt
20 g extra-virgin olive oil
600 ml refrigerated water

Sprinkle the dough in the mixer and add the crumbled yeast. Gradually add half the chilled water. Start to knead. Add the olive oil and the salt, followed by the remaining water. Knead for about twenty minutes (in the mixer) until the dough holds together well.

Place the dough in a bowl and cover the bowl with cling film. Proof the dough for 48 hours in the refrigerator. Divide the dough over baking trays that have been greased with olive oil. You should have enough dough to make three to four pinsas. You can use round or square baking trays. Make sure that the entire bottom of the tray is covered with a layer of dough. Press the dough down with your fingers so it fits snugly into the tray. Use your thumbs to press characteristic focaccia dents into the dough. The dough should be about one centimetre thick. Cover with a cloth or tea towel and let proof for another three hours.

GARNISH THE PINSA WITH WHATEVER YOU LIKE. HERE ARE A COUPLE OF SUGGESTIONS:

extra-virgin olive oil
800 g small, ripe tomatoes
21 mini mozzarella balls, cut in half (42 halves)
coarse salt to taste
oregano to taste

Drizzle olive oil over the proofed dough and rub the oil into the dough with your fingers. Place the crushed tomatoes on top. This is the pulp from chopped, fresh cherry tomatoes with the skin that you first cut in half and then squeeze with your hands to a cold pulp.

Garnish with the halved mozzarella balls by arranging them over the surface. Season with salt and oregano. The moisture seeps into the dough, making it wonderfully tender as soon as it comes out of the oven.

Extra layer: You can garnish your pinsa with chopped anchovies and capers.

Extra layer: after baking the pinsa, garnish with *prosciutto crudo* or Parma ham, or San Daniele ham, together with arugula, Parmesan cheese shavings and a bit of olive oil.

Bake the pinsa for 20 to 30 minutes at 200 °C in an electric convection oven or gas oven. Check to make sure that the dough doesn't dry out; the cooking time varies depending on the oven.

Sergio makes one of his legendary sandwiches

Mordi e vai – Bite and go

At the Mercato Testaccio, next to Da Teo, another stall captures my attention. The intoxicating smells and long line of waiting customers make me suspect that this is no ordinary stall. This is where Sergio Esposito and his son, Giugliano, serve their grandmother's cooking in sandwich form. Strong, simple, honest flavours. Simplicity meets genius. The display boasts various heated dishes placed neatly next to each other on heated chafing dishes. This popular bastion of street food keeps the Roman peasant cuisine tradition alive.

I want a taste of what I see and smell here. Giugliano makes me an *allesso di scottona* sandwich, topped with cooked young, lean meat. He spoons a piece of the tender meat from the simmering broth, places it on a cutting board and cuts it up into smaller pieces. He takes a crispy roll that is sliced lengthways down the middle and dips one-half of the bread in the warm meat sauce. He then arranges the finely chopped meat on the bread. In response to my request, he heaps some steamed *chicora* or chicory on top. The top bread half goes on top of the sandwich with a light press to keep everything in place. Then he wraps the filled bread in paper so I can eat it without making a mess. Delicious!

Sergio Esposito introduced this snack ten years ago and gave Roman cuisine fast-food allure. Sergio worked in the meat sector, and his wife Maria Cipriani was a chef. Today, his market stall is a beacon in the Roman street food scene. His sandwiches with *picchiapò* (soup meat in sauce), *polpette* (meatballs in tomato sauce) and *trippa* (tripe in a delicious sauce) are legendary. And well worth trying!

Mercato di Testaccio
Via Aldo Manuzio 66/B, Rome

SANT'ANGELO GETTO

'People always eat well in Rome,' journalist Maurizio Bianchini says. 'Rome never had a cuisine of its own but was always influenced by the various rulers. Emperors, kings, despots, and other rulers came, conquered, and disappeared. But the Jews remained. Jews and Romans have always lived side by side in Rome. This district was once segregated; today, it's one of the most popular places to be in town. Via Portico d'Ottavia is known for its Jewish-Roman restaurants. Connoisseurs from across the globe come here to taste their unique dishes.' I want to find out more about Rome's relationship with the Jews, so I immerse myself in the city's rich history. In 1555, Pope Paul IV issued a decree revoking all the rights of Roman Jews. The pope ordered the establishment of the Roman Ghetto, the Jewish district in the beautiful Sant'Angelo that also harbours Isola Tiberina, Tiber Island. Poverty once reigned supreme here. The residents living in overcrowded conditions had to make do with cheap, portable, deep-fried street food. The Jews didn't regain their rights until 1870, when the power of the popes was finally broken. The ramshackle buildings were torn down, and most Roman Jews sought a home elsewhere. Today, only a couple of hundred Jews reside in the district, which has retained its cultural significance and continues to be the heart of Jewish culture, with two synagogues, three Jewish schools and a Jewish museum.

RESTAURANT
Jewish-Roman cuisine

I walk down the ghetto's main street, Via del Portico d'Ottavia. Jewish restaurants flank the street on both sides, their menus displaying an interesting mix of Jewish-Roman dishes. Ilan Dabush runs Ba'Ghetto. His parents opened their first restaurant in Via Livorno, near Piazza Bologna. Together with his brothers Avi, Eran, and Amit, he opened four more Ba'Ghetto restaurants in Milan and Florence.

Ilan explains how the famous dish *carciofi alla giudia*, or fried artichoke, is made. This dish originated around the 16th century. Ilan: 'We use the tender, round Roman *cimaroli* artichokes. We first clean them with a knife. We trim the reddish parts and remove the outer leaves. We then soak the artichokes in a bowl of water with lemon juice. After ten minutes, we take them out of the bowl to dry. We then season them with a handful of salt and pepper. The artichokes are fried in oil for eight to nine minutes.'

I remark that fried food is typical of Jewish-Roman cuisine. Ilan: 'That's right. *Concia* is a popular dish made from strips of deep-fried Roman courgettes marinated in mint, parsley, and garlic. Another classic dish is the *tortino di aliciotti e endivia*, an oven-baked tart with layers of marinated endive and anchovies. Or *baccalà alla giudia*, deep-fried salted fish in batter.'

I can't wait to try all this delicious food. Ilan immediately orders a couple of plates of food.

Panino allesso di scottona

Yochanan and Angelo from Ba'Ghetto

Carciofi alla giudia

Annette at
Ba'Ghetto

'The *baccalà alla Romano* is also very popular,' Ilan continues. 'The restaurants here serve a combination of Jewish-Roman and kosher dishes, and the wine selection includes Italian, Israeli and French wines.

Yochanan and Angelo serve my chosen dishes with flair; *carciofi alla giudia, tortino di aliciotti e indivia* and concia. What a delight, all these dishes with a Hebrew touch! And what a wonderful place to spend time on the terrace! All the tables are occupied. The friendly Raoul at the table next to me confirms that the restaurant is immensely popular and lets me know that it's always better to make reservations beforehand. I look out over the wide pedestrian area of Via del Portico d'Ottavia, teeming with happy people. I take a sip from my glass of Israeli chardonnay. 'L'chaim', cheers, Ilan winks. Rome has conquered my heart!

Ba'Ghetto
Via del Portico d'Ottavia, Roma

TRASTEVERE

Just a kilometre away, the Tiber River reaches the colourful district of Trastevere. This funky, bohemian district is known for its artisanal cafés, fun shops, and traditional and hip trattorias. This is also where you'll find the more basic B&Bs and budget hotels. Time to explore the local food scene. I take a side street from Viale di Trastevere to Via San Francesco a Ripa in search of *supplì*. Supplì, together with *pasta cacio e pepe and pasta amatriciana*, are the city's most famous dishes. The I Supplì takeaway sounds like the perfect place to find out more. The takeaway's owner, Giacomo Lucarelli, greets me.

I supplì

Since 1979, I Supplì has dedicated itself to the jewel of the same name from Roman cuisine. A whole range of supplì glistens under a yellow lamp. Giacomo: 'Our rice croquettes are filled and finished according to Lazio's gastronomic tradition. The rice croquette looks like an *arancino*, and so I ask what the difference is. Giacomo:

'The *arancino* stems from Sicily; supplì are typical Roman fare. A supplì is shaped like an egg, while the arancino is round. With this elongated, oval shape, the cheese can spread out over the length of the supplì. When you break the supplì in two, the still-warm mozzarella or fresh pecorino cheese filling is drawn out in a string. That's why we also call this rice croquette *supplì al telefono*, or 'telephone-style supplì', referring to a telephone cord.

A hospital on a small island in the Tiber River next to Trastevere

⭐ Surprise

Behind every legend is a good story. The sparkle in Giacomo's eye tells me that there's more to the tale. Giacomo: 'The supplì may owe its success to our French neighbours. In the late 18th century, under Napoleon's rule, French soldiers discovered the deep-fried rice croquette. They named the croquette *surprise* after the stringy, melted mozzarella or young pecorino filling that delights on the first bite. Surprise soon turned into *surprisa*, followed by *supprì*, and finally *supplì*.'

Co-owner Loreto fills the counter with freshly baked supplì with cacio e pepe and joins in the conversation. Loreto: 'We follow the traditional recipe. The first supplì were sold on the streets. They were fried in a large pot of oil and then sold piping hot. Since the end of the 19th century, they've been served in Roman restaurants and inns. It took decades before the dish finally made its way into gastronomic circles.'

TAKEAWAY RESTAURANT
Variety

What makes the supplì here so special? Giacomo: 'We fill our supplì with all sorts of quality products from Lazio. The selection is endless. In addition to the *classico* with risotto and tomato sauce, minced meat and mozzarella, we also make fillings with typical Lazio flavours: *cacio e pepe* (risotto with pecorino cheese and pepper), *amatriciana* (risotto with pork cheek, tomato sauce and pecorino), *carbonara* (risotto with pork cheek, pecorino cheese and egg), *ragù di coda* (risotto with tomato sauce and oxtail), *baccalà e carciofi alla romana* (risotto with cod and artichoke), *endivia bufala alici* (risotto with endive, buffalo mozzarella and anchovies). We prepare supplì throughout the day, each time with a different filling. They're freshly fried and sold while they're still warm.'

Supplì Roma
Via San Francesco a Ripa 137, Rome

Supplì

Supplì cacio e pepe

300 g risotto rice (Vialone Nano or Carnaroli)
120 ml white wine
1 litre vegetable stock
   (water, 1 whole carrot, 1 whole onion, 3 sprigs parsley,
   3 sprigs celery, salt and pepper to taste, thyme, bay leaf;
   simmer everything over low heat for 1 hour)
100 g grated Pecorino Romano cheese
1 knob of butter

FOR THE FILLING AND COATING

100 g fresh pecorino cheese
   (this also works with mozzarella)
3 eggs
pepper to taste
salt to taste
breadcrumbs
peanut oil

The preparation doesn't require any special technique, but it helps if you make the rice a day beforehand and store it in the refrigerator until ready to use.

Roast the rice in a pan for a couple of minutes and add the white wine. As soon as the wine has evaporated, add the hot vegetable broth, one soup ladle at a time. As soon as the rice is al dente, remove from heat and stir the butter and grated Pecorino Romano cheese into the rice. Check to make sure the rice is properly seasoned with salt and pepper. Leave the risotto to cool.

Dice the fresh pecorino. Take a bit of risotto (a handful) and roll it out in the palm of your hand. Place a couple of pecorino (or mozzarella) pieces in the middle and wrap the risotto around the cheese. Seal each supplì with your hand and shape it into an egg. Coat each oval-shaped supplì first with the beaten egg, followed by the breadcrumbs.

Deep-fry the supplì in enough oil for three to four minutes until golden brown. Turn over regularly. Drain the supplì on a paper towel and serve warm.

Add some extra flavour to your supplì with pecorino and pepper by adding a piece of bacon or *guanciale* in the middle.

RIVIERA DI ULISSE ②

From Rome, I drive another 150 kilometres to Riviera di Ulisse, a protected coastal region with forest trails, Roman ruins, and gorgeous views of the gulf. Lazio also harbours golden sandy beaches on the shores of the crystal-clear Tyrrhenian Sea. Sperlonga, situated on a rocky outcropping high above the sea, is particularly worthy of note. Its narrow streets, white-stuccoed houses, an old Roman sea cave, and the Villa Tiberio make it one of the most beautiful villages in Italy. My next stop is the coastal town of Gaeta on Lazio's Riviera. Here I go hunting for a centuries-old city recipe, the *tiella*.

Tiella di Gaeta

I visit the Pizzeria del Porto in the town's small harbour. *Pizzaiolo* Ivan Branco is only too happy to introduce me to the Gaeta's tiella. Ivan: 'The *tiella*, made from pizza dough, looks like a pie. But we don't use any pizza dough; we only use stone-milled wholegrain flour. You can compare the tiella to a calzone in a round pie shape. It is a savoury pie made from two discs of soft dough that you press together with your fingers. A rich filling is inserted between the two dough layers. *La nonna* or *la mamma* used to make this classic family dish.' Ivan rolls out the dough into different round, flat shapes. The entire table is covered with tiellas, or pie tins – hence the name – as Ivan drapes a dough disc into each one of them.

Valentina Coreade fills each pie tin. I see reddish-purple octopus, tomatoes, and Gaeta olives and a second row of green-white endive leaves with onion and *baccalà* (cod). 'Homemakers used to use kitchen leftovers for the filling,' Valentina explains. 'It was a poor man's dish. The sea provided the octopus tentacles. But endive, olives and salted baccalà were also once ingredients from the peasant's kitchen. Today, they're expensive ingredients. We only use local ingredients and fish and seafood from the sea.'

Ivan places a second dough disc on top of the filling. Valentina carefully presses the two dough layers on top of each other. She presses them into *pizzoccole,* the wavy edges around the tiella.

⭐ Legend

This dish was known as far back as the Bourbon dynasty. Ferdinand IV of Bourbon (1751-1825) was a huge fan, and legend has it that he even invented the tiella.

During his stay in Gaeta, the young king would often disguise himself and mingle with his people. One day, he saw an attractive woman preparing bread dough. He was hungry – or perhaps he was just attracted to the beautiful woman – and he offered to help her.

He had her roll out the dough into a thin disc and place it on a baking tray (tiella). He also suggested placing vegetables and olives on top and adding a bit of olive oil.

A tiella made from pizza dough

He then asked her to roll out a second dough disk to seal the filling and place it in the oven. Ferdinand then spent some very enjoyable moments with the beautiful woman as the dish turned golden brown in the oven.

It was the first tiella ever, and the nobility was wildly enthusiastic. The fillings with baby squid, sardines, anchovies, octopus, endive and salted cod were particular favourites.

The legend is a well-kept secret in this countryside village. After the fall of the House of Bourbon in 1860, tiella became the iconic meal for immigrants who left Gaeta in search of work.

Pizzeria del Porto
Via Bausan 40, Gaeta

Frequently used ingredient: the Gaeta olive

The local Gaeta olives of the regional Itrana variety go with the tiella. Gaeto olives are purple-black and taste slightly bitter. The finished olives develop their characteristic aroma after pickling in brine for five months.

Gaeta olives

ARICCIA: PORCHETTA ③

Ariccia, some 80 kilometres towards Rome, is my next destination. I enjoy the trip through rolling gold-coloured landscapes dotted with fairy-tale-like villages and towns. The Castelli Romani were favoured as summer residences among the popes and the elite who wished to get away from the sweltering capital city and enjoy the cooler climate and fresh air. Ariccia sparkles among the beautiful hills south of Rome. In this city along the ancient Via Appia road, I hope to find the origins of the *porchetta*. Nicoló Romagnolo from porchetta business Cioli Egidio is my guide. Nicoló is a fourth-generation owner of this family business, named after his great-grandfather and founder, Cioli Egidio. He loves his porchetta. He explains how this meat dish developed into a classic in the central Italian region (Lazio, Abruzzo, Marche, Umbria, Tuscany, Emilia-Romagna). Today, this product is found on menus throughout Italy and far beyond. Porchetta has a proud thousand-year history and steals the show at village festivals and other celebrations.

1000 years of roast suckling pig on a spit

Nicoló: 'We're not sure where the original porchetta recipe comes from. But Ariccia can lay claim to its birthplace. What we do know is that the Roman nobility would organise hunting parties in the summer in the Ariccia hills; these were followed by extravagant banquets. The nobility was well-represented in Ariccia, and our artisans became very skilled in preparing porchetta. This tradition was passed on from father to son. In Umbria and in Abruzzo's Teramo province, pigs have been kept since Roman times. In southern Lazio, pigs were weaned during the time of the Etruscans.' So, what makes porchetta so unique, I wonder? Nicoló replies that the recipe has always remained the same throughout the centuries.

The preparation is simple. A female pig – porchetta – weighing 60 to 90 kg is chosen. Deboning the pig requires skilled hands. Moreover, seasoning and marinating the meat requires specific dosages. It's no secret that porchetta contains salt, pepper, garlic, olive oil and rosemary. The meat is rolled up into a 'sausage' with the skin on the outside. The ends are sewn together. The meat is tied up with cord to keep everything together.

Pork with a quality label

You then bake the suckling pig for about four hours in a convection oven heated to 180 °C for a deliciously crispy skin. The moderate maritime climate influences the flavour. Nicoló explains how the specific wind that blows through the hills dries the meat as it cools. It causes the meat to turn a lovely pink and makes the skin extra crispy.

In 2010, Porchetta di Ariccia was given an IGP quality label. For Nicoló, this was the guarantee that this artisanal tradition would never die. The quality label determines the regulations for its preparation, including the safeguarding of the product's originals and requirements for preparing the dish.

The name 'porchetta' refers to the entire piglet, including the head, or to the trunk – in that case, without the head – between the third vertebra and the last lumbar vertebra. Nicoló proudly tells me that only Ariccia has an IGP quality label for porchetta; Umbria, Marche and Tuscany don't. Besides Cioli Egidio, eleven other producers in Ariccia prepare porchetta the traditional way.

In most regions in central Italy, porchetta is seasoned with rosemary. In the higher regions of Lazio, Umbria, Molise and Emilia-Romagna, the meat is often seasoned with wild fennel. According to Nicoló, Umbria is famous for its use of different herbs.

Porchetta

With international allure

Porchetta di Ariccia has been well-known since 1950. That's when the *Sagra della Porchetta di Ariccia,* or the celebration of the *Porchetta di Ariccia* was first organised. Music, dancing, parades, and lots and lots of food were the main ingredients of this three-day popular festival in September. At the many festive stalls, you could eat porchetta served by the *porchettari,* or porchetta butchers, dressed in traditional costume. Today, the porchetta from Ariccia has conquered the world. Nicoló beams with pride: *'The New York Times* has rated our porchetta among one of the five best food products in the world!'

Cioli Egidio
Via Variante di Cancelliera, Ariccia

Ariccia

NEPI ④

I resume my journey from Ariccia to Nepi in the province of Viterbo. Nepi is situated in the heart of the historical Etruscan region of Tuscia and its beauty is breathtaking! The village, tucked away behind 16th-century walls, is located along the Cassia Road, some 40 kilometres from Rome.

Pecorino Romano is a staple ingredient in countless recipes from Lazio. Buonatavola Sini is the only large Pecorino Romano producer in Lazio. I meet the owner's sister, Elisabetta Capuani. Elisabetta: 'Pecorino Romano is a product from the Roman countryside. The cheese originated here two thousand years ago. Today, over 90 per cent of the production takes place in Sardinia; only 10 per cent is produced in Lazio and the Tuscan province of Grosseto. In the 1950s, the Americans discovered Pecorino Romano. Lazio couldn't keep up with the large demand and so asked Sardinian producers to help them.'

DOP *with a regional label*

Elisabetta: 'We have developed a brand with the name "il Pecorino Romano di Lazio". And, although the consumer may not notice the difference, we want to distinguish ourselves from the rest. The Pecorino Romano DOP designation applies to producers from Lazio, Grosseto (Tuscany) and Sardinia. We all belong to the same protected group, but we insisted on a separate regional label, and we're glad we did. There are still several small pecorino producers in the region, and they all produce excellent cheese. The flavour varies among regions according to the milk used. In Lazio, less salt is added, making the cheese less strong and suitable as a table cheese, not just as an ingredient.' Time for me to put this to the test. Elisabetta slices a piece from an enormous block of aromatic cheese. The pungent aroma immediately fills the room. The cheese is refreshing yet mature. The savoury flavour 'explodes' as it were on the tongue. Elisabetta: 'That spiciness is essential because Roman pecorino is often grated on or in Italian dishes.'

I Buonatavola Sini

Elisabetta: 'This cheese dairy, which used to be called *F. Illi Fulvi,* has been salting, seasoning, and cutting wheels of romano cheese since the end of the 19th century. Shepherds from Viterbo and Agro Romano, the region surrounding Rome, would supply the milk. Over a hundred years ago, we started exporting to the United States. The cheese is here to stay. Pasta cacio e pepe, carbonara and amatriciana are popular, traditional regional dishes and Pecorino Romano is a part of those dishes. I have always been familiar with these dishes from the peasants' kitchen and have eaten an awful lot of them over the years. Meanwhile, our cheese and these dishes have conquered the world.'

Pecorino Romano

Sheep in the countryside around Nepi

⭐ **Shepherds, a dying breed**

I ask what the future holds for *Pecorino Romano di Lazio.* Elisabetta weighs her words carefully before answering: 'We will continue to grow as we do now. We keep discovering new markets. But we are also dependent on agriculture here. We need to protect this important sector. There are hardly any shepherds left in Lazio, and that's a problem. We hope that agriculture here will receive more support so younger people can start to work here. Our basic ingredient deserves to be protected!'

**I Buonatavola Sini
Strada Statale Cassia Km. 41, Nepi**

RESTAURANT
Tortino di pecorino di Nepi

In Nepi, I visit Casa Tuscia, a small yet very elegant restaurant where you can try authentic Tuscian dishes. I park near the Piazza d'Armi and walk through the town centre to Via Porta Romani. Casa Tuscia is located near the Borgia fortress. The interior has an authentic atmosphere. Ex-journalist and television programme maker Maurizio Bianchini and his wife, Patrizia, started the business. This Garden of Eden is a testimony of their love for the country, the region and its products. Since 2015, this dining establishment has been run by Lupino Emanuele. I write this mouthwatering *tortino di pecorino di Nepi* recipe with a wink to his godfather, Maurizio.

**Ristorante Casa Tuscia Enoteca con Cucina
Via di Porta Romana 15, Nepi**

MAURIZIO'S RECIPE
Tortino di pecorino

200 g young or semi-aged pecorino
40 g grated Pecorino Romano cheese
200 g ricotta
2 eggs
fresh marjoram

Take the young/semi-aged pecorino. Remove the rind and dice into one-centimetre cubes. Add the ingredients (diced pecorino, grated Pecorino Romano, ricotta and eggs) to a blender and mix. Add the fresh marjoram and mix briefly. Take a muffin tray and line the cups with parchment paper.

Fill the cups with the cheese mix. Bake the pecorino pies in the oven. Place a baking tray with water underneath the pies while baking to keep the air moist. If you don't have much room in your oven, you can place the muffin tray in a shallow layer of water on the baking tray. Bake for about 25 minutes at 180 °C. Once the pies are cooked, you can place the pie on a bed of tomato sauce and garnish it with arugula pesto, for instance.

LEONARDO'S RECIPE

Tozzetti alle nocciole

MAKES 500 G OF BISCUITS

250 g 00 flour
130 g peeled hazelnuts
120 g sugar
50 g butter
2 eggs
½ sachet baking powder
grated zest of ½ lemon
pinch of fine salt

First, roast the hazelnuts in a pan or in the oven. Let them cool before coarsely chopping them. Combine the eggs and the sugar in a bowl, then add the melted butter and grated lemon zest. Add the chopped hazelnuts and stir in the sieved flour, baking powder and salt. Knead until you have a soft, compact dough. Dust your work surface with a bit of flour so the dough doesn't stick to the workbench.

Divide the dough into four equal parts and roll them into cylinders.

Place them on a baking tray lined with parchment paper and bake them in an oven preheated to 180 °C for about 20 minutes until golden brown. Remove the 'sausages' from the oven and slice the cylinders into diagonal slices (about 2 cm thick). Place the slices back on the baking tray. Bake the biscuits for 10 minutes in an oven preheated to 180 °C. Let the biscuits cool before serving. *Buon appetito!*

TIP The traditional Viterbo recipe calls for lard instead of butter, but you can also use extra-virgin olive oil for a lighter version of these biscuits.

Tuscia's pearl

The Tonda Gentile Romana hazelnut grows in the beautiful region of Viterbo in the Cimini and Volsini hills situated between Lake Vico and Lake Bolsena. The hazelnut thrives on the fertile volcanic soil surrounding Lake Vico. Experts ascribe excellent qualities to the Viterbo hazelnut. The hazelnut, rich in unsaturated fats, is an excellent source of nutrition.

Hazel trees on the shores of Lake Vico

As I leave Nepi and make my way to Lake Vico, I drive past a sea of green, a forest of chestnut and hazel trees. My journey takes me down panoramic roads through an endless forest carpeting the hills. The scene changes constantly, but it's always green. This landscape is completely different from what you find in the south of Lazio. This is pure nature in its most essential form. I'm just an hour's drive from Rome, but I might as well be on another planet.

Vico is one of the most beautiful and pristine lakes in Italy. The lake has a unique morphology, masked under a green blanket that stretches into the surrounding hills. The lake originated thousands of years ago, following eruptions of the Vico, or Vicano volcano. The underground natural springs and many rains filled the resulting crater, around which the hazels now flourish.

The rows of hazels around Lake Vico stretch as far as the eye can see

Lake Vico is surrounded by hazel trees

Hazelnut and chocolate paste

Leonardo Barbanti from *Azienda Agricola Gentilnocciola* tells me the story of the hazelnut. Leonardo represents the younger generation of a family of hazelnut growers. He recently started his own business so that he could grow hazelnuts, just like his grandfather, father, uncles and aunts before him.

Leonardo: 'Growing hazelnuts in Lazio is based on a centuries-old tradition. The Tonda Gentile variety has been around since before the Romans, but we didn't start cultivating them until the 15th century. The nut has travelled far and wide over the centuries and was a welcome addition to meals such as papal banquets. The fame of Lazio's hazelnuts reached new heights in the 20th century. Today, it's a basic ingredient in many baked goods and in chocolate. And, of course, it also led to several traditional, local delicacies such as the *tozzetti viterbese*, or dry hazelnut biscuits. They are similar in shape to Tuscan *cantucci*, but we use roasted hazelnuts here instead of almonds or pistachios. The preparation is simple. It's an excellent snack or dessert to go with a glass of desert wine such as *passito* or a white *vin santo*.'

The 15th-century fountain in the inner courtyard of Palazzo dei Priori in the medieval heart of Viterbo

VITERBO ⑤

I decide to remain in the province of Viterbo a little longer and visit the provincial capital of the same name. It is dusk, and the dew-covered hills reflect the setting sun in a delightful interplay of light and landscape. I see countless shades of green that vary with height. Green, dew and rays of sunlight follow me as I continue my journey. This is one of the many landscapes I want to capture on film. But it's a hopeless task. This unparalleled view is now etched into my memory for the rest of my life.

Health resorts are dotted around the outskirts of Viterbo. In the 13th century, this city, also known as the 'city of the popes', was briefly home to the papal throne. Various gorgeous historical palaces bear witness to those glory days.

Acquacotta

I walk to the Hosteria Dal Sor Bruno in the town centre. This restaurant is famous for its authentic Tuscia cuisine. You can order dishes such as gnocchi (a potato-based pasta) *alla viterbese*, chickpea soup with chestnuts, *pizzicotti pasta all'amatriciana*, rabbit *alla viterbese*, *porchetta* and much more. I choose the *acquacotta della Tuscia*, recommended to me by Bruno, the very charming owner. 'Acquacotta, which literally translates to "cooked water", is a traditional, hearty peasant's soup typical of the Maremma region: Maremma Grosseto (Tuscany) and Tuscia Viterbo (Lazio)', he begins. 'This was the typical afternoon meal for the farmers and the *butteri*, Italian cowboys who followed their herds on horseback through the countryside.

The soup was prepared in the open air in a pot over an open fire. They filled the pot with vegetables they had foraged along the way: wild chicory, potatoes, mint (*nepetella*), garlic and sometimes onions and tomatoes. The cowboys would occasionally bring some dried salted cod with them from home. The leather *catana* saddle bags were filled with bread, olive oil and salt. If the bread was too stale, they would break it up into pieces and place them on their deep plates. The chef of the day would then ladle a spoonful or two of vegetables over the bread, together with the broth. Nowadays, we add a raw egg to the soup.'

Acquacotta

Dessert with hazelnuts

⭐ Bomba or bomb

Bruno serves me a dish of acquacotta, beaming. I carefully sip the steaming-hot broth. The bitter chicory taste lingers on my tongue. This is definitely a hearty soup. The bread, the raw egg and the olive oil line the stomach. It's actually supposed to be a first course, but it's more than enough for me. Still, I venture to try the Dolce del Sor Bruno dessert purely out of curiosity. It is a spoon dessert with a base of chestnut biscuit crumbs, covered with a homemade hazelnut paste and topped with a layer of egg pudding. It hits me like a brick, or rather a bomb. Bruno looks concerned and asks me if everything's okay. I smile and suggest taking the rest of the dessert with me to finish later. I walk back to the car with this little gem in my bag. Even in darkness, this city exudes a mythical past and a rich, centuries-old culture.

Hosteria Dal Sor Bruno
Via San Pellegrino 30, Viterbo

MONTEFIASCONE AND LAGO DI BOLSENA ⑥

My final stop in Lazio is Montefiascone, 17 kilometres north of Viterbo. The road looks like a stairway to heaven in the light of the early dawn. Montefiascone is a jewel anchored on the highest hill of the Monti Volsini on the south-eastern shore of Lake Bolsena. I admire the spectacular view over the water. The city marks a crossroads along Via Cassia. Various wine and olive oil producers are located here. The region surrounding Europe's largest volcanic crater lake is exceptionally fertile due to earlier eruptions.

But Montefiascone owes its name mostly to the Est! Est!! Est!!! wine. Quinto Ficari awaits me in the historical wine house of Antica Cantina Leonardi. This man has dedicated his life to the history of Defuk, a legend that dates to the year 1111.

Medieval story

Quinto: 'The hero in this legendary tale is John Defuk, a noble in the court of the Holy Roman Emperor, Henry V. Defuk was a wine connoisseur, and he usually sent his servant, Martin, ahead during the imperial court's travels. Martin was tasked with finding the best wine cellars and taverns along the route. Martin wrote *Est!* – Latin for 'is' – on the doors of the better cellars or taverns, so his master would know where the best wines were. According to legend, Martin was so impressed by the Montefiascone wine that he wrote Est! three times on the tavern door. As soon as the noble tried the wine, he left the emperor's court behind him and settled down in the city. He drank so much wine that he fell ill and died two years later. He lies buried in the San Flaviano church. And as an homage to the local wine, Defuk donated all his worldly possessions to the town on the one condition that every year on the anniversary of his death, a barrel of Est! Est!! Est!!! wine would be poured on his tomb. This ritual continues to this day. Every August, during the *Fiera del Vino* festival, the residents of Montefiascone hold a procession in medieval costume through the town to Defuk's tomb.'

Bolsena reflected in an enormous crater lake

Antica Cantina Leonardi winery's stars

joins us. I notice the tattoos on his arms as he picks the cat up. 'These are various symbols and characters from the legend of Defuk,' he confides proudly.

A church full of secrets

I drive past the San Flaviano church and park in Via Defuk. The construction of this impressive Roman-gothic church started in the 11th century. A tableau with text and drawings in the church refers to the legend. His servant had the following words engraved on his tomb: *'Est est est pr[opter] nim[ium] est hic Jo[annes] De Fuk do[minus] meus mor-tuus est'*, which roughly translates to 'My Lord Johannes Defuk is laid to rest; he died from too much Est! Est!! Est!!!' Two goblets of wine are pictured next to the tomb. The legend lives on. *Salute!*

Antica Cantina Leonardi
Via del Pino 12, Montefiascone

The oldest wine label in the world

Everything starts with the wine. The legend is very popular among tourists and wine connoisseurs. But the wine has changed since Defuk's time. Quinto: 'This wine was originally made from the moscato grape. Today, wineries use a combination of local procanico, malvasia and roscetta grape varieties.'

The wine has a flowery scent with a refreshing, fruity, soft flavour. Quinto: 'It's a perfect accompaniment to Viterbo's many vegetable soups, as well as fish and white meat. Est! Est!! Est!!! is a DOC wine from the Lake Bolsena valley and the surrounding mountainside. This was the first wine label in the entire world. We found a document dating from 1500 with the Est! Est!! Est!!! label.'

⭐ A wine, a legend, and plenty of passion

Quinto accompanies me to the wine cellar beneath the Antica Cantina Leonardi domain. The impressive cellar, built on top of peat soil, is hewn into the rocks. I travel back in time and am completely enthralled by Quinto's story. My guide is a living encyclopaedia of this wine and its history. I have never heard anyone tell their story with so much passion. Quinto is so fascinated with the legend that he wrote a book about it titled *La leggenda di Defuk*. The man has devoted his entire life to the mystery of Defuk. He has researched every detail, and now he tells me all about him with great relish. We are back in the domain's courtyard, and Giorgio's cat

The interior of the San Flaviano church

UMBRIA

Umbria is situated between Tuscany, Lazio and Marche. The capital is Perugia. There's a reason why it's called the 'green heart of Italy'. I am entirely enthralled with the fairy-tale-like natural surroundings, from Monti Sibillini to the Marmore Falls. The hills are carpeted with trees, meadows, olive trees and vineyards. And with a bit of luck, you will come across a shepherd with his flock on the upland plains. The national park is home to wolves, ibexes, and birds of prey.

Umbria is a mosaic of landscapes. In the highlands, water and land alternate seamlessly in a picturesque whole as rivers twist and turn through impressive gorges and falls. Lago Trasimeno is the fourth-largest lake in Italy. I drive past medieval towns and villages surrounded by greenery. The pilgrim towns of Assisi, Cascia and Città di Castello add a spiritual dimension.

Perugia

The impressive Marmore Falls

Chiascio

Tévere

Lago
Trasimeno

Perugia

②
Montebuono

⑤
Montefalco

Topino

Castelluccio

③
Norcia

④

①
Lago di
Corbara

Orvieto

Nera

Nera

Tévere

Sagrantino grapes

FARMHOUSE FARE

The rustic Umbrian 'peasant cuisine' is based on ingredients straight from the land and centuries-old traditions. Gastronomy has always played a central role in daily life. The leading players are pork, truffles, pulses, cheeses, olive oil and wines. These natural ingredients give rise to unique flavours.

LIQUID TERROIR

Umbria produces a meagre two per cent of all Italian olive oil, but the region distinguishes itself with five separate DOP oils. Olives take their time growing here because of the climate. They are harvested just as they start to ripen. As a result, the olive oil is a clear green colour with a strong flavour palate.

This relatively small region brings a variety of often lesser-known wines to the table. Most local wines come from the vineyards around Orvieto. The dry, fresh white Orvieto wine is the best-known of these. But Montefalco delights with a treasure of its own. The sagrantino grape, a variety used for a complex, plum-like red DOCG wine, grows in vineyards around this hillside town. Umbria is also known for the sangiovese grape variety that is often combined with sagrantino for a lighter, fresher red wine.

ORVIETO ①

Along the Autostrada del Sole (A1) from Rome to Florence, the silhouette of a fairy-tale-like town appears on a rocky outcropping: Orvieto. I take the exit, follow the road for some 6 kilometres, and park on the outskirts of the town. I dive into the 3000-year-old history of this charming place. The *duomo's* facade is a fascinating sight to behold; the frescoes lining the interior are equally awe-inspiring. But Orvieto is much more than its cathedral. I lose myself in the picturesque streets and venture into an underground cave network dating from the Etruscan period.

BAKERY
Lumachelle orvietane

All that walking and wonder makes me hungry. *Panificio* Galleria Del Pane is a 600-metre walk from the Piazza del Duomo. Ronaldo and Eveline Salonga wait for me at their bakery.

I smell the intoxicating smell of fresh baked goods and pastries. Eveline beams as she says: 'Our speciality is *lumachelle orvietane*. This savoury pastry contains *pecorino* cheese and pieces of bacon.' Fascinated, I inspect an elongated tray containing freshly baked lumachelle. They look like round raisin cakes with pieces of bacon instead of raisins.
'You can eat lumachelle warm or cold,' Eveline continues. 'It's often eaten as a late-morning or *merenda* (late afternoon) snack. These pastries used to be very popular among the farmers, who would take some along with them into the fields.'

Lumanchelle

Marco and Mauro in the Fratelli Ricci butcher's shop

Circle of flavour and tradition

'To eat lumachelle is to taste tradition,' Ronaldo says. 'The recipe has never been recorded in a cookbook or an official document. It has been passed down by word of mouth through the generations. Perhaps the pastry owes its name to its shape. *Lumacha* means snail, and with a bit of imagination, you can recognise the spiral shape of a snail shell in the savoury pastry. We season the dough with pecorino cheese, lard and pork.

You will only find these pastries in the municipalities in the Orvieto department, where you can buy them in bakeries and occasionally in a café. The Slow Food Foundation has decided to protect the lumachella by adding it to the *Arca del Gusto,* or Ark of Taste. This is a project focused on maintaining diversity. We're afraid that this unique pastry may one day disappear.'

Galleria del Pane
Via Malabranca 6, Orvieto

BUTCHER
Mazzafegato

I walk another ten minutes to Fratelli Ricci, a butcher's shop. This very traditional butcher's, owned by brothers Marco and Mauro Ricci, is situated in Orvieto's historical centre. I want to try the unique *mazzafegato* sausage. Mauro: 'You will still find authentic cured meats here.

We work exclusively with meat from Umbria and process all the parts of the animal. Many butchers today turn up their noses at using everything, but our customers specifically ask for it, and we've never done it any other way.'

Marco: 'That's why we still make mazzafegato. This sausage contains at least 15 per cent pork liver. Mazzafegato goes under the name *salsiccia matta* in Marche and *sanbudello* in Tuscany. The production may date back to medieval times, but we think it's more likely a product from the first half of the 20th century when almost every family in central Italy owned a pig. The mazzafegati were the final sausages to be made when the meat was processed. First, people would make the more 'noble' sausages. The mazzafegato contains the heart, liver and lungs.

Black sausage

The dark, almost black colour betrays its unusual composition. 'This sausage has a highly robust flavour, and the many herbs and spices make it quite spicy,' Marco says. 'The name is derived from *"ammazza fegato"*, meaning to kill the liver. This sausage is seasoned with pungent herbs and is the fruit of peasant cuisine. We still make mazzafegato on the principle that nothing from the pig gets thrown away.'

Comeback food

Mauro resumes: 'Peasant cuisine lost its appeal with the industrialisation of the meat sector and changing dietary habits. But the tide has turned in recent years. Thanks to the slow food movement, mazzafegato is making a comeback. The presidium promotes production and consumption. The younger generations in the region have rediscovered this sausage, and the demand has grown.'

Ricci Marco
Via di Piazza del Popolo 22, Orvieto

MAKING SAUSAGES

'We finely mince the second- and third-choice pork cuts,' Marco explains. 'These include the tail, the tongue, and the liver. Fifteen per cent of the mixture must contain liver. We make a hearty seasoning mixture and add fruit. Every butcher has their own recipe. We use sage, rosemary, flat-leaf parsley, oregano, fennel flowers, pine nuts, orange peel or raisins... You will also find the sausages in semi-sweet varieties. We stuff the seasoned mixture into natural intestine casings and then twist them into sausages ten centimetres long and three centimetres thick. You can eat mazzafegato fried or grilled, with mashed potatoes or lentils, for instance. You can also eat this dried liver sausage cold.

Black sausage

Lamberto at the entrance to his laboratory

L'ORVIETAN

From the Piazza del Popolo, I walk another 500 metres to the L'Orvietan tourist shop near the breathtaking Duomo di Orvieto. The shop display features souvenirs and wine products. The owner, Lamberto Bernardini, tells me a highly intriguing story about his homemade digestif, l'Orvietan.

'When I started my business, I adopted the name l'Orvietan because I liked the sound of it,' Lamberto tells me. 'But I soon discovered that it's also the name of an old medicine. No one in Orvieto was familiar with this traditional medicine. The story was lost to history towards the end of the 19th century. But until 1850, you could find l'Orvietan throughout Europe. The herbal medicine disappeared with the rise of chemical pharmaceuticals in the second half of the 19th century.
I was able to find historical documents that corroborate the story. I was so fascinated that I tried to reproduce the preparation. It wasn't easy, and I had to ask specialists for help. After two years, we succeeded in replicating the original. L'Orvietan didn't exist anywhere else in the world, and my herbal digestif turned out to be a huge success. I am happy with its success, but I prefer to keep things small and artisanal. I only make a couple of thousand bottles a year.'

L'Orvietan (shop)
Via del Duomo 74, Orvieto

Laboratory

Lamberto makes the drink entirely by hand in his laboratory. I am invited to take a look. We walk another 150 metres down the road and turn into an alleyway known as Vicolo dei Dolci, which branches off from the beautiful piazza. Lamberto unlocks the door of a historical building overshadowed by the Duomo. I enter a treasure trove of pots, bottles, and antique books; a delightful herbal scent lingers in the air.

Herbal blend for l'Orvietan

Magic antidote

'Food poisoning was rife back in 1603,' Lamberto explains. 'Refrigeration, running water and hygiene barely existed. Foodstuffs were riddled with bacteria, and people needed something to counter its effects. Girolamo Ferrante had developed an antidote with two dosages: the first dose was a highly concentrated version for fast, efficient relief, and the second dose was a lower dosage with herbs to help the stomach recover.

Ferrante sold his drinks in Italy and France. The name referred to the vendor's origins: Orvieto, hence l'Orvietan, which translates to "the man from Orvieto". Ferrante was a salesman through and through. He even managed to get the pope involved in his project. A papal decree made it impossible for the recipe to be forged. Ferrante died in 1625, and in his will, he left the patents to his wife and son.'

A bottle of l'Orvietan, ready for a taste

Blessings from the pope, the Sun King and Molière

'But the story doesn't end there,' Lamberto continues. He leads me to a large bookshelf containing evidence of this history. Lamberto: 'Ferrante's son moved to Venice and opened a bottega on the Piazza San Marco to produce and sell l'Orvietan. Ferrante's widow stayed in Rome and remarried; as a woman, she was not allowed to produce and sell the elixir. Her much younger husband, Cristoforo Contugi, had direct connections to King Louis XIV in France. The Sun King was paranoid about poisoning, and that's why he ingested l'Orvietan daily as a precaution. He publicly proclaimed that he couldn't be poisoned because he used l'Orvietan. The French playwright Molière also referred to l'Orvietan in his comic opera, L'Amour médecin, in which he inferred that the elixir could also cure lovesickness. In those days, l'Orvietan could be found in courts and pharmacies throughout Europe.'

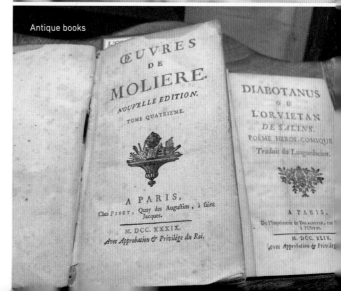
Antique books

Spiritual craftsmanship

Orvietan lasted 250 years, and then it disappeared completely. Lamberto is proud that he was able to re-introduce the herbal elixir. He started ten years ago in this laboratory. Lamberto offers me a glimpse behind the scenes: 'I make the elixir using 25 medicinal herbs. I crush them, place them on a cotton cloth and soak them in pure alcohol. The active ingredients from the herbs are infused into the liquid over the course of 20 days. I remove the bag of herbs and add water to dilute the alcohol content from 96 to 30 per cent.

This liquid is left to mature for at least another two months until it turns a light-yellow colour. And only then can I bottle the elixir. The original antidote from history was ten times stronger. Most herbs, including protected spices, come from the Italian hills. I use angelica, gentian, galangal, *carlina*, rhubarb root, mauveine, cinnamon, wormwood, myrrh, lavender... But I'm not going to tell you everything, of course.'

⭐ Finally, a taste

Lamberto pours me a glass in this beautiful setting with its delightful aromas. After almost two hours of stories and explanations, I can finally taste this illustrious elixir. As I suspected, the flavour is intense. A warm, powerful, pleasurable wave of flavour stirs my taste buds. Then, the bitter tones from the many herbs are released. The aftertaste is ever so slightly sweet. My mouth feels cleansed. The intoxicating wave passes from my palate to the brain and the belly. Divine!

L'Orvietan (Lab)
visit by appointment only, Vicolo dei Dolci 6, Orvieto

Annette's first taste of L'Orvietan together with Lamberto

MONTEBUONO ②

Lake Trasimeno is located some 70 kilometres from Orvieto. In the middle of this natural oasis lies Montebuono, where my search for the *torta al testo* begins. I have arranged to meet Luca Baldoni. Back in 1969, this spot featured a cosy, small kiosk where Luca's parents, Maria and Faliero, and his grandmother Pompilia prepared this flatbread over a perpetual fire. Today, the small kiosk has turned into a place where travellers can stop for a meal with views over the lake. Torta al testo takes centre stage in this cult restaurant.

An open fire crackles in the fireplace. Luca and Christiano's skilled hands prepare this famous dish. Their children (the third generation) and many other staff serve a variety of dishes. Next to the huge fire, salsiccie (sausages) are roasted on a skewer, and a couple of Chianina T-bone steaks await their turn. It smells delicious. The counter displays prepared pasta, fried fish from the lake, chickpeas, salads, grilled vegetables, beans with bacon, and much more. It all looks so good. But my eye is drawn to the golden-brown discs next to the large fire.

Luca: The torta al testo, also referred to as the *torta d'la Maria*, after my mother Maria, is the star of our trattoria, Faliero. Fire, wood logs, water, flour, oil, yeast, and salt; those are the ingredients for this crispy yet soft flatbread.'

Roman disc

The traditional Umbrian regional product, torta, owes its name to the *testo,* the fireproof stone on which the dough is baked. In ancient Rome, the *testum* was a terra cotta tile placed over hot coals for baking products such as flatbread. Maria: 'People here would use simple, cheap ingredients to still their hunger after a long day at work. Torta al testo was the perfect food. There were also variations with wheat, maize, barley, or spelt flour.

A story about water, flour, olive oil, yeast, and salt

According to *The New York Times*, Faliero is the perfect stop for the Umbrian torta al testo. The torta d'la Maria filled with grilled sausage and braised chicory is a must if you want to get acquainted with the authentic cuisine of yesteryear.

Luca explains how it's made: 'You'll find torta al testo everywhere you go in Umbria, but we're the only ones who make these flatbreads the traditional way. We bake them on stone over an open wood fire. We shape the dough into a smooth round disc measuring 40 centimetres by 1 centimetre thick, which we then bake on a red-hot testo. The bread is ready when the crust turns an even golden colour. I leave the pieces of bread to rest for another ten to fifteen minutes on a warm rack to make it lighter. After baking, we slice the still-warm bread horizontally for the filling and then divide it up into four, six or eight wedges.'

Luca has filled a warm torta slice for me. I take a seat at one of the many tables by the window with a view of the lake. I taste a deliciously fresh, crispy, stone-baked bread. The salty salsiccia and the bitter chicory complement each other nicely. Tasting authentic dishes like this in this out-of-the-way, breathtaking setting. It's a dirty job, but someone's got to do it...

Faliero
Via Case Sparse 23
Località Montebuono di Magione

Torta al testo, stone-baked flatbread

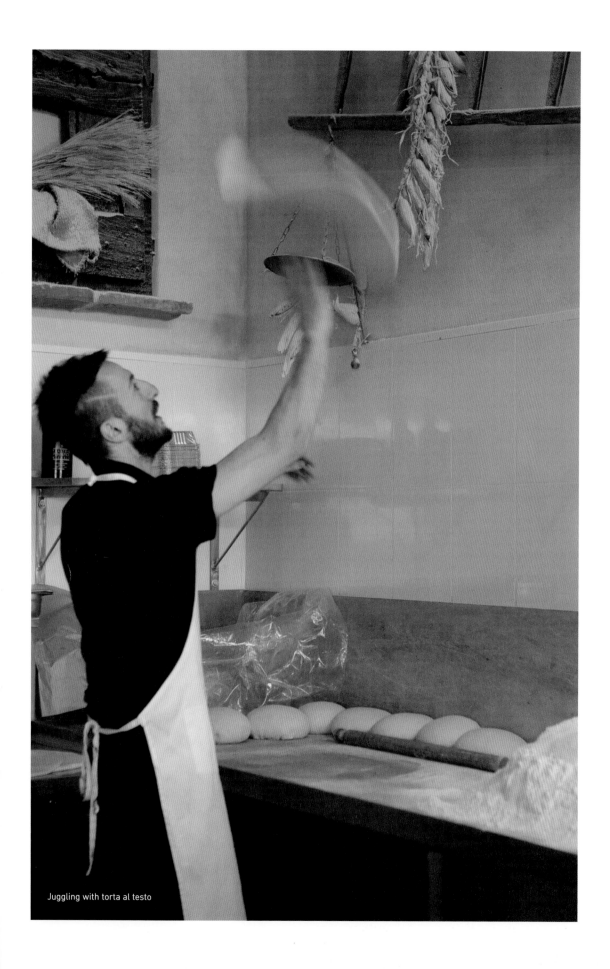

Juggling with torta al testo

Lake Trasimeno in San Feliciano

SWEETWATER FISH

Umbria is the only Italian region that doesn't have a coastline. But there's water aplenty with its many lakes, rivers, and waterfalls. Freshwater fish is part of Umbrian cuisine. This includes fish such as carp, perch, pike, smelt, tench, and eel from Lake Trasimeno.

Anguilla del Trasimeno - eel from Lake Trasimeno

I drive into a hidden harbour at a unique location in San Feliciano. A couple of fishing boats lie moored to the jetty, and the view is stunning. In the distance, the island of Polvese rises from the sparkling waters of Lake Trasimeno. It's an unforgettable sight. This picturesque harbour is home to Federica Trovati's Osteria Rosso di Sera. She is only too glad to tell me all about the locals and the local cuisine.

'Eel or *anguilla* has always been a king among the fish from Umbrian lakes,' Federica starts. 'With its snake-like, sinuous body, it's been winding its way upstream up the Tiber into the lakes for centuries. But since the 1960s, this fish has no longer been able to reach the lake because of man-made barriers. Still, this is a perfect

habitat for eels. The fish flourishes in the lakes' shallow, warm waters, rich in organisms. The eel reproduces in saltwater but then travels in search of freshwater environments such as rivers and watersheds. Now, thanks to human intervention, eels are once more able to flourish in Lake Trasimeno.

'I love them,' Federica continues. 'The meat is a true delicacy much-loved among the Trasimeni. The meat is slightly fat and exceptionally tasty. Tegamaccio is a typical eel dish. The fish is cooked for a very long time in an earthenware pot together with olive oil, tomato sauce, white wine, and herbs.'

Tegamaccio del Lago Trasimeno – Trasimeno fish stew

'Eel, carp, whitefish, pike, perch and tench are caught daily in this lake,' Federica knows. Tegamaccio is one of those characteristic dishes that does justice to the unique, unmistakable flavours of these fish. This preparation is named after the terra cotta pot in which the fish is braised. The fish from the lake have lots of bones. Tegamaccio used to be prepared with bones and all. But people nowadays don't want that. So now we just use the fillets. Filleting fish is a lot of work. But thankfully, we have specialists who do that for us. A little further down the road is the *consorzio*, where you can buy fresh fish daily. The cooperative removes the bones for you.

⭐ Evening red

Frederica and I sit together on the terrace and enjoy the view over the lake. As dusk settles, a red glow colours the water. And right then, I suddenly realise why the restaurant is called what it is. Rosso di Sera: evening red. 'The lake is our street. We also prepare street food dishes such as *polpette di pesce*, fish balls, or *panino con porchetta del lago*, a sandwich topped with 'porchetta' from the lake. Porchetta del lago is an ancient type of porchetta made with a large carp, seasoned with garlic, salt, pepper, wild fennel, and rosemary.'

As we talk, a steaming-hot, deliciously fragrant earthenware pot filled with fish stew is served at our table. Yes! Tegamaccio! Intoxicated by the scent, the warm evening glow, the sounds of the lake, and the great company, I feel myself melting away, a tiny pool of contentment in this vast oasis.

Rosso di Sera
Osteria di Strada, Via F.lli Papini 81, San Feliciano

Tegamaccio

SERVES 4 PEOPLE
1 kg fish (a mix of fish such as eel, swordfish, trout)
500 g peeled tomatoes
2 tablespoons concentrated tomato puree
2 cloves garlic
2 large onions
1 large glass of white wine
2 stalks flat-leaf parsley
1 chilli pepper
200 g cherry tomatoes
salt and pepper to taste
extra-virgin olive oil to taste

Clean the fish, remove all the innards, and then fillet the fish. Make sure that no bones are left in the fish (or ask your fishmonger to fillet it for you). Pour plenty of extra-virgin olive oil into a saucepan and add the minced onion (use an earthenware pan if possible). Brown over low heat for a couple of minutes. Add the crushed garlic, chilli pepper and concentrated tomato puree and combine the ingredients with a spoon. Briefly sauté the ingredients.
Now add the fish into pre-cut pieces measuring 4 to 5 cm and the fish heads for extra flavour. Browning the fish on both sides in the pan beforehand adds extra flavour to the stew. Add the white wine and give it a couple of minutes to evaporate.

Then add the peeled tomatoes, cherry tomatoes, salt, pepper, chilli pepper and parsley and let the stew simmer over very low heat for about an hour. The fish must not be stirred, otherwise it will break. Regularly shake the pan in a circular motion to make sure the fish doesn't stick to the bottom of the pot. Check occasionally with a fork to make sure the bottom doesn't burn. You can also make this dish in an ovenproof dish and leave it to simmer in the oven for 50 minutes at 160 °C. Serve the tegamaccio warm with toasted bread that can also be flavoured with garlic.

NORCIA ③

My journey takes me 120 kilometres south-east into Umbria to Norcia. This picturesque village lies in the Sibillini Mountains amidst stunning landscapes. This is truly breathtaking!

Norcia lifestyle

In this region, food is not just a form of nutrition; it's a lifestyle. You will find mostly healthy food here made from high-quality products. These mountain residents know that eating healthily and an active lifestyle in pristine nature makes people strong and resilient. The Norcia lifestyle is all about living in unique, unspoilt nature and enjoying the flavours that come from the land.

A shepherd crosses my path

I am 10 kilometres from Norcia's town centre. Here, on the outskirts of the Sibillini Mountains, I visit Prosciutto di Norcia, a business owned and run by the Patrizi family. 'Prosciutto di Norcia is one of the many high-quality products produced in this area,' Raimondo Cataldi explains. The brand-new company building stands in an isolated spot where the pastures meet the forests. As if by chance, I meet the 94-year-old Mario Cataldi, his sons Davide and Agostino Cataldi, and his grandson, Raimondo. 'I named my business after my wife, Almerina Patrizi. I still wonder to this day whether that was such a good idea,' the old man jokes. It feels surreal, as does the journey to get there and the many stops along the way to soak up my surroundings. At one of these stops, I meet a shepherd, Gregory. He's the one that sets me on the trail of these people and their unique story.

Heading out to Castelluccio

Prosciutto di Norcia IGP

'Admittedly, our hams are not as famous as the Prosciutto di Parma or the Prosciutto di San Daniele, but the craft did originate here,' Raimondo continues.

'Our market position has strengthened since the 1990s. Today, nine local producers are members of the Consorzio di Tutela IGP Prosciutto di Norcia. But our ham continues to be a niche product. We are incredibly loyal to the original production method and quality regulations. Prosciutto di Norcia IGP may only be produced in Norcia, Preci, Cascia, Monteleone di Spoleto and Poggiodomo. The production takes place at a minimum of 500 metres above sea level. This is an important condition.'

Salted, washed, dried and aged

Davide takes me to the back of the building. We enter a tall, cool space. A couple of people are standing next to a belt rubbing sea salt into the hams. Davide: 'Everything starts with the right raw materials. We only use the meat from heavy pigs because we need the right fat content to produce Prosciutto di Norcia's pear shape. A ham like this weighs at least 8 1/2 kilograms. The ham is coated all over with sea salt, as you see here.'

Davide opens a heavy door into the next chilled room: 'The salted hams are stored and chilled here for a week. We then remove the salt and massage the unsalted meat. That meat is salted once again and left to rest for another 14 to 18 days. After a second layer of salt, the ham is once again brushed and massaged. The hams are first stored horizontally before being hung up to dry.' I follow Davide to the next chilled room. Hams suspended from tall trolleys fill the room. 'We dry the hams for two to five months,' Davide assures me.

We now go to where the *sugnatura* takes place. Davide: 'This is the phase after the drying part. We cover the part of the ham that isn't covered with skin with seasoned lard. This protects the ham from outside influences. It also keeps the Norcia ham soft without drying it out. Once larded, the hams can be left to age for a very long time. The ageing period from salting to sale should take at least 12 months, according to IGP regulations. Our hams ripen about 16 months.'

Norcia ham

Hams at Patrizi

CURED MEAT PIONEERS

'Pig husbandry has been an important activity in this region since Roman times,' Raimondo tells me. 'The oak forests offered enough food for the animals. This is where people started to process and salt pork. We were the first true meat processors in the world. We have expanded our expertise to other regions. Norcino means "he who processes the meat" or pork butcher. It's an actual occupation; you will find it in the dictionary. The *norciniere* are the locations at which the cured meats are sold. It's something our region is very proud of.'

⭐ Gusto – flavour

After the guided tour, I return to the office where I share a small cup of strong coffee with all three generations: Mario, Agostino and Raimondo. I want to know what makes their ham extra special. 'You can taste the mountain air,' Raimondo replies. 'We have an excellent climate for curing meat. The specific wind that passes through this area makes the difference. Moreover, this is the predecessor of all Italian hams. The métier has its roots here!' Grandpa Mario adds that Norcia IGP tastes best when it's cut fresh from the ham *(con osso)*. 'Il più buono del mondo – the best in the world', Mario grins.

It's wonderful to see how happy these people are with their business, which they had to rebuild from scratch just six months ago. The building was completely destroyed during the 2016 earthquake; the entire stock went with it. The business was closed for five years. The owners spent that time searching for the financial means and required permits to rebuild the business. In May 2021, they took up residence in this brand-new fortress to practice the family tradition. My hat goes off to these brave people. It requires an enormous investment, and the hams need to ripen for 18 months before being put on the market. I hope everything goes well for them. Within a year, I'll be back to taste their latest product. That's a promise!

Patrizi
Via Leopardi 45, Fraz Frascaro, Norcia

RAIMONDO'S RECIPE

Bruschetta con crema di pecorino e prosciutto di Norcia

SERVES 6 PEOPLE

200 g ricotta
150 g semi-aged pecorino cheese
150 g young pecorino cheese
1 sprig flat-leaf parsley
salt and pepper to taste
bread, ciabatta or baguette
**   to roast in the oven**
100 g finely sliced Norcia ham (or other ham)

Combine the ricotta and both grated pecorino cheese varieties in a bowl. Add the parsley. Mix the cheeses (in a blender, if you prefer). When you add a little bit of extra-virgin olive oil, the pecorino cream will keep for up to four days if you store it covered in the refrigerator. Coat the slices of bread in olive oil and bake them in an oven at about 180 °C for about four minutes.

Remove the bread and spread the creamy cheese spread over the top. Top the cheese with pieces of finely sliced Norcia ham.

Tip You can also use the cream for pasta dishes.

TRUFFLE HUNTING

The black Norcia truffle is a gem in Umbria's culinary crown. I was about to go into one of the truffle shops in Norcia's town centre to get the story. But serendipity beat me to it. In Caffé Parigi, I meet truffle hunter Rocco di Muzzio. His dog, Pepino, settles down next to us as we strike up a conversation.

Rocco: 'Umbria is one of Italy's truffle paradises. This is where we hunt for the black gold with our tracker dogs. Truffles grow year-round, but you will find the best truffles between December and March.

Rocco unrolls a kitchen towel to reveal a couple of black truffles and lets me smell them. I smell a pleasant, aromatic scent. It reminds me of hay and chestnuts. The truffles are irregularly round in shape and blackish brown in colour. Rocco now breaks the truffle in two to reveal a brown-black pulp riddled with whitish veins.

'The flavour is unique and exceptionally intense, sometimes even sweet,' Rocco says. 'That's why we sometimes call this truffle the "sweet black" truffle. The Norcia truffle is also one of the most valued varieties, second only to the white truffle from Alba. The black truffle (Tuber Melanosporum) is known in the vernacular as *tartufo nero pregiato*. Umbria is not the only region where you will find the melanosporum in the wild. It also grows in the forests of Piedmont, Abruzzo, Molise, Calabria, and Campania. The truffle flourishes under oak, hazel, and olive trees in forests up to 800 metres high.

Truffle in the kitchen

A whole range of dishes uses black truffle. 'Italians have been experimenting with truffle for generations,' Rocco explains.
'We never throw anything away. So, if you have a lot of truffles, you have to find some way of preserving them. Truffle cream is a handy way of doing that. Rocco gives me his treasured family recipe. 'If you want a cream that doesn't include mushrooms, just scrap them and use more truffles instead,' he lets me know.

ROCCO'S RECIPE
Salsa al tartufo

SERVES 4 PEOPLE
**1 black truffle (about 10 g),
   or truffle slices preserved in oil**
250 g porcini, mushrooms, or wild mushrooms
1 clove or a pinch of ground cloves
1 salted anchovy fillet
1 clove garlic
2 tablespoons extra-virgin olive oil
salt and pepper to taste
bread

Trim and brush the mushrooms with a knife and a brush, mince them and set aside. Set a small saucepan with two tablespoons of olive oil and the garlic over heat and sauté for a minute. Add the anchovy fillet and briefly sear the fish, then add the mushrooms and simmer for five minutes. Stir regularly. Now add the thinly sliced or grated truffle, stir, and cook for another five minutes. Remove the clove and the garlic clove, and mix everything in a blender to a smooth cream. Season to taste with salt and pepper. The sauce is served on a crostino, toast, or bruschetta or as a dish accompaniment. You can eat this sauce warm or cold. You can store the cream in a glass jar. Cover the emulsion in the pot with a thin layer of extra-virgin olive oil. That way, it will keep for at least two weeks in the refrigerator. You can also store the cream in the freezer if you want to store it for longer.

* People in Umbria use this recipe to use up their leftover truffle. The truffles that aren't sold or are too small are, just like leftover pieces of truffle after shaving, ideal for processing into a cream.

CASTELLUCCIO DI NORCIA ④

Pulses from the region

I stay in the area and visit Azienda Agricola Brandimarte Maurizio. I want to learn more about the famous pulses that come from this region. I step inside the farm shop where I have arranged to meet Alessia Brandimarte. The enticing round cheeses on display exude an intoxicating scent. The shelves feature bags of *lenticchie* (lentils), *roveja* (wild pea), *farro* (spelt), *orzo* (barley) and *ceci* (chickpeas), as well as chickpea, spelt, wild pea flour, and lentil beer.

Roveja

I inspect a bag of brown-green pea-like pulses. Alessia: 'This is a variation of the wild pea that is now protected under the Slow Food Movement. The pulse has a high protein level and contains plenty of carbohydrates and minerals. Just like chickpeas, you need to soak roveja for at least 12 hours before you can use them in the soup. Once they're cooked, you can also serve them cold in salads. We also make rojeva flour for products such as *farrechiata*, a type of polenta. We season the polenta with garlic, anchovy and sage.'

Roveja

La lenticchia di Castelluccio di Norcia IGP

'These lentils are our most prized product,' Alessia tells me. 'They are grown on the rocky plains of Castelluccio di Norcia, spread out over an area of some 20 square miles at an elevation of about 1500 metres in the Monti Sibillini National Park. These lentils are unique because of their small size and distinctive flavour. This ancient pulse dates back to 3000 years before Christ.

Castelluccio di Norcia IGP lentils transform the plains into a colourful carpet of flowers during the flowering season. The lentils that grow among the rocks are picked by hand. It's labour-intensive work. It's important to know that you can cook these lentils straight away without having to soak them first. Our chefs love them.'

⭐ Tradition with a contemporary look

What this company does is genius. I ask Alessia whether her choice to go into farming was a conscious one. 'My grandmother founded the business,' Alessia replies. 'Together with my grandfather and their four sons, they managed to grow the farm into 100 hectares of land and 1000 sheep. They processed the milk into pecorino and ricotta. They grew the famous lentils and roveja peas, as well as spelt, barley and chickpeas in the hills around Castelluccio. We lost a lot during the 2016 earthquake. 76 sheep died when our barn collapsed. The hay, feed and all our milking equipment were destroyed. Today, we have a flock of about 400 sheep, and we cultivate 70 hectares of land. My father, mother, sister, and I work on rebuilding the farm and the fields of Castelluccio, some 50 minutes from here. We will continue the family tradition, and our production has resumed. We also experiment with new variations and flavours that we offer online. I studied economics, and now I want to offer traditional, high-quality products with a focus on nature, but with the help of modern technology. That is our future.'

Azienda Agricola Brandimarte Maurizio
Loc. Misciano, Norcia

A colourful patchwork of lentil fields near Castelluccio di Norcia

Colour symphony

Upon father Maurizio's recommendation, I drive through Castellucio to fully understand the region and its characteristic features. I travel to a small hamlet about 30 kilometres from Norcia. A long, winding road takes me up into the mountains. I end up 1450 metres above sea level in the majestic Monti Sibillini National Park. The landscape unfolds before my eyes after many twists and turns, and in the distance, I can see the village of Castelluccio perched on the side of a hill. The village was hard hit during the 2016 earthquake; about 60 per cent of its buildings collapsed. On the foot of Castelluccio lies the plain with a spectacular view of the mountains.

This is where the Castelluccio lentils flower from late May to early July, an impressive sight to behold. That's when the Colfiorito plateau turns into one vast colour symphony. No earthquake can beat that.

Each year, countless tourists experience the magic of these exuberantly decked-out fields. Lentil flowers, wild cornflowers, buttercups, daisies, and poppies spring up in an unsurpassed mosaic of colour. 'The colour spectacle is beyond compare,' Maurizio told me. Sadly, there are no flowers here today, so I can't confirm this. But the landscape is phenomenal, even without the flowers!

The Romanelli family's olive groves and vineyards

Sagrantino grapes are left to dry before being processed into Passito wine

MONTEFALCO ⑤

I resume my journey and drive 84 kilometres to Montefalco. On this mountain *(monte)*, the falcon *(falco)* finds its perch. This charming medieval mountain village is tucked away between hills covered in olive trees and grapevines. The Romanelli agricultural business in San Clemente di Montefalco is situated in the heart of Umbria. Devis Romanelli's wife, Moira Ugolini, has agreed to introduce me to their wines. On the terrace, she points out three silhouetted shadows of towns among the hills in the far distance: Foligno, Trevi and Spoleto. I breathe deeply, taking in the magic of this place.

⭐ The return of the falcon

'We only make organic slow wine here. We grow sangiovese, merlot, grechetto and sagrantino grapes on eight hectares of soil,' Moira explains. 'We do not use any artificial fertilizers, pesticides, or herbicides. You will find bird nests at strategic locations around the vineyards. They are home to bird species such as blue tits that hunt for insects. The bees feed and purify our plantations. A couple of large nests in the vineyard are for the falcon. He returns to our domain each year. He only shows up where the air is pure. He is our guest of honour.'

We move to a room where all the winery's wines are displayed. Moira: 'We use the sagrantino grapes for the red wines, Montefalco Rosso DOC, Medeo DOCG, Sagrantino Montefalco DOCG, Molinetta Riserva DOC, and a Grappa di Sagrantino. The Grecheto and the Umbria Bianco are our white wines. And, last but not least, we have our unique Sagrantino Passito.'

Passito

'Sagrantino is actually a Passito wine,' Moira mentions. 'People used to drink sweet wine with lamb dishes. Sagrantino is a permanent fixture in and around Montefalco. Monks have been making passito wine since as early as 1400. It is part of the region's agricultural history. People would drink the wine during religious festivals, or *sagra*, hence the name sagrantino. Monks made the drink of the gods from the sacred grape.' The dry sagrantino Montefalco wine has only been around for 40 years.

250 METRES ABOVE SEA LEVEL

'Sagrantino is typical for this region. You will only find this grape variety in five municipalities. The clay soil at 250 metres above sea level and the characteristic wind make the difference.'

We go out to the covered terrace on top of the main building. I see blue grapes drying on various shelves. Moira: 'For our passito, we first leave the grapes to *passire*, or turn, for three months. Here, they are protected from the rain, but the necessary north wind works its magic here. The grape completely dries out.

These grapes were harvested 14 days ago. This harvest will provide us with about 3000 bottles of passito sagrantino.' I pluck a grape from a bunch and taste it. Deliciously sweet.
Moira: 'That's right. The grapes are *dolce*, or sweet. You don't need to add sugar to make passito from the sagrantino grape. That's the difference from many other passito wines made from other grape varieties. Some people look down their noses at the sweet sagrantino passito, which is a shame. It is a very rich wine with a unique flavour palate and a long history. It was born here. And everyone who tries it says: Oh, but this one's different...'

Vendemnia or harvest

Tasting the wine sounds like a good idea. I try a glass of this holy drink. It tastes sweet, but I notice how the sagrantino grape's tannins cleanse my palate. That's unusual. The attack is sweet, yet the aftertaste isn't. The complex flavour palate is sublime.

Moira: 'Today, it's more common as a dessert wine, but this wasn't always the case. This wine goes equally well with aged pecorino cheeses, lamb or porchetta, or as an accompaniment to red fruit pastries, baked goods and pure chocolate. The sagrantino passito is in our genes, and we will always honour our deep-rooted traditions. With the first grape harvest, we organise a large buffet for the entire family and the staff. People of all ages enjoy our typical maritozzi pastry with the must from the first harvest. The earliest grapes are immediately pressed into grape juice, called must or *mosto*. The must has to ferment to produce wine. We use a small part of the first must for the maritozzi to celebrate the *vendemnia*, the harvest. Instead of water, we add grape juice to the dough.

I drive back down the hill armed with a couple of boxes of Montefalco wine and a handful of maritozzi pastries. As I descend the hill, I see the sagrantino grape vines to my left, and to the right are the sangiovese, grechetto and merlot fields – and lots of olive trees. 3000 in total, Moira told me. On my way back, I briefly stop to admire the beehives. Not sure if that's a smart idea. Oh well, life is good here, and what a truly spectacular location!

Agricola Romanelli
Colle San Clemente 129/A, Montefalco

Colle San Clemente in Montefalco

TOSCANA

Siena, Lucca, Montepulciano, Arezzo, Cortona, and unsurpassed Florence are all pearls in Tuscany's crown. I travel back to medieval times in these artistic cities with their rich past; it's like walking through one giant open-air museum. I drive over softly rolling hills among villages perched like eagles' nests and guarded by solitary fortresses. A patchwork of fields, rank upon rank of olive trees, oceans of sunflowers and vast vineyards set the scene for my gastronomic adventure.

Tuscany has fallen into numerous hands over the centuries. The Etruscans conquered what used to be 'Tuscia' in the fifth century BC, followed by the Romans. Florence, or Firenze, was already the capital back then. The legendary De' Medici family ruled over Tuscany from the 15th to the 18th century. They brought about an intellectual and cultural renaissance. Leonardo da Vinci, Michelangelo, Botticelli, and Galileo Galilei all left their distinctive marks and set the scene for the cultural world.

In the 18th century, agricultural practices flourished in Tuscany; later, the region was scarred by the Industrial Revolution and the Second World War. Still, Tuscany managed to retain its unique character. This world heritage region is protected by strict Italian legislation and rules.

Sunflowers in Val di Chiana

Collonata, Carrara

5

Firenze

1

Arno

Arno

Bettole, Sinalunga

2

Ombrone

3 Montepulciano

4

Monticiano

Montepulciano

Artusi

Pellegrino Artusi is no longer around to emphasise the influential role of Tuscany in Italian cuisine, but he did in the past. This literary critic, writer and gastronomic connoisseur lived in Florence from 1861 onwards. In 1891, he wrote the first edition of *Science in the Kitchen and the Art of Eating Well (La scienza in cucina e l'arte di mangiar bene).* His recipes form the basis for contemporary Italian cuisine. Artusi is instrumental in the development and dissemination of Italian gastronomy.

Salsa verde is a traditional dish linked to an important piece of Florence's gastronomic heritage, the *lampredotto.* Artusi's historic cookbook includes the recipe below:

ARTUSI'S RECIPE
Salsa verde

SERVES 4 PEOPLE
120 g mild olive oil
10 g capers
1 anchovy
1 clove garlic
10 g fresh parsley
10 g fresh basil leaves
10 g fresh mint
juice of ½ lemon
salt and pepper to taste

Blend all the ingredients together to form a smooth paste.

One of Florence's showpieces is the Santa Maria del Fiore cathedral.

FIRENZE ①

I park my car near Florence's central train station and travel to San Lorenzo, the 'Medici District,' on foot. This is where streetside vendors sell their wares. The stalls on the Piazza San Lorenzo open at the crack of dawn, and the streets instantly come alive. It's a maze riddled with history, art and *trippa.*

The Mercato Centrale forms the district's heart. The architect Mengoni constructed this market building in the 19th century. He was inspired by *Les Halles* in Paris, a revolutionary building at the time, also made from iron and glass. Mengoni wanted the ironwork to contrast with the city's old stone palaces and arches. The market opened in 1874 and soon became a popular attraction. Today, the regional farmers' stalls filled with high-quality Florentine products still draw people in droves. This indoor market is a must for lovers of delicious, authentic Tuscan cuisine. And the *trippa* and *lampredotto* are an essential part of that cuisine...

QUINTO QUARTO, THE FIFTH QUARTER

Enrico, proprietor of the La Toraia, a Chianina hamburger stand, bears witness to the market's success: 'Every day, we welcome about 1000 people in the Mercato Centrale.' On the first floor, some twenty-odd small bars serve street food dishes. On the ground floor, you will find mostly meat, fish, vegetables, fresh pasta, wines, dry foods, and a couple of *trippai*. They sell raw and prepared products from what they call the *quinto quarto*; the fifth quarter of the animal, as it were. Italians refer to the innards, heads, hooves, and tails of animals as *quinto*. The meat here is usually cut up into four quarters, and 'the fifth quarter' is the proverbial cherry on the cake.

Mercato Centrale, Piazza del Mercato Centrale, Via dell'Ariento, Florence

Lampredotto

Lampredotto is, without a doubt, the quintessential Florentine street dish, inextricably linked to this home of the De' Medici family. Lampredotto and trippa stalls have been livening up the streets and markets here for centuries. Lampredotto, a dish that has been known since the Renaissance, is delicious, fast, cheap, and nutritious.
Only Florentine cuisine makes use of the fourth and final stomach of the cow, the maw or abomasum. A sliced-open round bread roll (known in many places in Italy as *rosetta)* is filled with steaming lampredotto, sprinkled with salt and pepper, seasoned with *salsa verde* – green sauce – and often topped with an extra layer of spicy sauce. The top part of the roll is briefly dipped in the savoury broth before it goes on top of the sandwich. It's unique to Florence.

MARKET STALL
Bambi

Right next to the Mercato Centrale entrance is the market stall owned by the Bambi Trippa & Lampredotto family business. They have been here since 1890. I travel back in time to the days of *cucina povera*, or 'poor people's' cuisine. The lampredotto and trippa are favourites. Giacomo Trapani carries on the family tradition established by his grandmother Grazia Bambi. He developed a love for the traditional Florentine cuisine at his *nonna's* knee. Giacomo belongs to an entire generation of *trippai*, trippa makers. He brings the dishes from Florence's collective memory to life every day. Bambi is his grandmother's surname. She was cooking *al trippa*, bovine stomachs, for people as far back as the end of the 19th century.

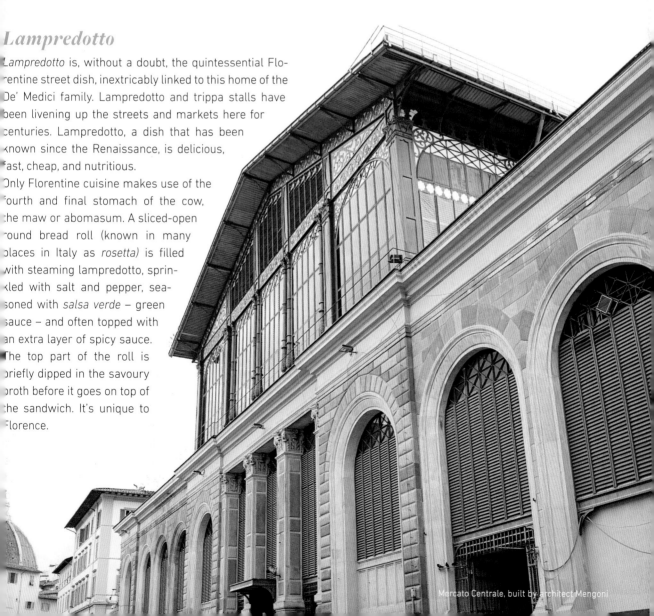

Mercato Centrale, built by architect Mengoni

Giacomo with a fine piece of the fourth stomach

The famous lampredotto with salsa verde and spicy sauce

Cheap culinary favourite in Florence

Giacomo: 'The De' Medici family ate a type of eel, *lampreda*, or lamprey, which only the rich could afford. The peasant variant, *lampredetto*, originated in the 15th century. The inside of the eel's maw looked like the piece of the stomach that the peasants ate; it may be where lampredotto got its name from. At the time, in Florence, the nobles donated animal innards to the peasants.

The resulting cheap culinary showpiece, lampredotto, is still very popular. Nonetheless, it continues to be a niche product because not everyone fancies eating stomach. With *trippa*, it's different. Trippa, or tripe, is not a product exclusive to Florence and has an international connotation. And trippa is less fatty.'

Cooking stomachs

The trippai from Florence buy the stomachs from the butchers who slaughter cattle and carve the meat. They only use the stomachs of bulls and calves because cows' stomachs contain too much calcium. The stomachs are cooked several times before being removed from the water and thoroughly cleaned by hand with a brush. There are only five businesses (*tripperie*) in Tuscany that do this preparatory work. Bambi is one of them.

Giacomo: 'I've been doing this my whole life. When I was a little boy, I would go with my father to sell the cleaned stomachs to shops, butchers, market stalls and supermarkets. In the afternoons, I would help stir the giant pots filled with stomachs with my mother, aunt, and grandma. The quinto quarto from the trippai is cooked in a vegetarian broth to season the meat and make it tender. The original broth recipe includes carrot, onion, and celery, with tomatoes to add colour if desired. The broth is seasoned with salt and reduced for 90 minutes to develop its strong flavour.

Giacomo argues that we need rules to preserve the lampredotto's quality. Giacomo sums up: 'Use only stomachs from bulls and calves, and only from Italian ruminants. It is also important that all vendors in Florence stick to the same recipe for their broth and sauces. Heaven forbid someone puts mayonnaise or ketchup on your sandwich!'

Bambi
Mercato Centrale di San Lorenzo, Florence

TRIPPA

Trippa is made from the first, second, and third stomachs of the cow. The fourth stomach is reserved for lampredotto. The cooked stomach is cut into fine strips.

First stomach – Rumen (paunch)
the fattiest part of the stomach

Second stomach – Reticulum (honeycomb)
the hardest part, looks like a sponge

Third stomach – Omasum (manyplies)
the least fatty part

Fourth stomach – Abomasum (rennet-bag or maw), the true stomach, dark, fatty and flavourful; this is used for lampredotto

Chianina hamburger

I also meet Enrico Lagorio at the Mercato Centrale. 'The godfather' of the Chianina burger introduced this street food delicacy. Enrico is one of the owners of the La Toraia brand and the Tenuta La Fratta agricultural business in Sinalunga. The Chianina hamburger has become just as popular in Florence as the iconic Bistecca Fiorentina, or the Chianina T-bone steak. And yet, this hamburger wasn't introduced until 2009. Both are the product of 'il Gigante Bianco', a large cattle breed that has been taking the national and international culinary world by storm. Gentleman farmer and entrepreneur Enrico linked this white giant to the burger: 'With my family business, I combined the tradition of eating on the streets with a modern product. An affordable product with respect for quality. The Chianina burger contains meat from a cattle breed that was initially used to work the land and was later bred for its meat. We mince the lower-quality cuts of meat to hamburger meat; cucina povera, but with superior-quality meat.'

Chianina hamburger

TENUTA LA FRATTA

Chianina is synonymous with La Fratta. Tenuta La Fratta is a centuries-old gentleman's farm (1208) in Sinalunga. Enrico: 'La Fratta is one of the oldest and most famous authentic Chianina farms in Valdichiana in southern Tuscany. Our animals eat local grain products. The environment, people and animals still go hand in hand here.'

The beautiful Chianina breed lives in its natural biotope at La Fratta, where the Chianina hamburger is prepared and sold. The story began around the year 2000. A group of intellectuals wanted to make sure that Chianina cattle were not only bred for steaks. Local entrepreneurs took the initiative and introduced the Chianina hamburger – and the rest is history.

Tenuta La Fratta
Località La Fratta, Sinalunga

The perfect hamburger

In Firenze Lungarno, Massimiliano Brogi, one of La Fratta's three owners, awaits my arrival. Massimiliano: 'We supply our points of sale from our own lands and with our own cattle. We don't want blind expansion; we want to keep things the way they are now. With our *filiera corta*, or short supply chain, we go straight from production to consumption.'

Since 2011, La Fratta has opened Chianina burger outlets in various cities and expanded its in-house retail and catering division – with success. You need to wait in line outside on Lungarno del Tempo for a burger.

Massimiliano is straight to the point: 'Less is more. This pure meat doesn't need much. The hamburger is made from 95 per cent Chianina beef and 5 per cent pork to make the hamburger juicier.

I order a Chianina burger with onion (fried in home-brewed beer), lettuce and a little bit of mustard. That tastes good!

La Toraia
Lungarno del Tempio, Florence

The La Fratta farmstead dates from 1208

Chianina at La Fratta

SINALUNGA ②

The Chianina breed is a beautiful, elegant cattle breed – stately because of its height, yet graceful with its long rump and limbs. Bulls can grow up to two metres tall and weigh up to 1900 kg. A fully grown cow weighs between 900 and 1000 kg. The cattle breed first appeared near Tevere and Valdichiana; today, you will also find them in Siena, Pisa, Perugia, and Rieti. In Valdichiana, the largest bovine breed in the world is called 'Il Gigante Bianco della Valdichiana', or Chiana valley giant. We are currently in the 'zona d'origine' with its own IGP, or Identificazione Geografica Protetta indication. This is a geographic indication and delineation for the original breed that has been grazing in these pastures for almost 2000 years.

AMICI DELLA CHIANINA

The Amici Della Chianina present the culinary potential of Chianina beef during workshops, events, and demonstrations. They encourage local producers, butchers, and chefs to look beyond the traditional Florentine steak.

In Bettole (Sinalunga), I meet Giovanni Corti, chairman of the Friends of the Chianina society. Giovanni is an architect by profession, but he is also dedicated to protecting the Chianina breed: 'The Chianina hamburger is part of what we call *cucina povera*, or peasant cuisine. The steak was the most valuable part of the cow. The demand for Chianina steak kept growing. This meant that other cuts of meat would often be discarded. Chefs were not interested in the less valuable cuts of beef because the preparation requires a lot of time and effort.'

Crostino nero Toscano

I decide to remain in the area and visit chef Walter Redaelli at this restaurant in Bettole. I want to learn more about the star of the *antipasti* (appetizers) on Tuscan tables: The *crostino nero,* or black toast. This dish has countless variations and recipes. Each village has its own interpretation. That is why I turn to chef Redaelli so he can share his expertise with me. I arrive at an impressive 18th-century farm that has been renovated into a high-class restaurant and sit at the table across from Walter next to a majestic fireplace. Redaelli is known for his delicious Tuscan dishes prepared solely using local ingredients and his love for Chianina beef.

Walter: 'The ingredients for a crostino nero are a synthesis of traditional country life: offal, herbs and stale bread. The pantries of Tuscan farms always had these ingredients tucked away somewhere. The recipe has changed over time because we now add more refined ingredients. The name crostino is derived from the Latin *crustulum*, meaning crust. It is basically a slice of bread that is hardened to a crust by toasting or baking it.

⭐ Love it or hate it

Walter: 'In Tuscany, we will sometimes use the word "crostino" to refer to an annoying person that complains all the time. I don't know if there's any correlation between the crostino nero and this vernacular use of the term. The original recipe dates from the Middle Ages and can be found in one of the oldest cookbooks in existence: the *Liber de Coquina* from the early 14th century.

It contains the following passage: 'Pigeons or chickens: take their livers or other offal. Roast them and then grind them finely with pepper in a mortar. Dilute with wine and vinegar. Cook however you like. Use toasted bread.'

I notice that this recipe sounds very primitive compared with today's crostini neri. But offal has always been an essential part of the recipe, and it's probably not for everyone, I conclude.

Variations

Walter: 'In the provinces of Arezzo, Firenze, Prato, and Pistoia, only chicken liver is used, fried with onion and Tuscan olive oil. Some versions add celery and carrots.

The mixture is cooked in a bit of meat broth and wine. Anchovies and capers are added after cooking. The mixture is then passed through a food mill or blended with a hand blender. I don't recommend using a hand blender because the mixture will then lose its texture.'

He resumes: 'The Senese variation uses the spleen. This recipe is common throughout the province of Siena, including here in Bettole. We use spleen from calves or cows in addition to the chicken livers and add a bit of minced veal. The meat and offal are sautéed with onion, celery, and carrot. The rest of the preparation is similar to how it's made in other provinces. In the province of Pisa, they also add minced veal to the chicken livers.'

Signature dish

Walter: 'I have tried a lot of variations in my time, and I personally fell in love with the recipe I'm about to give you. This version goes straight to my heart, and my guests also appreciate this recipe very much. I wanted a flavour that combined well in an antipasto with fine, salty Tuscan cured meats such as *prosciutto crudo*, *capocollo*, and our salamis. My crostino nero provides an essential bitter contrast. My recipe uses the spleen from the Chianina cattle. I believe that the spleen is essential because that's what makes the crostino black, or *nero*. Using chicken liver alone makes the composition brown. We serve the resulting cream on authentic – unsalted – Tuscan bread. The anchovy and salted capers in my recipe contain enough salt for the entire dish. People used to dip the hard bread in broth before spreading the paste over the top. Today, only the older generation still does that. We briefly roast the bread in the oven to soften it up.'

Annette and Walter Redaelli

I remark that some recipes also use pear or apple to sweeten the bitter flavour. Walter replies that he's not a fan of this option. He prefers a sweet *vin santo* instead. This Tuscan dessert wine is a far more effective addition, according to him.

Walter: 'Patience and refinement are characteristic of my work. The sauce needs to simmer and stew long enough to develop the right flavours. We work with raw ingredients that need to spend enough time over heat to do them justice.'

La Leopoldina
Via XXI Aprile 26, Bettole (Sinalunga)

Walter's tips

'One thing that's good to know is that you need to remove the gallbladders from the chicken livers before preparing them, without breaking them. They would give the sauce a bitter taste. You can best do this in a bowl of water. As soon as the sauce is ready, you can store it in the refrigerator for a week, preferably in a glass jar with a layer of lard or olive oil on top. People used to add a thick layer of lard over the top. That was their way of preserving the paste.'

Crostino nero

SERVES 4 PEOPLE

100 g veal or beef spleen
   (if you can't find spleen,
   use chicken livers instead)
150 g chicken livers
200 g veal mince
olive oil
1 large white onion
1 clove garlic
1 stalk flat-leaf parsley
beef stock
50 ml vin santo (a small glass of dessert wine)
50 ml red wine
30 g salted capers
1 anchovy fillet
pepper to taste
bread

Clean the spleen and the livers. This is essential to the success of this dish. For the spleen: cut in half and open it up. Remove the inner, softer part and remove the hard outer part. Don't use this. The livers: clean and finely chop them with a knife. Sauté the minced onion, garlic, and parsley in extra-virgin olive oil over medium heat.

Add the spleen and simmer for seven to eight minutes. Add the livers and cook them until they change colour. Cook the veal mince in a separate pan and separate with a fork. As soon as the veal mince is browned, you can add it to the liver. Now, gradually add the beef stock; you will need about two to three soup ladles of broth. Simmer over low heat for about 25 minutes.

Add the red wine and the vin santo. Simmer everything for an additional 30 minutes over very low heat. Finely chop the rinsed capers and anchovy with a knife. Add to the pan and stir for two to three minutes. Add some extra olive oil.

Cook everything for another 20 minutes over very low heat. Check regularly to make sure the bottom doesn't burn. Turn off the heat and leave the mixture to cool slightly. Toast the bread. Spread the (slightly) warm sauce on the slice of bread and serve. The sauce can also be served cold on toast.

MONTEPULCIANO ③

And what do you drink with a crostino nero? Walter pours me a delicious glass of red wine: Nobile di Montepulciano from Avignonesi's vineyards. This wine is garnet coloured. The flavour is full-bodied yet smooth. This is interesting. I look at the label and read: 100 per cent sangiovese.

The sangiovese grape: the prince of Tuscany

Walter: 'It is the most cultivated red grape variety in all of Italy. You will mostly find them in the central regions: Tuscany and Emilia-Romagna, Umbria, Marche, and Lazio. The glass of wine leaves me with a taste for more, so I drive 20 kilometres further to Montepulciano to visit the Avignonesi domain that has been in the hands of the Belgian Virginie Saverys since 2009. The Avignonesi brand has a long wine-growing tradition, and Vino Nobile di Montepulciano is probably the most famous wine from this part of the world. I drive along the winding roads through the hillsides flanked by charming vineyards and olive groves in happy anticipation. I am completely overwhelmed by the romance of this remarkable Tuscan landscape. I turn off the road onto a driveway lined with stately cypress trees. I park my car further down the lane and walk towards the reception and *enoteca* near the entrance to this majestic estate.

Ilaria Roccanti gives me a warm welcome. She proudly tells me of the famous liquid produced here and how it has seduced connoisseurs from this part of the world for over half a century. Ilaria: 'Sangiovese is also known as the prince of Tuscany because the grape is found in many red wines, including the region's most famous wines: Chianti, Brunello, and Vino Nobile di Montepulciano. The Tuscan soil is ideal for cultivating the sangiovese grape variety. Here, we have sun, water and a clay soil that keeps the earth moist.

The soil on our lands in Cortona, for instance, contains more rocks and sand and is more suitable for grape varieties such as chardonnay, cabernet, and merlot. We have 180 hectares on which the sangiovese di Montepulciano grows. It is our most important grape. The Avignonese wine labels with 100 per cent sangiovese grapes include the Nobile di Montepulciano, Rosso di Montepulciano, DADI, Grandi Annate, La Tonda, Cantaloro rosato, and our Vin Santo Occhio di Pernice.'

The Avignonesi Le Capezzine winery

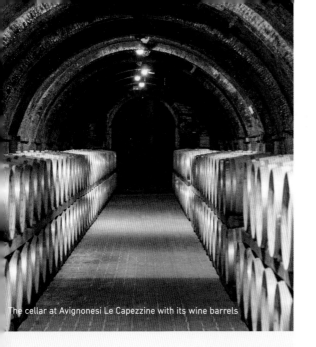
The cellar at Avignonesi Le Capezzine with its wine barrels

BALANCED WINE

'You can keep sangiovese wines for a very long time, and that's necessary,' Ilaria resumes. 'We soften the tannins by ripening the wine in oak barrels for long periods. It is important that we preserve the full-bodied flavour of the sangiovese grape, but at the same time, tone down the after-taste. We create balanced flavour palates.'

Nectar of hospitality

'According to Tuscan tradition, serving vin santo is one of the oldest gestures of hospitality,' Ilaria continues. 'This means that you see in the other a valued friend or respected person.'
Ilaria serves two types of vin santo. One is made from white trebbiano and malvasia grapes, the other is 100 per cent sangiovese and carries the name Vin Santo Occhio di Pernice, the eye of the pheasant. I feel honoured to be offered this liquid gold. Ilaria: 'Its sugar content is very high because of the prolonged ageing process. The taste is sweet, yet it cleanses the palate.'

The first van santo is a viscous, caramel-coloured liquid. I taste a delightful combination of sweet and sour, with a whole spectrum of flavours that includes coffee beans, marmalade, figs, and almonds.

The second wine, the Occhio di Pernice, is even more syrupy and has more of a sweet and spicy flavour profile. The palate includes flavours such as dried prunes

or apricots, gingerbread, smoked hazelnut, and even tobacco. What an experience!

You'd be mad to dip a *cantucci* (almond biscuit) in this wine, I remark. 'You're right. That's not such a good idea with this vin santo,' Ilaria explains. 'I know it's tradition-al with this type of wine. But because of the prolonged ageing process, our vin santo is so concentrated and outspoken in its flavour that it goes much better with aged cheese or cured meats.'

Yeast starter or madre

These dessert wines are so heavenly, so it wouldn't surprise me if making this elixir of the gods is an ar-duous, time-consuming process. Ilaria: 'For both these dessert wines, the grapes are harvested by hand in September. Vin santo is produced by leaving the best grapes to dry on mats for four months. The must that we retain after pressing the grapes has a very high sugar content. The moisture is then transferred into wooden barrels called *caratelli*. The must is then fer-mented for ten years in the wooden barrels, together with the yeast starter, or *madre*. This is must that was used in an earlier batch of vin santo. It is a priceless in-gredient that we protect at any cost. During the ageing process, the wine's volume is reduced by half. It is then kept for another year in aluminium barrels, followed by an additional year in bottles. And only then do we put our vin santo on the market.'

⭐ Holy wine

One question that I've been dying to ask is where the name comes from. Vin santo literally translates to holy wine, doesn't it?
Ilaria: 'The origins of this wine go far, far back. How far? We don't know. One story about the origins of the vin santo name is linked to the plague which struck Siena in 1348. It is believed that monks gave their sac-ramental wine to the afflicted to ease their suffering. After drinking the wine, they would cry out "vin santo!" or "holy wine!" because of the relief they felt. But its origins can most probably be attributed to its frequent use as a sacramental wine,' Ilaria winks.

Avignonesi Fattoria Le Capezzine,
Via Colonica 1, Montepulciano

Drying grapes for the production of vin santo

Schiacciata

Back to the region's capital. Florence is sun, tradition – and a long line of people waiting in the old town for *schiacciata*. This *focaccia* lookalike has been a household name in this city for years, in part thanks to Tommaso Mazzanti from All'Antico Vinaio. His sandwich shop near the Piazza della Signoria is an institution. I visit this historical shop next to the Uffizi Gallery and spy three more All'Antico Vinaio shops further down the street. The schiacciata is baked on the spot and filled with Tuscan delicacies.

The street dish looks delicious. Tommaso: 'It's pure nostalgia for the local Tuscans. As a child, almost all of us were served something like this for our *merenda*, or late-afternoon snack, often baked by the *nonna*, or grandma. A sandwich like this is something to treasure for the rest of your life. You can recognize the real Schiacciata Toscana by the irregular handmade shape, with extra-virgin olive oil soaking the holes in the bread and the sprinkling of sea salt on top. The bread is prepared by hand. Skilled, nimble hands knead the dough. A sandwich like that delights with the intense olive oil flavour and the coarse salt on the crust.'

Ancient bread

Schiacciata dates back to ancient times, as far back as the first agricultural and animal husbandry practices. The shape back then was primitive. The ancient bread only contained water and grains that were crushed on stone. People would bake a thin, round disc on a hot stone. In ancient Egypt, yeast was added, and the Romans added wheat to the dough. Thus, the tradition of Italian bread was born. Since the Middle Ages, the dough has been baked in an oven. The filled version of schiacciata dates from the 18th century.

The Florentine nobility loved schiacciata Toscana. In one of his letters, Lorenzo de' Medici wrote: '*Doman t'arrecherò una schiacciata*,' – I will bring you a schiacciata tomorrow.

Almost the best sandwich in the world

Tourists find these to be the best sandwiches in Florence and its surroundings. But you must be prepared to spend some time waiting in line to try one. Still, who could resist enjoying a treat like this under the watchful eye of Michelangelo's David – or rather, a replica – or on the Arno near the Ponte Vecchio?

A filled schiacciata sandwich

Schiacciata from the oven at All'Antico Vinaio

Enjoying a schiacciata sandwich with a view of the Arno

You can choose à la carte fillings or make your choice from a set menu. The *Favolosa* is a favourite. The schiacciata bread is sliced in half and filled with *sbriciolona* (fennel salami), *pecorino* cream, slightly spicy grilled aubergine, and an artichoke cream. According to the online edition of *Saveur* magazine, this sandwich belongs among the world's top three.

All'Antico Vinaio
Via dei Neri 76R, Florence

Franca in her amazing kitchen

MONTICIANO ④
Cucina casalinga - home cooking

My journey takes me in the direction of Grosseto. After 97 kilometres, I arrive at a remote little village, Monticiano, located on the border between the provinces of Siena and Grosseto. I have arranged to meet with Franca Anesa. She is a midwife, a healer and a lightworker. Her home resembles a fairy-tale cottage without a single trace of bad energy. Franca is a passionate advocate of the region's unique cuisine. Here, people cook with seasonal ingredients from the local soil. Even her pots and pans reflect the farm kitchen of days gone by.

Franca epitomizes *cucina casalinga*, home cooking. She knows all the classics by heart. 'I don't need a cookbook,' she says with a smile. Her sparkling eyes and genuine laughter colour the entire room. 'I learned to cook from my mother and my grandmother, and the rest is a matter of course.'

Panzanella

Franca suggests making *panzanella* together. This is a typical Tuscan summer dish. Franca: 'It's a salad made from stale bread soaked in water and vinegar, finely chopped red onions, cucumbers, tomatoes, basil, and plenty of extra-virgin olive oil. The dish's name is a combination of two words: *pane,* or bread, and *zanella,* terrine.'

As we chop the vegetables, Franca explains that this was originally a peasant dish eaten here primarily by farmers and fishermen. 'They used whatever leftover vegetables and bread they had in the salad. It is even believed that the fishermen would dip their bread into the briny water to soften and season it. Traditional Tuscan bread is unsalted,' she notes.

So, the bread is essential to this dish, I continue. Franca: 'Bread has always been a very important part of our culture. It was a staple in both noble and peasant kitchens. They would soak bread that had gone stale in water and vinegar before crumbling it and mixing it with other ingredients in a salad. In the winter, they mostly make soups with bread. The famous bread soup *ribollita* is an example of this.'

221

Although a form of panzanella has been around since the 15th century, cucumber wasn't added until the 16th century, and tomatoes in the 18th century.

'Today, it's considered an open-ended dish where everyone can add whatever ingredients they want,' Franca continues. 'Some people add tuna and hard-boiled eggs, but other options are corn, olives, fennel, lettuce, celery, sausage, carrots, various types of cheese and pickles.' Franca: 'What's important is that you add a bit of salt and pepper at the end and pour a generous splash of olive oil over the top. Then, leave everything to steep in the refrigerator before serving. The flavours need to be well-blended.'

FRANCA'S RECIPE

Panzanella

SERVES 4 PEOPLE
300 g stale bread
2 tomatoes
1 cucumber
1 onion
1 sprig basil
2 tablespoons white vinegar
water
salt and pepper
extra-virgin olive oil

Slice the stale bread into thick slices and soak it for 20 minutes in a bowl with cold water and two tablespoons of vinegar.

Wring the moisture out of the soaked bread and crumble it into a large salad bowl.

Slice the cucumber into not-too-thick slices, dice the tomatoes (seedless, so remove the insides first), and thinly slice the onion.

Place the sliced vegetables on top of the breadcrumbs.

Season the salad to taste with olive oil, salt, pepper and coarsely chopped basil.

Store the panzanella in the refrigerator at least one hour before serving.

The flavours need to be well-blended.

Large parts of the Maremma are protected nature reserves

MAREMMA

We enjoy this refreshing dish together before heading off on a day trip by car. Franca takes me on a journey of discovery to a little-known part of Tuscany: the Maremma.

It is situated along the Tyrrhenian Sea in southern Tuscany and in a tiny part of northern Lazio. Franca: 'The Maremma is home to countless natural riches, such as nature parks, beaches, dense pinewood forests, rolling hills, thermal springs, and archaeological sites. Moreover, this region is still preserved from tourist exploitation.

It's a beautiful ride. There is hardly any traffic on the roads, and the road winds through a panorama of descending hills towards the sea. Franca: 'The Maremma used to be a wild, rugged area with lakes, marshes, and lagoons. Living in the coastal area was dangerous because the marshes were a breeding ground for diseases such as typhus, cholera, and malaria. And, if you didn't succumb to some terrible disease, you could always fall victim to the bandits that terrorized the region. The dangerous marshland was reclaimed during Mussolini's Fascist regime. The malaria mosquito disappeared, and the region became habitable. Nature has profited from the centuries-long absence of human interference. That's why large parts of the Maremma are still protected nature reserves.'

⭐ Tuscan cowboys

I see cattle with long horns in the fields. Franca: 'Those are the typical Maremma cows that are still herded by Tuscan cowboys, the *butteri*. These animals roamed the Maremma when it was still a giant marsh. After the reclamation, they remained together with the cowboys. They still herd the Maremma cattle on horseback and keep an eye on the entire region while doing so. In addition to cattle, the land and shrubland are also home to wild boar, hares, deer, weasels, martens, and badgers. Herons, flamingos, and countless other bird species inhabit the ponds.

Lardo di Colonnata

I drop Franca off at her home in Monticiano and travel the 210 kilometres to Colonnata alone. The famous white charcuterie named *lardo* is still on my list of local delicacies that I need to try. Lardo di Colonnata is a unique delicacy with a refined, rich flavour. This is another example of how peasant cuisine found its way from the countryside to the city. Lardo was the food of the workers in the marble quarries in and around Carrara. Historians believe it's what kept them alive during the Middle Ages. Whatever you do, don't call lardo 'fat'. It is a delicacy, melted on toast or *bruschetta* or spread on a sandwich.

CARRARA ④

The town of Carrara in northwest Tuscany owes its worldwide fame to the approximately 300 marble quarries in the Apuan Alps. These marble quarries, dating from Roman times, are the oldest still active industrial sites in the world.

Michelangelo imported his marble from Carrara. It is also home to the village of Colonnata, the birthplace of the pure, authentic, soft, exquisite lardo di Colonnata. Lardo is bacon with highly pronounced aromas and exceptional qualities. This culinary highlight develops in marble tubs where the fat is left to ripen for months at a constant, cool temperature. With the right seasoning, the lardo develops its distinctive aromas and flavours. Lardo di Colonnata, produced in the village of Colonnata, has an IGP quality label. The recipe is as old as the village itself.

BUTCHER
Giannarelli

Marino Giannarelli is the owner of the family business that his father founded in 1953. I follow him down a marble staircase to one of the cellars. The scent of herbs, cinnamon and meat welcomes me. In a large, underground, cool cellar, several rows of similar-sized, white-grey *conche di marmo*, all sealed with the same lids, stand like toy soldiers perfectly in line next to and behind each other.

Toast with lardo di Colonnata

Marino says: 'We have about 100 marble tubs in our cellars. We place various layers of bacon fat seasoned with sea salt, black pepper, herbs and spices, fresh rosemary, and cloves of garlic in the marble tubs. The tubs remain sealed for six to ten months. The lardo di Colonnata becomes so soft that it melts between your fingers. The marble conche is coated on the inside with garlic. This is the only place where you can make lardo di Colonnata. The marble, the climate, the sea, the herbs, and the people make this product. Only Colonnata holds the IGP label. There are about a dozen producers in our village.'

Larderia Giannarelli
Via Comunale di Colonnata 2, Carrera

Marino next to the marble tubs
where the lardo di Colonnata ripens

Carrara's marble quarries

HEALTHY

Is lardo di Colonnata healthy? 'The fat contains few calories because the bad fats are removed during the ripening process,' Marino replies. 'We add fresh rosemary. This herb contains antioxidants which cause fat loss. A transformation takes place during the ripening process. The rosemary plays and important role in this transformation. This natural antioxidant converts the unsaturated fats into mostly unsaturated fats. The combination of garlic and rosemary makes the transformation possible. We do not use any preservatives or other additives,' Marino assures me. 'The sea salt in the cool marble tubs helps preserve the lardo.'

UNIQUE SPICE BLEND

Lardo di Colonnata links the terroir and the marble with the hard work in the stone quarries. One glance at the landscape, the mountains, the marble veins running down the hillside says it all. The bacon fat is processed with aromatic herbs from the region, dried in the sun and stirred by the sea breeze. The choice of herbs dates to ancient times. Greek stonemasons showed the Tuscans how to cut the marble from the mountainside. They brought their own herbs with them to season their food according to Greek tradition. The rich spice blend in Colonnata has Greek heritage, with black pepper, cinnamon, nutmeg, cloves and star anise seeds, fresh garlic, and rosemary leaves. According to Marino Giannarelli, there is no other charcuterie in existence with such a diverse range of herbs and spices.

LIGURIA

The Liguria region is home to the city of Genova (Genoa) and the world-famous Cinque Terre fishing villages. Liguria is situated in the northwesternmost part of Italy, nestled between mountains, Mediterranean shrubland and a sea of blue. Liguria shares its borders with Piedmont to the north, Emilia-Romagna and Tuscany to the east, and France to the west. The Ligurian Sea in the Mediterranean forms its southern border.

The breathtaking landscapes are a celebration of colour. The Riviera di Levante between La Spezia and Genoa, with its Golfo Paradiso, Golfo del Tigullio, Cinque Terre and Golfo dei Poeti attracts tourists in droves. On the other side of Genoa is the Riviera dei Fiori, a gorgeous stretch of coastline stretching from Imperia to the French border. The shore is high, rocky, and rugged, especially in the region surrounding La Spezia and Genoa; to the west, steep cliffs alternate with fine sandy beaches.

The typically coloured houses of Genoa

The rocky Portovenere coastline in La Spezia

Savona
3

Genova

1

2 **Recco**

Golfo di Genova

San Remo
4

The port of Genoa

TERRA LIGURIA

Ligurian cuisine holds no secrets for historian Paola Cordiviola. I meet her in Genoa. 'The soil here is hard and stingy,' Paola tells me. 'So how do you still get a fine harvest? By making smart use of different heights. Terraces were built and planted with crops such as olive trees and vineyards. Paola: 'Olive oil, dairy products, fruit, vegetables, and aromatic herbs are the building blocks of the *cucina povera* that our gastronomic culture stems from. Our culinary heritage includes *focaccia, farinata, panissa, brandacujun, frisceu, torta pasqualina, fritti misti* and pesto.

Seaport

If you want to discover new products and recipes, a port like Genoa is a perfect place to start. The history of the pasta alone speaks volumes. As early as the 18th century, freshly made and dried pasta from workshops throughout the city conquered the entire world. Today, the quality of Ligurian pasta is renowned far beyond its borders. Pesto genovese is the proverbial 'sauce on the pasta'. This iconic sauce is a permanent fixture in Italian cuisine.

GENOVA ❶

Genoa, *La Superba,* is Liguria's capital. The historical town centre, measuring 113 hectares, is one of the largest in Europe. Together with Venice, Genoa was historically one of the greatest maritime superpowers in the Mediterranean. Trade with the east and the Crusades turned Genoa into a powerful, rich seaport.

I almost get lost in the maze of alleyways called *caruggi.* These alleys are the beating heart of an authentic city. The smell of fish and herbs is everywhere. I see people eating at sidewalk cafés wherever I go. I have to push my way through the crowds. I can't stress this enough: don't take the car into town. The steep town centre is not easily accessible, but the walk is more than worth the effort. Each alley leads to some beautiful historical *palazzo* or church. This city is one giant spectacle of former triumph and grandeur, poverty, and decline, captured in a vast amalgamation of styles and impressions.

Caruggi

The street names betray the trades, personalities and traditions of days gone by. I walk from Via degli Orefici (the former jeweller's way) to the Piazza Campetto (the old blacksmiths' district), climb up Via Garibaldi and land in one of the most beautiful and important districts in the city, the Macelli di Soziglia. Abattoirs and butchers have made this district their home since 1200. The narrow alleyways connect myriad plazas, each with their own churches, all owned by noble families. The thirty historically recognized shops in the old town encompass a variety of trades. They include a chemist's shop, a bottega, pâtissiers, a *tripperia* (where offal is sold), a chocolatier, a silver smith, a bookshop, *trattoria...* You can't help but be taken in by all this authentic splendour. The spirit of Genoa is found in these alleys and shops, where scents, flavours, languages, and cultures blend together. The historical centre is one giant melting pot.

SOTTORIPA

The historical neighbourhood of Sottoripa is situated on the Piazza Caricamento in the old port district around the Piazza Cavour. The fish markets stretch out to Via al Ponte Calvi. These are the oldest public arcades (1125-1133) in Italy. Sotto means 'under' and ripa 'river banks'. The sea used to lap against the foundations of these houses. Sottoripa offered space for trade along the harbourfront. A part of the arcade was destroyed during the Second World War. You will find fish shops and stalls selling fried fish and vegetables.

Farinata fresh from the oven

Trippa being prepared at tripperia la Casana

These savoury pies are typical examples of sciamadde

TORTA di ZUCCA

TORTA DI CIME DI RAPA

TORTA DI RISO

Iconic street gastronomy: sciamadde

Eating 'on the street' is very popular in Italy nowadays. 'What else is new?' my guide, Giulio Burastero, laughs. 'Street dishes have coloured our city since ancient times. *Sciamadde* is the plural for *sciamadda*, the Arabic word for "flame". It refers to the deep-fryers and ovens in the harbour district where people used to make cheap food for the camalli (porters) and sailors. Sciamadde taste like a city that thrives on trade, travel, and the sea.'

Looking for a fast, traditional meal? Try the sciamadde. Which ones? *Farinata, panissa, focaccia, torta pasqualina, frisceu,* fried seafood, fish, or vegetables... Wrapped in *cartocci,* or paper bags, to eat standing up or seated. Savour them as you look out over the sea or as you wander through the old town.

I climb onto the back of Giulio's moped for a tour of sciamadde that have written culinary history in Genoa.

DELICATESSEN
Delizie dell'Amico

Manuel has been a pie maker in a sciamadda since he was 19 years old, making him the youngest in all of Genoa. Twenty years later, he carries on the tradition with passion and an eye for detail. He prepares the most popular pies from the Ligurian recipe book: from *pasqualina* to artichoke pie or savoury pies such as one made with beetroot and a type of ricotta. In addition to pies, he also sells stuffed or fried anchovies and cod beignets.

Le Delizie dell'Amico
Via di Canneto Il Lungo 31, Genoa

DELICATESSEN
Antica Sciamadda

This delicatessen has been making golden, crispy *farinata* in the same oven since 1800. Their other specialities include fried *baccalà, panissa, frisceu,* fried and stuffed anchovies, and savoury pies.

Antica Sciamadda
Via S. Giorgio 14/R, Genoa

The entrance to the Mercato Orientale in Genoa

DELICATESSEN
Tripperia La Casana

Trippa (tripe) has been prepared here since 1890, in the heart of the medieval district, with Annetta Cavagnaro as the erstwhile owner. This shop is perhaps the most intriguing in the entire city. It remained in the family for almost 100 years. Since 1984, Gabriella Colombo has been the driving force behind this centuries-old establishment. The interior feels antique and exudes simplicity. The traditional floor, the vaulted ceiling, the white tiled walls, and the large hood hanging over the copper pots and pans all add to the atmosphere. The shop still has furniture and equipment from the early 20th century. The locals would eat at the marble tables on stools. Their regulars were workers and dock workers who would stop here on their way to work for a bowl of hot trippa soup.

Tripperia La Casana
Vico Casana 3/R, Genoa

MARKET
Mercato Orientale

Giulio and I drive on to the Mercato Orientale (1899). We end up close to the eastern city gate, at the site where a convent once stood, near Via XX Settembre, a shopping street.

The fruit and vegetable stalls look like still-life artworks. The Mercato Orientale is one giant colour palette with plants and fragrant flowers, bright red meat, fresh blue fish, yellow and white cheese varieties, bread, and fresh pasta. You will also find regional herbs such as *basilico di Prà*, the main ingredient of pesto genovese and the olive oil typical of the Ligurian Rivièra.

The heart of the Mercato Orientale is home to a variety of food stalls, bars and the *osteria* owned by one-Michelin star chef, Daniele Rebosio. Traditional Ligurian cuisine with an international touch. You buy your dish at one of the food stands and eat it at one of the tables.

MOG Mercato Orientale,
Via XX Settembre 75/R, Genoa

FISH IN GENOA

If you love quality fried foods and beignets, Liguria is definitely worth a visit. Caterina Conti from Fish'n Street introduced me to street food dishes such as *baccalà fritto*, *brandacujùn* and *sardine ripiene alla genovese*. Her business is situated right next to the Mercato Orientale. Caterina prepares street food dishes with market-fresh fish. The penetrating, pure fish scent is a testament to the fish's Ligurian origins. For her traditional recipes, Caterina uses traditionally prepared batter. And, of course, all these ingredients are closely linked to the region.

Fish stall in the Mercato Orientale

Baccalà fritto

Baccalà fritto

Baccalà, dried salted cod, led to simple yet very refined Ligurian dishes. In the olden days, baccalà was sold along the famous *vie del sale*, the 'salt roads' (read more about this in the Piedmont chapter). The baccalà dishes have a distinctive flavour. Centuries ago, this was cheap food for the poor. Nowadays, you have to dive a lot deeper into your wallet for this relatively scarce cod. Nonetheless, fried cod continues to be very popular.

Brandacujùn

Brandacujùn is a typical Ligurian dish made with potatoes and cod. The baccalà is cooked in water with the potatoes. Garlic, parsley, olive oil, lemon juice and/or lemon zest (slivers), pepper and salt are then added. You vigorously shake the pan – with a special lid – so all the ingredients melt into each other.

There are many legends regarding the origins of the name brandacujùn. Branda is derived from *brandare*, which means to 'shake' in Genoese dialect. That part is pretty much established. The origins of the second part of the name are more nebulous. According to some people, the *cujun* – the dumbest of the group – had to shake the pot. Other people believe that this was the task assigned to the man of the house. He would shake the pot sitting down, causing the pot to touch his private parts, or *cujun*.

Dried stockfish is sometimes used instead of baccalà. You eat brandacujùn cold. It goes wonderfully well with Taggiasca olives and *bruschetta*.

Acciughe ripiene alla genovese

'Stuffed anchovies are a traditional Ligurian peasant dish that was served to use up leftover vegetables and stale bread,' Caterina explains. 'People would finely chop the leftover scraps and combine them with soaked bread to make a tasty, savoury stuffing. People would stuff the mixture into the cheap and highly nutritious anchovies.'

Caterina gladly shares her recipe for stuffed anchovies. 'You need to work with ultra-fresh fish,' she says. When cleaning the anchovies, place them lengthways belly-side down so you can easily remove the backbone and the head. 'But keep the tail on. You can also make this dish with sardines,' Caterina adds.

Fish'n Street
Via Colombo 26/R, Genoa

Acciughe ripiene

Sardine ripiene alla genovese - stuffed fresh sardines

SERVES 4 PEOPLE

400 g fresh sardines
20 g stale bread
60 ml milk
1 clove garlic
5 g parsley
olive oil
2 anchovy fillets in oil
15 g Parmesan cheese (grated)
1 sprig marjoram
1 egg yolk
fine salt to taste

Clean the sardines; remove the heads, innards, and bones. Make sure that the sardines remain whole. Rinse them and leave them to drain.

Pour the milk into a bowl together with the stale breadcrumbs to soak the bread. Finely chop the garlic and parsley and sauté in a pan with the anchovy fillets and the extra-virgin olive oil. If you're aiming for three sardines per person, you will need 12 sardines that can be cut into 24 halves.
The remaining sardines are finely chopped together with the breadcrumbs. Wring the moisture out of the soaked bread. Combine all the ingredients along with one egg, the Parmesan cheese, the marjoram, and a pinch of salt. Mix thoroughly and leave to set for about 10 minutes. You should end up with a firm emulsion.

Take a spoonful of the stuffing and spread a layer over each sardine. Cover with the other half of the fish. Coat the entire fish with the beaten egg, followed by the breadcrumbs, and leave to rest for a bit.

DEEP-FRYING

Fry in hot oil. Fry only a couple of sardines at a time so they don't break. Drain on a paper towel and serve the stuffed sardines with a squeeze of lemon or grated lemon zest.

Torta pasqualina

'Another traditional classic from the Ligurian cuisine is the torta pasqualina,' Giulio Burastero tells me. 'This delicious vegetable pie is available on the menu year-round. You will find them at the *fornaio* (oven bakers), the *pasticceria* (patisseries), and the *panetteria* (bakeries) and in shops, bars and *sciamadde* throughout Genoa. Torta pasqualina contains a filling of chard, cheese, eggs, fresh marjoram and *prescinseua* (a type of ricotta cheese). Traditionally, this pie was made during Easter. The 33 layers of puff pastry reminded people of the age at which Jesus Christ died. Cheap chard was the basic ingredient for the original torta pasqualina. Today, you will also find versions with spinach or artichokes.'

'The "queen of savoury pies" is a typical Genoese dish. According to legend, the whole eggs in the filling referred to the birth of Jesus Christ. The yolks firm up in the oven, and you instantly see them when you slice through the pie. People used to carve symbols into the pie. That's how they would distinguish their own pies from others in the communal village or town oven.'

Torta pasqualina on display

Focaccia genovese straight from the oven

La focaccia genovese at Panificio Mario

You haven't been to Genoa until you've tried *fügassa*. The *focaccia genovese* or fügassa (dialect) is baked over a fire, just like the equally famous *farinata*, the embodiment of street food. Focaccia means 'friendship' in Genoa. 'We give it to each other and eat it together,' Graziano from Panificio Mario in Via San Vincenzo declares. And you will find focaccia everywhere, but Genoa's focaccia is unique. Perhaps it's the sea air and the Ligurian extra-virgin olive oil. At Mario's, the highest quality focaccia has been baked since 1938: golden-coloured, not too thick, well-greased, with the perfect amount of salt, slightly crispy on the outside and soft on the inside.

Graziano: 'The best place to go to for good focaccia is a *panificco* or *fornaio*. They have enough room for the flat bread to proof long enough. The preparation process takes some eight to nine hours. Focaccia is a piece of world heritage for us. We eat it around the clock: for breakfast, with the cappuccino, as a snack, as *merenda*, or with a digestif. Focaccia with flavourful fillings is our comfort food.'

In 1996, 35 Genoese bakers introduced the 'Focaccia genovese' brand. This label protects the product in its traditional form. Focaccia genovese is exclusively prepared with flour, extra-virgin olive oil, yeast, sea salt, water, and malt extract.

Graziano suggests I turn my focaccia upside down before taking a bite. My taste buds instantly taste the salt crystals. Genius!

Panificio Mario
Via S. Vincenzo 61, Genoa

Graziano kneads the dough for a perfect focaccia

FOCACCIA

A typical carùggio or alleyway in Genoa

RECCO ②

Recco lies to the east of Genoa, along the Golfo Paradiso towards La Spezia. Here, the twins Gianni and Vittorio Bisso from restaurant Daö Vittorio tell me how to make real pesto. 'Pesto represents our entire lives!' connoisseur Gianni assures me. 'We grew up with it. We can't do without. We make pasta, vegetable pies and soups with it. Daö Vittorio is a historical restaurant. You come here for traditional Ligurian dishes – and pesto, of course. Vittorio and Gianni are fourth-generation owners. 'Our *nonno* made pesto in the same marble mortar that we still use today,' Vittorio says. 'Pesto is the perfect fit for this region. This simple, flavourful sauce has stood the test of time, just like us!'

Pesto: the quintessential Ligurian sauce

Pesto is an undisputed icon of the Ligurian cuisine. The current version with olive oil, basil, and dried cheese dates from the early 19th century. The pesto was made from a mixture of oily seeds, pine nuts, walnuts, and sour cheese.

DOP

The main ingredient is basil. Real *pesto alla genovese* is made with DOP basil from Prà. This basil is harvested while the leaves are still young, and these smaller leaves have a much stronger flavour. The Ligurian olive oil is extra-virgin olive oil. The cheese varieties also have a DOP label in accordance with regulations from the *Consorzio del Pesto Genovese*.

The sauce is still prepared today as it was centuries ago, preferably the artisanal way: by hand, crushing the leaves in a marble mortar and adding garlic, coarse salt, pine nuts, olive oil, and cheese.

Daö Vittorio
l' Eredità dei Sapori,
Via Roma 160, Recco

The bay at Recco

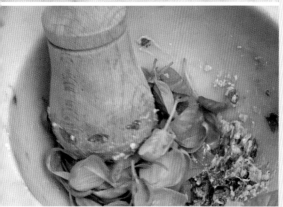

Pesto genovese

SERVES 4 PEOPLE

4 bunches of Genoese basil DOP
  (60-70 g leaves)
One or two cloves of garlic
10 g coarse sea salt
30 g pine nuts (from Pisa or the Mediterranean)
60 g Parmigiano Reggiano DOP
40 g Il Fiore Sardo DOP
60 cl extra-virgin olive oil DOP from Liguria

Roberto, the chef at Däo Vittorio in Recco, shows me how to make authentic Ligurian pesto. You need a marble mortar and a wooden pestle. Wash the basil leaves and leave them to dry on a cloth. Crush the garlic with circular motions in the mortar, then add the coarse salt and pine nuts. Keep crushing the ingredients.

Now, gradually add the basil. Roberto: 'You can't use basil from Naples. It's too dark, and its veins are larger, making it more bitter.' The basil from Prà, a district in Genoa, is light-green in colour with small, crisp leaves. Roberto shows me how the coarse salt soaks up the moisture from the basil. 'This is very important,' he stresses as he continues to grind. 'And it's not as easy as it looks. You need strong wrists and shoulders and a lot of stamina!' I now smell a powerful basil scent.

Roberto adds the Parmigiano Reggiano DOP and the Pecorino Il Fiore Sardo DOP. The emulsion is diluted very slowly with the extra-virgin olive oil. Roberto: 'The Taggiasca olives from near Imperia are sweeter than those from Puglia. A Ligurian DOP olive oil is, therefore, an excellent seasoning for fish dishes, vegetables, and sauces.
Roberto continues to grind the pesto, and I savour the scent of pure basil.
'Never blend basil in a blender,' Roberto advises. 'The leaves become warm and lose some of their flavour. You can only blend basil if you freeze the blades in the freezer before-hand so they're ice-cold during the blending process.'

I try the freshly prepared pesto on a bruschetta. It is a lot of work with the mortar and pestle. This preparation took 20 minutes. A blender only needs 2 minutes. But what a difference! This is phenomenal!

FOCACCIA DI RECCO

My next meeting is in the Golfo Paradiso along the Riviera di Levante in Recco on Liguria's eastern shore. And Recco is synonymous with focaccia with cheese. The *focaccia di Recco* has an unmistakeable flavour. The extravert Biagio Palombo turns this focaccia into a celebration of flavours in his Baracchetta on the sea wall. He has been baking them since 1975, and his thin focaccia filled with cheese is legendary.

RESTAURANT
Il padrino di Recco

I want to know what the secret is of delicious focaccia with cheese. Biagio points at his heart: *ci vuole l'amore.* Love! It's the passion of a man who delivered bread from a local baker on his bicycle as far back as 1955. He now runs his Baracchetta di Biagio together with his wife Anna, his sister Teresa, his daughters Giovanna and Valentina, and his co-worker Andrea. Biagio, born on Saint Biagio's day, is a living institution for the focaccia di Recco. This snack should be eaten at a table with views of the Golfo Paradiso or as you stroll along the sea wall.

With thanks to the Saracens

'Did you know that focaccia with cheese dates back to the Saracen invasions around the year 1000?' Biagio asks. 'The Saracens were notorious pirates and pillagers. People escaped into the mountains. Cheese, flour, and oil were readily available, and that's how the ancestor of the focaccia di Recco started. Our star product was born!'

Biagio Palombo with a focaccia di Recco in his shop

Crescenza cheese is spread between two thin layers of dough

The flatbread has also been designated as a geographically protected product in the past 25 years. The Consorzio Focaccia di Recco col Formaggio promotes the authentic focaccia with cheese. Every year, on the final Sunday in May, they organise the Focaccia di Recco col Formaggio festival.

La Baracchetta di Biagio,
Via Marinai d'Italia 3, Recco

How do you make focaccia di Recco

No one knows how to make focaccia di Recco like Biagio. The man has almost 60 years of experience. 'The dough is made from wheat flour, extra-virgin olive oil, water, and salt. *È tutto!* That's it. Let the dough rest for about half an hour and then roll it out to a slab 1 mm thick.' Biagio: 'This is precise work that requires a lot of practice!'

He now places the thinly rolled-out dough on a greased baking tray on which he places tiny heaps of fresh, pasteurised cow milk cheese. 'We use a crescenza cheese called *invernissi.* It's made from 100 per cent cow milk, produced specifically for focaccia bakers.'

The cheese is covered with a second thin layer of dough. Biagio presses the edges down so the cheese doesn't escape. He pours a drizzle of extra-virgin olive oil over the top. He presses the dough closed and pricks a couple of holes in the top. '*E pronto!* It is ready,' Biagio says. The focaccia goes into the oven, where it is baked for six minutes at 300 °C.

Biagio's friendly and enthusiastic daughter, Giovanna, serves me a plate and a glass of white wine *della spinna*, from the tap. Let the celebration begin.

SAVONA ③

The *farinata* awaits at my next stop. The Vino e Farinata restaurant is situated in the historical centre of Savona, a seaport some 55 kilometres from Genoa in the direction of Riviera dei Fiori.

Ligurian dishes are the stuff of legend. Luca Tortarolo from Vino e Farinata regales me with the story of the farinata. Luca: 'This Savonese dish owes its origins to a historical naval battle. A couple of barrels of oil and sacks containing chickpea flour were destroyed in the hold of a Genoese ship returning from the Battle of Meloria in 1284. The contents mixed with the briny water, turning it into pulp. The following day, the pulp dried in the sun, and the farinata was born.' Fact or fiction? The fact is, once the farinata arrived, it was here to stay.

The 'diva' of 'cucina povera'

Farinata is a peasant cuisine classic, like so many dishes in Liguria. This thin polenta made from chickpeas only contains chickpea flour, water, salt and olive oil. Farinata is a 'child of the streets', wrapped in paper and freshly cut from the typical flat, round, copper testo pot. Preparing farinata requires patience and skilled hands, according to Luca. The mixture of flour and water is left to rest for at least four hours before it goes into the wood-fired oven. Pizzaiolo Pasquale Dell'Apa manoeu-vres the trays into the 400 °C oven with his stick like a skilled acrobat. I'm impressed. Under the watchful eye of customers, he slides the trays to and from the fire until they're ready to cut or serve. Meanwhile, he pushes fresh wood to the fire in the back of the oven without once touching the trays of dough.

⭐ Farinata di Grano di Savona

Farinata is a flat, savoury cake made from chickpea flour. At Vino e Farinata, you'll also find the white version with plain flour. The white farinata is a Savonese speciality. The preparation is the same, but the resulting pastry is crispier. When, in 1528, a sudden heavy tax on chickpeas was imposed – by Genoa – Savona retorted with their own Farinata di Grano di Savona with plain flour. Luca points at the wall. On the wall is a cartoon about the levied tax and what the crafty Savonesi had devised.

Chickpeas were a staple in Ligurian cities at that time. In the interior, people were dependent on chestnuts. The city residents used chickpeas in soups and as flour for the farinata or *panissa*. In Savona, people circumvented the chickpea flour shortage by mixing it with white flour or wheat flour. You will only find this white version in Savona.

Vino e Farinata
Via Pia 15/R, Savona

Farinata, a thick, savoury pancake made from chickpea flour

Fette Panissa

In an alley off a side street from Via Pia in Savona, you will find Marissa Poggi's Fette Panissa. This tiny, well-hidden shop is a magnet for lovers of authentic panissa.

I can barely move in the cramped space. I see a fryer near the entrance, a counter, two racks with shelves stacked with cooked panisse, a table, and a bench for the guests... The furniture has stood the test of time. This eatery is an institution in Savona. Marissa is the fourth-generation owner. She runs this family business together with her husband, Antonio di Sarto. She tells me how she has spent her entire life in the shop of her great-grandmother, Teresa Ferro. The women ran the shop; the tradition was passed down from mother to daughter.

Polenta lookalike

Panissa is a typical Ligurian peasant dish made from chickpea flour, water and salt. The same ingredients are used for farinata, but without the olive oil. For panissa, the mixture is left to cook for at least an hour to form a hard emulsion similar to polenta. You need to stir constantly. The set and cooled mixture is then cut into slices. You can use panissa in a variety of ways. Marissa recommends using panissa in a salad. Marissa: 'In thin slices and garnished with delicious extra-virgin olive oil, salt, pepper, a tiny dash of vinegar and onions. You can also order the panissa fried, as fries or served on a delicious roll.

Marissa: 'I have always made panissa with my heart and soul. Our recipe is the finest of them all!' As it turns out, for real panissa, you need to go to Savona. 'No one still makes them as pure and authentic as we do,' she says decidedly.

Fette Panissa
Vico dei Crema, Savona

Fried panissa

Cooked panissa made from chickpea flour

SAN REMO ④

San Remo lies 100 kilometres from Savona as you head towards France, along the Riviera di Ponente. This is the birthplace of the *sardenaira*, a street dish that even made it to the pages of the American business magazine *Forbes*. I quote: 'This seaside resort is known for sardenaira, a focaccia-style treat with tomatoes, anchovies, olives and capers, a culinary cousin to *pissaladière*, popular across the nearby French border, which uses many of the same ingredients, minus the tomatoes.' That's quite a mouthful.

Carlo Rovere from Pasta Madre in San Remo takes me on a culinary journey through time. The *pissaladière* from the Provence and the French Riviera paved the way. Carlo: 'The sardenaira originated in the 14th century. It was a soft dough, like focaccia, and garnished with onion and salted anchovies.' Not long afterwards, the scent of fried anchovies and onion made its way throughout western Liguria and the valleys.

Pomodori

The tomato was added to the recipe upon its arrival here from South America. The sardenaira from San Remo has a couple of other tweaks. The onions were replaced by tomatoes, garlic and capers, and the anchovies made way for sardines, hence the name sardenaira. Black Taggiasca olives are the proverbial icing on the cake.

DE.CO.

Carlo and a few other artisanal bakers submitted this recipe as a traditional speciality of San Remo. As of 2014, it was awarded the DE.CO. local denomination. The recipe, which is unique to San Remo, is now safeguarded. Carlo is the oldest baker in town with his *fornaio* Pasta Madre. Since 1890, the business has been handed down through the family – from his great-grandparents to Carlo, his wife Vittoria Silvano, and their daughters, Marta and Sara di Paolo Santi. Both daughters run a similar bakery and eatery with the same name in the historic heart of San Remo.

⭐ Don't call it pizza!

'You are not allowed to call a sardenaira a pizza,' Carlo says fiercely. He immediately goes on to highlight the unique character of the dish, particularly the double-proofing process, one of which takes place directly in the baking tray. The ingredients are flour, water extra-virgin olive oil, brewer's yeast and salt. Carlo: 'We do not use any butter or fat, only olive oil!' The thickness and height of the dough also varies. And finally, a lot of attention is given to the way the bread is baked to create a soft product with a crispy base.

San Remo's harbour

Mare e monti

Every municipality has their own recipe. In Imperia, for instance, you have the *pizzallandrea*. 'The San Remo version is the most richly filled,' Carlo believes. The different flavours 'from the sea to the mountains' – *dal mare ai monti* – make the dish. The sardines are fruits from sea, the Taggiasca olives, the garlic, and the olive oil come from the countryside, and the oregano comes from the mountains. The entire terroir is represented in the sardenaira, and that translates to a whole range of aromas and flavours.

Pasta Madre, Corso Matuzia 209, San Remo
Pasta Madre, Via Francesco Corradi 54, San Remo

GAMBERO ROSSO

In San Remo, I also pay homage to a gem from the Ligurian seas: the *gambero rosso*. This delectable crustacean is exclusively bred off the coast of San Remo. Gaetano and sous-chef Paolo Tropiano from Mare Blue restaurant are only too glad to explain. Paolo is convinced that this large, bright red shrimp has the tastiest flesh of them all. Paolo's father, Gaetano, adds: 'Only the San Remo fishermen are allowed to catch gambero rosso.' In October and November, fishing is suspended, so the creatures are given time to reproduce.

'The gambero rosso is sweeter and firmer than an *argentino* or a Sicilian *gambero del Canale di Sicilia*. Both of those are more tender. The San Remo gambero rosso is firmer, even after cooking,' Gaetano assures me.

You can eat this shellfish in a variety of ways, but Paolo likes them best raw, even without salt and pepper. I try a raw gambero rosso outside on the terrace. They do supply me with a separate plate with a lemon wedge, salt, and pepper. The prawn on my plate is completely translucent. 'That means that it's fresh,' Paolo explains. 'The San Remo prawn keeps its eggs in its head; that's why it's so delicious. The absolute finest in the world, according to the real connoisseurs.' Who am I to prove them wrong?

Ristorante Mare Blu
Via Carli 5, San Remo

Sardenaira

The gambero rosso remains firm after cooking

A fisherman on the docks checks his nets

PIEMONTE

Piedmont, situated 'at the foot of the mountains', is a paradise for epicureans. The snow-capped peaks of the Alps form a spectacular setting. Piedmont lies nestled between Switzerland, Valle d'Aosta, France, Liguria, Lombardy, and Emilia-Romagna. It has been the gate to Europe since Roman times. The region fell under the rule of the House of Savoy (Italian: Casa Savoia) after Lombard and French rule. The Savoy nobles followed in the marquis of Ivrea and Turin's footsteps and reigned over the Alps, the French Savoy region, and Sardinia. Grand baroque palaces and fortresses remind us of their glory days. Piedmont led attempts to unify Italy. Victor Emmanuel II, King of Piedmont and Sardinia, assumed the Italian throne in 1861. The Alps, the hills, and the plains are Piedmont's strengths. Both industry and gastronomy found fertile soil here.

However, in this chapter, you will look for wine, *spumante,* truffles, rice, cheese, nuts or chocolate in vain. Other authors have already written extensively about these divine fruits of Piedmont's soil. I discovered a relatively unknown piece of Piedmontese culinary heritage with inspiring dishes from the tradition of 'cucina povera' – peasant cuisine. They thrive in the shadows of the gastronomic greats. Currently, this rich heritage is experiencing a revival thanks to initiatives by the Piedmontese and their organisations.

Turin, Piedmont's unconventional capital

You can explore Turin by tram

Borgofranco
d'Ivrea

2

Torino

1

Asti

3

Bra

4

Genola

5

TORINO ①

Piedmont's elegant, unconventional capital is situated on the Po plain, with the majestic Alps rising in the background. Turin was the first capital of unified Italy. The residences of the Royal House of Savoy have added allure to the city and its surroundings since the 17th century and have been listed as a UNESCO World Heritage site since 1997. Like many cities, Turin is subdivided into districts, each with its own market square. Yet the Turin Porta Palazzo is different. City and regional residents have been selling their wares since time immemorial on this enormous four-square marketplace that marks the crossroads between Via Milano and the Sottopasso Repubblica.

PORTA PALAZZO

I reach the Porta Palazzo from Via Garibaldi and find myself in an outdoor marketplace with stalls. The 'fruit and vegetable zone' lies on the other side of Via Milano. And further along, there's a market hall with delicious fish. I cross the road and spot the meat stalls in the splendid indoor Antica Tettoia dell'Orologio. An antique timepiece hangs over the entrance. From the meat market, I follow Via Milano to the fourth indoor marketplace.

Food market

My guide, Valentina Masuelli, tells me that the large grey building was renamed Mercato Centrale Torino in 2019, following the formula's success in Florence and Rome. Valentina: 'The area around Port Palazzo has been revived thanks to the Mercato Centrale. This 19th-century trade centre is, by far, the most vibrant, colourful place in all of Turin. This is where people trade, yell, sing, talk and eat. Artisanal bakers and millers prepare their own bread and flour on the spot. Farmers from the region sell high-quality snacks. You can choose from *frittura* (fried snacks), hamburgers, *arrosto* (grilled meat), pizza, *arancini, supplì,* artisanal ice cream and much more.

Mercato Centrale
Piazza della Repubblica 25, Turin

Palazzo Castello in Turin with the Palazzo Reale, the Royal Palace

In Turin, water sports are allowed on the Po

LE ANTICHE GHIACCIAIE

Underneath the city, you can find the remains of Antiche Ghiacciaie, or 'antique ice houses' from the late 18th and early 19th centuries. There were no refrigerators back then, so vegetables, fruit, meat, and fish were chilled naturally. A series of subterranean domes was linked by corridors. Valentina takes me to a beautifully restored dome in the cellars of the Mercato Centrale. 'People would line the sides of the dome with ice and place the foods in the middle. The ice was brought in burlap bags from the Valle de Susa. Do you see those thick walls? They kept in the cold, typical for these *ghiacciaie*,' Valentina explains.

I spot the giant, antique city gates, the Porte Palatine in the distance. 'That once used to be the entrance gate to the city,' Valentina says, pointing at the gates. The "Porta Palazzo" was the heart of Turin; as soon as you entered the city, you found yourself in the market square. The ice carriers would bring in the sacks of ice through those gates and then drive their carts filled with sacks to the cellars underneath the Mercato Centrale.'

Antiche ghiacciaie inside the Mercato Centrale

A tramezzino with salmon

Tramezzino

This Italian sandwich is made from two slices of crustless, soft white or wholemeal bread, cut into triangles, and liberally filled with various ingredients. It is the most popular bread in Turin. Millions of Italians eat this delightful sandwich daily, and throughout the day, you see Italians and tourists around the city with this iconic snack in hand. Coffee bars display a fine assortment of homemade *tramezzini*. Laura Vesco from the trendy coffee bar Costarda Social Coffee Factory in the Turin city centre loves the tramezzini filled with anchovies, lobster, truffle, or *bagna cauda* the most, alongside about thirty other popular variations.

**Costarda Social Coffee Factory,
Via Teofilo Rossi di Montelera 2, Turin**

Caffè Mulassano

The first tramezzini were served in the early 20th century at the historical Caffè Mulassano on the Piazza Castello. An worn sign in the bar reads: *'Nel 1926 la signora Angela Demichelis Nebiolo, inventò il tramezzino'*: in 1926, Madam Angela Demichelis Nebiolo invented the tramezzino. The Italian poet and writer Gabriele D'Annunzio (1863-1938) devised the name tramezzino on the spot. D'Annunzio was a longstanding regular at Caffè Mulassano. He would often sit on the terrace outside. His name for the sandwich refers to *spezzafame*, which literally translates to 'hunger-breaker': a sandwich to still the hunger *tra* (between) *mezzo*, between breakfast and the evening meal.

**Caffè Mulassano
P.za Castello 15, Turin**

TURIN, HOME OF THE TRAMEZZINO

Italian cities and regions like to lay claim to ownership of popular dishes. The story of the tramezzino is a straightforward one in that respect. Everything has been fully documented since the birth of this delicious variant of the English sandwich.

Angela Demichelis Nebiolo's husband brought the toaster with them from the United States around 1925. They also experimented with using the bread from the special toasting loaf without toasting it. The trend caught on; from then on, people spread and filled their sandwiches made with two slices of crustless bread. Anchovy and butter became a classic, but nowadays, you will find plenty of other delicious variations.

A tramezzino with anchovies

Caffè Mulassano is situated on the Piazza Castello

Classy and bold, just like a bottle of vermouth

Vermouth

Vermouth is the best aperitif in all of Turin, according to insiders. 'And here it's also referred to as "bibi"', Roberto Bava, chairman of Il Consorzio del Vermouth di Torino, confides in me. Roberto is also the owner of the Bavi and Giulio Cocchi Spumanti Srl wine taverns. Roberto: 'Vermouth is making a comeback. Bartenders offer the finest quality. Vermouth is a basic ingredient in classic cocktails such as Negroni, Manhattan and Americano.' The drink originated in 1786 in Turin with a recipe created by Antonio Benedetto Carpano. He sold vermouth in his wine shop on the Piazza Castello. The shop drew a lot of customers because everyone loved this delicious drink.

A glass of vermouth with ice and lemon peel

Mythical drink

Vermouth turned out to be a big hit as an aperitif, and soon, over thirty local producers were offering the drink on the market. In the 18th century, the Cinzano family started producing vermouth. Their Turin vermouth took the world by storm. Another household name is Martini & Rossi. This company from Chieri, southeast of Turin, dates from the 18th century.

Today, the drink has acquired a cult status, and Piedmont has been officially declared 'zona geografica Vermouth di Torino' since 2017.' Poor imitations are kept at bay with strict quality criteria. 'Each producer has its own product and recipe,' Roberto says. 'The consortium currently consists of 17 authentic companies that produce and export Turin vermouth worldwide: Amarot, Cav. Pietro Bordiga, Fratelli Branca Distillerie, Davide Campari – Milano, La Canellese, Giulio Cocchi, Compagnia dei Caraibi, F.lli Gancia & C., Gruppo Italiano Vini, Martini & Rossi, Valsa Nuova Perlino, Del Professore, Antica Distilleria Quaglia, Giacomo Sperone, Torino Distillati, Tosti1820 and Turin Vermouth.'

Il consorzio del Vermouth di Torino,
www.vermouthditorino.org

Authentic and vintage

Roberto Bava was 20 years old when he started working at his father's wine business (Bava). His father had just taken over the business from Giulio Cocchi, a spumante and vermouth producer. After 30 years of research and development, Cocchi Vermouth has become the most valued Vermouth di Torino internationally. They remained authentic with vintage allure. Roberto and his brother, a herbalist, experiment with new flavours, ingredients and recipes.

Secret recipe

The basic ingredients of vermouth are wine, wine alcohol and *Artemisia* (wormwood, *Artemesia absinthium*). Those are essential. All the other ingredients are kept a secret. You can make your own recipe with any of the following ingredients: liquorice, caramel, aniseed, clove, cinnamon, saffron, rosemary, yarrow, quinine bark, lemon verbena, tarragon, ginger, sweet flag, chamomile, bay leaf, nutmeg, sage, honey, water, sugar. 'Making vermouth isn't difficult,' Roberto argues. 'You can come a long way with just wine, herbs, and sugar. But finding the right balance is no picnic. The exact proportions of the various ingredients are what make the recipes such a well-kept secret.'

⭐ What else?

Roberto lets me taste a selection of cocktails with vermouth, each one purer than the last. We discuss the recipes behind them. Vermouth di Torino is classified by colour (Bianco/White, Ambrato/Amber, Rosato/Rosé, or Rosso/Red) and sugar content. A vermouth with less than 50 g sugar per litre is 'extra secco' (extra dry), and 'dolce' from 130 g sugar per litre. A separate category of Vermouth di Torino includes 'Vermouth Superiore' (17 per cent alcohol) with local herbs and 50 per cent wine from Piedmont.
I decide on the pure Vermouth di Torino with ice and lemon peel. What do you eat with this? Roberto recommends a typical tramezzino or *fritto misto Piemontese*. Bring it on, I think. Vermouth di Torino, what else!

Giulio Cocchi Spumanti Srl.,
Via E. Liprandi 21, Cocconato (Asti)

Grissini Torinesi Artigianali at Sotto i Portici

You eat *grissino* on the street, on the go, with an aperitif or as a *merenda* (afternoon snack). In and around Turin, you will find fresh grissini at the *panifici* (bakeries). Piedmontese don't want to have anything to do with pre-packaged grissini.

I visit penetteria Sotto i Portici in Andazeno. The owner, Vitrotti Luigi, shows me how to make these elegant, crispy breadsticks. I taste freshly baked artisanal grissini.

Sotto i Portici was established by his *bisnonno,* or great-grandfather, Luigi Vitrotti, in 1958. Massimiliano (fourth generation) explains how, before the war, everyone baked their own bread in the community village or town oven. Until the Second World War, the farmers would grind their own flour and then bake bread in the village oven for personal use. After the war, entrepreneurs opened bakeries. At Sotto i Portici, they produce handmade grissini with natural yeast and without preservatives.

Sotto i Portici
Corso Vittorio Emanuele II 18, Andezeno

What are grissini made from?

The flour is refined but not too refined: between 0 (*zero*) and 00 (*zero zero*). Water and salt are added to the dough. At Vitrotti, they make a variety of types. The softest version includes flour, water, salt, and two per cent lard. The traditional grissini contain flour, water, salt, and olive oil. If you use just flour, water, and salt, you end up with a crispier, more brittle version. Other variations include grissini with olives, turmeric or with grains. The artisanal grissini are not only crispier but also much longer. The better you knead the dough, the longer you can stretch out the grissini. Some grissini are 70 centimetres long.

Rubatà

A typical Turin variation is the *grissini rubatà* that you also find at Sotto i Portici. *Rubat* is Piedmontese dialect for 'to drop'. And so, just like in the olden days, the baker throws the grissini on the workbench, making them slightly bent. They are baked in that shape. Massimiliano adds that you usually eat this type of grissini wrapped in *prosciutto crudo.* A grissino is also delicious with *lardo* (a certain type of pork fat from the back of the pig), salami, tapenade, soup, or cheese.

Massimiliano weighs the freshly baked grissini on a scale

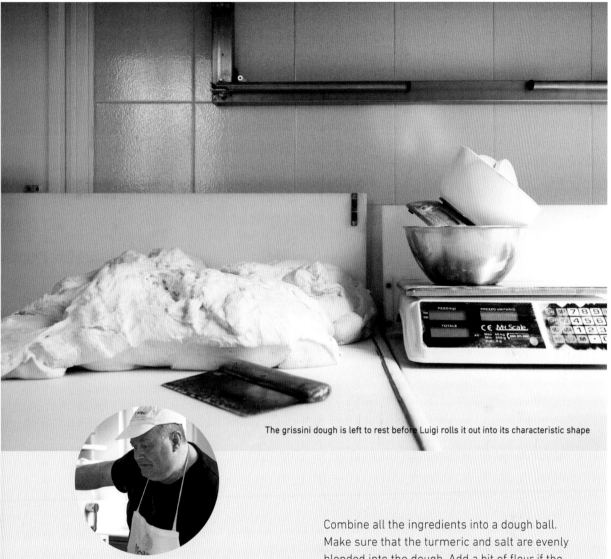

The grissini dough is left to rest before Luigi rolls it out into its characteristic shape

Grissini

MAKES ABOUT 40 GRISSINI

250 g flour
30 ml olive oil
1 teaspoon baking powder
1 teaspoon salt
2 teaspoons turmeric
100 ml water

Combine all the ingredients into a dough ball. Make sure that the turmeric and salt are evenly blended into the dough. Add a bit of flour if the dough is still too wet or sticky. Leave the dough to rest for two hours.

Pull small balls of dough (about 2 to 3 centimetres in diameter) from the dough and roll them between your hands and your work surface into long cylinders about one-half to one centimetre thick.

Bake the grissini on parchment paper in an oven preheated to 200 °C until they turn light golden brown (10 to 15 minutes, depending on the oven). It's best to turn them over as they bake so they brown evenly on all sides. Leave them to cool to room temperature.

ASTI ②

Via del Sale and bagna cauda

The story of *bagna cauda* speaks to the imagination. Anchovies play the starring role. The salted fish has been closely linked with Piedmontese gastronomy since the Middle Ages. But this region doesn't have a coastline, right?

Antonio Campagna from Asti's Angelo del Beato restaurant unveils part of the mystery. He refers to the region's 'past poverty'. People used to bake bread once a week in the village oven. They would knead by hand a dough made from water, flour, and yeast, leave it to proof, and then bake the bread in the oven. Each family was assigned one baking slot per week. And naturally, this was a treasured moment. Antonio's 'mamma' also made sweet bread and grissini for the entire week. Antonio: 'I will never forget those precious moments.' Life was simple back then. Large families enjoyed 'peasant cuisine'. Antonio continues: *'Polenta*, polenta today, polenta tomorrow, and the day after that... more polenta. The menu was predictable, to say the least. Or was it? Because we had anchovies! Polenta with a piece of anchovy made a world of difference. Anchovies provided variation and added flavour to simple dishes. What a revelation! "Finché c'era un'acciuga c'era speranza": "As long as there was one anchovy, there was hope,"' Antonio sums up his story. The anchovy was an inspiration to household chefs, and many Piedmontese dishes to this day contain anchovies: *vitello tonnato, acciughe al verde, salsa verde, salsa rosso, bagna cauda, tramezzini, peperoni alla piemontese, trippa e acciughe* ... it's *un porto senza mare* – a harbour without a sea. What a remarkable story!

Acciughe e sale

The anchovy myth is based on hard facts, such as the story about the 'contrabbando del sale' or salt smuggling along the *vie del sale*, the salt roads. Salt was a valuable preservative. The word 'salario' (salary) dates to Roman times. Back then, soldiers were paid in 'sale' (salt).

If we travel back in time to 800 AD, feudal lords were responsible for the people's safety. They developed protected toll roads, which promoted trade in the centuries that followed. The people, worn and weary from constant plundering from pillagers and barbarians, finally had some sense of perspective.

Many Piedmontese dishes contain anchovies as a seasoning, but the fish can also be eaten raw

The safe through roads were the driving force behind economic development. But this military security came at a cost. The feudal lords often requested excessively high tolls whenever people crossed their territories. If you entered their lands without permission and refused to pay the toll, corporal punishment awaited.

Smart smugglers found a way around that problem. They concealed the valuable 'white gold' (salt) under layers of anchovies. That's why so many anchovies were supplied, sold, and used in peasant cuisine. The anchovies ensured that salt became cheaper. The trade in anchovies continued to be very important in the centuries that followed. It was killing two birds with one stone.

Bagna cauda

Antonio believes that bagna cauda is the most characteristic Piedmontese dish. I try the *piatto povero* with anchovies in Antonio's restaurant, Angolo del Beato, in Asti. Antonio started his business 44 years ago. He has passed the torch to his son, Marco. The menu boasts highly traditional regional dishes with a nod to peasant cuisine.

The chefs, Francesco Galluzzi and Silvio Gai , prepare the delicacies. Before I take a seat at one of the tables, Antonio brings me a large bib. In line with tradition, I wear a beautifully decorated bib for the bagna cauda, which I'm supposed to eat with my hands. And with it, a delicious local wine, of course. The Barbera Nizza is an intense, ruby-red DOCG wine from the province of Asti.

Angolo del Beato
Vicolo Giuseppe Cavalleri 2, Asti

⭐ Bagna cauda kiss
Bagna Cauda Day is celebrated annually worldwide on the last Friday, Saturday, and Sunday of November. This initiative was introduced five years ago by the Associazione Astigiani, which is responsible for promoting the region in and around Asti. In every Italian restaurant, chefs with Piedmontese roots serve bagna cauda. According to Antonio, even restaurants in Tonga (near Australia), Los Angeles and New York serve this dish on Bagna Cauda Day. During the most recent edition, 25,000 dishes were sold worldwide. And on Sunday night, a unique event takes place on Asti's central square: the Bagna Cauda kiss. At midnight, lovers give each other the famous garlic kiss.

The Via del Sale runs high into the mountains

SALT ROUTES
The Via del Sale ran all the way into France. The anchovies from Liguria were transported to Piedmont. The elevated Le Langhe is a mountainous region in Piedmont's Cuneo province. The road to the Alps takes you past villages and hilly ridges offset with deep valleys. The journey was traditionally made by donkey and, starting in the 19th century, with wooden carts. Today, adventurers have rediscovered this route with its secret passageways.

The Alta Via del Sale is a spectacular white *piste* that links the Alps to the Ligurian coast. You walk at an elevation of 1800 to 2100 metres among the mountains.

The road from Limone (Piedmont) to Monesi di Triora (Liguria) runs over 45 kilometres and can only be accessed in the summer – from early June to late September – because of the snow.

Bagna cauda

SERVES 6 PEOPLE

12 cloves garlic
1 egg
water or milk for cooking
1 glass extra-virgin olive oil and
 1/3 glass walnut oil
5 salted anchovies
raw vegetables such as: cardi gobbi or chicory,
 artichoke, white cabbage hearts, endive,
 sweet pepper, fresh onion
cooked vegetables: red beetroot and potato
grilled vegetables: pumpkin and sweet pepper

Cook the garlic cloves in water or milk.
Drain them in a colander once they're soft.
You will no longer need the cooking liquid.
Rinse the anchovies with red wine, and melt
them in a saucepan over heat with a bit of olive
oil. Add the remaining oil and garlic.
Blend everything with a hand
blender and simmer over low
heat for about 30 minutes,
stirring regularly.
Add a knob of butter at the end
to soften the flavour, if desired.
Pour the bagna in a special
fujot. This is an earthenware bowl
with a tea light beneath it to keep the
sauce warm.
Arrange the vegetables in a circle on a plate.
At the end, when almost all the sauce has been
used up, fry a raw egg in the bowl, sprinkled
with grated fresh truffle, if desired.

** Antonio's recipe for bagna cauda is the official
recipe from the Accademia Italiana della Cucina
di Asti.*

BORGOFRANCO D'IVREA ③

Borgofranco d'Ivrea is situated at an exit between Aosta and Turin. Two hundred charming Balmetti houses surround Via del Buonumore at the foot of the Mombarone. Sadly, most of them are empty.

Marco Omenetto, proprietor of the Farinel bar and beer garden, adds life to this party. He is my guide in this desolate village. Marco: 'The people once built these lovely houses because of how the capture the air from the mountains. It is a unique natural phenomenon. The mountain air enters the house through a hole in the cellar. The temperature in the cellars remains constant at 7 to 8 °C throughout the year thanks to this mountain air. Wine growers and brewers used to live here, which explains the barrels in the cellars (17th century). The houses are situated along a street half a kilometre long, named Via del Buonumore, the street of good cheer. Because people visited the cellars to drink and party. I want to bring that back with my project "al Balmet dal Farinel". This village has become a forgotten mystery, just like the *miasse,* a centuries-old street food dish that is rarely served these days. People here used to bake miasse instead of bread. With Farinel, I want to give the miasse – and this village – a new lease on life.'

Miasse al Farinel

To try miasse these days, you have to travel to northwest Canavese, to Borgofranco d'Ivrea and the Biellese Alps. Two years ago, Marco purchased an empty Balmet house with a large garden. Together with his wife, Alexandra, he runs a bar with a terrace and a street food stand in this idyllic location. Marco has been baking miasse for 12 years. When I ask him what miasse are exactly, his reply is brief: 'Crispy, traditional cornbread cooked over the fire.' The flames rise higher in the metal stove. We're going to make miasse over a wood fire. 'Do you see those iron supports?' Marco asks me. 'That's where we'll be attaching the miasse irons later on.'

We bake the thin sheets of cornbread on special preheated iron plates. Marco's skilled hands knead the dough. The original recipe calls for ground maize and water (just like polenta). This used to be food for the poor because you could find maize everywhere. Nowadays, you can find variations with oil, cornmeal, wheat flour, water, egg, and salt, but Marco keeps to the original recipe. He greases the hot irons with bacon fat (strutto) and briefly returns them to the fire.

Freshly baked miasse

Marco prepares the dough for the miasse

Miasse with meat and cheese as a merenda

Miasse on an iron plate in the fire

Simplice e genuine – simple and authentic

The heating irons are warm enough. Marco uses a metal spatula to spread out a thin layer of the maize mixture over the iron plates. He spreads the dough thinly over the plates before returning them to the fire until the dough sets. This takes about three minutes. The miasse are ready. They are at their most delicious when eaten warm. I immediately try one. They taste like a delicious, firm cracker in their plain form. *Semplice e genuine.* Simple and authentic.

Marco now fills the miasse with homemade soft cheese. The Salignùn Canavese is a fresh ricotta cheese with cumin seeds, finely chopped chilli pepper and a sprinkling of coarse sea salt. We also make a miasse with ricotta cheese, anchovies, and sundried tomatoes. Delicious!

The miasse is just as big as the iron plate upon which it is baked: 20 cm x 40 cm. On the counter, I see Toma cheeses, Salignùn Canavese, a boudin (sausage with potato), and a beef salami... all local.

⭐ Birra in Mombarone

We enjoy all this delicious food on a shady terrace with a glass of artisanal wine or beer. The hum of guests' voices fill the background. Marco, laughing: 'This is me reliving my second youth. In my past life, I used to be a pizza baker in Andalusia. But I wanted to return to the mountains and the *balmetti*. Those are the characteristic natural cellars carved from the morainic rocks of the Mombarone massif.

Marco met Alexandra along the way, and they both decided to establish themselves permanently in this abandoned village. Marco exchanged sunny Andalusia for the magical rocks of Mombarone. And with it, he found a new life goal: to put miasse back on the Italian culinary map. I step into the car after all that delicious food and drink. My eye is drawn to the old Birra Livorno brewery along Via del Buonumore. What a shame that this gorgeous building has been empty since 1939.

A hamburger with juicy, flavourful fassona beef

BRA ④

I couldn't continue my journey without stopping in the town of Bra near the hills of Le Langhe first. Different buildings in 17th- and 18th-century baroque styles add colour to this vibrant town centre. What brings me here is the legendary *fassona* or *Razza di piemontese* hamburger. Fassona is a part of this town and this area. I walk to Via Mendicità Istruita. Number 53 has Ox-Burgers printed in large letters on the front of the building. Paola Mechelozzo and Christian Forbes-Bell welcome me warmly. They started this hamburger joint in 2019. And meat from the unique Razza Piedmontese cattle breed features on the hamburger menu. 'If the foundation is good, the rest will follow,' Paola believes. 'Fassona meat is softer, juicier and much tastier than other meat.'

OX Burger
Via Mendicità Istruita 53, Bra

Salsiccia di Bra

You can also order *salsiccia di Bra* on a roll. It is a sausage made almost exclusively from fassona beef. *Sautissa di Bra* is what the Piedmontese call it. And this product has a remarkable story. Fact or fiction? Traditionally, you were only allowed to make salsiccia di Bra with beef. That was good news for the Orthodox Jews because they

didn't eat pork. In all of Sardinia – of which Piedmont was a part at the time – it was forbidden to add pork to the salsiccia. Since 1847, under the reign of King Alberto and the Savoy dynasty, the – certified – butchers in Bra have used beef for their salsiccia. Since then, Bra has been dubbed the capital of salsiccia di fassone.

The meat is mainly eaten raw, but can also be cooked. The salsiccia di Bra is recognized as a DOC product. This protective designation guarantees that only certified butchers from Bra are allowed to make and sell this type of salsiccia. Nowadays, you're allowed to mix a little bit of pork into your beef.

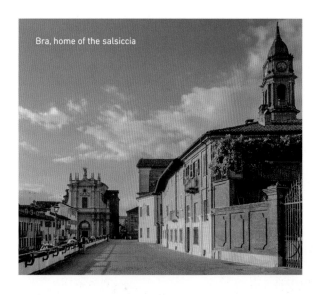
Bra, home of the salsiccia

GENOLA ⑤

After having tried the sausage and the hamburger, I go off in search of the real thing: Razza Piedmontese cattle. My next stop is the La Piemunteisa farm in Genola in the vicinity of Cugno, about 25 kilometres west of Bra. The owner, Paolo Solaveggione, tells his story: 'The *Razza Piemontese* goes back to 1886. One sunny day, an unusual bull was born in the village of Guarene d'Alba in Cuneo province. It was the first time a bull with enormously muscular thighs and buttocks, a so-called "groppa doppia" (double rump), was born. The bull became the forefather of the *Vitelli della coscia,* thick-thighed veal. This natural mutation makes the animals highly suitable for milk, dairy and working the fields. The castrated male calves become larger and fatter.'

I ask Paolo if he knows how many head of Razza Piemontese cattle are in the region. His son, Matteo, immediately surfs the internet to the Anaborapi databank of the association of cattle breeders, or Associazione Allevatori della Razza Bovina Piemontese. Matteo: 'The current count is 300,000 head of cattle.'

It's an exceptional breed, father and son explain enthusiastically. Cattle driver Paolo has only recently become a cattle breeder. He loves to spend time with his cows. In the summer months, he heads into the mountains with his herd. There, the animals enjoy fresh grass, fresh air, and crystal-clear fresh water.

Bull Zalino at the La Piemunteisa farm

PRESIDIUM

The La Granda presidium is the governing body for the various farms where Piedmontese cattle are kept. Sergio Capaldo designed an agricultural model for La Granda: the environment, the land, and the animals form a closed cycle based on symbiosis. It reads like a convention for sustainable farming. The terroir needs the soil and the animals to develop to its full potential. Cattle breeders, farmers, horticulturalists, and foresters work together with one shared goal: quality life and production. Capaldo condemned industrial cattle breeding and offered an alternative. Since the beginning, he has been a proponent of non-genetically modified animal feed. In the presidium, he is a proponent of animal reproduction on the farm and keeping the mother cow with the calves.

Stress-free environment

'Il dottore Capaldo' tells me more about the meat. Sergio leads a commendable project in La Granda in Genola. In 1996, together with 12 cattle breeders, he founded an association for re-evaluating the Piedmontese cattle breed. Today, membership is at 75 cattle breeders. Sergio: 'Our association imposes a few important rules. For instance, the feed needs to be 100 per cent natural and from local soil.' Under no circumstances are antibiotics allowed, I read on the list. 'For high-quality meat, you need the best grain and hay,' Sergio continues. 'Animal welfare is also very important. The calves remain with their mother and grow up in a stress-free environment. We can only produce quality meat from a breed with such unique genetic qualities if we strictly abide by the rules.' Sergio knows what he's talking about. As an experienced veterinary surgeon, he has studied how the animals develop in their habitat.

He linked an economic business model to strict quality regulations. The cattle breeders now cater to a stable market at a correct price. As a result, they put a stop to rural depopulation.

Sergio Capaldo

Slow Food Movement

The Slow Food Movement started in 1986. Their international headquarters are located in Bra. That is also the home town of the movement's founder, Carlo Petrini. Moreover, Bra is situated in a region known for its wine, truffles, cheese, and beef. Carlo Petrini and Sergio Capaldo are good friends. They have strongly influenced each other with their projects, research, and vision. Slow Food means preserving the biodiversity of food sources.

Lean, tender and nutritious meat

The morphology differs per breed. The Piedmontese cattle breed is very muscular, and those impressive muscles are encompassed by a thin layer of fat. The muscles make the meat so tender that you can even eat it raw. The meat contains few veins and digests easily. It is also highly nutritious, rich in unsaturated fats, omega-3, and omega-6 fatty acids, and low in cholesterol, just like fish.

Il dottore

Capaldo lives among the animals in the countryside. He believes that you need to treat animals like children: with love and passion. He proudly shows me a video from one of his partner farms. A farmer rewards a cow for good behaviour with a spoonful of jam. 'That's what I mean,' Sergio laughs. He feels incredibly engaged with the agricultural side of the business, but in his heart, he'll always be a vet. 'I ensured that the stalls were made bigger and that the cattle grew fatter.' Capaldo explored how the animals could add balance to their surroundings. 'We need to be smart about our animals and the pastures in which they graze. We only use organic seeds and manure, so the soil retains its nutrients and minerals. The plant gives life to the soil, and the soil gives life to the plant. Both need to balance each other. You can't reinvent nature. You can only guide them to work together as efficiently as possible,' Sergio explains.

Slow Food

Sergio: 'With this mission in mind, I'm also involved with the Slow Food movement, in particular with regard to the Piemontese breed. Industrial cattle breeding doesn't work for this exceptional breed.' The veterinarian wants to keep the animals in their original surroundings. 'We discovered that the animals suffered more from infections outside their natural habitat,' Sergio says. 'Since we stopped removing the animals from their habitat, they no longer need antibiotics. This indigenous cattle species eats from the soil and gives manure back to the earth. It's an important natural filter.'

Paolo and Matteo Solaveggione

From head to tail

Sergio Capaldo also invested private funds into researching the transformation from meat to dish. He brought chefs together. He promotes the idea that the animals should be consumed in their entirety. Sergio: 'We need to use all the parts of the animal! We haven't forgotten about tradition. People spend less time in the kitchen nowadays, so they only use the quickest and easiest parts. But you can prepare the entire animal, from head to tail.

Eataly

Sergio: 'I was a veterinarian when I met Oscar on vacation, purely by accident.' Oscar Farinetti is an Italian businessman and investor and the owner of the high-quality Italian Eataly food outlet chain.
'One night, we started talking, and before we knew it, we were eating together and making plans until four o'clock in the morning,' Sergio remembers. 'Our project was starting to take shape! Oscar asked me to stop working as a veterinarian and join the Slow Food movement. That was in 2002, but I waited another two years and did some thorough research. I introduced Oscar to my work, the Piedmontese cattle breed and the meat dishes. We started to experiment, and in 2007, we founded Eataly. I was responsible for the meat.' Sergio is now a partner in the international Eataly business. He selects the butchers and agricultural businesses for membership, and he determines the rules – in Italy and abroad.

Slow Food is founder Carlo Petrini's life's work. Sergio and Carlo have been friends from the very beginning. Sergio: 'Everything started with my passion for wine. Petrini shared my passion, and that's how we got to know each other. One day, he said to me: "If you can organise a label for high-quality meat, just like we do for wine, I will help you," And that's how we got the ball rolling.'

Fritto Misto piemontese

This fried dish is a Piedmont classic. You cut parts from the cow's head and the *animella,* or veal sweetbread, into fine pieces and coat them with flour before deep-frying them. The cow's spinal cord is another deep-fried delicacy. The fried meat is served in a bag or placed on a piece of cardboard. A couple of drops of lemon over the top, and that's it. Or would you rather have enjoyed this dish in blissful ignorance?

Three fine Razza Piemontese beauties

Tartare with Piedmont beef

Alternative cuts of meat

'The best dishes come from the peasant cuisine,' Sergio explains. *'Il carre* (loin) and *il filetto* (fillet) don't belong in traditional Piedmontese cuisine. People used to mainly eat the liver, the spleen, and the stomachs. In contrast to the Tuscans, the Piedmontese didn't eat the fourth stomach but did eat the three other stomachs: the *rumine, reticolo* and *omaso.'* The *guanciale* (beef cheek) is also delicious. Add a bit of lemon on top or a salad on the side, and you have a delightful meal. Sergio loves its sweet taste. All you need is a dash of salt and pepper for a first-class dish. 'Nothing from the animal goes to waste!' Sergio says. 'And this is also important from a commercial viewpoint. You will only earn a profit if you use all the parts of the animal. The meat from Piedmontese cattle is very delicate. You need to prepare it properly, and this takes time. You should never add too many other flavours. The tail, for instance, is skinned and deboned, a time-consuming process. The tail meat is delicious in a roulade.

⭐ Sono Italiano e mi piace mangiare!

We explore the Razza Piemontese's culinary qualities with a menu where the less evident pieces of meat are also used. The chefs let their imagination run wild: finely ground liver on toast, tripe kebab, raw hamburger, roasted steak tartare... And I discover that the pure meat is delicious. Sergio joins me at the table. He clearly enjoys the dishes he has helped devise. Sergio: *'Sono Italiano e mi piace mangiare!'* – I am Italian, and I love to eat!' I'll definitely drink to that. We have a bottle of nebbiolo wine to go with this delicious food. A wonderful experience at La Granda in Genola that I won't easily forget!

La Granda
Via Garetta 8/A, Genola (Cuneo)

Landscape in Cuneo province

VALLE D'AOSTA

Valle d'Aosta, Italy's smallest region, is grand. I feel like I'm in a movie in this valley surrounded by impressive mountains. It's a fairy tale with an edge. Four mountains more than four thousand metres tall tower above the valley: the Matterhorn, Monte Rosa, Mont Blanc and Gran Paradiso. Only the latter is entirely on Italian soil and the nature reserve that is named after it, which also happens to be the oldest in the country, is my favourite place in the Alps. The valley owes its name to the town Aosta, which has proudly withstood numerous natural disasters and foreign rulers. Impressive castles stand watch over the important through route that Valle d'Aosta has always been.

Fontina cheese production
in Valle d'Aosta

Valpelline
2

1
Aosta

3
Saint-Marcel

Aosta, the city of emperor Augustus

The Lillaz waterfalls near Cogne

AOSTA ①

My journey of discovery starts in the city of Emperor Augustus. Aosta was founded in 25 AD as a garrison town along one of the routes to Gaul. The Arco d'Augusto welcomes me to the city. A straight road cuts through the car-free city centre from east to west. The city's importance flourished with the increase of trade in the 10th century. Aosta became a part of the Savoy region in 1027. This county later became the Duchy of Savoy. Aosta is bilingual, just like the rest of the valley; the second official language is French.

Merenda valdostana

The *merenda valdostana* or *merenda sinoira* are perfect for eating with your hands and standing up. Everyone loves them. This type of merenda has the simplest, purest, and most authentic flavours and is typical of cucina povera (peasant cuisine) in the Aosta Valley.

★ Asterix-style

In the Aosta Valley, not only what you eat but also how you eat counts. When you order a merenda valdostana in a bar, café or restaurant, this afternoon treat is always lovingly prepared in Asterix-style. The cheese and cured meats are a homage to father (*papa*) and grandfather (*nonno*). For them, the merenda or afternoon snack was not just a quick snack, but a coming home after a day of hard work. The warm stove and the food kept the cold and the exhaustion at bay.

The *Valdostani,* the residents of the Aosta Valley, looked forward to the evenings as a time to warm themselves up. During the merenda (from 16:00 to 17:00), they liked to sit down with a large plate of cheese and cured meats, 'Opinel' knife in hand. This French knife with a wooden handle reminds me of Asterix. The meats and cheeses were eaten with dark bread and a glass of homemade wine. Later in the evening, a light meal of soup, pasta or milk with bread would be served. The merenda sinoira is a journey back in time.

PURE NATURE

The Aosta Valley is home to Italy's oldest nature reserve, Gran Paradiso. These lands were once Victor Emmanuel II's private hunting grounds. Thankfully, everyone can enjoy this park's natural beauty today. It's a paradise for walkers, hikers, mountain biking enthusiasts, and climbers. The region boasts 475 kilometres of walking trails. You come across dense forests and picturesque villages, luscious Alpine meadows and babbling brooks. The deep mountain lakes and impressive waterfalls are a sight to behold. Along the way, I see chamois, ibex, and entire colonies of marmots, hawks, and owls.

Nostalgia on a plate

The magical merenda was – and still is – a moment to look forward to. The bartender who prepares your order spreads the honey over the black bread with care and a touch of nostalgia, respectfully places the cooked chestnuts, the piece of goat's cheese and the salami on your plate. You're allowed to use your hands, and you're welcome to talk, laugh, roar, sing and cry. If you order this merenda in a bar after a day of hiking, mountain biking or skiing, you'll experience how a farmer feels after a day of working the fields.

BAR
Taglieri tipci

Paola Arvat and her husband Alex Creter from Bar Risto Celebrity in Aosta treat me to a merenda valdostana. This eatery recently opened its doors. Their impressive menu boasts regional products. More impressive still are their merenda dishes, or *taglieri tipici*, typical dishes with various types of cheese, ham, fruit, jam, nuts and bread. It is hard to choose, but I eventually settle on the traditional valdostano. They serve mostly craft beers and local wines with their dishes. I select a local red fumin wine on Alex's recommendation.

Bar Risto Celebrity
Via De Lostan, 27, Aosta

Jacopo enjoys a delicious sandwich with artisanal cured meats

Pane nero

Regional products

This merenda valdostane is served throughout the region. The ingredients vary from town to town. Dark bread (*pane nero*), Vallée d'Aoste Jambon de Bosses DOP, a type of black pudding: *il Boudin*, La Mocetta di Bovino (similar to *bresaola*), Toma di Gressoney (a typical mountain cheese), *formaggio di capra a pasta molle* (a soft raw goat cheese), Bleu d'Aoste (blue cheese), Fontina DOP and nuts, chestnuts, or figs, are standard. Paola and Alex tell me about the region's history and products with great relish.

And when I taste all that delicious food, I decide that you should probably eat the merenda on an empty stomach and scrap any plans for a heavy evening meal.

Merenda valdostana

VALPELLINE ②

Non è un fromaggio, è fontina!
This is not cheese; this is fontina!

I drive 43 kilometres from Aosta to Valpelline. This is where I hope to find out more about the Aosta Valley *fontina* cheese, at an elevation of 1147 metres. I meet Ezio Toscoz, director of the Cooperativa Produttori in Latte e Fontina. We meet in a building beautifully situated among the rocks above the village of Valpelline.

The milk and fontina producers' cooperative (1957) coordinates the ripening, marketing, sales and logistics of the cheese. Fontina itself has been around for over 800 years. The first mention of fontina appears in a document from 1270.

A small army of farmers and cheesemakers is involved in the production of fontina. The consorzio collects the cheese wheels for ripening and processing. The cooperative has about 200 partners, 150 of which are producers. Thanks to the association, fontina has become a homogeneous product, production costs have been lowered, and no milk is wasted. This has allowed fontina to grow and conquer the global market. The optimal use of natural (mountain) resources safeguards sustainable production, and high-tech production techniques contribute to the cheese's quality. The entire process is under strict regulation. The farmers can't produce everything themselves. You need 100 litres of milk for one wheel of fontina, and you are not allowed to reuse milk from the previous day or morning milk in the afternoon. That means the smaller farmers bring their milk to a cheesemaker from the consorzio.

The ritual of washing, turning, and salting fontina cheese wheels

DOP

Since 1996, fontina has been recognised by the European Union as a DOP (Denominazione di Origine Protetta) product. A law guarantees that only fontina cheese from the Aosta Valley may be sold. The cooperative has been monitoring the cheese quality for over 50 years by imposing very strict production processes and rules. The raw milk is processed into cheese within two hours of being milked. The cheese is made twice a day because the cows are milked in the mornings and the evenings. The milk comes from indigenous breeds such as the *Valdaostana bianca-rossa* (light-brown and white), *Valdaostana nera-bianca* (black and white), *Valdaostana castania* (brown). The animals eat exclusively local feed, grass and hay from the fields and hills of the Aosta Valley.

This is how the tradition, the original character of the cheese and its unique flavour are preserved. Cattle breeding is still an important sector for the region's economy; about 17,000 head of cattle produce milk for fontina cheese.

Cows enjoy pure water and fresh grass in the more elevated areas during the summer

Alpeggio

Every year, in late May, the farmer takes his cattle to the *alpeggio* (pasture) high in the mountains according to tradition. The cows eat fresh grass there at different elevations. Each elevation has stations with stalls, materials and milking facilities. The cattle farmers take their animals higher each time, looking for fresh grass. The milk is immediately converted into cheese.

The alpeggio season lasts about 100 days. The low meadow grass is highly nutritious, with lots of flowers. The resulting milk is much fattier and more aromatic. Moreover, the animals drink pure mountain water.

In September, the animals descend from the mountains, stopping at the dairies along the way. Some cows are adorned with a bouquet of flowers on their heads. The most dominant cow wears a bouquet of red flowers, and the milk champion is adorned with a bouquet of white flowers. The herds are welcomed back to their villages in festive triumph. By then, it's early October. Some villages organise huge celebrations with parades featuring the cows and lots of delicious food. Isn't it wonderful to see how traditional and artisanal mass production can be!

Staggionatura

The elevation is very important for the cheese ripening process. The temperature must not exceed 10 °C, and the air must be very humid (almost 100 per cent humidity). And those conditions are only found in a unique location. Ezio is my guide. We walk to a cave. A delicious scent wafts up from the cave, and the view is spectacular. A seemingly endless supply of fontina cheese wheels rests on wooden shelves in the rock face. They all undergo the daily ritual of washing, turning and salting. I lose myself in this maze of passages among the ancient rocks and the countless wheels of cheese.

'The production of fontina has been of great social-economic and cultural importance over the centuries. Fontina is an essential ingredient in many dishes worldwide, such as risotto, gnocchi, cannelloni, ravioli, portobello mushrooms...' Ezio continues.

Centro Visitatori Fontina
Frazione Frissonière, Valpelline

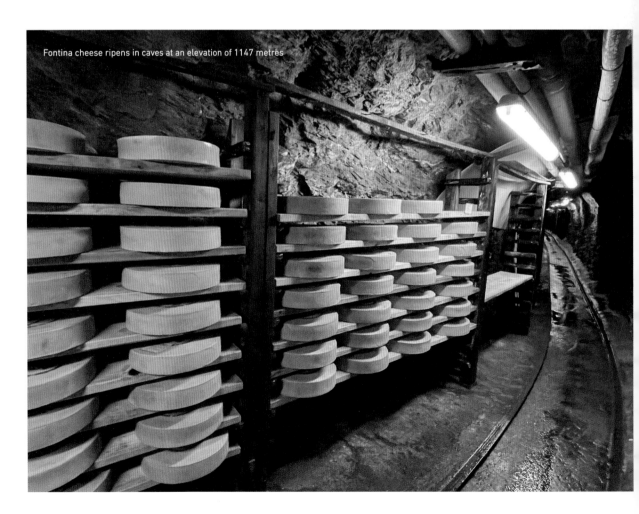

Fontina cheese ripens in caves at an elevation of 1147 metres

Zuppa valpellinese

SERVES 5 PEOPLE

½ savoy cabbage
200 g fontina
200 g rye bread
100 g lardo (bacon)
50 g butter
750 ml meat
   or vegetable broth
salt

Make a delicious meat or vegetable broth for this dish. Wash the savoy cabbage. Remove the outer leaves and the hard centre. Fry half the butter with the lardo over low heat.

As soon as the butter and the lardo have melted, arrange the savoy cabbage leaves on top. Add a pinch of salt and simmer everything covered over low heat. As soon as the savoy cabbage is tender, turn off the heat.

Slice the fontina into thin slices and set aside. Take a round, tall oven-proof dish and grease the dish with butter. Place the rye bread on the bottom of the dish. Arrange a layer of savoy cabbage on top, followed by a layer of fontina cheese. Top with a second layer of bread, followed by another layer of savoy cabbage.

Pour the meat or vegetable broth over the top and finish with a final layer of fontina. Place the dish on a tray to catch any broth or cheese that may run over. Bake the dish for about 40 minutes at 180 °C.

Artisanal processing of Saint-Marcel ham

SAINT-MARCEL ③

From Valpelline, I drive another 23 kilometres to Saint-Marcel. Great things happen in this mountain village. The air is pure, the water sparkles, and everything smells of wildflowers. Since the 15th century, people in Saint-Marcel have been making ham for the Aosta Valley's rich nobility. From time immemorial, pigs have been farmed in the Alps for personal use. And whenever the pigs were slaughtered, they would stock the meat. Meat and bacon were coated in salt and seasoned to be preserved. A few families succeeded in curing ham with salt and mountain herbs. The recipe has been lost to time because the farmers processed their meat at home, behind closed doors. But in 1985, the age-old recipe was resurrected by La Valdôtaine.
A few passionate businessmen decided to re-introduce the original recipe. The Prosciutto Crudo di Sain-Marcel brought local tradition back to life. And suddenly, the Aosta Valley was a first-rate ham richer.

Unique flavour

Paolo Fabris from Valdôtaine explains what makes this ham so special. 'It's about Italian DOP meat. We season the ham with herbs and sea salt and leave the meat to ripen naturally in conditions with a dry microclimate. The saturated fats are converted into healthy fats. It's also how the meat develops its unique flavour. There are countless producers of *prosciutto crudo* or raw dry-cured ham in Italy. Nine million Parma hams and three million San Daniele hams are sold each year. It is believed that each year, a total of 30 million whole prosciutto are sold in 58 different varieties.'

Paolo strives to produce quality. Saint-Marcel represents a unique flavour. Paolo: 'We limit our annual production. Saint-Marcel is an artisanal niche product.

This ham is relatively unknown outside of the Aosta Valley. We focus on the local market. Promotional activities such as our Via del Prosciutto help us gain local recognition.'

Ripening the ham is a highly delicate process. At Valdôtaine, the ham is left to ripen in dry air in a well-ventilated area with a stable temperature. During the ripening process, the herbs that are rubbed into the fat seams on the outside of the ham penetrate deep into the ham. Saint-Marcel's dry micro-climate completes the picture. The pure ham tastes like a fruit of nature, an experience I savour to the fullest. Valdôtaine in Saint-Marcel undoubtedly has plenty of potential, but I agree it should remain a niche product.

PROSCIUTTIAMO

In 2015, Paolo opened his own *merenderia* at the foot of the mountain, inspired by the success of the merenda and the *tagliato e mangiato*, or cut-and-eat formula. Here, you can try hams, beverages, and regional products from the Aosta Valley.

Valdôtaine's merenderia became the starting point for the Via del Prosciutto, a route that you can follow on foot, by bicycle, or by car. Paolo designed an entire route with stops at bars, restaurants and viewpoints. The route is 18 kilometres and ends at an elevation of 1819 metres at the 'Servettes' viewpoint.

In the third week of July, the local Prosciuttiamo team organises an annual three-day event around the Via del Prosciutto, with the Saint-Marcel Prosciutto in the starring role. Together with the eateries along the route, the organisation offers tastings and other fun events. You taste cured hams at different elevations. It's a three-day extravaganza with cycling, Nordic walking, yoga, country dancing, concerts... and food!

Sciatt

You will also find 'Sciatt' on the menu during the festivilies. It is a typical snack from Valtellina in the Alps, a member of the *fritture* or fried delicacy family. What makes them special is that they're made with buckwheat flour, with a delightful piece of fontina cheese in the centre. It is an easy and quick dish.

Sciatt

SERVES 5 PEOPLE
150 g flour
100 g buckwheat flour
20 ml grappa
250 ml blonde ale
750 ml sparkling water
fine salt
pepper
200 g fontina cheese
peanut oil for frying

Make sure that the liquids for the dough are chilled. Remove the crust from the fontina cheese and dice it into 1- to 1 1/2-centimetre cubes.

Freeze the diced cheese cubes in the freezer so they don't immediately melt when they're being fried. Freeze them for no longer than 15 to 30 minutes.

Combine the flour with the buckwheat flour in a bowl and add the salt and pepper. Combine everything with a whisk. Add the beer and the water. And last but not least, the grappa. Whisk everything with a whisk until the batter is runny and doesn't contain any lumps. Briefly chill the batter in the freezer.

Meanwhile, heat the oil in a cooking pot until it's warm enough that it sputters when you drop a drop of water into it. Take the cheese and the batter out of the freezer. They should be well-chilled by now.

Coat a cheese cube with the batter. Use two tablespoons to do this. This is also how the sciatt gets its irregular shape when you slide it into the oil. Gently drop the batter-coated cheese in the soup ladle into the oil.

Each cheese fritter should fry for no longer than a minute. Turn them over regularly so they brown evenly on all sides. Eat the sciatt while they're still hot.

At Valdôtaine, essences from the finest alpine plants are transformed into unique alcoholic beverages

Alpine distillery

Ham isn't the only product produced in Valdôtaine. I also visited a small distillery from 1947 with the same name. The alcohol and its derivatives follow an impressively convoluted path through the antique copper distillation flasks and pipes. Time has come to a standstill here. Anna Maio explains: 'We operate the alembic, or still, by hand. We produce small quantities of alcohol using artisanal methods: gin, vermouth, vodka, grappa, bitter liqueurs and amaros. The rare mountain flowers and herbs in the grappas and other liqueurs create a unique flavour palate. Water from the Acqueverdi spring near Valdôtaine adds character to these spirits. Rare minerals colour the spring water, giving it a turquoise hue. Truly magical,' Anna reveals.

**Valdôtaine and Le Merenderie,
Zona Industriale 12, Saint-Marcel, Aosta**

Wine in the Aosta Valley

Francesco Agresti from the Les Crêtes winery says that the Aosta Valley is a challenging environment for wine production because of its extreme conditions. 'We have a lovely, dry microclimate. We keep the vineyards and harvest the grapes by hand on the steep flanks. Our region has the smallest appellation with just 750 are of vineyards. You will not find vineyards at elevations like these anywhere else in Italy. We are nestled between the peaks of the Mont Blanc and the Matterhorn. And it's those peaks that give the grape its distinctive character. The cold and the variation in temperature means the grapes take longer to ripen, giving them an intense flavour. I discover a whole range of local, unique grape varieties: petit rouge, fumin, petite arvin, torrette ... 'Wine is still the second-largest product in the Aosta Valley after fontina,' Francesco says.

You will not find vineyards at elevations like these anywhere else in Italy except the Aosta Valley

Small houses on the hills

Les Crêtes is a pioneer in wine production and sales in the Aosta Valley. Today, the region is famed for its wine. Les Crêtes was established in 1980 by Constantino Charrère. The founder of the Mont Blanc ski school saw potential in the production of wine. During a drive through the hills of the Aosta Valley, particularly around Aymavilles, I recognize the Les Crêtes vineyards by the tiny houses atop the hills.

**Les Crêtes,
Soc. Agr. di Charrère & c.s.s. Aymavilles, Aosta**

BLENDING WITH REGIONAL PRODUCTS

Constantino's daughter, Elena Charrère, recommends a red Fumin Valle d'Aosta because it has a lot of texture and pairs nicely with the local cheeses and charcuterie. But the Syrah Valle d'Aosta is also a fine accompaniment to fontina or toma cheese. On the white wine front, the complex Fleur Petite Arvine Valle d'Aosta is a good choice with antipasti.

In the autumn, the cows descend from the mountains and return to the Aosta Valley

LOMBARDIA

Lombardy, the fourth-largest region in Italy, borders Switzerland to the north, Trentino-Alto Adige and Veneto to the east, Piedmont to the west and Emilia-Romagna to the south. Milan, Lago Maggiore, Lake Garda and Lake Como are famous tourist attractions. Lombardy has also been Italy's wealthiest region since the 18th century. The region has been able to retain this position through a strong artisanal tradition combined with Germanic and Anglo-Saxon innovations.

I Navigli, the district between Milan's two canals, the Naviglio Grande and the Naviglio Pavese

Rice is grown near Pavia

Lago Maggiore

Lago di Varese

Lago di Lugano

Lago di Como

Adda

Como

6

Valtaleggio

5

4 **Gandino**

Adda

3

Bergamo

Lago Idro

Lago di Garda

Milano

1

Ticino

Adda

2 **Pavia**

Po

Po

Po

TOP-QUALITY PRODUCTS

Lombardy delights with its versatile products and flavours. The region's economy is based on industry, the service industry and dynamic agriculture. Moreover, Lombardy values its high-quality products.

Food is inextricably linked to the cultural identity of Italy's regions. Various areas within Lombardy have their own specialities: wine from Oltrepò Pavese, Franciacorta and Valtellina, olive oil from Garda Bresciano, rice from Lomellina, meat and cheese from the Alpine valleys.

High-quality food is anything but an empty slogan here. Lombardy is home to 34 DOP and IGP products, 41 DOCG DOC and IGT wines and 250 traditional products. And it's no coincidence that it's the birthplace of numerous world-renowned specialities such as Grana Padano, Bresaola, Taleggio, Gorgonzola and Franciacorta that have all been elevated to world heritage status.

Where does all this richness come from? The region's favourable location, in combination with the tremendous organisational talent and innovative power of local businesses. This culture of excellence is embedded in Lombardy's DNA.

Cucina povera born of necessity

Until the 1950s, Lombardy was a region with a varied social strata and great social-economic diversity. While the rich had everything they could wish for in terms of food, the poor had to make do with what little they could find. The result? Original experiments and improvised dishes that add colour to the local cuisine. The Lombards are experts in transforming scarce foods into culinary delights and cleverly using last week's leftovers in this week's dishes.

Rice and polenta form the historical foundations of the region's cuisine. The menu also boasts a variety of filled pastas. But, you won't find any pasta in this chapter. Instead, we will pay homage to lesser-known yet unique regional dishes.

My journey starts in Milan, Lombardy's capital, with the story behind the typical street food known as a *panino*, a filled sandwich. The panini cult has achieved religious status here.

It didn't take long for the panino to capture Milanese hearts

Numerous terraces line the waterfront in Milan's trendy Navigli district

MILANO ①

Milan is the capital of the province of the same name and the Lombardy region. Art, fashion, history, and delicious food reign supreme here. The cathedral or Duomo (dedicated to Santa Maria Nascente), the Castello Sforzesco and the Galleria Vittorio Emanuele II are musts during any city visit.

Italians from all over the country moved to Milan and brought with them new impulses for the food scene, leading to a varied selection of foods. The Milanese panino, the stuffed sandwich roll, conquered Milanese hearts. The *spezzafame*, or 'hunger-breaker' snack of the past, is now a richly-filled panino.

Real panini breathe Milan

In the 1980s, panini culture was inspired by young people with their distinctive language and specific clothing styles. They were casual, hip, and hung around at the sandwich bars, which sprang up after the crisis in the 1970s. The Milanese panini contain ingredients from all over Italy, and the toppings were designed to catch the eye. In Milan, a panino is a fashion item, a visual delight. The more beautiful and original the sandwiches, the more famous the clientele flaunting them. Panini are often displayed in beautiful showcases or served in trendy bars with a delicious cocktail or espresso. A real panino just breathes Milan.

Sandwich at bar Quadronno

Panini culture led to the rise of retail chains in and beyond Milan. It became a triumphal procession for countless visionary entrepreneurs specialising in the art of daily fast food. I wander through the city in the footsteps of these unique urban icons. What explains the Milanese panino's tremendous success? My quest takes me past breathtaking monuments and spectacular shops, the inspiring Navigli district, beautiful squares, clean streets, and friendly, well-dressed people.

Très m'as-tu-vu

My starting point is the Porta Romana, one of the four side gates south of the city (easily accessible via the Porta Romana metro station). Even celebrities often come here for a Milanese panino or to take one to go. The Pasticceria Gattullo is one of those historical patisseries. Giuseppe Gattullo, alias 'Peppino', established the bakery in 1961. To keep up with the times, he supplemented his traditional sweet pastries by introducing aperitifs, cocktails, and his cousin Domenico's legendary sandwiches. Milan's elite instantly fell in love with his creativity. Now practically a household word, his *triplo special* features cooked ham, *fontina* cheese (warm), goat cheese, foie gras and a pink sauce divided between three slices of bread (hence the name 'triple special').

Pasticceria Gattullo,
Piazzale di Porta Lodovica 2, Milan

Trendsetter

I walk along Via Quadronno to Bar Quadronno. This bar is a pioneer among Milanese sandwich bars. This is where, in 1964, the idea originated to top bread with gastronomic delicacies and sauces. It was a minor revolution because, at the time, bread was simply topped with ham, cheese or salami. The formula was an instant success. The panini Quadronno with tongue, tomato, tabasco, and a secret sauce were always sold out. Quadronno has been a Milanese 'must' ever since. You can visit at any time during the day or night, even until 2 AM.

Bar Quadronno,
Via Quadronno 34, Milan

Giuseppe Zen from Macelleria Popolare

DARSENA

I continue my walk to the Corso di Port Ticinese until I reach the Porta with the same name at Piazza XXIV Maggio. This square was renovated for Expo 2015. This is where Milan's old port is situated: the Darsena. This canal system originally linked the Po River to the region's various lakes. The harbour and the canals – which were used at the time for freight transport and as a water supply – are now back in use. The stroll along the waterfront, past the canal district's restaurants and bars, is an enjoyable one. My panini compass has me firmly pointed in this direction.

Lampredotto sandwich at Macelleria Popolare.

Visionary 'hunger-breaker'

Macelleria Popolare is located in the indoor market in the city's port district of Darsena. My senses are on high alert as I enter this delightful slice of Milan. The owner, Giuseppe Zen, has built his own piece of gastronomic paradise in this waterfront market. The only thing that matters here is quality: from the meat to the cheese, the grains for the bread and the wines served. Giuseppe Zen is a visionary butcher known throughout Milan as the owner of Mangiari di Strada in Via Lorenteggio. At Macelleria Popolare, he personally greets his guests and explains to them which meat is on offer and what makes it so special. You can try the meats and cheeses accompanied by a glass of wine, or you can take meals with you to go. There's seating room along the counter and at the tables outside. The focus here is on honest, sustainable food. I order a delicious crunchy toast with tartare. Pure perfection. On Giuseppe's recommendation, I order a refreshing glass of white Manzoni Bianco Fontanasanta Foradori wine from the Dolomites. Passionate, pure, authentic; let the sparks fly!

Macelleria Popolare
Mercato della Darsena, Piazza XXIV Maggio, Milan

Urban riviera

New neighbourhoods with inspiring locations give rise to amazing projects. I find myself in Ripa di Porta Ticinese by the waterside, where I discover a slice of Riviera Romagnola (from Emilia-Romagna) along the Naviglio Grande. Luca Zaccheroni and Omar Casali have opened a bistro there with street food delicacies based on piadina, or flatbread.

Maré
Ripa di Porta Ticinese 67, Milan

A trapizzino sandwich alla parmigiana

The chic Camparino has been housed in the Galleria Vittorio Emanuele II since 1915.

A pan'cot club sandwich at Camparino

Rome in Milan and the world

The Ripa di Porta Ticinese is also where you will find the unusual Trapizzino sandwich. Rome has clearly found a home in Milan. Trapizzino is originally a Roman snack but is a favourite throughout Italy and the world. The brand has outlets in Rome, Milan, Turin, Florence, Trieste, and New York. Pizza baker Stefano Callegari invented the Trapizzino ten years ago. The sandwich, shaped like a pizza wedge, is filled with all sorts of fillings. The bread is crunchy on the outside and soft on the inside. Fillings include *melanzane alla parmigiana,* stracciatella cheese and anchovies, meatballs in red sauce, tongue in green sauce, and so on.

Trapizzino
Ripa di Porta Ticinese 2, Milan

Celebrity sandwiches

Galleria Vittorio Emanuele II along the Piazza del Duomo is Milan's main attraction. With its beautiful, vaulted iron and glass arcades, this galleria has earned its place as one of the most beautiful indoor shopping arcades in Europe. In addition to Vuitton and Prada, the galleria boasts high-quality restaurants and bars. Camparino comes highly recommended. This is probably the most famous bar in the heart of Milan. In addition to cocktails and food, you will also find a fascinating piece of art history. The business dates back to 1867 when the Galleria Vittorio Emanuele II had just been completed.

On the corner looking out over the Piazza del Duomo, Gaspare Campari – the inventor of the drink of the same name – opened Il Caffè Campari, which became Camparino in 1915. The largely still-intact art nouveau interior contains works from the famous furniture maker Eugenio Quarti and master blacksmith Alessandro Mazzucotelli. Camparino in the gallery is a daring combination of iconic history and contemporary allure.

This is where celebrity chef Davide Oldani creates his panini. The warm sandwiches look like cakes. Oldani combines flavours according to the rules of traditional gastronomy. His dishes are true works of art. On the menu, you will find: *Pan'cot Zafferano alla Milanese* accompanied by a Campari Seltz cocktail, a Pan'cot club sandwich with crispy ham and an Americano cocktail, or a Pan'cot with salmon, dill, and carrot and a Campari Spritz on the side. A pan'cot here costs twice as much as a normal panino, but the difference is worth it. Unforgettable.

Milan's Duomo on the Piazza del Duomo.

PIAZZA XXV APRILE

I set a course for Piazza XXV Aprile, just outside the historical city centre. The square is the focal point of a pedestrian street that links the historical centre to the trendy Isola district. It's a paradise for graffiti lovers and shoppers alike, with its narrow streets filled with trendy boutiques, organic food stores and thrift shops.

Tramezzino

Tramé is a fun address on the Piazza XXV Aprile. This is another Tramezzino Veneziano concept that has become a chain store. Tramé caught my attention because it headed the list under the 'sandwiches' category during the 2019 Food Service Awards in Italy. Tramé's tramezzini are gems in food form. They are Venetian because they are made with soft white or wholemeal bread. You can choose from some thirty-odd very rich toppings. I try a sandwich on wholemeal bread with scampi and spinach, accompanied by a refreshing Aperol Spritz. Mmmm. Tramé also has outlets in the Milanese districts of Brera, Pisani and Milanofiori.

Tramé
Piazza XXV Aprile, Via Monte Grappa 22, Milan

Sandwich shop chain

Il Panino Giusto was founded in 1979 on Corso Garibaldi in the old part of Milan. The owners innovated with authentic Milanese and Italian panini, a formula for success. Milan today has 18 Panino Giusto outlets. Il Panino Giusto can be found in many Italian cities as well as in London, Paris, Geneva, and Tokyo.

Panino Giusto
Corso Garibaldi 125, Milan

Pescaria welcomes me 400 metres down the road to the northwest. This fish fast food concept is very popular in Milan. The fish is prepared and served deep-fried or raw on rolls according to Apulian tradition. The menu boasts *panzerotti,* bagels, fish burgers, salads, and tartare. Chef Lucio Mele, an Apulian native, is the brain behind Pescaria. According to his staff, Mele is a true artist. He combines fish with vegetables, dairy products, and cured meats.

Pescaria, Via Nino Bonnet, 5, Milano
en Via Andrea Solari, 12, Milano

A sandwich with a variety of fish preparations at Pescaria

Southern traditions

I walk further in a north-westerly direction until I end up at Sbunda along the Piazzale Baiamonti. Sbunda offers sandwiches with Calabrian ingredients. Two Calabrians from Catanzaro, Marco Rizzitano and Giampaolo Cardamone, set up this establishment in 2019. 'Here, you will find traditional village delicacies with a contemporary twist,' Giampaolo explains. 'We work with regional artisanal suppliers. Which means that we have unique cheese and cold meat varieties. Calabria is more than just 'nduja, you know,' Marco adds.

My eyes are drawn to the 'a nonna piace' sandwiches inspired by their grandmother, Caterina. The typical Calabrian toppings include *parmigiana* (aubergine casserole), fried pork, or meatballs in spicy tomato sauce. The well-presented food looks incredibly delicious. A slice of southern authenticity among the chain shops.

Sbunda Panini di Calabria
Piazzale Antonio Baiamonti 1, Milan

Gourmet Toast

The Turro district is situated in the northeastern part of Milan, some ways away from the historical centre. This is where you will find the Parco Trotter, a beautiful urban park. First, I visit Toasteria Mi Casa. Toast has always been a highly popular snack in this city. This Toasteria is a favourite among young Milanese, where you can enjoy real gourmet toast.

On the menu, I see a *prezioso* with bacon, fresh mozzarella, courgettes, and saffron cream next to a boscaiolo with cooked ham, smoked *scamorza* cheese, mushrooms, truffles, and Parmesan shavings.

My toast with bacon and saffron cream is incredibly tasty. As I sit under the trees, I am briefly transported to another world.

Mi Casa Toasteria,
Piazzale Governo Provvisorio 5, Milan

Traditional village fare with a contemporary twist at Sbunda

Marco and Giampaolo in their shop, Sbunda

Typical toast at Mi Casa

PAVIA ②

From Milan, I head south to the province of Pavia, home to the cities of Pavese, Lomellina and Oltrepò Pavese. Lomellina is the land of rice, with over 1000 kilometres of rice paddies. This is where well-known rice varieties such as Carnaroli and Arborio are produced. Thanks to this region, Lombardy and Piedmont are the most important rice producers in Europe.

Oltrepò Pavese is situated in the heart of the northern Apennines and strongly resembles the Emilia region in terms of geography and morphology. The city is literally pinned in between Emilia-Romagna and Piedmont, close to the Ligurian border.

Zuppa alla Pavese

The zuppa alla Pavese is what brings me to Pavia. This soup gets right down to basics: a broth, egg, and stale bread. This is typical for a region where people hate to waste food.

This soup has a fascinating history. Zuppa alla Pavese was created by accident. During the battle of Pavia on 24 February 1525, King Francis I lost to Charles V (the Roman-German emperor and King of Spain). After the battle, an exhausted Francis I sought and found refuge in a shack halfway between Pavia and Borgarello. The king asked the peasants for a warm meal. The peasants prepared a soup with everything they had at the time: a broth made from herbs, stale bread, and eggs. The recipe made history. The French king valued the peasants' hospitality and the warm soup. The king was taken prisoner and later released. Back in France, he ordered his chefs to make the same soup the Pavian peasants made – *la soupe à la Pavoise*. The soup was an instant success in the king's court. And so, this frugal fare found its way to international gastronomic circles. Although many centuries have passed, this soup still enjoys a tremendous amount of respect to this day. The preparation has hardly changed over the years.

Piera Spalla, from the Selvatico restaurant in Rivanazzano Terme, and I make this soup together. We use meat broth and wholemeal bread (instead of white bread). Both ingredients add more flavour and are highly nutritious.

This meal fit for a king is a fine start to my journey of discovery in the province. Piera is the patroness of Oltrepò Pavese. She was born and raised here and is proud of her region's rich heritage. I can't imagine a better guide for this relatively unknown part of Lombardy.

The *Ponte Coperto* (covered bridge) spans the Ticino River in Pavia

PIERA'S RECIPE

Zuppa alla pavese

SERVES 4 PEOPLE

8 slices of bread
20 g butter
4 eggs
60 g Grana Padano
1 litre meat broth

Slice the bread into the right shape so it fits on the bottom of the serving plates. Melt a knob of butter in a pan, toast the bread on both sides and sprinkle the grated Grana Padano over the top at the end. Take the soup bowls and place the bread on top.

Place one egg yolk on the bread in each bowl. Make sure that the yolk remains intact and doesn't break. Pour the boiling broth into each bowl so the yolk sets slightly.

Cover everything with plenty of grated Grana Padano cheese and serve.

You can also serve this with a couple of extra slices of toasted bread.

BUON RETIRO: OLTREPÒ PAVESE

I travel through Oltrepò Pavese. Piera: 'You will discover a whole variety of aromas and flavours here, south of the Po River. Oltrepò Pavese used to be agricultural lands. In recent years, intellectuals and artists from the city found their 'buon retiro' (pleasant retreat) here. The tranquil, beautiful natural surroundings serve as an inspiration for their creativity. Even Armani bought a 17th-century villa here not too long ago. We drive past hills with terraced vineyards, medieval villages and castles. Everything is still pristine. Tourism has not left much of a mark here yet.

Renaissance south of the Po Valley

'A strange country. A no-man's land, according to many,' Piera tells me. 'Stuck between Piedmont, Emilia-Romagna and Liguria. But we love our region. Our gastronomic tradition is a mixture of specialities and traditions. "Good food, hospitable people and enormous wooden barrels" is how the Greek geographer Strabo described this area when he passed through Oltrepò in 40 BC in the footsteps of Roman troops.'

Several of the younger generation and foodies are joining forces to put niche products on the map. Agricultural and horticultural businesses produce and market high-quality products with respect for the region's characteristic properties. Among the group are intellectuals and chefs who draw inspiration from traditional recipes and techniques. Exceptional businesses put forgotten regional products back on the map with the blessing and support of the Slow Food Movement. Examples include Pomella Genovese apples and old grain varieties such as Grani di Tradizione Dell'Oltrepo. I meet a determined young entrepreneur who breathed fresh life into a saffron plantation. Young British bankers are now growing strawberries using aquaculture.

'These are wonderful tales of entrepreneurial derring-do,' Teresio Nardipo from the local Slow Food Movement tells me during a conference in Voghera. 'These young people believe in the power and sustainability of organic products, and that's why they return to the countryside to start their own businesses.'

Oltrepò Pavese

WINE DOMAIN
Vino vino

The wine marks my odyssey through Oltrepò Pavese. My eye is drawn to the grapevines standing out like beacons among a sea of green, and I long for a good glass of wine. I find myself in Lombardy's largest, yet little-known, wine-growing region. The pinot nero grape is Oltrepò Pavese's pride and joy. It is not an easy grape variety to cultivate. But, on these hills, the grape provides excellent results. The red pinot nero wines are very flavourful, and the 'spumante metodo classico' wines (sparkling wines) made from pinot nero grapes are also excellent. They use a 19th-century technique to make sparkling wines. The bottles are flipped upside down at different stages. The robust, ruby-red Buttafuoco wine, another favourite, may only be produced in a limited geographical area.

Cristina Carri Comi waits for me at the Tenuta Travaglino wine estate in Calvignano. 'Travaglino is the oldest wine-growing business in Oltrepò Pavese,' Christina tells me.

'The region's main grape varieties, pinot noir and riesling renano, are cultivated on over 80 hectares of land. We make both the classic red wines and the white and rosé sparkling wines.

The Travaglino estate in Calvignano dates from around the 12th century. The wine estate's inner courtyard is gorgeous, and the wine cellars have been tastefully renovated. 'In 1868, the wine estate was bought by the Milanese knight Vincenzo Comi, my great-great-great-grandfather. The estate has remained in my family for all this time. I'm the fifth generation,' Cristina smiles.

Tenuta Travaglino is definitely recommended if you want to discover wine in Oltrepò Pavese. Try a pinot nero or spumante metodo classico wine in this phenomenal setting, and you can cross another item off your culinary bucket list.

Tenuta Travaglino
Località Travaglino 6, Calvignano

Mondeghili on the menu

From the wine back to food. *Mondeghili* is another typical Lombardy dish. It is better known as *polpette*. The name refers to the meatballs from the Italian *cucina povera* tradition. I have scheduled a meeting at the Park Hotel restaurant, owned by the Milanese Preti Torlaschi family, so I can get to know this unique dish better.

Francesco Preti has done some in-depth research into his region's culinary history. He tells me that the mondeghili was eaten as far back as the 16th century. Francesco: 'They are an expression of the Milanese spirit and form the main cultural heritage left behind by the Spaniards. This dish spread throughout the region during the century and a half when they ruled our capital city.'

Recycled food

'Mondeghili, which is now a gourmet dish, used to be a recycled dish,' Francesco explains. 'The oldest recipes refer to scraps of beef enriched with *mortadella,* soaked bread and eggs. The meatballs were fried and served warm. Today's version of the recipe is more refined while still preserving the dish's rustic character,' Francesco concludes.

Is there a set recipe for this dish? 'Not really,' Francesco replies. 'In 2008, the Milan municipal council awarded mondeghili the De.Co. quality label. The dish now belongs to the municipal area. The recipe leaves plenty of room for variation, such as adding extra minced onion or garlic, and you can also add sausage or grated Parmesan cheese.'

Park Hotel (Salice Terme),
Via Enrico Diviani 8, Salice Terme

Polpette della nonna Attilia

SERVES 4 PEOPLE

400 g leftover meat scraps
  such as roast beef, pork or veal
400 g mixed pork-veal
  or pork-beef mince
100 g minced mortadella
1 egg
1 onion, minced
1 clove garlic, minced
1 tablespoon finely chopped fresh parsley
2 tablespoons fine stale breadcrumbs
3 tablespoons grated Parmesan cheese
  pepper, salt and paprika powder to taste
finely chopped fresh marjoram to taste
1 sachet of 'La Saporia'
  (powdered spice mix) or a pinch of ground
  cinnamon and ground nutmeg
breadcrumbs

Combine all the ingredients. Shape into meatballs (3 to 4 cm in diameter)

Coat the meatballs with breadcrumbs. Brown the meatballs in a pan with butter or olive oil.

Once the edges are browned, leave them to simmer in the covered pan for about 30 minutes over very low heat.

This recipe comes from my late mother-in-law, Attilia Pomini, from Cremona. She had her own recipe for making meatballs. And when the large pan with polpette was served at the table, that was always cause for celebration for her thirteen children.

Malfatti del Selvatico

Piera Spalla from Selvatico introduces me to another classic from Pavia's *cucina povera*. Her *albergo ristorante* opened in 1912 as a place where people could hitch their horses. It is now a hotel with five rooms, a renowned restaurant and an impressive wine cellar. Piera registered her homemade recipe in the Italian 'Ristoranti del Buon Ricordo' guide. This society has been promoting and preserving Italian food and wine culture since 1960.

Piera, together with her daughter and fellow chef Michele Spalla, added their own interpretation to the dish. Their *malfatti del Selvatico* is prepared with chard, spinach or nettles, depending on the season. They are actually gnocchi made from bread instead of potatoes. That is how stale bread is given a new lease on life.

Albergo Ristorante Selvatico
Via Silvio Pellico 19, 27055 Rivanazzano

Malfatti del Selvatico

SERVES 4 PEOPLE

500 g chard, nettles or spinach
150 g breadcrumbs made from stale bread
250 g flour
250 g Grana Padano cheese
150 g ricotta cheese
50 g butter
2 eggs
1 sprig marjoram
1 clove garlic salt
a pinch of nutmeg

Cook the nettles, chard or spinach straight in the pan without any water. As soon as they are tender, leave them to cool before mixing them to a puree. Melt the butter in a pan. Add the marjoram, followed by the nettle, spinach, or chard puree and cook so the flavours are allowed to blend. Add the breadcrumbs to the same pan and combine into a smooth mixture.

Pour the mixture onto the pastry board and add the flour, Parmesan cheese, eggs, ricotta and nutmeg. Add salt to taste.

Knead the dough. Divide the dough into pieces and shape the pieces into thin rolls using the palms of your hands. Dust your work surface and the palms of your hands with flour if desired to prevent the dough from sticking. Divide the thin rolls into pieces measuring about three centimetres.

Toss the malfatti into boiling salted water and remove them with a skimmer as soon as they start to float.

Spoon the malfatti onto separate plates and top them with melted butter and Grana Padano cheese.

Polenta

BERGAMO ③

Heading back past Milan and turning northeast towards the province of Bergamo, I find myself in the foothills of the Italian Alps, some 40 kilometres beyond Milan. The area lies forgotten between the bustling tourist attractions of Milan, Venice, Lake Como and Lake Garda.
But there is plenty to discover here, and the history of the *paesani* or the peasants intrigues me. Their yellow pride and joy, *la polenta,* is inextricably linked to paesani life.

Grano turco

Christopher Columbus brought polenta to Italy after discovering maize on his voyage to America. His log book entry marked 6 November 1492 reads as follows: 'The land was very fertile and cultivated with those 'niames' and kidney beans and broad beans all very unlike our own; likewise, Indian corn [maize].' Maize soon reached Italy via Spain. The fast-growing plant introduced an entirely new gastronomic tradition to Lombardy and far beyond. The new, exotic grain was given the name *grano turco* or Turkish grain because it came from an exotic country. Polenta from maize flour or grano turco is emblematic of celebration, tradition and motherly comfort in Italy.

The cultivation of maize dates back to the 16th century, although the new grain was not yet considered a household

FOOD FOR THE POOR
The farmers and mountain residents survived for long periods on this yellow, soft, steaming-hot food. Today, polenta is a beloved gourmet dish that is highly valued and praised, perhaps because it has saved so many people from starvation in the past. Polenta symbolises warmth and sharing. You cook it in a copper pot and then pour it out onto a large wooden plank called a *spianatora*. Polenta is the dish that kept the large families of many poor northern Italians fed. Polenta forms the cultural identity of Northern Italy, in particular Lombardy. It's a staple at every table, from the Po Valley to the Alps and even the Abruzzo Apennines.

ingredient in Italian kitchens. Two centuries later, maize had become a staple of Italian cooking everywhere. In the 18th century, maize was planted in abundance to keep hunger at bay. Maize was a staple for the paesani who worked and lived on the large estates.

Polenta flour from spinata maize

Gandino

This one-sided diet, with polenta for breakfast, lunch and evening meals, was hardly healthy. Agricultural workers developed pellagra, a skin disease caused by a lack of essential vitamins. Thankfully, this later changed as dietary habits improved.

Polenta is always cause for celebration

The traditional way to make polenta is very simple. You just need the following ingredients: maize meal, water and salt. The method is simple. As soon as the water boils, add the maize meal and keep stirring with a wooden spoon until the polenta is firm enough. You serve the polenta atop a large plank and let guests help themselves at the table in a convivial setting.

Each region has its own tradition. The *polenta taragna*, typical for the valleys around Bergamo, contains a mixture of ground maize and buckwheat combined with ingredients such as leftover cheese scraps from the refrigerator. In the valleys around Brescia, polenta with chicken and mushrooms is a true delicacy.

GANDINO ④

From the city of Bergamo, I drive another 24 kilometres towards the Alps. The village of Gandino in the Seriana valley is situated at an elevation of 550 metres. This is where the ancient spinato maize variety was rediscovered. I have seldom met more dedicated people. Chef Emanuele Caleca studied this ancient grain and gave it a second life at his restaurant, La Spinata. 'The spinato grain variety came to Gandino in 1632,' Emanuele tells me. 'We have been re-evaluating this valuable maize variety since 2007. We found a couple of ears with seeds, which were preserved at Ca' Parecia, an old farm in Gandino. Spinato di Gandino maize is yellow and has a *spino* or point. The colour, the shape and the flavour differ from other types of maize. The stone-ground meal is coarser and has the texture of wholemeal maize flour,' Emanuele explains.

Giambattista Gherardi has devoted his entire life to the promotion of spinato. He points out that this grain stems from central and southern Mexico. 'Back then, the Incas produced maize in abundance. This grain variety came here through the port of Venice,' Gianbattista explains. 'The flour in the supermarket is not produced with our maize. Spinato is unique; you will only find it here.'

LE CINQUE TERRE DELLA VAL GANDINO

Spinato di Gandino maize is a product from Gandino, which is part of the touristic Le Cinque Terre della Val Gandino region (Gandino, Leffe, Casnigo, Cazzano Sant Andrea and Peia). A marketing campaign thought up by the five municipalities. 'It is also of economic importance,' Gianbattista adds. 'The textile industry in Val Gandino has practically disappeared. This region was one of Europe's main textile producers. Our maize has replaced the dwindling textile industry,' Gianbattista explains. 'The local authorities awarded this product a De.Co. quality label in 2007. This grain grew in an isolated valley and has, therefore, never been cross-pollinated with other grains from areas such as the Po Valley. The crops disappeared because farmers from our valley went off to work in the textile mills. No one cultivated maize anymore, but thankfully, the tide has turned. Spinato is grown, processed and sold once more in the Cinque Terre della Val Gandino. This new economic growth doesn't fully compensate for the loss of textile industry jobs, but it does provide us with hope for the future,' Gianbattista says resolutely.

Not a pizza

La spinata is maize's star product and a registered trademark. You can try this certified delicacy on La Spinata's patio, or take it with you to eat on the go. Spinata has been on the menu of this eatery, owned by the Caleca family, since 2010. The spinata looks a lot like pizza, but I am not allowed to call it that. It is baked as a wholemeal, four-grain flatbread that includes spinato. The dough is topped just like a traditional pizza in numerous variations. While we enjoy the delicious spinata, Gianbattista points out the strong flavours that dominate this ultra-light dish. For now, you can only eat this mouth-watering not-a-pizza here.

Spinato meal is perfect for Bergamo's classic polenta. Emanuele uses it in both sweet and savoury products, such as pasta, pizza, ravioli, flatbread, waffles, biscuits, bread, crackers, bread sticks, cakes, and even an ice cream as well as biscuits and beer!

La Spinata
Piazza Vittorio Veneto 11, Gandino (Bergamo)

La spinata is a type of pizza based on Spinato maize meal

Holes are punched into the strachitunt to allow the natural moulds in the cheese to do their work

VALTALEGGIO

Valtaleggio is a gorgeous small valley in the province of Bergamo. The mountains, the water and the valleys are pristine and breathtakingly beautiful. I smell the Alps in the air, a promising sign of the mountain cheeses I'm about to discover. After a long, winding road, I end up at CasArrigoni where Marco Arrigoni and his daughter Guglia welcome me. The family business owned by Marco, his sister Tina and her husband, Alvaro, is located in Taleggio, right between the mountains. This is where the raw milk *taleggio* and *strachìtunt* cheeses are produced.

'We collect the milk for our cheese from small farms in the Valtaleggio and process the raw milk in the dairy cooperative around the corner from us. They make fresh cheese. Our job is to ripen and store them,' Marco explains. 'The taleggio has a thin, pink crust and a creamy paste. It owes its unique flavour to the ageing process, which lasts at least 60 days. The strachìtunt ripens at least 75 days.'

Keepers of the mould

Marco and Guglia take me to one of the subterranean ripening cellars that have been carved out of the mountain. 'These cellars are made from reinforced concrete, a living material that mimics the ageing conditions of natural caves. The cheese wheels ripen in pinewood crates covered with cotton cloths, which also disinfects them naturally,' Marco explains. He shows how he washes the cheese wheels each week with water and Sicilian salt. 'This artisanal technique is necessary because that's how we see and feel what our cheese needs at any given moment.' Large piles of wooden crates are stacked throughout the various rooms. Every week, six people work from early morning to late evening to individually wash and brush each one of these wheels of cheese by hand. 'You could call us the keepers of the mould,' Marco says. 'The mould gives our products their typical flavour, colour and aromas.'

Strachìtunt, the layered cheese

Until a couple of decades ago, the local dairy was mostly used for *strachchino* cheese varieties, which were also called *tunt* or *quader* (round or square), depending on

The freshly moulded cheese is ready for ripening

Monitoring the strachìtunt's ageing process

Delicious aged taleggio at CasArrigoni

Along the way to Val Taleggio, I pass the medieval village of Gromo

their shape. Strachìtunt or round stracchino stems from this tradition. Raw, full-fat milk (still warm, fresh from the cow) is used for the preparation, and the double-paste method is used where the cooled curd from the night before is combined with the still-warm curd from the following morning. The cheese is formed in layers.

The thick, rough, brown rind tends towards grey as ageing processes. During this process, holes are punched into the cheese by hand to foster the growth of the natural moulds in the milk and the surrounding environment. This gives the cheese a natural, irregular, marbled look. The flavour is aromatic and intense, ranging from mild to sharp depending on the degree of ageing. Strachìtunt was neglected for decades but has been rediscovered and reintroduced to the market in recent years. In 2013, strachìtunt was awarded the DOP quality

label. Marco explains that this cheese is the father of the gorgonzola. 'The strachìtunt came first; the formula wasn't applied to gorgonzola cheese until much later.'

Taleggio

This cheese boasts a very long tradition. Taleggio dates as far back as 1200. Its history is closely linked to the Val Taleggio, after which the cheese was named. Over the centuries, the production and ageing territory has extended to include most of Lombardy (Bergamo, Brescia, Como, Cremona, Lecco, Lodi, Milan, Monza and Brianza, Pavia), as well as provinces in the Piedmont, Veneto and Treviso regions. Taleggio is designated as a DOP cheese.

CasArrigoni srl
Fraz. Peghera 575, Valtaleggio

Crespella al taleggio

Taleggio is a popular ingredient in many dishes, including polenta. Marco and Guglia from CasArrigoni accompany me to Albergo Ristorante Liberty in their village. Everyone knows each other here, but chef Alida is a close friend. Here is where you can taste all the CasArrigoni cheese varieties. You will find the cheese in dishes such as their linguine with strachìtunt and their polenta with a Taleggio cheese fondue. But you will also find cured meats from the Val Taleggio region here.

'This building used to be a café where travellers could hitch their horses. I remember how my grandfather used to cook here for the travellers,' Alida recalls. She shows me how she makes crespella al taleggio. 'This is a savoury crepe filled with Taleggio cheese, potatoes and pears,' Alida explains as she stirs the batter.

Albergo Ristorante Liberty
Via Antonio Arnoldi 314, Taleggio

ALIDA'S RECIPE
Crespelle

MAKES 8 CRESPELLE
– SERVES 4 PEOPLE

80 g flour
140 ml milk
1 egg
cognac
salt and oil

FOR THE FILLING
2 potatoes
300 g Taleggio cheese
1 pear
rosemary
Grana Padano cheese
béchamel sauce

Sieve the flour in a bowl and add the eggs and a pinch of salt. Combine everything with a fork. Add the oil and continue to mix.

Add the milk and whisk until you have a smooth, homogenous batter.

Add a couple of drops of cognac and leave the batter to rest in the refrigerator for half an hour. Meanwhile, dice the potatoes, blanch them for a couple of minutes in salted boiling water and let them cool.

Dice the pears and the Taleggio cheese.

Once the potatoes have cooled, place them in a stew pan together with the Taleggio cheese, béchamel sauce and rosemary.

Combine everything and add the pears, coating them with the rest of the filling. Cook the crespelle in a pan like you would normally cook crepes.

Fill the crespelle with the filling, place them in an ovenproof dish and add a drizzle of béchamel sauce and a sprinkling of Grana Padano cheese over the top. Bake for 20 minutes in an oven at 180 °C.

LAKE COMO 6

The Como region's star dish brings together the flavours of land and water. *Missoltini* bears witness to the culture and traditions of people who have always stood with one foot in the lake and the other in the mountains. I decide to take an in-depth look at this speciality in Cernobbio on Lake Como.

Silvia from Le Specialità Lariane serves me this typical regional dish with the lake's impressive shoreline as the backdrop. 'Missoltini with polenta and cheese is a centuries-old peasant dish,' Silvia confides in me. 'The *agone* fish from Lake Como are dried and pressed using a special technique. You will hardly find them anywhere else.' I remark that the meat reminds me of sardines. Silvia explains that the innards are removed after the fish are caught – with a line or a net. Silvia: 'The fish are then coated in salt and placed in a barrel to which more salt is added. After 48 hours, the fish is rinsed, threaded onto a string and hung or laid to dry outside for a couple of days.'

Pressing as a preservative

The heads are removed, and the dried agone are then layered with bay leaves in between in special *missolte* tins. These are then sealed and pressed shut with a press or weights. This is how the oil is removed from the fish; the oil tastes bad and causes the fish to rot. After four or five months, the missoltini are ready to eat.

Unique freshwater fish

How do you prepare missoltini in the kitchen? 'First, you wash them with salt and vinegar to remove the excess salt and congealed leftover fat,' Silvia replies. 'Then season them with oil, vinegar and parsley, grill them and serve them with roasted polenta. This dish, from the *cucina povera* tradition, has become popular because it's an exclusive regional speciality.'

Le Specialità Lariane
Via Cinque Giornate 59, Cernobbio (Como)

The village of Menaggio on the shores of Lake Como

TRENTINO - ALTO ADIGE

Trentino-Alto Adige is located in the northernmost point of Italy, bordering Austria and Switzerland between the central and eastern Alps. The region borders Veneto to the southeast and Lombardy to the southwest.

This is where the mountains are at their most beautiful, with the Dolomites crowning them all. The landscape is a mosaic of majestic mountaintops, vast forests and broad valleys, criss-crossed with rivers and lakes featuring panoramic views, interspersed with charming villages in the rich colour palette of the pristine natural surroundings.

Trentino Alto Adige has been an autonomous region since 1948, with Bolzano as its capital. The region comprises two provinces: Alto Adige to the north and Trentino to the south. Alto Adige is named after the Adige River, and people speak German in Bolzano. Before the Second World War, this region was officially known as Südtirol or South Tyrol. Trentino, named after Trento, is purely Italian. Until the end of the Second World War, this region was known as Venezia Tridentina.

Bretzels in Bolzano

The San Giovanni church from 1180 is
one of the Dolomites' hidden treasures

Lago di
Resia

Adige

Solda

Plima

Valsura

Adige

Passirio

Bolzano

1

R. gardena

Barnes

San Romedio

Avisio

Noce

Avisio

Avisio

Vanoi

Sorino

Lago di
Caldonazz

Brenta

2

Trento

Chise

Lago
d'Odro

Lago di
Garda

Two cuisines

Trentino and Alto Adige also differ in terms of culinary traditions. In Alto Adige, Central-European cuisine has left its mark. The South-Tyrol Würstel, *canederli* (German: *Knödel*), *Bauerntoast* and *Bretzel* betray the strong influence of German and Austrian traditions. Trentino has mainly preserved the local *cucina povera*, with dishes such as *canederli, polenta, tortelle di patate, smacafam* ... accompanied by meat dishes for those who could – and can – afford it.

MOUNTAINS AND BEER

Both regions share the mountains and a passion for beer. Towards the end of the 19th century, a mildew infestation destroyed many vineyards. That is why you will find beer on the menu instead of wine in many places today. This hoppy brew has a tradition of high-quality. Artisanal breweries flourished and continue to be active to this day. The *birrerie* are a tradition. Throughout the region, you will find countless small craft beer breweries with annexed taverns or osterias where fresh beer flows from the brew kettles on a daily or weekly basis. Such birrerie also often put traditional peasant cooking on the map along with their traditional beers. The beer movement has been an economic incentive for both regions.

Characteristic Bolzano or Bozner Beer

BOLZANO ①

Frugal fare served in dirndl and lederhosen

This region has always been a crossroads of languages and cultures, and that is reflected in its cuisine. These include fine cured meats, sausages, mountain cheeses and many different types of bread.

South-Tyrol is a region with a thousand faces, where apparent contrasts live side by side in harmony. The valleys in the snow-white Dolomites enjoy a mild climate. Here is where the Alpine and Mediterranean worlds meet, and that includes at the table. Pizza, pasta, espresso, grappa, and so on – they're everywhere.

I have come to the right place to experience the local cuisine: the Osteria Hopfen & Co in Bolzano.
Diego Bernardi started the business in 1998. He brews Bozner beer (beer from Bolzano) in his own birreria. 'Beer tastes best with fine food; that's why we combine our beers with authentic dishes,' manager Nicoletta Angeli explains. On the menu, I find *canederli, Weisswurst* with *Bretzel, Biergulasch,* lentil soup, and Nürnberger sausage: typical Tyrol cuisine, in other words. The male wait staff wear lederhosen, and the ladies are dressed in lovely dirndl dresses.

Recycling

My first dish is *misto di canederli,* a selection of Knödel. Canederlo, canederli (plural) or Knödel in German is – under the guise of various names – also a typical first course in southeastern Germany, Austria, the Czech Republic, Slovakia and Poland. 'We serve large *gnocchi,*' Nicoletta assures me. 'We make them from a mixture of stale bread to which we add speck (diced bacon) or cheese.'

The history of the canederli goes back a long way. Nicoletta: 'Such Knödel were already made in the 12th century. A mural dating from 1180 in the chapel of the gorgeous castle of Appiano proves this.
The castle, Hocheppan, is situated high above the Adige valley and offers panoramic views of the Dolomites and the capital, Bolzano. Hocheppan is the perfect match between natural beauty and the romanticism of a medieval castle.

Terrace in Bolzano, where Alpine and Mediterranean cuisine come together

Canederli

SERVES 4 TO 5 PEOPLE

300 g bread
120 ml milk
150 g speck (diced bacon)
1 small onion
40 g flour
40 g butter
a few sprigs of chives
1 sprig of flat-leaf parsley
800 ml meat broth
3 eggs

Fill a large pan with meat broth before
preparing the canederli.
Sauté the minced onion for a couple of minutes
with butter in a pan over medium-low heat.
Add the speck and brown it. Set aside.

Put the cubed slices of bread in a bowl.
Add the milk, the lightly beaten eggs, the
browned speck and onion mixture, the flour,
the chopped parsley and the chives.

Season to taste with a pinch of salt. Combine
everything with your hands. Cover the bowl
with cling film and leave the mixture to rest for
10 minutes. Then, shape portions of the dough
into balls weighing about 50 grams each.

Bring the meat broth in the pot to the boil.
Boil the dumplings a couple at a time in the
simmering broth for about 10 to 12 minutes
until cooked through.

Strain the dumplings and serve with the
hot broth, melted butter and grated cheese,
or another sauce of your choice.

Soaked bread

It's a simple dish, according to Nicoletta: 'Stale bread is
first soaked in milk or beer before mixing it with eggs,
diced speck or local cheese, spring onions and parsley. The mixture is then rolled into balls and cooked
in meat broth. We also fill the canederli with pieces of
red beetroot or kale with apple. The canederli are very
popular and a perfect accompaniment for our beer.'
I get to taste three varieties. The canaderlo with cheese
is subtly flavoured, the bacon version is typical of
South-Tyrol and quite spicy, and the third one with the
red beetroot filling has a fruitier flavour. The third is
my favourite.
I also spy *canederli dolci* on the dessert menu. These are
large gnocchi filled with apricots or plums, depending on
the season.

Hopfen & Co.,
Piazza dele Erbe / Obstmarkt 17, Bolzano

The maestro's Bozner beer

I try the homebrewed beer with the canederli. Brewer and beer sommelier Matthias Obkircher pours me a glass of blonde ale from their assortment. The light blonde beer (four per cent) tastes pure. An excellent refreshment!

Hopfen & Co's focus is on the Bavarian beer tradition. 'We always make a blonde, a dark and a wheat beer and a whole range of special craft beers, depending on the season. I brew a batch four times a week, so we always have fresh beer that doesn't need any filtering or pasteurising. And the beer story doesn't end there. 'Beer in moderation is good for your health,' Matthias says as he places a pint of one of his latest special brews in front of me. 'I have developed this authentic Bozner beer myself,' he explains. 'It is a unique recipe that combines familiar basic ingredients with a malt of the highest quality. I even made the yeast myself.' I taste an exceptionally pure, refreshing, bitter and intense beer. An experience worth repeating. Nicoletta and Matthias proudly show me the many beer awards they have managed to earn over the years.

Weisswurst on Sundays

Weisswurst is the next classic dish on the menu. This is a white veal sausage. The Bavarian-style dish is accompanied by homemade sweet mustard and Bretzel.

Here, it's tradition to eat a Weisswurst with sweet mustard and a glass of beer at one of the street stalls after Sunday mass. 'The tradition continues to this day,' Nicoletta says. 'Bozner beer with sausage is the perfect aperitif after mass and before the Sunday family lunch.'

Bretzel, praying with your arms crossed

My plate also features a Bretzel. Pure folklore. The shape and distinctive salt grains on top make this bread unique. 'This is a gastronomic symbol of South-Tyrol and German-speaking countries,' Nicoletta says decidedly.

The Bretzel, or pretzel as we call it, with its loose-knot shape, is a favourite street food item across the globe. Nicoletta: 'You can eat Bretzel plain or with a filling. In Bolzano, we prefer to drink beer with it. The sweet Bretzels are coated in chocolate or a sugar glaze. You will find them at street food stalls and in bakeries, restaurants and bars.'

Many stories about the Bretzel link this food to the Catholic church. The Bretzel gained in popularity during the fasting period when meat, dairy, lard or eggs were off limits. This product – made from water, yeast and flour – was allowed. The oldest references date back to 610. Italian monks gave Bretzel-shaped pastry

Tradition on a plate with Weisswurst and Bretzel

scraps to pupils who were able to say their prayers properly. The Bretzel symbolized prayer. In those days, Christians would pray with their arms crossed. Is the story true? Who knows? Whatever the case, the Bretzel is immensely popular in Bolzano and Alto Adige.

The inn of a thousand stories

After sharing food, drink and countless stories, Nicoletta shows me around the historic building that houses Hopfen & Co. 'This building has been around since 800 AD,' she explains. 'This was once a tower along the city wall. Back then, a river flowed in front of the building, but the river was made dry centuries ago. In a past life, this also used to be Bolzano's town hall. Prisoners were locked up in the basement. A farmers market sold their wares in front of the building and on the "Obstmarkt". Our street still has a vegetable and flower market. This house used to be an inn and a place where travellers could reshoe their horses. It was strategically situated along the road to Brennero and a through road to Austria and Germany. This building has so many stories. This is where legendary parties, concerts and operas were performed.

In one of the rooms, I spot a beautiful painted portrait of a young man. Nicoletta: 'This is the son of the former owner. He died in the war when he was only 19 years old. We couldn't bring ourselves to hang the painting somewhere else. One glance at this innocence makes you feel instant and genuine empathy.

Another inn near the Tre Cime di Lavaredo

TRENTO ❷

The cucina povera revival

From Bolzano, I drive 60 kilometres south to Trento. When I ask people what some examples of typical peasant dishes are, they all reply in unison: canaderli. The bread dumplings are considered a true delicacy here in Trento as well. Other characteristic dishes include *tortel di patate* and *smacafam* (pie with sausage). You won't find either of these dishes in Alto Adige.

I visit the traditional *trattorie* or *birrerie* to try some of these traditional dishes. This town is experiencing a revival of frugal fare but in combination with beer instead of wine. Microbreweries are popping up everywhere, and they are taking over the city with their fine craft beers. Nicola Malassoni is my hostess at the oldest birreria in town, Birreria Forsterbräu Trento (1906). Moreover, this café-restaurant is located in one of the city centre's oldest buildings. With this café, they aim to promote their beers in combination with traditional dishes. It all fits together. The menu boasts canederli, Würstel, hamburgers, Goulash and tortel di patate; each dish comes with a beer selection. Because the beer takes centre stage here.

Tortel di patate for good company

I try the *tortel di patate* in this beautiful, classic setting. '*Il tortello* is very distinctive because you will not find the potatoes in Alto Agide like we make them here.' Nicola says firmly. '*Il tortello* comes from the Val di Non valley. This valley is situated in the northwestern part of the Trento province, where you will find white potatoes for this dish.'

I watch how she prepares the *tortel* with potatoes, flour, beer and water. Nicola: 'This dish should be served with cured meats, seasonal vegetables and cheese. You eat this dish with others; it's all about enjoying food together, which is why it's a perfect match with our beer!'

I try the dish before it cools and wash it down with a homebrewed pilsner. Perhaps not the best option if you're trying to lose weight, but oh my, this tastes so good!

Birreria Forsterbräu,
Via Paolo Oss-Mazzurana 38, Trento

NICOLA'S RECIPE
Tortel di patate

SERVES 4 PEOPLE
1 kg potatoes, preferably white Kennebec
80 g flour
a splash of beer (2 tablespoons)
a pinch of salt
oil and lard or pork fat for frying

Peel the potatoes and grate the raw potatoes with a coarse grater. Strain the grated potatoes in a colander, pressing the remaining moisture out by hand.

Put everything in a bowl and add half the flour and the salt. Carefully stir with a wooden spoon. Add a splash of beer and the remaining flour. Keep combining to a batter. Shape the batter into fritters using your hands. Add the oil and lard to a non-stick frying pan. Place the fritters in the oil once the pan is hot. Turn them over repeatedly until a golden-brown crust forms. Remove the fritters from the pan and drain on paper towels.

FRIULI – VENEZIA GIULIA

Friuli-Venezia Giulia in northeast Italy is a border region, hemmed in between Austria and Slovenia, with the Adriatic Sea to the south and Veneto to the west. A region with three names, indicative of its unique composition. Friuli-Venezia Giulia is the sixth least populated region in Italy. Its residents are mostly Italians and Slovenians. Over the centuries, Romans, Slavs, Venetians and Austrians have left their mark on the local language, culture and cuisine.

After the Second World, Trieste and its surroundings became an autonomous region. In 1954, Trieste returned to the Italian fold and became the region's capital. I travel from the rocky highlands and the Dolomite foothills to the north to the arid and sometimes marshy lowlands to the south. Natural pastures in the north are a testament to abundant rainfall. In the valleys, maize and various types of grains flourish, and around Udine, the landscape is dominated by horticultural lands. In the southeast, the province of Trieste forms a narrow corridor between the Carso (Karst) limestone plains and the Adriatic Sea, right down to Trieste.
Seaside resorts such as the famous Lignano Sabbiadoro border long, sandy beaches and idyllic lagoons from the Veneto border to Monfalcone; the shoreline becomes rocky as it descends further south towards Trieste.

Bay of Sistiana in the Duino-Aurisina region

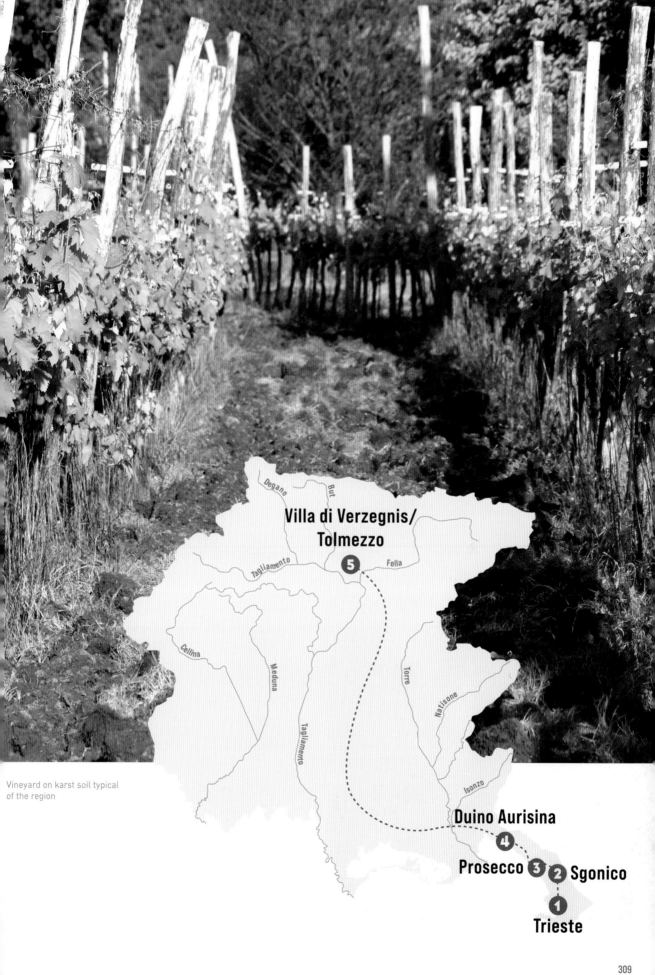

Vineyard on karst soil typical of the region

Villa di Verzegnis/Tolmezzo

Degano

But

Tagliamento

Fella

5

Cellina

Meduna

Torre

Tagliamento

Natisone

Isonzo

Duino Aurisina

4

Prosecco **3** **2** **Sgonico**

1

Trieste

MELTING POT

Friuli-Venezia Giulia is a cultural melting pot. The cuisine is distinctive in its ingredients, dishes and flavours. This region, where the mountains meet the sea and which has been influenced by so many peoples and cultures, is a delight with its unusual aromas and flavours. Polenta from white or yellow maize, gnocchi and ravioli, sometimes with a slightly sweet filling, are reminiscent of Veneto and Lombardy. San Daniele prosciutto, from the village of the same name in the province of Udine, is a cut above the rest among the region's characteristic fine cured meats. Cevapčići betrays Slavic influences. These minced meat sausages look like Turkish kebabs. And then there are the excellent cheese varieties, some aged in deep subterranean caves. Of these, Montasio is probably the best-known. This cheese forms, together with potatoes and onions, the basic ingredient for the delicious *frico*. The Adriatic coast and the lagoons provide an extensive banquet of fish and shellfish.

Strolling past the historical buildings along the Canal Grande is a wonderful way to pass the time

TRIESTE ①

My journey of discovery starts in Trieste. The city has seen many different rulers over the centuries. Caesar, Charlemagne and Napoleon all coveted this strategic seaport. So, it's no surprise that Trieste played an important role in almost every noteworthy regional conflict. According to my guide, food blogger Chiara Giglio, her city was a transit location for spies during the Cold War. Chiara, proudly: 'Trieste was once the third most important city of the Austrian Habsburg Empire after Vienna and Prague. Trieste was a gateway to Europe and a world-class trading centre. The various ethnic groups that made their homes here have left their mark. Churches, temples, and synagogues all reflect our long, multicultural tradition.

Eclectic and idyllic

'We celebrate life in our elegant cafés, bars and restaurants in our vibrant sea port,' Chiara says. 'Everyone lives and works together in this pocket-sized metropolis.' Trieste looks like an eclectic and idyllic location for film sets. I enjoy the city's allure and the pleasant salty breeze from the Adriatic Sea.

The art of living

'We Triestines are a special breed,' the local philosopher Manuel Laghi explains to me during lunch. 'We celebrate life. We go outside as soon as a single ray of sunshine breaks through the clouds. We feel cosmopolitan. Trieste, which shares a border with Slovenia, is a gateway to the east and yet quintessentially European. Experience Trieste and you will immediately discover that the city lives and breathes with you.'

Habsburg culinary decadence

Manuel is right: this city is alive. At night, I walk through an immense crowd. Happy people settle down on countless terraces. They sing, yell, argue and laugh. Trieste fell into Italian hands after the First World War, but the city has managed to retain its Viennese charm. The large cafés betray the Viennese architecture. The Strudel in café and patisserie display cases are a slice of Austrian cultural heritage. The typical buffets that you find in several places are reminiscent of the empire's heyday.

The Canal Grande from the 18th century is located in the Borgo Teresiano district

Habsburg culinary decadence lives on in the Trieste buffet, entirely in the style of this Italian yet cosmopolitan border city. The Buffet da Pepi is an institution here. Here is where you can find Central-European-style pork and sauerkraut alongside goulash, hams and sausages.

⭐ The power of the imagination

Pepi's holds its own somewhere between an Alsace brasserie and a New York-style deli. I feel like I've just walked into a spy novel. A man with a black moustache and a white, starched shirt with a gold chain quietly asks me: *'Cosa desidera signora?'* or: 'What would you like, madam?' This is Luca Bellanti. Trieste has made a name for itself with its traditional 'buffet' from the Austrian-Hungarian empire days. The establishments that have this buffet on the menu serve pork 'from snout to tail' with sauerkraut, mustard, and freshly grated horseradish, accompanied by the obligatory foamy pint of beer. 'The pork is cooked for two to three hours in a flavourful broth in a *caldaia* or boiler,' Luca explains. 'We use all the parts of the pig, just like in the olden days. This includes smoked loin, bacon, cheek, head, innards, ears, sausages and *cotechino*. Only the tongue is beef.'
Buffet da Pepi (1897) was founded by Pepi Klajnsic and passed on to the Pepi family. Today, former employee Paolo Polla runs the establishment together with his son, Andrea. Da Pepi hasn't changed a bit since it was founded.

Not for the faint of heart

I order a *misto caldaia* with pieces of cooked pork, a dish unique to Trieste. Luca prepares the dish in front of me as I wait. A buffet like this is a work of art. The meat is cooked fresh daily, and its preparation requires skilled hands. Luca lifts the pork pieces and beef tongue with a large fork and reheats the meat by dipping it into the boiling broth. He takes a large cleaver and cuts the meat, the fragrant hams, ears, snouts, neck, and sausages into pieces on a plate. He garnishes the plate with a sprinkling of salt and grated horseradish. And crowns his work with a spoonful of mustard. This is something else. Luca serves me the dish. I suddenly realise that this dish is not for the faint of heart. But the local beer to go with it does wonders – or is it the gentle sea breeze? Before I know it, my plate is empty.

Buffet da Pepi
Via Cassa di Risparmio 3, Trieste

Retro romanticism

At the Antico Caffé San Marco, I meet philosopher and conversationalist Manuel Laghi for coffee. I've barely sat down at our table when he hits me with a quote from James Joyce: 'My soul is in Trieste.' Let this be the opening for my story about retro romanticism and Trieste's coffee culture.

'Trieste is the birthplace of Illy and the city of retro cafés,' Manuel declares. 'Our cafés are rooted in the Central-European intellectual culture and literature. Trieste is a city of authors. Italo Svevo, Umberto Saba and James Joyce were regulars here!' Manuel points out that the names of the cafés are spelled with a capital C here. 'Caffè Tommaseo, Caffè degli Specchi and Antico Caffè San Marco are all places with a mystical charm.

I feel like I've been transported back to 1914 in Antico Caffè San Marco, where the interior has stood the test of time. The enormous mirrors, the cast-iron and marble tables, and the dark wood of the bar haven't changed since those days. Only the customer's faces have changed over the years. I see them playing chess or reading papers clamped tightly between newspaper sticks. Here and there, a student sits hunched over a book in deep concentration.

Luca prepares
a misto caldaia for me

'Caffè Tommaseo is the oldest café, and Caffè degli Specchi has the finest views from the Piazza dell-Unità d'Italia. You can also enjoy your coffee on the terrace and watch the sea sparkle in the distance,' Manuel announces.

Coffee port

Coffee has become a part of Trieste's DNA; their story dates from the 18th century, when the city was still a part of the Habsburg Empire. In 1719, Trieste was awarded the status of 'free port', and the first ships carrying green coffee from the Ottoman Empire were allowed to dock.

⭐ Love story

Illycaffè is the product of a love story, which is typical for Trieste. After the First World War, Francesco Illy, a soldier in the Austrian-Hungarian army, ended up in Trieste. He decided to stay there when he found the three loves of his life here: the charming city that had captured his heart, the coffee served in the historical bars where the intelligentsia met, and Doris, who later became his wife and the mother of his children. And Illycaffè. And so, Francesco applied for Italian citizenship and started to sell spices, chocolate – and valuable, exotic coffee beans. Trieste became this widely-travelled, multilingual world citizen's anchorage.
The company logo bears the red and white of Trieste, the city where the business was founded, where its headquarters are located, and where the family runs the business to this day. And even though it has grown into a global brand name, Illy stands for Italian-style coffee and espresso, or as they say in Trieste: *un nero!*

Un nero per favore – an espresso, please

Trieste residents have developed their own vocabulary for the many variations on the unfinished coffee symphony. Don't just order an 'espresso' or 'caffè' in a bar. You need to explain what you want using the lingo. A coffee in the bar is a nero, and a cappuccino is a *caffè latte*. When you're in a bar, don't be surprised to hear someone order a *capo in b*. This is a *caffè macchiato* (coffee with milk foam) in a glass. Manuel helped me draft the following list:

Un nero in b on the left and un caffè latte in b on the right

How do you order coffee in Trieste?

Un nero
an espresso in a cup

Un nero in b
an espresso in a glass

Un deca
a decaf espresso in a cup

Un deca in b
a decaf espresso in a glass

Un capo
an espresso macchiato (with milk) in a cup

Un capo in b
an espresso macchiato (with milk) in a glass

Un capo deca
a decaf espresso macchiato (with milk) in a cup

Un capo deca in b
a decaf espresso macchiato (with milk) in a glass

Un goccia
a coffee with just a drop of milk foam

Caffè latte
what we know as cappuccino

313

SGONICO ②

The Karst Plateau is situated between Italy and Slovenia. It's home to a Slovenian-Italian community. Pure folkloric magic awaits me among the green vineyards and picturesque limestone streets. And this is where I let fate guide me. I go off in search of wine estates or farms with a *frasca* (climbing vine) in front of the entrance. The dried twigs are a symbol that I can join the *osmiza*.

Gregor and Alice Budin

Every osmiza has a charcuterie board with cured meats and cheese

This frasca means that an osmiza is being held here

I walk through the gates at Gregor and Alice's Budin's vineyard. Simple, long trestle tables and benches line the courtyard next to the vineyard. I discover an entirely new culinary world.

Gregor is a passionate wine maker. His white vitovska and malvasia and his red terrano are produced as naturally as possible, with as little intervention as possible during the ripening process. During the osmiza, you get to taste these delicious wines, accompanied by boards with an abundance of home-made charcuterie and cheeses. You eat from plastic or paper plates. It all looks very simple, but the meat is beautifully cut into paper-thin slivers and everything is market fresh.

'The osmiza tradition dates from the time of Maria Theresa of Austria. In 1784, farmers were given permission to purchase their own farm-produced wines and agricultural products tax-free for eight consecutive days. The name comes from the Slovenian word for eight – *osem* – referring to the number of days the sale was allowed,' Gregor explains. 'Today, this period varies from 8 to 45 days a year depending on how much wine is produced.'

An osmiza is organised at a hospitable, homely, informal location. 'You will often come across exuberant groups of people. The meal is frequently accompanied by a repertoire of folk songs from Trieste or Slovenia, and the terrano grape ensures that all these songs start to sound alike after a while,' Gregor laughs. You will always find hard-boiled eggs during osmiza, an ideal remedy for the hangover that inevitably follows after so many glasses of wine, as it turns out.

Osmiza Budin
Località Sales 122, Sales

How do you find an osmiza?

An open osmiza makes use of a very unusual signpost. Just keep your eyes out for the frasca at crossroads along the main roads close to the locations and follow the red arrow. The osmiza period varies each year.

You can find out which winegrowers organise an osmiza per village at **www.osmize.com**. Each osmiza is unique. The home-made products, the wines, the location, the view, the owners, the service, the songs... the atmosphere is different every time.

The Karst Plateau's red soil is also highly suitable for growing vegetables

ZONA AGRICOLTURA DEL CARSO

Gregor is a Slovenian from the Karst, a region that joined Italy after the Second World War. Gregor: 'We have always spoken Slovenian here, and we still have Slovenian schools. Everyone lives together in harmony. Trieste has always been a melting pot. It's a mini New York.' I point at the charcuterie board. 'But this looks very Italian,' I remark. Gregor agrees: 'If there's one thing we've learned from the Italians, it's their art of cooking. The Italians are masters in preparing fine cured meats!' Gregor is proud of Karst's contemporary gastronomy. 'The quality of the wines has greatly improved, and that also goes for the osmiza. We owe this to the efforts of several leading producers, and we hope to follow in their footsteps. The agricultural sector is growing once more.'

He resumes: 'Trieste has always been a trading hub. After the Cold War, we returned to the countryside. And that's just as well. I'll admit that the many slopes make it hard to cultivate the land, but the soil here is perfect for quality wines. More and more young people are finding their way to the countryside; they develop projects in the Zona Agricoltura del Carso. That's how we create our own territory with food and drink that will appeal to tourists.'

Osmica u Kutu

My next stop is the Azienda Agricola Bukavex Vesna in Prosecco, where Zarko Bukavec welcomes me with the warm words: '*Fate come a casa vostra*', or 'make yourself at home.' This is what makes *Osmiza u Kutu* so great. 'Kutu is Slovenian for "in the corner".' And who ends up in corners? The daredevils,' Zarko explains. Clearly, my host does more than just grow grapes and make salami. I sense the passion of a man on a mission.

Don Quixote

I try a *prosekar*, a sparkling wine – or more accurately, a prosecco from the village of origin. This tastes like a real prosecco. Zarko makes about 500 bottles each year.
'The grapevines in Prosecco are a part of our cultural heritage,' Zarko explains. 'Anyone who cultivates grapes for the production of wine here deserves our unconditional admiration. The growers preserve the vulnerable sandy slopes. We want to give our agricultural sector a new lease on life with products such as prosekar, our version of prosecco. Prosecco was originally produced in Slovenia, after the village of the same name that was once part of the country. Veneto has taken glera grape variety used to make prosecco from us, as well as the name. An entire wine culture lies hidden in these hills, which we want to spread to the rest of the world,' Zarko says with conviction.

Zarko shows me the hatchet people used to open the bottles

When I ask who Zarko is, he replies: '*So di non sapere, come Socrates,*' in other words: 'I know that I know nothing, just like Socrates.' Zarko describes himself as a communist and an anarchist. 'I am a Slovenian with Venetian blood. Here in Trieste, we need to remain defiant. When does Don Quixote die? When he starts listening to others!'

⭐ Il vino della passione

For his prosekar label, Zarko selected a portrayal of a beautiful young woman who, after drinking this delicious wine, didn't know when to stop and ended up having an orgasm. '*Quel prosekar, quel amore, quelle gocce di passione*! – This prosekar, such love, such drops of passion!' the label reads.

'In our Bukavec winery, we have been producing local wines with respect for nature and tradition for several generations. Our vineyards are situated on the Karst Plateau and ridge of the village of Prosecco, with views of the 19th-century Miramare Castle and the Gulf of Trieste. In this idyllic location, we try to make a difference with our prosekar. We strive to produce high-quality, authentic, pure products.'

Slovenian siren

The osmiza in the courtyard is coming to life. A group of men savour the passionate wine, the fine home-made cured pork, the cheese, the bread and the hard-boiled eggs. The sun is shining, the sky is blue, and this farm is now officially an osmiza. I can't hear a single word of Italian now that the entire Slovenian village choir has assembled here. Everyone is enjoying themselves, and the atmosphere is exuberant. This is life, this is Prosecco, the Karst, and Italy!

I ask if they want to sing a song for my blog, and they immediately consent. Prosecco has had its own Slovenian men's chorus since 1887, and these 20 men sitting in this courtyard are keeping the tradition alive. Their repertoire includes Slovenian, Russian and Italian folk and protest songs. I listen to a Slovenian and a Russian folk song. Goosebumps! You can listen to clips by scanning the QR code below.

Osmica U Kutu
Località Prosecco, Contovello 82,
Prosecco

Prosekar with a voluptuous young woman on the label

Miramare Castle is situated near the village of Prosecco

PROSECCO ③

The prosekar at Osmica u Kutu has sparked my interest. I turn to Alessio Stoka, chairman of the Associazione Prosekar, for more background information. We arrange to meet at the Klin winery, owned by his niece, Katrin Stoka in Contovello.

In recent years, a battle has been brewing between the big world of Prosecco DOC production in Veneto and the tiny Carso vineyards around the village of Prosecco. But all is quiet and peaceful at the Klin winery. The location atop a hill is breathtaking. To the left, we see Croatia and Slovenia and straight ahead, the shadowy outline of Venice rises up in the distance. We have the world at our feet.

Klin Vina
Azienda Agricola Stoka, Contovello

From Prosek

Prosekar's origins date from around 1548. It was the economic driving force behind Trieste, which was fully focused on agriculture. The wine was produced in the stretch of land along the Adriatic Coast between the Karst Plateau – 200 to 300 metres above sea level – and Mirmare Castle along the coast. This area includes the villages of Prosecco (Prosek in Slovenian), Contovello and Santa Croce. *Prosekar* in Slovenian literally translates to 'from Prosek', a clear reference to its origins.

David versus Goliath

Thirteen years ago, the decision was taken to expand the Prosecco DOC area to nine provinces in Veneto and Friuli-Venezia Giulia. The wine's original territory in the hills between Conegliano and Valdobbiadene expanded to include the province of Trieste – and the village of Prosecco. And with it, the Veneto wine growers were allowed to claim the territorial name prosecco as per the denomination. It is important that you can associate the name of the grape or wine with a location; otherwise, this name can be stolen by others. The few wine growers in the Carso region didn't oppose the decision at the time because they were promised a series of investments in return (a promise which, according to Alessio, still hasn't been kept).

Katrin and Alessio Stoka at the Klin Vina winery in Contovello

⭐ Che cavolo, il prosecco è il nostro!

'Prosecco DOC then changed the name of the grape variety to 'glera', just like we have here,' Alessio explains. 'In the past, they always referred to it as prosecco. Anyone who had glera grapes in their vineyard was then allowed to call it prosecco. That's why the name was changed to glera, and the decision was made that only Veneto and Trieste were allowed to produce wine under the prosecco name. The protective designation shifted from the grape to the territory. Suddenly, wine growers in Valdobbiadene started to produce billions of bottles of prosecco. It was a thorn in our side: *"Che cavolo, il prosecco è il nostro!"* – "Prosecco belongs to us, damn it!" But we no longer make the wine because of rural depopulation, the challenging soil, and a government that apparently couldn't be bothered to invest in the local infrastructure. There was nothing we could do because we had nothing.'

Alessio and the society are now looking to write up a disciplinarium or procedure for their own version of prosecco wine, prosekar. This distinctively local wine can bring new life to the territory and tradition. The grapes used for its production are historically glera, vitovska and malvasia.

This is not Coca-Cola

Various young people in the region started their own vineyards in the hopes of becoming full-time wine growers. Karst is a wine region under development. Alessio: 'We need to plant a lot of grapevines together, and it will take quite a bit of time before we can produce enough grapes. Our approach is different: small-scale, organic and with respect for our natural surroundings. We don't want to become another Valdobbiadene, but a place where wine is an experience. This is a beautiful region along the Adriatic Coast. There isn't any wine tourism yet, but we're convinced that our concept will catch on.'

When I ask why they don't want to associate their sparkling wine with the prosecco name, Alessio is adamant: 'Prosecco is like Coca-Cola, a global brand name. We can't compete with that. We want to target people who are looking for more and explain to them that this is where prosecco really comes from. Our approach focuses on the experience and on our history. Prosekar is a unique story!'

Grapevines at the Klin winery

Glera grapes harvested for prosekar

DUINO AURISINA ④

The Karst Plateau or Karst region stretches along the southeast Slovenian and northeast Italian border. It is a Central European region marked by strong winds and rocky terrain, sometimes inhospitable and not always suitable for agriculture. This swathe of land between the Alps and the sea starts at Duino-Aurisina and Sgonico and runs through Slovenia to the Istrian coast.

Kante: painter and wine grower

I decide to stay in the wondrous Karst region a little longer. Teresa Renzi from Azienda Agricola Kante tells me about her wine domain. 'The combination of the red soil, the limestone rocks, the sea winds, the bitterly cold winters and arid hot summers produces wines with a unique acidity, mineral and salt content.

Edi Kante is one of the leading figures in the wine scene. The painter and inventor fell in love with the Karst region in 1980 and instantly saw great winegrowing potential. Edi Kante started to make his own wine in Duino Aurisina and built an extremely impressive wine cellar. I enter a giant cave, some 20 metres deep, that has been carved out of the natural rock face in different layers. The air is chilly, and I hear moisture dripping from the ceiling through a labyrinth that has its own unique acoustics. 'This is the perfect place for storing barrels and bottles throughout the year at an ideal temperature and humidity,' Teresa assures me.

Kantes' vineyards are situated some 250 metres above sea level, all of them facing the sea. The vineyards produce mostly white wines made from the two local grape varieties, vitovska and malvasia, but they also have chardonnay and sauvignon grapes. The red wines include a terrano and a pinot nero.

I have the pleasure of trying the malvasia in my lazy chair among the grapevines; it tastes refreshing and exceptionally delicious. Mild yet with an intensely fruity aroma.

I promise to visit Teresa again in ten years' time because the area is still fully under development. 'There aren't that many wine growers here yet, but there's certainly potential,' Teresa concludes.

Kante
Loc. Prepotto 1/A, Duino Aurisina

CARNIA

From the province of Trieste, I drive on to the geographic region of Carnia. After travelling 120 kilometres towards the northwest, I find myself back in the Alps and close to the Austrian border. Situated in the Friulian Dolomites, Carnia is absolutely stunning: a pristine nature reserve, almost unmarked by tourism, with rivers, mountains, picturesque villages and, above all, an authentic culture.

The mountain people speak Ladino as well as Italian. The people here carry Italy in their hearts alongside Austria and Slovenia, and that is clearly reflected in their cuisine.

Wine barrels in wine grower Kante's fantastic cellar

Carnia's natural surroundings are breathtakingly beautiful

Wild fennel grows in the hills around Villa di Verzegnis

VILLA DI VERZEGNIS ⑤

Friuli's cuisine embodies traces of a vast, complex region. Potatoes, barley, turnips, maize, pork and cheese form the basis of the traditional frugal fare with Habsburg, Jewish, Greek, Hungarian, Russian and Bohemian influences. Its beauty and originality can be found in the unique combinations of salty with a hint of sweet or sweet with a hint of salt. *Cjarsons* are probably the best example of this.

I visit the Antica Osteria Stella d'Oro to try this unique dish. This historical tavern is situated in the green Villa di Verzegnis valley and is a gastronomic landmark that is also greatly valued among the local residents. The welcoming restaurant with its beautiful terrace is located in the heart of a quiet village. The menu offers traditional dishes such as cjarsons, goose gnocchi, along with wild and local vegetables, including the famous *radic di mont.*

The owner, Francesco Marzona, also runs an *azienda agricola* or agribusiness with his brothers, where they grow the vegetables, fruit and grains for the restaurant. Moreover, they gather their own honey in this surprisingly biodiverse area.

Cjarsons

The name *cjarsons* or cjalzons, depending on the area, refers to a special type of herb ravioli.

They come in a variety of sizes and shapes, such as round, half-moon-shaped and boat-shaped. The filling varies from region to region and even from family to family.
The contrast between sweet and salt determines its unique flavour. The salty filling can also contain ingredients such as raisins, dark chocolate or cocoa, cinnamon, apple, pear or jam. The cjarsons are traditionally served with melted butter and cooked, grated ricotta.

According to a local legend, the huge variation in fillings is linked to the history of the *cramârs*, the travelling herb salesmen who crossed the Alps on foot from the 18th century. They kept their goods in a *crassigne*, a type of wooden backpack with small drawers. Cramârs crossed the Alps to sell their exotic Venetian wares in the Germanic countries. Their arrival home after the long journey was always cause for celebration.
The women would prepare cjarsons, a type of ravioli made from potatoes with a ricotta filling mixed with spices, dried fruit, sultanas, aromatic herbs, cocoa and whatever else was left in the crassigne's drawers. As a result, no two fillings were ever the same.

Cjarsons are a type of half-moon shaped ravioli

Cjarsons di Cercivento

SERVES 4 PEOPLE

FOR THE DOUGH

350 g 00 flour
350 ml lukewarm water (approx.)
1 pinch of salt
1 egg to seal the dough

FOR THE FILLING

400 g potatoes
1 small onion
50 g butter
fresh lemon verbena, mint and
    flat-leaf parsley: 1 sprig of each
peel of 1 lemon
60 g sultanas
1 tablespoon sugar
cup of white wine
    (or sweet dessert wine)
2 ground cloves
ground cinnamon
salt and pepper

FOR COOKING

meat or vegetable broth

FOR THE GARNISH

smoked ricotta cheese to taste
80 g butter
ground cinnamon

On a pastry board, shape a classic heap of flour with the salt added in, and gradually add the lukewarm water until you have a malleable dough. Keep a close eye on how much water the dough absorbs, and add more water if needed. Make sure that the dough is soft yet homogenous.

Transfer the dough to a work surface dusted with flour and knead it for a few minutes. Then roll it into a ball, cover, and leave it to proof for half an hour.

Meanwhile, cook the unpeeled potatoes. While the potatoes are cooking, soak the sultanas in white wine. You can also soak them a few hours beforehand for added flavour. Drain the sultanas, pat them dry, and coarsely chop them with a knife.

Finely chop the parsley together with the mint and lemon verbena. Melt the butter in a small pan, add the minced onion and sauté the onion without letting it turn brown.

Once the potatoes are cooked, pass them through a potato ricer and collect the mashed potatoes in a bowl. Add the chopped herbs, the minced onion with a bit of butter, the raisins, the lemon peel, the cinnamon, the cloves, one tablespoon of sugar, salt and pepper. Combine everything thoroughly and set aside.

Roll the dough out into a thin layer with a rolling pin. Dust your work surface and your rolling pin before rolling the dough. Using a dough ring or a glass, cut round discs measuring 7 to 8 cm in diameter. Place a bit of potato filling in the middle of each dough disc. Lightly beat the egg and coat the sides of the dough circle around the filling with the egg wash. Close the half-moon-shaped ravioli, press the edges down firmly and press small folds into the edges. Don't use too much egg, or else the ravioli won't seal properly.

Melt the butter for the garnish. Bring the meat or vegetable broth to a boil. As soon as the broth starts to simmer, dip a few pieces of the pasta at a time into the broth and bring the broth back to a boil. As soon as the ravioli start to float, cook them for a couple more minutes before taking them out of the pot with a skimmer.

Once all of the cjarsons are cooked, top the pasta with melted butter, a generous sprinkling of smoked ricotta and a pinch of cinnamon.

An isolated area

Sara is not entirely sure about this story. But she does know that the people here in the Alps lived in very isolated conditions and had to fend for themselves. 'This is an isolated area, and the people are self-sufficient, which is reflected in our culture and our cuisine,' she explains. Sara: 'The recipe for cjarsons is something personal that you don't easily share with others. This culinary tradition is cultivated in every family. Every Friulian family has their own codified recipe, passed on from generation to generation and safeguarded like a precious heirloom. Each valley has a different type of filling, which in turn varies from family to family.'

Even the restaurant here has its closely guarded secrets. Asking for the recipe is 'not done', and chef Mattia is brought in just to be on the safe side.

⭐ Tantalising the taste buds

I finally try the cjarsons according to Mattia's secret recipe. Will I be able to discern the flavours and ingredients?

The flavour palate varies from salty to sweet and back to salty again. Incredibly fresh and pure flavours. The sweet fruit, the fresh mint and basil dominate next to the sweetened cinnamon, the salty smoked ricotta and the pasta. I've undoubtedly missed a couple of flavours. What an experience. You really have to try this. Preferably right here in this restaurant.

I wasn't made privy to the restaurant's recipe, but Francesco did give me the official recipe from a neighbouring village, Cercivento. 'This dish is at its best in the summer when all the fresh herbs are readily available,' he adds. 'The dough used to be made with potatoes, but now we make it with water and flour.'

Where time stands still

Villa di Verzegnis in Carnia is a match made in heaven between nature and art. Sara speaks incredibly highly of her famous neighbour, Egidio Marzona. Marzona has described this place as follows, citing Goethe in the process: *To me the mountain's mass is nobly dumb*, and time seems to have stood still.'

'Marzona is the son of a Friulian emigrant to Germany. He collects art on a global scale. But he has always felt a close bond with the village of his birth and his beloved mountains,' Sara explains. 'In 1989, he designed

HERBAL OASIS

Mattia believes that the herbs make all the difference. 'You don't find them everywhere, and they're linked to a particular valley. The cjarsons filling is dependent on what the surroundings have to offer, such as mint, tarragon, nettles, and so on. And that also varies depending on the season. The herbs are foraged in the wild. You combine the herbs with something sweet like apple or pear. Some work with fig jam or make a plum filling.'

Francesco confirms this: 'Carnia has always been a paradise for herbs. It is Europe's richest herb garden.'

Egidio Marzona's garden

an art park featuring items from his modern art collection. These works of art stand out in the open air, and some are displayed in his personal museum that looks out over the park.

Open-air opera

I walk together with Francesco through the park with its contemporary art collection. 'Mostly minimalism and arte povera,' Francesco reiterates. 'Every summer, Egidio organises fantastic open-air opera performances in this park. The performances draws visitors from far beyond Italy. It's an experience we all want to be a part of: the village and the valley are then transformed with a magic wand!'

My dessert and the view at the Antica Osteria Stella d'Oro

Tiramisu

I walk back to the restaurant, because I'm still owed a dessert. And not just any dessert.

Tiramisu, the most famous Italian dessert worldwide, was invented in Friuli-Venezia in the 1950s – in Tolmezzo, Carnia's capital, to be precise. It all started with Norma Pielli, who ran the famous Albergo Roma restaurant in Tolmezzo together with her husband, Giuseppe (Beppino) Del Fabbro. Norma regularly prepared the traditional dessert 'Dolce Torino' in her kitchen, a dish also familiar to Pellegrino Artusi (the author of: *Science in the Kitchen and the Art of Eating Well, La scienza in cucina e l'arte di mangiar bene)*. Dolce Torino was made from butter, chocolate and ladyfingers.

But Norma felt that something was needed to spice it up. And so, she replaced the butter with a mascarpone cream and the chocolate with bitter coffee syrup. The tiramisu was born! The original recipe that the Del Fabbro family had certified with documents that prove the dessert's

provenance doesn't include any liqueur. Beppino chose the name tiramisu because the combination of coffee and mascarpone served as a real pick-me-up: *tirami su.*

This scrumptious dessert was an instant success, and connoisseurs found their way to Albergo Roma. Today, tiramisu is the quintessential spoon dessert in Italy and the rest of the world.

Of national importance

For years, the regions of Veneto and Friuli-Venezia Giulia competed over the tiramisu recipe's authorship. It was a matter of national importance. Journalist Gigi Padovani and author Clara Vada did some extensive research and discovered that the dessert didn't originate in the restaurant Le Beccherie in Treviso. The owners published their recipe in a book for the first time in the 1970s. They discovered an older recipe for tirami su, that had been on the menu of Albergo Roma in Tolmezzo since the 1950s. Would you like to learn more? Read all about this wondrous dish in the book *Tiramisù. Storia, curiosità, interpretazioni del dolce italiano più amato* by Clara and Gigi Padovani (2016).

Meanwhile, Friuli-Venezia Giulia's claim to be the birthplace of the dish has been officially recognized. The official recipe has been recorded, together with the criteria which the original tiramisu must meet. Today, 25 patisseries and restaurants are allowed to serve the original tiramisu, including Antica Osteria Stella d'Oro. These certified establishments receive a porcelain plate marked with the text 'tirami su' to hang in their place of business.

⭐ Niente amaretto – no amaretto

Chef Mattia makes a much lighter tiramisu than I'm used to. The biscuits have been thoroughly soaked beforehand for an intense coffee flavour. I don't taste any amaretto. Mattia had no idea that amaretto is often added to this dish. He sighs and frowns before decidedly answering: *'Niente amaretto!'* Mattia: 'The recipe is very simple. We use a sweet rum, but alcohol is often not used at all. We don't add cream. Only eggs, mascarpone, sugar, cocoa powder and biscuits.'

**Antica Osteria Stella d'Oro,
Via Tolmezzo 6, Villa di Verzegnis, UD**

Tiramisu by the rules

SERVES 6 PEOPLE

4 whole eggs
300 g white sugar
500 g mascarpone cheese
40/50 savoiardi biscuits or ladyfingers
300 cl bitter, strong coffee, left to cool
  and with rum added in, if desired
100 g bitter cocoa powder

Prepare the coffee (mocha or espresso) beforehand and leave it to cool. Put the egg whites in a bowl and beat them into stiff peaks with a pinch of salt. Whisk the egg yolks with the sugar, then fold the mascarpone in with a spatula and slowly fold from the bottom up to make a cream. Finally, add the stiff egg whites and combine everything very slowly, from the bottom up, so the resulting cream doesn't collapse.

Place a layer ladyfingers that have been soaked in the coffee and drained beforehand on the bottom of a tureen or an oven-proof dish. Spread half the cream mixture over the biscuit layer. Top the cream with a second layer of ladyfingers that have been soaked and drained, just like the bottom layer. Spread the remaining cream out on top. Leave the dessert to set in the fridge for twelve hours. Dust the dessert with unsweetened cocoa passed through a sieve before serving.

VENETO

Veneto is hemmed in between Trentino-Alto Adige, Emilia-Romagna, Lombardy, Austria, Friuli-Venezia Giulia, and the Adriatic Sea. The Dolomites and Carnic Alps form a natural border to the north. To the southwest lies Lake Garda, while a fertile plain to the south stretches all the way to the Gulf of Venice.

The region's very rich cuisine betrays Veneto's historical importance through its many different types of crops and cattle. Rice dishes and spices hint at the Eastern and other exotic influences from its many trading partners.

Venetian cuisine is very versatile, with an abundance of fish dishes in the coastal areas and vegetable and grain-based specialities in the hills.

In terms of wine styles, Veneto boasts Italy's largest wine territory. This region is one of the country's most important producers of high-quality wine. The vineyards extend over 75,000 hectares of land over the plains, hills and mountains. Veneto means fine wine; the people here are wine lovers and connoisseurs.

A typical terraced vineyard in Veneto.

Venice, Veneto's water-rich capital

Lago
di Garda

Verona
④

Vicenza
③

Padova
②

Venezia
①

Piave

Adige

Po

VENEZIA ①

My journey of discovery starts in Venice. I soak up the atmosphere in this city of doges and dive into the world of the *ombra*, which literally translates to 'shade'. Ombra means wine here. Drinking an ombra is an ode to friendship and solidarity. This ritual refers to the wine trade that took place in the shadow of St Mark's bell tower. In the olden days, the wine merchants would follow the tower's shadow. They would move their cart into the shifting shade to keep their wine cool.

A gondola is a unique way to explore Venice

At Bàcaro Cà D'Oro alla Vedova

BÀCARI

The wine bars are called bàcari here. The name is perhaps derived from the Venetian *far bàcara,* which means to celebrate in honour of the wine god, Bacchus. You need to have visited a bàcari in Venice at least once in your life, and not just for the delicious wines.

Cicchètti

Bàcari resemble bars or pubs; this is where people go to socialise and have fun while they enjoy small side dishes with bruschette, stewed beans, grilled squid, smoked baby squid, sardines in a saor sauce, marinated eel, egg halves with anchovies, grilled *polenta, baccalà, trippa,* meatballs or fried anchovies.

These snacks are known as *cicchètti* in the Venetian dialect, which means a small or modest amount. You serve them with a glass of wine or ombra. If you hear a Venetian say *andar per ombre*, or let's find some shade, they are referring to the ritual of snacks with a glass of wine.

The bàcari don't serve full meals like in the trattoria or restaurants. You can recognise a bàcaro by the dark wood of the bar, chairs and tables, and the grand selection of cicchètti in the glass display counter.

To sum up, a cicchètto is a quick snack that you eat on the go, and 'un ombra' is a glass of wine that you drink as an aperitif in the shade of a bàcaro, or bar/osteria. Remember those three key words when you go hunting for tradition street or apéro food in Venice.

BAR
75 recipes

In the Cantine del Vino già Schiavi, I meet Alessandra De Respinis, the owner of this bàcaro. We find ourselves in the picturesque Dorsoduro district. Alessandra makes hundreds of cicchètti, baguette slices with countless different toppings. This *schiavi bàcari* or tavern has been around since the late 19th century. In 1945, Sisto Gastaldi took over the business. His son Lino kept the business going, together with his wife Alessandra De Respinis whom he met here by coincidence in 1960. Lino has sadly passed away.

A chichetto with brie and anchovies

Cicchètti as art

I step inside the bar and am immediately impressed by the display of exquisite *cicchètti*. Each and every one of them is a tiny work of art. Countless bottles of wine await thirsty customers on shelves lining the wall. But the display counter, with Alessandra standing behind it, is the central showpiece. Alessandra beams with pride as I stare in wonder at the display. But what are all those ingredients so artfully displayed on the baguette slices? Alessandra sums up: 'Shrimp and sweet and sour cabbage, gorgonzola and walnuts, ricotta and caviar, truffle eggs and mushrooms, cream cheese and pesto, pumpkin cream and Parmesan cheese, *primo sale* cheese and radicchio, brie and nettle sauce...'

Mio giardino segreto – my secret garden

What a rich and gastronomic selection of mini dishes! I try several of them and realise it's hard to pick a favourite. The mini slices of bread are crispy yet soft, savoury yet sweet, earthy yet briny. And every single one of them is perfectly balanced. A seamless combination of modern and classic. I award Alessandra three stars in my non-existent Michelin guide for cicchètti. 'I'm constantly thinking up new creations such as this

cicchètto di castagna with chestnut puree and creamy robiola cheese,' Alessandra confirms.

I tell her how much I enjoyed the cicchètto with tuna tartare and the one with the egg and the flowers. The rose, daisy, violet, lemon verbena and marigold all come from her personal garden. 'Mio giardino segreto. I have a private garden in Venice where I go to relax and unwind,' she explains.

The tuna tartare is a story in its own right: 'My customers will rebel if I stop serving the tuna tartare. It's a combination of tuna, capers, egg yolk, parsley and mayonnaise, dusted with unsweetened cocoa powder. With this combination, I won second prize in a culinary competition in Mexico City,' she declares proudly.

Cicchèttario

In 2020, Alessandra introduced a 'Cicchèttario' in memory of her husband. This cookbook contains the most fantastic cicchètti recipes. Each recipe comes with a wine suggestion recommended by her son, oenologist Piero. 'This book is the product of my brave, dedicated mother's creativity and innovative drive. This is the story of her life, her family and this place,' Piero adds.

Alessandra points out that she puts a lot of love and passion into these refined recipes. Alessandra: 'The bread is just as important. We use freshly baked baguettes. The bread must be fresh and crispy and sliced into slices measuring about a centimetre and a half thick.'

Wine by the glass

Every day, Già Schiavi serves about 25 different wines, mostly from Veneto, which you can order by the glass. Piero: 'You eat, drink and pay at the counter.' This is an important detail because this is not a restaurant. He continues with a slogan from the book: '*Un cicchètto non ha senso senza un'ombra e un'ombra non ha senso senza un cicchètto!*' In other words, you always drink a glass of wine with a cicchètto, and you always have a cicchètto with a glass of wine!

Cantine del Vino già Schiavi
Dorsoduro 992, Fondamenta Nani, Venice

A cicchètto with gorgonzola and walnuts

Cream of asparagus with courgette and sundried tomatoes

WINE TIP: VESPAIOLLO

Put about twenty green asparagus tips (pre-cooked for 10 minutes in salted water) in a blender together with a spoonful of extra-virgin olive oil, salt and pepper. Blend to a smooth paste. Slice one courgette lengthways into thin slices, salt them and let them rest for 15 minutes. Then, grill the courgettes for a couple of minutes.

Spread the asparagus cream on a baguette slice measuring 1 1/2 cm thick, place a grilled courgette slice on top and garnish with a piece of sundried tomato.

Melon mousse with ham and pistachio

WINE TIP: GRILLO

Blend a quarter of honeydew melon and combine with 125 g ricotta. Season to taste with salt and pepper. Blend to a smooth cream. Place a slice of *prosciutto crudo* (Parma ham, San Daniele ham or another Italian cured ham of your choice) on a baguette slice measuring 1 1/2 cm thick. Spread the melon cream over the top and garnish with chopped pistachios.

Cauliflower florets in a spicy sauce

WINE TIP: SAUVIGNON

Blend a grilled sweet pepper with a clove of garlic, extra-virgin olive oil, pepper, salt and spicy spices such as *peperoncino* or cayenne pepper. Blend to a cream. Spread a layer of this spicy pepper cream on a 1 1/2 cm-thick baguette slice, top with raw cauliflower florets and finish with a couple of dollops of extra pepper cream. Garnish with a lettuce leaf.

Tuna tartare with cocoa powder

WINE TIP: PROSECCO BRUT

Take two cooked egg yolks, 100 g tuna in oil, half a spoonful of capers, a pinch of parsley and two spoonfuls of mayonnaise. Combine everything into a homogenous whole. Place a lettuce leaf on a baguette slice measuring 1 1/2 cm thick, spread the tuna tartare over the top and lightly dust cocoa powder over the tartare.

Brie with a nettle cream

WINE TIP: VERDISO

Braise 250 g nettle leaves and blend with 50 g grated Parmesan cheese, 50 g pine nuts, salt and a spoonful of extra-virgin olive oil. Top a baguette slice 1 1/2 cm thick with a slice of brie covered with the nettle cream, followed by another slice of brie and another layer of nettle cream. And the cicchètto is ready!

You can buy fresh fish at the Mercato di Rialto in Venice

MERCATO DI PESCE

For fish and shellfish, I make my way to the Rialto fish market along the Campiello de la Pescaria. The name is derived from Rivo Alto, the part of the city with the highest banks. Today, Rialto is the beating heart of Venetian trade, but it hasn't always been. This used to be where the seat of government was located. The impressive loggia at the Rialto fish market is now the place to be for aperitifs and cicchètti.

**Mercato di Rialto,
Sestiere S. Polo 122, Venice**

Fritolin

In addition to bàcari, Venice also has small *fritolin* where fish is fried and served in paper cones, *scartosso di pesce fritto*. The smell of fritolin has been gracing Italian alleyways since 1700. People would prepare the small fish from the day's catch supplied by the fishermen. And what else did you need? White flour, a sieve and a large pot of boiling oil.

BAR
The right way

Today, you will still find *scartosso di pesce fritto* in Venetian bars and restaurants. 'We fry our fish the right way,' Luca Franchin from WEnice seafood bar says. 'We coat the cleaned fish in the right flour and fry them in the perfect amount of oil. Today, we prepare a larger variety of fish, crabs, squid and shrimp. We also sell fried polenta, pumpkin, broccoli, courgettes, artichokes, and asparagus.'

**WEnice
Calle de le Beccarie o Panateria 319, Venice**

Moeche

Luca: 'In the spring and the autumn, when the lagoon crabs moult, we fry another Venetian delicacy, the *moeche*. That's when the crabs exchange their old shell for a new one, making them very briefly incredibly soft and tender. Dedicated *moecanti,* or crab fishermen, fish the crabs one by one from the lagoon's shallow waters around the islands of Giudecca, Chioggia and Burano. These skilled fishermen learn how to select the moeche during the moulting period and this knowledge is passed from father to son.

Moeche means 'soft' in the Venetian dialect. The silky soft crabs from the lagoon are rare and valuable, real jewels of the sea. The Slow Food Presidium supplies the necessary quality guarantee. 'The crabs are so soft and intense in flavour that you eat them in their entirety in a light, crispy crust made from just eggs and flour. We sell them deep-fried or with Veneto's typical white polenta. You will find the crispy, fried version wrapped in paper in restaurants and on the streets, but the moeche are also excellent when you boil and season them with oil, garlic and parsley.'

Pesce fritto

LIVE CRABS IN THE FRIDGE

I decide not to try this delicacy because of the way it's prepared. The moeche is eaten when it's at its freshest, just a couple of hours after the catch. The crabs are cooked alive. People wash them, cut into their backs so all the moisture seeps out and then leave them in a bowl with beaten eggs and a pinch of salt for a couple of hours. The crabs eat part of the egg mixture in the bowl. They are then coated in flour and deep-fried in boiling oil until golden brown. The moeche are served with extra salt and a couple of lemon wedges. A real Venetian tradition, but thankfully also rare.

Piazza della Frutta in Padua

PADOVA ②

I leave Venice and head to Padua, 40 kilometres further west. La Folperia of Max and Barbara Schiavo is my next stop. This is where you can buy cooked *moscardi*, or baby squid, called *folpetti*, just like in Venice. Folpetti are among the most famous street food dishes that have their origins in the lagoon. This was once cheap fare, but the folpetti on Padua's Piazza della Frutta have become incredibly trendy. La Folperia in the city's historical centre comes highly recommended. This simple kiosk with local fish specialities served in paper plates is located right in front of the Palazzo della Ragione in the Canton delle Busie, or the 'corner of lies'. The name refers to the trade among merchants back in the day.

Max and Barbara Schiavo's La Folperia

Folpetti

Max: 'You will find folpetti mainly in Venice and Padua. The baby squid are also a tradition in Padua because the Venetian lagoon used to stretch all the way to Padua. The water reached as far as this square. In the 19th century, the canals in the city were drained. You will find folpetti in street food stalls and in the bàcari in Venice. 'They're boiled baby squid seasoned with oil, garlic, and parsley,' Max explains. 'We don't remove the head and the innards, and that makes the moscardini or squid so unique.' Barbara shows me the pots containing the warm *folpi*, or squid. I also see a display counter with *bovoetti* or land snails, *moeche* or crabs, *peoci* or mussels and small fish.

Squid and nostalgia

I try a plate of warm folpetti with a splash of extra-virgin olive oil and salsa verde; the big smile and the touch of nostalgia are an added bonus. What a flavourful delight in this wonderful place! 'Eat this with a fine spritz or a glass of prosecco,' Max recommends.
'Our parents started this kiosk 40 years ago,' he explains. 'Only about a dozen polpari or squid stands remain in Veneto today. We are the last in Padua's historical centre.'

La Folperia
Piazza della Frutta 1, Padua

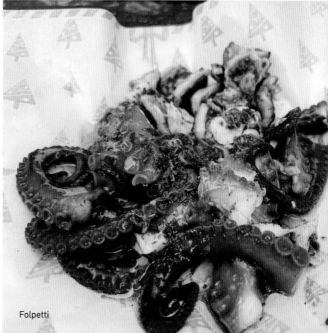
Folpetti

Barbara, Alexa and Luisa at the 'La Folperia' folpetti stall.

Authentic Veneto aperitif

I pass tables coloured with glasses of a red aperitif. This bitter-sweet cocktail is the ultimate thirst-quencher. *Spritz* is Veneto's characteristic aperitif, made from a red liqueur, prosecco and soda or sparkling water. This world-famous aperitif is light and versatile. I quench my thirst in Bar Margherita on the Piazza della Frutta. The waiter, Pietro, is only too happy to tell me all about this spritz. Piero: 'Padua plays a very important role in the history of this drink of the gods, of which several versions exist.' He has caught my attention.

Spritz bianco

Spritz turns orange with Aperol and red with Campari. But spritz was originally white or translucent. The drink owes its origins to soldiers from the Austrian empire, who ruled the Lombardo-Venetian Kingdom in the 19th century. The military normally drank beer, but the Venetian wines here had a much higher alcohol content. And so the wine was diluted with water or soda. Nowadays, people still water down the wine, especially in Trente and in the smaller cities in Veneto and Trieste. *Vino sprizato* is even well-known in Milan. If you want to try the original spritz in Padua, order a spritz bianco.

Symbol of economic growth

Colour was added to the spritz, and it gained popularity as a cocktail in the 1920s. Aperol from the Fratelli Barbieri company (from Padua) was added during the first Paduan trade fair in 1919. Select from the Venetian brothers Fratelli Pilla & Co later became an alternative to Aperol from 1920 onwards.

The spritz instantly conquered Padua, Venice and the entire region. Sophisticated Aperol advertising campaigns made the spritz a household name throughout Northern Italy in the 1950s. The advertisements with the Aperol bottle in art nouveau style became symbolic of economic growth in Italy.

Fratelli Barbieri started to establish an international profile after it was acquired by the Campari Group (Milan) in 2003. Campari had accurately gauged Aperol's potential. Pietro believes that Padua is the uncrowned capital of spritz because of Aperol's rich history. But not everyone agrees. The 'Venetian spritz' has been an official cocktail since 2011, according to the IBA, the International Bartenders Association...

Bar Margherita
Piazza della Frutta 44, Padua

Drinks are supplied by boat in Venice

The bartender at Caffé Martel prepares a spritz

PIETRO'S RECIPE

Spritz

PER GLASS

100 ml prosecco
50 ml sparkling water
50 ml bitters from one of the following brands:
 Aperol, Campari, Select, Cynar, Luxardo or Fiero
ice cubes
a slice of orange

First, pour the ice cubes into a large glass, followed by the prosecco, the soda or sparkling water and finally the bitters. Make sure that you turn the bottle as you pour the bitters. Combine everything with a bar spoon and garnish with half a slice of orange.

Bitter variations

Pietro shows me the various combinations for spritz:

Spritz with Select: 'The little-known authentic Venetian spritz.'

Spritz with Campari: 'In Venice, people will ask you whether you want a spritz with Campari (red) or Aperol (orange).'

Spritz with Aperol: 'This is the classic spritz with Aperol, which gives the cocktail its orange colour.'

Spritz with Cynar: 'The famous bitter Cynar made from artichokes, the most "amaro" of them all.'

Spritz with Luxardo: 'The latest addition to the spritz range with a deep orange colour, less sweet than with Aperol.'

Spritz with Fiero: 'A fine blend of bitter and sweet.'

'Aperol is for the purists, Select for the nostalgic, Cynar for people who love bitter, and Luxardo for the avant-garde... And last but not least: spritz is sacred to all Venetians!' Pietro concludes.

Spritz is a must in Padua. The aperitif is inextricably linked with the city. Drinking a spritz on the terrace or in a bar at the Piazza delle Erbe or the Piazza della Frutta is one of those things you have to do when you're in Padua.

VICENZA ③

Vicenza is located 50 kilometres northwest of Padua. I arrange to meet chef Luca Chemello, the leading expert regarding the sacred *bacalà alla Vicentina*. His Locanda Veneta is situated in the suburbs. Here, you can order traditional local dishes. Luca is obsessed with Venetian gastronomy and is a member of the local brotherhood. He prepares the characteristic dishes of this society.

Cooking at his mother's knee

Luca teaches cooking lessons to tourists and takes them on a culinary tour of Veneto. The *fagottini* (a type of ravioli) filled with ricotta and pear is a coveted dish. These fagottini are typical for Veneto's cuisine, where salt and sweetness often go together. Another example is the *sarde in saor*, which I will come back to later in this chapter. Luca is an ambassador for traditional, local cuisine, which he disseminates in places as far away as Melbourne, Australia. Luca: 'The large Venetian community there organises an annual bacalà festival. Bacalà is a real tradition in Vicenza; we even established a brotherhood in 1987, of which I'm a proud member. I started in my father's kitchen when I was barely five years old. I am of the third generation of chefs in our family.'

Locanda Veneta
Via Battagione Valtellina 138, Vicenza

Luca Chemello

Stoccafisso

The province of Vincenza has a unique bond with Norway, more specifically, the Lofoten Islands. That is because Veneto is the largest importer of *stoccafisso*, stockfish from Norway. The bacalà in Vincenza is not made from salted cod but from Norwegian stockfish.

Stoccafisso

Cod baccalà is salted and dried, while stockfish bacalà is only dried on wooden racks in the cold Norwegian air. Stockfish is not only made from dried cod but can also be dried ling, cusk, hake, pollock or haddock. Bacalà alla Vincentina is spelled with one c instead of the double c for the traditional salted cod baccalà.

Lofoten fish

Stockfish bacalà is unique in the province because of an important historical event. 'Messer Piero Querini introduced the stockfish to these parts,' Luca explains. 'In 1431, this Venetian merchant was looking for trade opportunities beyond the Mediterranean Sea. He left Candia, what is now called Crete, with a ship loaded with malvasia wine, spices and cotton for Flanders in the Low Countries. He was shipwrecked along the way. At the mercy of the waves and the winds, he and his surviving crew eventually washed ashore on a small island covered in snow: one of the Lofoten islands. The sailors were taken in, fed and cared for by the locals. That's how they discovered 'tørrfisk' and the special technique used to preserve the fish. The fish was cleaned and then left to dry in the wind until the fish were 'as hard as a stick'. The Venetian took this remarkable food back home with him. Many of the region's poor benefitted from the fish and this unique preserving technique. Stockfish became an affordable yet profitable popular product that stored well.'

⭐ Bacalà brotherhood

'Every September, a Festa del Bacalà all Vicentina is held in Sandrigo in the province of Vicenza,' Luca says. 'The stockfish takes centre stage. It is prepared according to regulations set forth by the honourable Confraternita del Bacalà alla Vincentina. This is where you eat the fish according to tradition: with polenta. The Bacalà brotherhood protects and promotes the over 400-year-old original recipe of Bacalà alla Vicentina. In Vicenza, people make the most wondrous dishes from this woody, hardy stockfish that has been beaten, soaked and cooked with endless patience. The variations are countless, but they all agree on one thing: never stir the bacalà!

Bacalà alla Vicentina Brotherhood
www. baccalaallavicentina.it

Vicenza

Bacalà and polenta

VERONA
ta Borsari, 3 – tel. 045/00 487
0A (zona stadio) tel. 045 57 66

Every bakery in Verona has its own recipe for the torta russa

VERONA ④

Verona, the city of love, lies 60 kilometres west of Vicenza. If you love someone, take them to Verona. This is where Shakespeare's tragic love story of Romeo and Juliet took place. Juliet's home with its famous balcony, her tomb, and Romeo's house are major tourist attractions. Verona preserves the myth in its old squares, alleyways and courtyards.

The city's overt sweetness is reflected in its cuisine. The city and the province have made a name for themselves with their sweet treats. According to Alessandro De Rossi, 'Verona has always been home to excellent pâtissiers, and even our industrial bakers have achieved great success in marketing sweet pastries.' Verona is the birthplace of the pandoro, first devised by Melegatti. Bauli, Paduani and Melegatti are the three most important industrial bakeries in Verona. They make panettone and pandoro.

Alessandro De Rossi and his wife

Torta russa

Alessandro runs *pastificio* De Rossi in Verona's city centre. The enticing *torta russa* in this bakery's display window immediately catches my attention. It is pure dolce amore, or 'sweet love' in food form. This exquisite sweet treat is a puff pastry filled with a delicate mixture of almonds, amaretti and eggs. Alessandro: 'The cake owes its name to the *colbacco* or *oesjanka*, or the Russian fur hat shape with ear flaps that is typically worn in Russia, Armenia and Afghanistan. The cake is believed to be the invention of a Veronese pâtissier on a cruise ship. He dedicated the cake in Odessa to a beautiful Russian girl with whom he had fallen in love.' According to Alessandro, there could be some truth to this story, and the cake must have been made somewhere else because the almonds in the cake are not native to Verona. Torta russa is a relatively recent Veronese delicacy dating from after the Second World War. Alessandro grew up with the cake. 'This popular pastry is mostly eaten in family circles as a *dolce di casa*, or a pastry for at home,' he explains.

We slice the cake, and I take a bite. The cake holds its own between dry and soft and tends towards bread, but it's clearly a dessert. The puff pastry is lightly salted, and the almond filling is deliciously sweet. 'A torta russa will keep for up to six days, and you don't store it in the refrigerator. The cake retains its flavour because of the almonds,' Alessandro adds. 'This is 100 per cent Veronese and one of the most commonly sold local desserts. Tourists come and visit Verona just for this cake. This cake hasn't been awarded an official De.Co. designation because every baker in Verona uses a slightly different recipe, which is why we don't want to patent it. Torta russa is available for sale in all the finest bakeries.'

De Rossi,
Corso Porta Borsari 1/A, Verona

The De Rossi bakery

Baci di Giulietta and baci di Romeo

Kisses from Romeo and Giulietta

Before I leave, I try two other Veronese delicacies, *baci di Giulietta* and *baci di Romeo*. They are small hazelnut-almond biscuits covered in a cocoa or vanilla glaze. Traditionally, men give women Juliet kisses, and women give men Romeo kisses as an expression of their love.

According to historical sources, the story of the two starcrossed lovers dates from 1303, when the Scaligeri family ruled Verona. The feud between the Montecchi and Capuleti was so fierce that the poet Dante referred to it in his writings. Afterwards, Luigi Da Porto recorded the story in his *Historia novellamente ritrovata di due nobili amanti*. The tragedy became known throughout Europe in different versions by various authors. In the late 16th century, William Shakespeare used the story for his most famous play of all time. It's a love story that has gained great symbolic value over the centuries, an undying icon shaped by the collective consciousness, immortalised not only in books but also in music (Tchaikovsky, Prokofiev, Gounod, Bellini) and film.

Pandoro towers

I say goodbye to Alessandro, cookies in hand. Images and snatches of music from the Romeo and Juliet saga drift through my mind as I stroll along the picturesque streets and impressive buildings of this romantic city. A hundred metres further down the road, I stop in front of the shoe shop where Melegatti's pandoro was once invented. The building's facade still boasts a large vertical sign with the word 'Melegatti' painted in blue. But my eye is particularly drawn to the two towers shaped like pandoro on top. How cool is this! Alessandro tipped me off to this little piece of culinary history. 'It's a very well-kept secret. Almost no one knows of its existence,' he tells me.

Do not leave Verona without having seen Juliet's balcony first

The Adige River flows through Verona

Sarde in saor

I also visit the Osteria da Ugo in Verona where I have arranged to meet owner Ezio Martel and chef Daniele Colletti. Ezio used to travel the world as a watch salesman. 'I like to eat, so I thought, why don't I start my own restaurant?' he smiles. The osteria is a fine place that only serves dishes with local ingredients. 'We Italians like to eat from our own land,' Ezio assures me.

I want to learn more about *sarde in saor*, one of the leading culinary dishes in Veneto. Sarde in saor is one of the region's oldest dishes. The tantalisingly refreshing, sweet and sour snack is an excellent accompaniment for an aperitif. Both the accompanying soave and the glass of sauvignon are a perfect match.

'Saor means flavour in the Venetian dialect. The ingredients are simple and frugal but artfully combined. The recipe calls for sardines, onions, raisins, pine nuts and vinegar. This cold dish dates back to 1300,' Daniele says.

Sweet and sour

Daniele: 'With saor, you prepare the fish with vinegar so it keeps longer. Saor is typical for Veneto: the browned, sweetened onion comes from gardens on the lagoon islands. The sultana raisins from grapes and pine nuts are reminiscent of the former "gateway to the East". The Venetian fishermen who prepared this dish on board at the time only used ingredients that they had in the hold. Valuable raisins and pine nuts were not among those ingredients back then. Our sardines come from Lake Garda,' Ezio adds.

Osteria da Ugo,
Vicolo Dietro Sant'Andrea 1/B, Verona

Sarde in saor

SERVES 4 TO 5 PEOPLE

500 g sardines
white 00 flour, as needed
1 kilo onions
neutral oil for frying
extra-virgin olive oil, as needed
1 teaspoon sugar

1 glass of white wine vinegar
sultana raisins and pine nuts,
as needed
salt and pepper to taste

Thoroughly clean the sardines and remove the heads. Coat the fish with flour and fry them in a generous amount of neutral oil. Drain on paper towels to remove the excess oil.

Peel and trim the onions. Slice them in very thin slices. Sauté the onion slices over low heat in extra-virgin olive oil in a pan with high sides. As soon as the onions turn brown, add the spoonful of sugar and the vinegar. Let the liquid evaporate over high heat. Continue to simmer the onions over low heat. Take your time; the onions need to be nice and soft. Add the pre-soaked raisins and pine nuts. Season with salt and pepper.

Layer the ingredients in a serving dish. Use the fried sardines for the first layer. Add a second layer with the sweet onions. Continue with the sardines, followed by the onions, and continue to layer until all the ingredients have been used up. Marinate the fish for at least a day. This softens the bones and gives the fish added flavour. Eat the dish at room temperature with slices of grilled polenta.

EMILIA-ROMAGNA

Emilia-Romagna is situated between Veneto, Lombardy, Piedmont, Liguria, Tuscany and the Marche region. Bologna is the region's capital. Emilia-Romagna owes its name to the ancient Roman road – Via Emilia – that crosses this territory and has been connecting Rome with the European heartland for over 2000 years. This is one of the most prosperous regions in Europe.

Emilia-Romagna is an important centre for culture and tourism. Bologna boasts the oldest university in the world, while Modena, Parma and Ferrara betray Romanesque influences and are a testimony to the richness of the Renaissance period. The coastal towns of Romagna Cervia, Cesenatico, Rimini and Riccione are major tourist draws.

Countless beach parasols provide shade for the many sun worshippers in the seaside resort of Rimini.

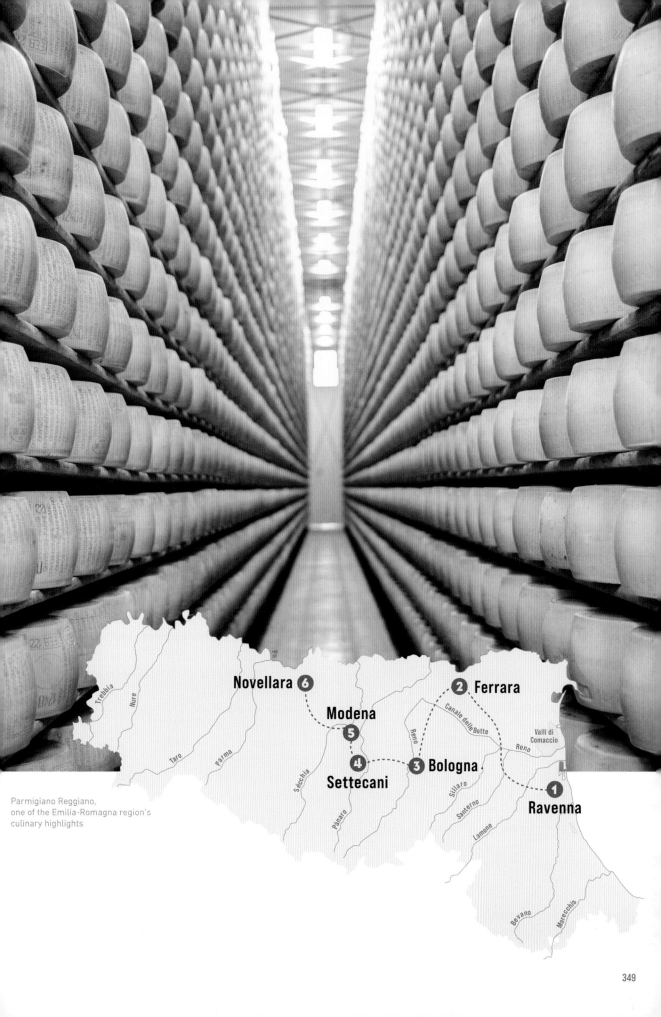

Parmigiano Reggiano,
one of the Emilia-Romagna region's
culinary highlights

Novellara ⑥

Modena
⑤

④
Settecani

② Ferrara

③ Bologna

① Ravenna

Trebbia
Nure
Po
Taro
Parma
Sécchia
Pánaro
Reno
Canale della Botte
Valli di Comaccio
Reno
Sillaro
Santerno
Lamone
Bévano
Marecchia

Broth with tortellini in Bologna

RAVENNA ①

I start my journey along the Riviera Romagnola in Ravenna. This town became famous thanks to the gorgeous mosaics that grace the interiors of Ravenna's religious monuments, which have been listed as a UNESCO World Heritage site. But the *la piadina* also deserves an award. This street food is very popular in Ravenna and Romagna. The uncrowned queen of Italian street food is a favourite among millions of people across the globe. The piadina or *piada* has been a mainstay of the local gastronomy for centuries.

Federico Lorenzo from La Piadina del Melarancio waits for me in Ravenna's historical centre. I ask him what piadina means to the local residents. '*È il nostro pane* – it is our bread! We have all been raised on piadina. It is a tradition we gladly share with the entire world,' he replies.

Culinary heritage

As we see so often in gastronomic history, the truly popular flavours often originate from frugal fare. Federico: 'The piadina is a simple dish with a long history. The filling is whatever you want it to be. The flatbread makes a perfect single meal or snack, but you can also use it for delicious appetisers. Piadina goes very well with the fine cured meats from Emilia Romagna and flavourful cheeses such as *pecorino, squacquerone* or *stracchino*.'

Piada or piadina

Federico: 'In Cesena and Ravenna north of Rimini, they eat piadina, and from Rimini to Cattolica, they have piada. Some prefer the thinner piada alla Riminese to the thicker piadina from Ravenna.'

Both on the shore and further inland, I come across piadina or piada stands *(piadinerie)* and small specialised shops. I find numerous variations on the 'flatbread' theme on the menu. Piadina or piada is often served as a side dish in high-end restaurants.

La Piadina del Melarancio
Via IV Novembre 31, Ravenna

FOOD VALLEY

Gastronomic and winegrowing traditions flourish here in Emilia-Romagna. Opera star Luciano Pavarotti was a great fan of the region's typical flavours. During my travels, I come across the finest quality products, artfully displayed at the butcher's or in artisanal grocery shops. The menu boasts filled pasta made from soft wheat flour. The tortelloni, lasagna, and tagliatelle belong to Bologna, but you can also find them elsewhere in the region. The Parmesan cheese known as Parmigiano Reggiano is produced in workshops in Reggio Emilia, Parma, Modena and Bologna, while Grana Padano is produced in other parts of the region. Eel and mussels are reflective of the fish caught on the Adriatic coast, but the region is particularly famous for its meat products. The charcuterie is legendary. Pork is processed into Parma's *prosciutto, coppa, culatello* and *salame felini*, Piancenza's *pancetta*, Bologna's *mortadella*, Modena's *cotechino* and Ferrara's salami. Emilia-Romagna is home to an extensive selection of IGP and DOP products.

Food for the poor

The *piadina romagnola* originates from the Etruscan period. Throughout the centuries, the simple yet versatile piadina was a meal for farmers and poor people. The grain was meant for bread. But around 1300, during the plague years, the farmers were too poor to afford bread. They ate polenta and flatbread made from poorer-quality grains, dried pulses and acorns.

The courts and manors flourished during the Renaissance period, and the large noble banquets were the talk of the town. This is where the finest chefs earned their patents of nobility. Examples include the much-treasured *Cristoforo di Messibugo* in Ferrara, who put the House of Este on the culinary map. He made sure that the poor could eat flatbread during times of food scarcity.

In the early twentieth century, the piada was given a new lease on life. The combination of maize and wheat flour made a fine dough, and the flatbread was cheap. Five and six-year-old-girls learned to make the dough and bake the aromatic piada or piadina.

But the real breakthrough didn't come until the 1940s and the 1950s when the piadina became a popular snack among seaside tourists. The first stands appeared along the side of the coastal roads and have been an indispensable part of Romagna's food culture ever since.

Piadina in Ravenna

Federico heats piadinas on the stovetop

Art nouveau, hats and Benigni

I visit Al Cairoli in Ravenna's historical centre. The proprietor, Attilio Bassini, is a surveyor and has his own construction business, but he also belongs to a family of millers. He runs this eatery together with his wife, Raffaella. Al Cairoli is a shop and a restaurant featuring local dishes. 'For a hundred years, this building housed a hat shop. I was blinded by the beauty of its art nouveau facade and the interior,' Attilio says. 'This is the most beautiful shop in Ravenna, if I do say so myself.'

I love the pictures lining the wall, they're of actor Roberto Begnini, who filmed a couple of scenes here for the hilarious film *Johnny Stecchino*. Everything exudes vitality here. I am allowed to watch as the piadina is made. Raffaella: 'The piadina romagnola's recipe is one of the cornerstones of the regional gastronomy, which explains its IGP designation.' There is an official recipe, but there are also a lot of variations out there.

Al Cairoli
Via Cairoli 16, Ravenna

ATTILIO AND RAFFAELLA'S RECIPE

Piadina

MAKES 6 TO 8 PIADINAS

500 g 00 flour
220 g water
80 g lard (official recipe)
   or 80 ml extra-virgin olive oil (alternative)
10 g salt
10 g baking powder

Sieve the flour into a bowl and add the water, baking powder, salt and lard. Combine everything in the bowl to form a dough. Place the dough on a (wooden) board. Knead well with your hands until you have a homogenous whole. Shape the dough into a ball and place it in the bowl. Cover the bowl with cling film. Leave to proof for one hour at room temperature. Remove the dough from the bowl and place it back onto the wooden plank. Roll out into a cylinder. Divide the cylinder into six or eight pieces, depending on the size of the frying pan. Each piece of dough should make one piadina. Roll out the balls of dough with a rolling pin on a work surface dusted with flour (or lined with parchment paper) to a thickness of 2 to 3 mm. Bake the piadinia one by one in a hot non-stick pan and turn the piadina over by hand so it warms evenly on both sides. The piadina should cook a couple of minutes on each side; as soon as it turns a light golden-brown with dark spots on the outside, the piadina is ready.

Put the piadina on a cutting board and fill them with ingredients such as:
• Parma ham
• soft stracchino cheese and rocket
• boiled ham and soft squacquerone cheese
• *porchetta* and rocket

FERRARA ②

I drive 90 kilometres northwest from Ravenna to the picturesque town of Ferrara. This small, charming town lies nestled behind medieval walls, a castle and renaissance palaces. Ferrara is proud of its rich history and equally rich gastronomy. I discover its valuable ingredients as I walk through the town. The cuisine is essentially wintry, with very flavourful, rich dishes that taste like the past, the renaissance, the courts and the popes. The hearty *salama da sugo*, a type of salami, is its showpiece. This sausage is little known outside of Italy and is much loved in the region. Salama da sugo is a flavourful, almost round sausage that needs to be cooked for a long time. The *pasticcio ferrarese* or ferarese pie is another dish bursting with flavour that you find on almost every menu. This pastry is filled with macaroni, meat sauce, béchamel sauce, mushrooms, truffle and nutmeg.

An ode to the pumpkin, la zucca

The pumpkin is the odd man out among these delicacies. But pumpkin is an essential part of Ferrara's cuisine, and the vegetable grows abundantly throughout the region. It is one of the many products that turned up in Italy after Christopher Columbus' voyages to America. Pumpkin seeds from Central America came to Europe through Spain.

Trattoria da Noema is located in a beautiful medieval building (1400) in Ferrara's historical district. I immediately feel right at home here. Traditional Ferrara dishes steal the show on the menu. I want to learn more about the pumpkin from this town that is home to the impressive Castello Este. I can't help but see Cinderella leaving the castle in a giant pumpkin. Luca Matteucci from Trattoria da Noemi brings me back down to earth. 'Our town's traditional main course is *cappellacci di zucca*, round pasta with pumpkin, served with butter and sage. We eat pumpkin in *tortelloni di zucca*, or pumpkin tortelloni, and as

Ferrara boasts amazing sights such as Castello Estense

a flavourful ingredient with many other types of pasta. We also use this tasty vegetable in almond cakes, in soup, sliced and baked in the oven, fried, dusted with sugar, in risotto, in gnocchi or as a puree...

Real pumpkin fans love the *sformatino di zucca* from Ravenna, a warm pumpkin pie with Parmesan cheese sauce. It's an exceptionally light dish.' That pie sounds particularly good. I accompany Luca to the kitchen to see how it's made.

Sformatini di zucca su crema al parmigiano

The owner, Maria Cristina Borgazzi, stands behind the stove. 'It's a relatively simple dish made from pumpkin puree, cream, eggs and cheese,' Maria Cristina lets me know. 'And it's a great success because it's so pure and light. One tip: work with high-quality pumpkins. For the sauce to go with the pumpkin, we prefer to use Parmiggiano Reggiano over Grana Padano . Reggiano adds that extra touch of flavour that's needed for such a subtle dish.'

Pumpkin is essential to Ferrara's cuisine

Sformatini di zucca

FOR 10 MINI PIES

the pulp of half a pumpkin
1 white onion
1 glass dry white wine
a couple of fresh sage leaves
2 sprigs of fresh rosemary
salt
pepper
nutmeg
4 eggs
fresh cream (about 100 ml)
grated Parmesan cheese (about 70 g)
breadcrumbs

FOR THE SAUCE

70 g milk
70 g cream
35 g grated Parmesan cheese

Sauté the minced onion for fifteen minutes over low heat. Add the sage and rosemary. Tie the fresh herbs together with kitchen twine so the rosemary doesn't lose its leaves. Add the diced pumpkin (cubes of ± 2 cm).

Sauté everything lightly, then add the wine and let the alcohol evaporate. Sprinkle salt over the top and cover the pot. Turn the heat all the way down. Stir occasionally and keep an eye on the cooking process. Check to see whether the pumpkin is soft enough. Remove the fresh herbs and blend everything with a mixer to a creamy pumpkin puree. Add the four eggs, cream, grated Parmesan cheese, salt, pepper, and a pinch of nutmeg and continue to blend.

Preheat the oven to 175 °C. Grease mini cake tins with butter and dust the insides with breadcrumbs. Pour the mixture into the tins until they're 2/3 full. Place the tins on a large baking tray and place everything in the oven. Pour a layer of water into the baking tray so the pies cook au bain marie. Bake for about 40 minutes at 175 °C. Remove the tins from the bain marie and let them cool before re-moving the pies from the tins.

Meanwhile, prepare the cheese sauce: heat the milk and the cream until it's not quite boiling, then add the Parmesan cheese and a pinch of nutmeg. Stir everything well with a whisk over low heat. Heat to the desired consistency.

Serve the warm pumpkin pies with a large spoonful of Parmesan cheese sauce on top.

The city of Bologna

BOLOGNA ③

I leave Ferrara and travel to Bologna, 50 kilometres further southwest. Il Chiosco is located in Villanova di Castenaso, seven kilometres from Bologna. I want to learn more about the *crescentina di Bologna*. Dania Morelli once started a piadina stall here; today, it's a lunch & dine situated in the middle of a quiet park. Here, you will find snacks such as piadine, crescentine and *tigelle* with the finest quality cured meats along with different types of cheese and vegetables.

Crescentina

'Crescentina is a puffed bread made from flour, lard, salt, milk and a leavening agent. The dough differs from piadina because it needs to rise,' Diana explains. 'When you bake the dough in oil, it puffs up; the dough is much lighter than what you would use for piadina. People used to bake the crescentine in a round, copper cooking pot suspended from the fireplace with chains. The pot would tilt, and the leftover liquid lard was collected in a smaller pan for the next dish. Nothing went to waste!'

Dania treats me to a crescentina. I take a seat at a table outside with a view of the park. I enjoy the sunshine and savour the refreshing Lambrusco wine. This crescentina tastes very light, and the cooked ham in the filling goes extremely well with the fried onion and soft cheese. I can hear myself think: this is close to paradise on earth. I have a tigella with Nutella for dessert. Because the proof of the pudding is always in the eating!

The two towers of Asinelli and Garisenda symbolise medieval Bologna

A typical puffed-up crescentina

LA GRASSA AND LA ROSSA

From Villanova di Castenaso, I drive on to Bologna's historical centre. The city is a surprising contrast between contemporary elegance and medieval grandeur. I discover a hard-working, high-tech city on the ultra-rich Po Plain with grand theatres and some of the best restaurants in the country. Here, politics is the talk of the town, and the graffiti-clad squares are works of street art.

Bologna has a whole range of historical nicknames. La Grassa, or 'the fat one', refers to its rich culinary tradition. This is where *ragù* or bolognese sauce was born. La Rossa, 'the red one', is reminiscent of the medieval terra cotta buildings with their long galleries and their love for left-wing politics.

Freshly made tortellini

Tortellini is an ancient dish

In Emilia-Romagna Christmas dinner is not complete without fresh pasta in broth. *Agnolotti, tortelli, cappelletti,* there are countless variations, but the king of the Christmas meal is the tortellino. This tradition is passed on from family to family.

Two provinces vie for the title of the tortellino's birthplace, and as with so many dishes, there's a legend associated with it. The feud between Modena and Bologna goes back a long way, but what was it all about?

Once upon a time, there was... a young noblewoman. One fine day in 1200, she was resting at the Locanda Corona in Castelfranco Emilia, which was Bologna's territory back then. The innkeeper was so taken in by her beauty that he spied on her through the keyhole to her room. His gaze fell to her navel as he rolled out a sheet of pasta, cut it into squares, filled the squares with meat, and wrapped the squares around his little finger. The tortellino was born.

Others claim it was Venus' navel. After she had spent the night in an inn, the innkeeper who was sent to wake her found her naked. The bewitched man tried to recapture her features, especially her beautiful navel, with thinly rolled-out dough. The inn where the tortellino was believed to have originated is situated in the province of Modena, but this territory belonged to Bologna until 1929. As a result, both provinces lay claim to the dish's origins.

A history lesson

Historians have placed tortellini's origins at the Christmas table at around 1200. The first literary references date from 1300, with a recipe written out in the dialect of Modena. Boccaccio also refers to them in 1348 in his *Decamerone:* 'And there was a mountain of grated Parmigiano cheese, with people standing on top who were doing nothing else but making macaroni and ravioli and boiling them in capon broth.'

The most important date is 1904. That's when the Bartani brothers took part in a fair in Los Angeles where they presented their tortellini. They had discovered a conservation method for the pasta. The tortellino has been gaining in popularity ever since. On 7 December 1974, the original recipe for tortellini in broth was registered by the Dotta Confraternita del Tortellino at the Chamber of Commerce in Bologna.

SETTECANI ④

The tortellino, or 'Navel of Venus', is typical of Emilia-Romagna. Divine or not, I haven't gotten to the bottom of this story, and so I travel to Settecani, 40 km towards Modena. Marisa Vandelli waits for me at her business, Zoello. She has made tonnes of tortellini in her lifetime. I have read and heard the legends, the poems, and the stories of historical figures and gods; and now, at Je Suis Marisa's pasta workshop, I finally get to see and feel the pasta as Marisa tells her own story.

Marisa's parents, Zoello and Imelde Vandelli started hotel-restaurant Zoello in 1938. 'I have been making pasta since I was just 11 years old,' Marisa begins. 'Heaps of tortellini passed through my hands every day. We served them to customers from all over the province. And I don't know how many romantic relationships flourished in our garden. Too many to count! Those were wonderful days. The tortellini were a set item on our menu. I have learned everything from my parents. My sister went away to study, but I wanted to keep working in the family business. We also made tortelloni, tagliatelle, lasagna and rosette by hand and using the finest ingredients from our own fields.' In 2018, Marisa and her daughter Isabella also opened a pasta shop in the indoor Marcato Albinelli in Modena with the name Je Suis Marisa. 'I don't have a French background, but I chose the name because I was reading a French book at the time,' Marisa smiles.

Marisa at work

⭐ Singing meat

Marisa: 'We briefly fry the meat for the filling, while in Bologna, the meat is added raw. We lightly fry minced pork, veal, and fresh sausage in a pan, and when the meat 'starts to sing,' it is ready. Voilà, that's our kitchen secret. We also add a generous helping of love, which makes the dish even more delicious!'

Rolling with love

Marisa: 'You make the dough with eggs and flour, very simple. You knead it into a ball. You then wrap the ball in cling film and leave it to rest in the refrigerator for 12 hours. We always used to knead the pasta by hand, but we have a machine that does that now. After the dough has rested, you roll the pasta out with a wooden rolling pin. The wood contains the energy through which our emotions are channelled into the dough, and it improves the elasticity. Nature on nature. It works wonderfully well on our tortellini.'

'You always take your ring off first so it doesn't get dirty from the flour.' Marisa has a small plate in front of her on which her ring rests while she works. 'That's how you do it,' she says emphatically.

Settecani's surrounding countryside

Ombelico – navel

A large ball of meat rests on the workbench, and the dough has been rolled out into one giant sheet cut into four-centimetre squares. Marisa places a dollop of meat filling in the middle of each square. Each square of dough is folded one by one into a tortellino. Marisa patiently shows me how to fold a tortellino. The tortellini are very small. 'The pasta is shaped like an *ombelico* or a navel, did you know that?' she asks as she folds a dough square with filling into a triangle. I nod. She presses the edges lightly. She then folds the two sides down to form a sort of valley. Finally, she twists the tortellino around her index finger and seals the ends together. Now it's my turn to try, and I soon discover that it's not as simple as it looks. Marisa (77) is incredibly fast and nimble. 'You need to seal the tortellini properly because they're not allowed to open up when you cook them in the *brodo* or broth.' She continues to fold, twist and seal. 'We used to eat tortellini every day because it contains everything,' the chef continues. 'Pasta, meat and vegetables from the broth. The broth is made from chicken or capon – castrated rooster – celery, carrots and onions. People eat it nowadays with cream as well, but that's not really my cup of tea. I can still hear my mother growl whenever people would ask her. "*Non si fa*!" or "That's not done!" she would say. Tortelloni, on the other hand, have different fillings and are made with different sauces.'

The Mille Miglia race for classic cars stops in the heart of Modena

Tortellini shaped like a navel

⭐ E allora?

I ask Marisa whether tortellini came from Bologna or Modena. 'Here, it's a tradition that's passed down from generation to generation, so it's always been ours. But this dish belongs to all of Emilia,' she says with conviction. 'There are differences between the Modena and Bologna versions. You seal the tortellino around the index finger in Modena and around the little finger in Bologna. In Modena, we use chicken broth for cooking, while in Bologna, they use capon and beef bone broth. *E allora* – So what?

Zoello
Via Modena 171, Settecani

Home of the
Italian sports car

Many customers have a bond with Ferrari or Ducati. Marisa: 'They come here to visit the factory, or the Autodromo circuit, or even the museum. We know Enzo Ferrari very well. He had a son, Piero, born out of wedlock, the child of his mistress, Lina Lardi, who lived right around the corner. Enzo would often come to eat here. My father was his confidant. I grew up with his son, Piero. We always used to play together. We even learned to ride a bike together. The third house to the left of the restaurant was Enzo's mistress' home.

Emilia-Romagna is the birthplace of Italian sports cars. Ferrari was established in Maranello near Settecani in 1929. Lamborghini, Maserati, Pagani, De Tomasco and Ducati also found a home here.

Coincidentally, I was able to watch the Mille Miglia pass through Modena during my visit. This endurance race spanning one thousand miles was run 24 times between 1927 and 1957. Today, the Mille Miglia is an annual race for classic cars. An event that still speaks to the imagination!

MODENA ⑤

Modena, the birthplace of the opera singer Luciano Pavarotti, lies 15 km further north. This world-famous tenor always came here to stock up on his tortellini or Parmigiano Reggiano before he went on tour. I visit La Consorteria in the city centre. To find out more about another local celebrity: *aceto balsamico*.

The statue honouring Luciano Pavarotti in front of Modena's Teatro Comunale

Modena's historical centre is certainly worth a visit

Il tradizionale

Elisa welcomes me at La Consorteria. 'We represent some twenty-odd artisanal products from the region,' she tells me. 'You can try and compare products from different producers here.' The balsamic vinegar in their assortment is all 'aceto balsamico tradizionale'. Elisa: 'It is a DOP product, which means that everything is produced in Modena or within 50 km of the city within the province of Modena. It's all about the grapes, the wood, the ripening and bottling process... we're talking about a very small area with a production of some 8000 litres per year, in contrast to the industrial producers from the region, with an IGP label, who produce 90 million litres per year. The balsamic vinegar you find in Belgium or the Netherlands has a IGP label. Aceto balsamico tradizionale is not for sale outside of Italy.'

No fewer than 30 bottles of aceto balsamico are displayed on a shelf. Some bear labels indicating an aging time from 12 to 25 years. The tastes range from very sweet to sour, with often surprising aromas. I am introduced to a whole new world of balsamic vinegar.

Only grape juice

Aceto balsamico tradizionale contains only boiled grape juice. Elisa: 'Nothing more. We don't add wine vinegar, colouring agents or sugars. This is pure, natural and 100 per cent grape. The label only has one ingredient: "mosta di uva cotto" *e basta!* Only grape juice. That's it! The subsequent aging process takes at least 12 years. Otherwise, it isn't awarded the DOP label. The aging process is what gives the vinegar its flavour.'
'An IGP aceto balsamico ages at least two months,' Elisa adds. 'It will contain at least three ingredients: grape juice, wine vinegar and caramel. The producer's profit is based on volume and a short production time.
Tradizionale vinegar also comes in an *extra vecchio* version. This is balsamic vinegar that has aged for at least 25 years. Even older versions exist. These are the bottles that families pass on from generation to generation. They produce small quantities, so it's not enough to make a living. The wooden barrels in which the balsamic vinegar is left to age are responsible for the flavour. The specific aromas and characteristics are determined by the wood used for the barrels. That's why the customer always has a taste before he buys something in our shop. And that makes our shop unique. You know you're buying the best.'

La Consorteria
Piazza Giuseppe Mazzini 9, Modena

Artisanal aceto balsamico is aged for at least 12 years in wooden barrels

Crescentine wedged between tigelle stones

Apennine bread from Modena

The *tigelle*, also known as *crescentine*, are a typical Modena product. I have arranged to meet Annamaria Resca and Andrea Brighenti at La Chersenta in Modena's city centre. Annamaria: 'The terra cotta stones used to bake the bread are called tigelle, but were originally called crescentina.
Tigelle is now the name for the bread throughout Italy. The half-moon-shaped crescentina is characteristic of the Apennines around Modena. This mountain bread is a traditional speciality. The preparation is very simple. You use only natural ingredients: white or wheat flour, water, lard, salt and brewer's yeast.'

Terra cotta bread

'The terra cotta tigelle stones with the raw dough in between used to be placed in the front in the fireplace,' Andrea adds. 'The different stones were piled on top of each other like a tower, with pieces of dough trapped between the stones. The heat from the fire would then bake the dough. The tigelle were terra cotta discs about 1 1/2 cm thick and 15 cm wide. Each side of the disc was engraved with geometric and flower motifs that were imprinted into the bread during the baking process.'
'The crescentina or tigella are filled immediately after baking,' Annamaria continues. 'The most traditional filling is a mixture of finely chopped lard, rosemary, gar-

lic and plenty of Parmigiano Reggiano. Today, we work with all kinds of gourmet fillings and combinations.'

'Tigelle or crescentine are timeless,' Annamaria explains. This is our traditional bread. They're very popular here in Modena. Restaurants serve crescentine or tigelle in a basket with other dishes or as antipasti.

La Chersenta
Via Luigi Albinelli 46, Modena

MERCATO ALBINELLI

'Another popular bread in Modena is *gnocco fritto*. Here in Mercato Albinelli, I meet Monica from the food stall I mentioned before, Je Suis Marisa. 'Gnocco fritto is one of the many flatbreads native to Emilia-Romagna,' Monica explains. 'It's impossible to list them all. Especially because they go by different names at different locations, such as the *crescentina Bolognese*, *torta fritta* in Parma, *penzino Ferrarese* and *chisolino* in Piacenza.
'These fried bread delicacies are very popular today,' Monica resumes. 'This is Emilia-Romagna's pride and joy. You will find them in many restaurants and trattorias and at village festivals, with *mortadella di Bologna*, *culatello di Zibello*, *coppa di Parma*, *squacquerone* or *stracchino*. Have one of these with a fine glass of Lambrusco wine, and that's when the magic happens!'

Je Suis Marisa, Stand 9/10,
Mercato Albinelli, Via Luigi Albinelli 1, Modena

Annamaria in Mercato Albinelli

NOVELLARA 6

My next stop is Novellara in Reggio Emilia, some 50 kilometres further north. Time for a wine course. I am curious about the Lambrusco that has been constantly recommended to me thus far.

Lambrusco

'Lambrusco is a very versatile wine,' Mattia from Cantine Lombardini explains. 'When you hear Lambrusco, you often think – and wrongly – of an average-quality wine. The wine has evolved; it's a refreshing, rich sparkling wine, our region's showpiece,' Mattia says with enthusiasm. 'The Made-in-Italy tradition is reflected in the large number of DOC and IGT labels. The types of Lambrusco currently on the market stem from a very long tradition. Their origins are linked to the evolution of the wild grape, Vitis sylvestris, that has always grown in the area, which now encompasses the provinces of Modena, Reggio Emilia and Parma (all three in the Emilia-Romagna region) and Mantova (in the Lombardy region).

The production technique has been perfected over time. The contribution the monks made during the Middle Ages was exceptionally valuable in that regard. After the fall of the Roman Empire and the arrival of barbarian forces on Italian soil, a form of prestigious wine-growing tradition mostly linked to monasteries and fortified towns continued to survive. During this period, the cultivation of the classic rows of grapevines that we know today was widely disseminated.

Lambrusco wine is made from the grape of the same name. Mattia: 'Lambrusco grapes are aromatic, red, and perfect for sparkling, sweet, dry and even rosé wines. Reggio Emilia's wine and cuisine, with its simplicity and quality, is a perfect match for fine cured meats, flatbreads, warm pork dishes, filled pasta dishes and cheese.

I try a dry *vino frizzante:* Il Campanone, crowned the best Lambrusco in 2019. This amazing bright ruby-red Lambrusco is elegant yet delightfully vibrant in flavour.

Cantine Lombardini
Via Cavour C. B. 15, Novellara

Vino frizzante: Il Campanone

LE MARCHE

Marche is a surprisingly beautiful and versatile region. In addition to the hills and mountains, the region boasts sandy beaches on the Adriatic side of the Umbrian-Marchigian section of the Apennines. The breathtaking Riviera del Conero, which includes Sirolo, Numana, Camerano and Portonovo near Ancona, has stunning panoramic views. Whole stretches of virgin territory are often solely accessible by sea or via footpaths through the green Mediterranean shrubland. Napoleonic forts and steep staircases that wind down to beaches together with the azure-blue Adriatic Sea form the ingredients of this heady cocktail.

National and regional nature reserves such as the Monti Sibillini and Monti della Laga are a walker's paradise with unrivalled landscapes.
Endless orchards and vineyards on the hilly slopes of Piceno stretch out as far as the stunningly beautiful Esino Valley. Farmsteads still offer the genuine hospitality and authentic flavours of days gone by.

The characteristically furnished caves at Ancona

One of the most beautiful beaches along the spectacular Riviera del Conero

Foglia

Urbino
❶

Metauro

Esino

Ancona
❷

Musone

Potenza

Chienti

Tenna

❸
Camerino

**Ascoli
Piceno**
❹

Tronto

369

Artistic towns

The artistic towns of Urbino, Ancona and Ascoli Piceno, with their magical buildings and piazzas, are a testimony to the region's grand history. Urbino's historical centre has rightfully earned its spot on the UNESCO World Heritage list. In the port town of Ancona, I visit numerous impressive historic monuments. Marche regional councillor Carlo Ciccioli is my guide. I gaze in silent awe at the fantastic Piazza del Plebiscito, the Loggia dei Mercanti, the Arco di Traiano and the Mole Vanvitelliana by architect Luigi Vanvitelli. We drive uphill to the old part of the city. The Cathedral of San Ciriaco rises high above the sea on the site of a former Greek acropolis. 'This is one of the most interesting medieval churches in Marche,' Carlo explains.

REGIONAL PRODUCTS

Marche is a region of culinary delights with an extensive assortment of regional products. Beef from the valued Marchigiana cattle breed, *carne marchigiana*, is a feather in the cap of breeders who guarantee the highest quality with a highly regulated IGP designation. Famous figures from the past, such as Michelangelo, greatly valued the cheese known as *casciotta di Urbino*. This DOP cheese, made from a combination of sheep and cow's milk, owes its fragrance to the flowers and herbs that grow here in the pastures, such as thyme. Pork is processed to produce exquisite cured meats such as Ciauscolo salami, salsiccia, Fabriano salami, Carpgena ham and much more.

The fish from the Adriatic Sea is some of Italy's finest. Regional seafood products include mussels (*moscioli*), cod, stockfish, sardines, prawns, shrimp and Venus clams.

URBINO ①

My journey starts in Urbino. This small hillside town flourished as a cultural centre in the 15th century, drawing artists and intellectuals from all over Italy and beyond. Urbino's most popular street food dish is one of those gems from the Renaissance period.

Crescia di Urbino

Valerio Piergiovanni from the restaurant Il Ragno D'Oro introduces me to the secrets of the *crescia di Urbino*. 'The shape is similar to the *piadina* from Emilia-Romagna, but how it's made and the ingredients differ,' Valerio begins. 'The *crescia sfogliata* from Urbino dates to the Renaissance period. This was a favourite dish of the Dukes of Urbino back in the 15th century.'

Valerio: 'You combine flour with eggs, milk, salt, pepper and a little bit of lard. The dough is left to rest for half an hour before it's rolled out, shaped into two layers and then coated in lard. This flaky crescia pastry is unique to Urbino. Crescia is the forefather of the millefeuille. At the time, puff pastry was a real delicacy, served mainly during festivals.'

Ragno D'Oro
Via Don Minzoni 2, Urbino

Urbino's old town centre is listed as a UNESCO World Heritage site

Perfect fillings and combinations

I talk to Pietro from Fagiolo Pizza in Urbino's town centre. The *crescia sfogliata* turns out to be quite a hefty dish. 'Every crescia weighs 150 grams on average and is richly filled. It's a meal in itself. The perfect filling is with *prosciutto crudo* and casciotta cheese from Urbino. 'In the summer, a filling with grilled vegetables and cheese is very popular. You can choose your favourite combination here. Every bar, restaurant and trattoria in Urbino has crescia on the menu,' Pietro concludes. I try a creamy crescia sfogliata di Urbino filled with crescenza cheese and rocket. The dish is rich, in part because of the lard. It's delicious, but I save the last bit for later.

Fagiolo Pizza
Via Vittorio Veneto 19, Urbino

Sunday lunch and football

I drive 100 km onwards until I'm almost in Ancona. I have been invited as a guest at casa Sandroni on the shore in Montemarciana. Today is the European football championship final. Stefano has invited his family and friends for Sunday lunch, *pranzo della domenica,* long before the game is due to start. This extensive Sunday lunch is a tradition that spans generations. And despite the many differences among Italian regions, they all have one thing in common: Sunday lunch is sacred throughout the country. Italians like to spend long hours at the dining table; they start with antipasti, or appetisers, followed by a *primo* or first course with fresh pasta or risotto, a second course with meat or fish accompanied by a side dish, dessert and finally, coffee. Stefano: 'We make the sauces and the fresh pasta the day before. Spending time together around a well-laid table gives a feeling of warmth, happiness and contentment. We also have extensive feasts for weddings, harvest celebrations and when a child is born; that's how it's supposed to be.'
'On Sunday, we make traditional dishes that reflect our culture and the region. The recipes have been handed down by our grandmothers. Sunday lunch is tradition, and we Italians love tradition,' Stefano explains. 'This day of rest follows a strict schedule for most Italian families: a morning walk, the smell of food, the laid-out table, family and friends that come trickling into the house, the lunch, the fine company and loved ones at the table, the sofa, the television, and the inevitable king of sports: football!' And today just so happens to be the spectacular final between England and Italy.

Menu at casa Sandroni

We drink a refreshing spritz and take our seats at the festively set table on the terrace overlooking the sea on the other side of the street. We sate our hunger with bruschetta and divine fish roe from Sefro, *uova di trota di Sefro.* Alessandro has prepared a delicious *inslata Russa.* This traditional cold dish originates from Belgium and Russia. Diced cooked potatoes, carrots, celery, peas, capers and gherkins make up the ingredients. The vegetables are combined with a homemade mayonnaise, and the dish is garnished with artichokes marinated in olive oil and hard-boiled eggs. This is followed by a delicious *pasta all chitarra* with plenty of garlic and crisp, fresh seafood. The main course is *sepie con pisello,* squid with market-fresh peas from Macerata (Marche). Stefano was responsible for bringing the sea to the table. And all of it was mouth-wateringly fresh and pure. Giada took care of dessert: *babà al limoncello,* or cake soaked in limoncello and garnished with fresh fruit. The lunch, the company, the food: perfect! Now for the game. After the walk, the siesta and a game of cards, everyone returns to the table. The leftovers are heated up, but no one's really hungry. Tensions are mounting. Drinks are passed around freely. Maurizio pours wines from his own Marchetti winery: a Rosso Conero, Verdicchio dei Castelli di Jesi and Metodo Martinotti sparkling wine.

The game is a nerve-wracking match with a strong Italian team ending the match with an *'Abbiamo vinto!':* 'We won!' This is followed by a lot of yelling, dancing, singing, and the honking of car horns out in the streets. The Sunday lunch gradually turns into dinner. And then all that's left is the washing up and *dolce far niente, e calcio!* In other words: doing nothing and football!

Pasta alla chitarra with seafood at casa Sandroni

Wine in Marche

The Marche region boasts excellent wines such as Rosso Conero, Rosso Piceno, and Lacrima di Morro d'Alba, Bianchello, Bianco Piceno, Passerina, Verdicchio, and much more. I visit Maurizio Marchetto for an introduction. Maurizio meets me at his domain on the outskirts of Ancona, in the heart of the Rosso Conero DOC district. The vineyards, planted with montepulciano and sangiovese grapes all face south. The grounds are home to a small castle and a large manor. Maurizio is a true gentleman. He blends in perfectly with this setting.

Maurizio's Azienda Agricola, or agricultural business, produces both Rosso Conero and Verdicchio dei Castelli di Jesi. The vineyards planted with the grapes for the Rosso Conero: montepulciano and sangiovese stretch out over the Ancona hills. In this unique region, the red grapes grow close to the sea in the shade of the Monte Conero, while the white wines are produced further inland. Maurizio shuttles back and forth to nearby Castelli di Jesi for his Verdicchio. The Verdicchio is a mild white wine made from 100 per cent verdicchio grapes. Rosso Conero contains 85 per cent montepulciano and 15 per cent sangiovese grapes.

Azienda Agricola Marchetti
Via Pontelungo 166, Ancona

ANCONA ②

It's nine o'clock in the morning, and Capitano Roberto Sandroni and his wife Alberta are busy in the kitchen of their cave. Capitano owes his name to a long-standing career as a sea captian. What do the nets have for us this morning? A few kilos of *moscioli*. These wild mussels only grow here, clustered on the limestone rocks of Conero. After washing the moscioli, Roberto prepares the fish menu that will bring friends and family to the table on the duckboards with views of the sea. And with it, everything that matters to those that live here: the sea at your doorstep, and the rocks because Ancona natives don't like beaches. They hunt for fish and shellfish among the jagged rocks. 'True Ancona natives love to fish, eat and drink,' Capitano laughs.

A LITTLE BIT OF PARADISE AMONG THE LIMESTONE ROCKS

Capitano's *grotta* is one of the last caves along the Spaggiola, a bay carved out of the immense limestone rocks of Conero. I descend a steep set of stairs and count 227 steps. The view is breathtaking. I see a brightly coloured mosaic of wooden gates and terraces among the wave-battered constructions.

⭐ Cave dwelling as a philosophy

According to Capitano, being a cave dweller is a philosophy. There are two rules: 'You never run out of work because there is always something to do or repair in the cave. And the cave is always open to everyone. You don't ever refuse someone a shower, shade and a handful of *moscioli*.' Roberto continues: 'After the war, when living standards rose, we spent more and more time at the seaside, not at the beaches, but in the caves. We came to swim under the "monumento ai caduti" the monument to the fallen in World War I. The economic boom in the 1960s ensured that people had more free time to spend, and they started to claim the caves. People came down to the shore, marked a cave with a cross, and said: "This one's mine." There were plenty of caves to go round.'

Roberto: 'The current municipal laws didn't exist back then. We got along fine with each other, and whoever felt like furnishing their cave simply did so. Those living above the caves were happy because the cave dwellers made sure that the caves didn't erode any further. We built jetties to protect the caves from the sea. We also built the stairs and the footpath.'

THE SEA IS OUR STREET

The municipality decided to do something about it and make it official. Although not a single resident had anything officially on paper, in 2011, the municipality purchased the entire area and gave the cave dwellers permission to stay there. Alberta: 'These caves give us an immense sense of freedom. We come here to cook, and we almost always eat fish because the sea is our street.'

A typically decorated cave
below the town of Ancona

On the street menu

I taste this amazing little piece of paradise on earth. Roberto and Alberta prepare the following dishes: First, a paté of grey mullet roe on toast. Capitano dubbed this dish *caviale dei poveri*, or poor man's caviar. This is followed by *alici marinate con aglio orsino*, marinated sardines with wild ramson (Allium ursinum) personally harvested by Roberto in the woods. The sardines are garnished with parsley and lemon. Roberto also serves *moscioli al naturale*, or cold mussels marinated in extra-virgin olive oil and lemon juice.

And finally, *linguine con moscioli* or linguine pasta with mussels. Which you make just like *pasta alle vongole*. You wash the mussels and then put them in a pan with onion and garlic and leave the shells to open. Once the shells are open, add the cooked linguine and chopped parsley. The mussels develop a strong flavour because they open while they're still raw. They cook in their own water instead of being boiled. According to Capitano, mussels lose a lot of their flavour if you leave them in the water too long.

Ritual

Capitano throws the mussel shells back into the sea after the meal is finished. 'We take from our street, and we give back.' It does me good to see how close Capitano feels to the cave. 'We find our meals here in the sea. We are the happiest people in all of Italy with this paradise at our doorstep,' Capitano alias Roberto concludes.

ROBERTO'S RECIPE

Caviale dei poveri, or poor man's caviar

SERVES 4 PEOPLE
150 grams fish roe sacs
salt and pepper
juice of ½ lemon
2 tablespoons
   extra-virgin olive oil

Use the roe from sea bass, grey mullet or other fish for this dish. Mackerel or red mullet are also delicious if you can find them. Use small or large fish depending on the flavour and how much work you need to put into it to remove the roe. Clean the sacs and make sure all the blood has drained out. Then, bring a pan with water to a boil, submerge the sacs in the pan and keep a steady boil going for 15 minutes.

Drain well and leave to cool. Slice the sacs, carefully remove the membrane, remove the eggs, pour them into a dish and mash them with a fork until you have a homogenous paste.

Season with salt and pepper and add extra-virgin olive oil and lemon juice to taste until you have the right consistency. If you don't plan to serve the paste immediately, store it in the fridge (eat preferably cold) in a jar covered by a thin layer of olive oil.

Spread the 'caviar' on crostini or bruschetta. The flavour is very delicate. Make sure that the bread has a mild flavour so you can still taste the caviar.

Moscioli alla selvaggia or wild mussels

SERVES 4 PEOPLE

1.5 kg mussels
3 cloves garlic
½ chilli pepper
extra-virgin olive oil

In Ancona, moscioli from the Adriatic Sea are used. You can also make this dish with North Sea mussels. Make sure that the moscioli are very clean, with gleaming shells. Place them in a covered pan over high heat. The mussels only need to open; you don't need to cook them.

Remove the opened mussels from the pan and set aside. Repeat this process until you have the desired amount of mussels.

Don't put them all in the pot at once because then they will cook. Set aside a glass containing the released mussel juice. You can pour this over the shells if there isn't enough moisture left in the pan.

Finely chop three cloves of garlic for 1.5 kg mussels. Pour olive oil into the pan, just enough to cover the bottom of the pan. Sauté the minced garlic and chilli pepper in a large pan with high sides. As soon as the garlic starts to brown, pour the moscioli and stir with two wooden spoons so the mussels are coated evenly with the condiments. Make sure your heat is turned right up!

Stir for at least three minutes and make sure that a little water is left at the end. The water you have set aside will come in handy for extra sauce. Turn off the heat and serve the mussels with the sauce while still piping hot.

If you eat Adriatic moscioli, make sure you remove the beard first.

Alessandro Ascoli

Ancona's harbour

Tutti a Tavola, con gli amici a casa mia

"Everyone at the table, with my friends at my house," is the name of Alessandro Ascoli's catering business. He makes *pollo in potacchio*, a typical Marchigian dish, at my request. We cook for friends in Stefano Sandroni's fantastic penthouse apartment with views over Ancona's harbour and the sea.

'*La buona cucina è la vita, e la compagnia*', Alessandro says. Good cooking is life and friends. 'Make your guests feel at home, and you're already halfway to a successful meal. That's why cooking and food are all about passion,' according to Alessandro.

Pollo in potacchio

'This is one of the region's oldest dishes,' Alessandro explains. 'To make potacchio, you need chicken pieces, rosemary, garlic and white wine. The name comes from the French *potage*, meaning soup. This dish came to our country in the 16th century. Sunday chicken cooked in potacchio at grandma's table is a familiar tradition in Marche.'

METHOD

Together, we make a basic sauce from garlic, peperoncino (chilli peppers), rosemary, tomatoes, marjoram, thyme, and sage. 'I add more fresh herbs for a more intense flavour,' Alessandro explains. We now place the chicken pieces in the pan, with the liver if you want, and cook everything over high heat until the meat browns. We drizzle the chicken with white wine as soon as the chicken starts to develop a nice brown crust. We then lower the heat. The moisture seeps out of the chicken. 'Once the moisture has evaporated, I turn up the heat to roast everything thoroughly,' Alessandro continues. He takes a dish with grilled potatoes, seasoned with rosemary and sea salt, from the oven. A perfect side dish for the chicken.

The doorbell rings; our guests have arrived. We set the table for six people. The chicken is truly delicious. '*Molto saporito*', 'with plenty of flavour'. I have put my heart and soul into this potacchio, as per Alessandro's recommendation. I hope the guests notice the difference. I think they do!

Ciauscolo from Camerino is tender, refined and very aromatic

CAMERINO ③

Camerino is a 70-kilometre drive inland from Ancona. This city in the Apennines borders Umbria. It's also home to the famous University of Camerino, which was founded in the Middle Ages. I visit artisanal butcher Macellaeria f.lli [=brothers] Bellesi, where a renowned salami is made: *ciauscolo*.

Ciauscolo

I find both brothers, Venanzio and Giovanni Bellesi, in the shop. They're cutting and preparing the meat while serving customers. The counter is filled with a variety of specialities made from Marchigiana beef, alongside a large homemade porchetta and other local cured meats. Salamis hang on ropes behind the counter. I recognize the famous soft Marchigiana sausages by their colour and shape. 'Ciauscoli', Giovanni confirms.

'Ciauscolo IGP is a finely ground sausage from twice-minced noble cuts such as the shoulder and loin from Italian pigs,' he explains. 'The meat is combined with red wine, spices, salt and pepper. The mixture is aged for three months in a natural casing. The salami is very soft on the inside. The IGP Ciauscolo production area encompasses several municipalities in Marche.

Giovanna places a sausage on my plate, and I cut a slice. The sausage is cylindrical in shape and measures about 6 cm thick and 40 cm long. The inside is pinkish red. Giovanni drizzles a dash of extra-virgin olive oil over the top for extra flavour. The ciauscolo is tender and delicate, with a spicy aroma and a savoury after-taste. Fabulous.

Macelleria f.lli Bellesi
Via Madonna delle Carceri 47, Camerino

Panino con braciola

I continue on my way and stop at the da Alberto food truck at the crossroads between Castelraimondo, Camerino and Pioraco. People are constantly coming and going here. 'Alberto's *braciola* sandwich is an institution for thousands of people in and around Camerino,' Sofia tells me as she and her boyfriend join me at my table. Tasty, well-seasoned and freshly roasted slices of pork on a crispy bun. That's the foundation. Alberto also serves other dishes such as homemade porchetta, sausages, and ham and cheese sandwiches. I bite into a braciola sandwich. The meat is tender, well-seasoned and incredibly tasty.

Ristoro da Alberto
Strada Provinciale 36, Castelraimondo

Ascoli Piceno

GROTTE DI FRASASSI

Before I resume my food road trip, I drive past Genga, where I visit one of the wonders of the natural world. Frasassi's underground caves are so large that they could hold Milan's Duomo. Genga's mayor, Marco Filipponi, guides me through a network of galleries, tunnels, shafts and cavities spanning five kilometres. I admire the hanging stalactites and rising stalagmites. These limestone formations form from water drops that seep and drip into the caves through the ground. These caves also harbour picturesque underground lakes, some up to 25 metres deep.

The surprisingly large Grotte di Frasassi

ASCOLI PICENO ④

I drive 150 kilometres from Camerino to Ascoli Piceno. I have arranged to meet Primo Valenti, Micaela Girardi and Giuseppe Maria de Nardis at Lorenz Café on the Piazza del Popolo. This is the home of the Oliva Ascolana Del Piceno DOP. I sit across from Primo, chairman of the consortium for this unique type of olive.

Oliva Ascolana

A plate of fried, stuffed olives appears at our table. The olive surrounding the meat gives it an incredible flavour. The queen of street food is used as a garnish for main courses and is highly popular as an aperitif and antipasto. 'The fried olive all'Ascolana is crispy, juicy and flavourful,' Primo adds. 'The centre contains 100 per cent Marchigiana meat, and the typical Oliva Tenera Ascolana is covered with a coating of breadcrumbs.'
Among the fried courgette and artichoke slices on my plate lies a small, deep-fried cube of pudding coated in breadcrumbs. 'We almost always serve this cremino with the olives,' Primo explains. 'It's sweet, but it's often also eaten as an aperitif or antipasto.' I drink a white pecorino wine to go with all this delicious food. The tone is set. We're clearly talking about quality products here. 'You can recognize the DOP quality by the way the olives are coated,' Primo says. 'Inferior Ascola olives have a thicker coating that isn't only made from breadcrumbs. The crispy, thicker crust masks what's inside.'

Lorenz Cafè
Piazza del Popolo 5, Ascoli Piceno

Spritz and oliva Ascolana

Resourceful Benedictine monks

The Ascolana olive has its roots in the Roman Empire. Giuseppe, professor of law and political science, explains that the Piceni – the region's original residents – soaked the Piceno olives in salted water in terra cotta jugs and transported them to Rome. 'Historical documents show that *il pranzo piu raffinato,* the most refined lunch, started with the *olive piceno,*' Giuseppe adds. 'The Benedictine monks at Ascoli succeeded in improving the preservation method around 500 AD. The quality of the olives improved, and they were often given as gifts to cardinals, princes and popes. *Oliva piceno* became *oliva Ascolana.*'
'But it was the inventive chefs in service of the noble houses in the 19th century that first came up with the idea of seeding and stuffing the olives,' Micaela adds.

⭐ Sparkling olives

The olive's characteristics and the recipe have been registered by the 'Consorzio Tutela e Valorizzazione Oliva Ascolana del Piceno'. I visit Ugo Marcelli's Cooperativa Agricola Case Rosse for more background information.

'You recognise the olive by its soft flesh,' Ugo begins. 'The flesh is soft yet crisp; it feels like a balloon pops on your mouth when you crush the olive between your teeth. The *frizzantino* or sparkle is typical for this type of olive. We sell the olives preserved in glass jars. They also form the basis for the famous stuffed Oliva Ascolana del Piceno DOP.'

Ugo is an agricultural engineer with his own agricultural business. Twenty years ago, he decided to devote himself full-time to the Oliva Ascolana del Piceno DOP and manage the entire *filiera* or production chain, from product to consumer, in-house.

Ugo and I stroll through his olive orchard, with the southern Marchigian hills in the background. 'Even the trees receive my undivided attention.' he tells me. 'What you give to the plants, you will get in return.'

Cooperativa Agricola Case Rosse
Contrada Case Rosse 173, Ascoli Piceno

Ugo admires the trees in his olive orchard

THE FILLING FOR ASCOLANA OLIVES

Ugo: 'After seeding the olives, you slice the olive down the middle and place the minced meat in the cavity where the seed used to be. The pre-cooked mixture contains pork, beef and a bit of chicken. It is a type of ragout to which carrots, celery, onions and fresh herbs have been added. The meat mixture is drizzled with white wine. As soon as the meat has cooled, the mixture is ground, and we add nutmeg, egg yolks and grated Parmesan cheese.

The olives are stuffed and then coated in flour, followed by lightly beaten egg and breadcrumbs. As soon as the olives are ready, they're deep-fried in plenty of (preferably extra-virgin) olive oil.

He stirs in the meat sauce and then shows me how the meat is ground down. I see the simple machines that cut the olives in half. The olives are then submerged in an egg bath and dusted with breadcrumbs. It's an artisanal production process, but everyone seems dedicated to their task. But they still have a long way to go to position and protect their product in the global market. Every year, during the second or third week in August, a festival is held in Ascoli Piceno to honour the oliva Ascolana. 'For now, you'll only be able to eat the real Oliva Ascolana del Piceno DOP in the region,' Ugo concludes.

Ascolana olives

Oliva Ascolana snack

Soaking up the atmosphere of Ascoli Piceno on the Piazza del Popolo

L'Anisetta from Meletti

The historical Caffè Meletti is one of Ascoli Piceno's draws. I order a glass of world-famous Anisetta Meletti and delve into this drink's past. Matteo Meletti, the fifth-generation offspring of founder Silvio Meletti, after who the aniseed liqueur is named, helps me discover its origins.

Caffè Meletti looks out over the Piazza del Popolo, the heart of the city. The building's soft-pink neoclassical facade is three storeys high, with a spacious terrace on the top floor. This café was the setting for box-office hits such as *I delfini* in 1960 with Claudia Cardinale and *Alfredo, Alfredo* in 1972 starring Dustin Hoffman.

A visit to this café is like travelling back in time. 'The art nouveau interior has been perfectly preserved, and that also goes for the layout, which is still in its fully original state,' Matteo tells me. The 'Anisetta Meletti' is the house's speciality. There is little room for doubt on that score. The shelves lined with bottles of Meletti and the artistic posters are a dead giveaway.

Matteo: 'This liqueur, based on aniseed and other aromatic herbs, is an original recipe from 1870 from my great-grandfather, Silvio Meletti. Only three people in the entire world know the secret recipe, which is kept in our family. And we'd like to keep it that way.'

Bartender Silvio pours me a chilled Anisette Meletti in a glass with a coffee bean, the so-called *mosca* or fly. I chew on the coffee bean after my first sip. The drink is sweet with an overpowering aniseed flavour. The coffee bean gives the liqueur a finishing touch: a hint of bitterness to offset the sweet aniseed liqueur. Wow!

'Anisetta Merletti's versatility makes it a popular addition to pastries, fruit salads, desserts, coffee and cocktails,' Matteo says proudly.

Caffè Meletti
Piazza del Popolo 56, Ascoli Piceno

Caffè Meletti

The Navigli district in Milan

Nonna Matilde from Genoa

ACKNOWLEDGEMENTS

I have met many Italians during my travels, and they have all helped shape this book in their own way. I have also had many unique encounters with people who became friends for life.

I would first like to thank Giulio Burastero, with whom I struck up a conversation as we were both stuck in a long traffic jam somewhere between Turin and Genoa. We instantly hit it off, and our friendship has continued to this day. Giulio became my guide in and around Genoa and helped me get in touch with many other important figures from this book in Liguria and far beyond. I will never forget his charming consideration.

I met Rosella Pepa through Giulio. A fiery, fascinating lady. Thank you for taking me into your home and your circle of friends. Stefano Sandroni helped me discover Italy's Epicurean side. Those delicious dinners and excellent wines on that amazing rooftop terrace with views of the harbour will always remain with me. The same goes for Sergio Capaldo from Genola.

I experienced some of my finest moments with 'Il Capitano' alias Roberto Sandroni and his wife Alberta in their cave underneath the city of Ancona. I thank Councillor Carlo Ciccioli from the Marche region for the many introductions in the cities and in several other regions. And thank you to Alessandro Ascoli for the wonderful time we spent cooking together during those magical moments.

I have also maintained valuable friendships from the 'share your garden' gardens where I parked my camper van. Stefania (Il Gerbas) was my guide in Piedmont, and I received plenty of tips from Nadia (Casa Costanza) during my travels in Veneto. Marta Barcella from Ponte Nossa guided me through Lombardy, and Lidia Sabato's advice helped me on my way in Abruzzo.

A very special thanks goes out to Giovanni Corti and Claudio Bambini from Sinalunga. I spent about half of my adult life in this village. They inspired me with a passion for the authentic *cucina povera*. As far back as twenty years ago, we were already philosophising about the Chianina cattle breed and its 'zona d'origine'. Back then, our little slice of Tuscany was yet to become famous. It must have been a foreshadowing of this journey.

Erik Verdonck's efforts were essential to the success of this book. I appreciate his support and encouragement.

I would also like to thank the staff at Lannoo Publishers. Karolien Van de Velde and Lieven Defour for their professionalism and trust in me.

Of all the various photographers, I want to thank Suzanne Simons in particular. The road was not without its bumps, but aside from the pictures, she deserves a special mention for her infectious enthusiasm and irrefutable admiration of beauty. A thank you to Myrthe Van Rompaey for her courage and endless patience with the design.

Thank you to the test panel that helped me refine the recipes. They are: Maria Canini, Tina Canini, Ramona Canini, Vittorio Canini, Lorena Canini, Chiara Vanstiphout, Nele Driesen, Viki Daems, Martine Daems, Yenthe Daems, Magda Vandebos, Kris Flossie, Chris Van Roey, Anne Vermiert, Chris Verlinden, Stephy Germano, Peggy Vuybert, Anastasia Bilozor, Mary Horbach and Bert Cuyvers.

I want to share my exceptionally warm affection for my loved ones because none of this would have succeeded without amore.

And a heartfelt thank you for the support from my husband, Giovanni Canini (Gio), and my children, Ramona, Vittorio and Lorena. Gio, thank you for your indispensable help with the photography part.

I want to say a special thank you to my parents, who have always encouraged me to try new things and who have boundless faith in me.

Thank you to my brothers and sisters for your unconditional support.

And my family-in-law and nonna Attilia, who taught me to love Italy. I thank my colleagues at Sette Piatti for the many fine years we spent together in the Italian kitchen.

Every amazing journey has to come to an end at some point. But I believe that this book hasn't marked the end of mine... this adventure has given me a taste for much, much more!

Dear Caroline,
I have taken your ode to wondrous amazement with me in every encounter and in the many stories in this book. And with it, your beloved Italy has taken you into its welcoming heart.

An idyllic place to spend the night in Ortona, with breakfast served on top of a Fiat 500

Gioia, Paola Piccioni and Annette during the England-Italy football final
Giulio Burastero from Genoa
Alberta, Stefano and Roberto Sandorini from Ancona

INDICES

Place names

Recipes

Culinary glossary

Horse meat stew in Lecce

Moscioli in Ancona

BIBLIOGRAPHY

Books

Acciavatti Giancarlo & Mirabilio Gemma, 2009, La Cucina d'Abruzzo, Terra Lannoo publishers
Ascoli Alessandro, 2021, Storie di vita e di svendite
Bacchia Paola, 2021, Italian Streetfood, Smith Street Books
Bonifazi Gabor, 2009, L'Osteria dei Pettorossi
Bunnik Miriam, Kleurrijk Liguria, Edicola Publishing
CasArrigoni, Storie di formaggi
Comune di Gandino, 2012, Gandino, La Storia, Comune di Gandino
Cooperativa Produttori Latte e Fontina, 2007, 50 anni di ricette
Cooperativa Produttori Latte e Fontina, 2008 Fontina DOP in forma
De Rooij Evert, 2018, Calabria & Basilicata, Edicola Publishing bv
De Rooij Evert, 2017, 2019, Lombardije Oost, Edicola Publishing
De Vogel Hetty, 2019, Puglia, Edicola Publishing bv
Fancello Giovanni, 2004, Sabores de Mejlogu. L'arte della cucina Sarda. Archivi del Sud Edizioni.
Felicioni M., Seghetti L., De Angelis M., 2019, Oliva Ascolana del Piceno, Piceno University Press
Gambero Rosso, 2019, Street Food del Gambero Rosso
Gambero Rosso, 2021, Streetfood del Gambero Rosso
Golding Matt, 2018, Pasta Pane Vino, Roads and Kingdoms
Mainardi Giusi, Berta Pierstefano, 2018, The Grand Book of Vermouth di Torino, OICCE
Marche Gente e terra, 2007, Banca Marche
Marche in bicicletta, Le Guide, La Repubblica,
Marche, Un territorio magico, Condé Nast Traveller
Martinelli Gianluca, 2019, Valle D'Aosta Top 100 Esperienze che non potete perdere
Mathiou Francesco, La Fontina, Dove e come nasce, IV Edizione, Cooperativa Produttori Latte e Fontina
Oliveri Maria, 2019, I segreti del chiostro, Il Genio Editore
Paardekooper Ingrid, 2019, Mooi Molise, Edicola Publishing bv
Padovani Clara e Gigi, 2013, Street Food All'Italiana, Giunti, Piccinino Fulvio, 2015,
Il Vermouth Di Torino, Storia e Produzione del più famoso vino aromatizzato, Graphot
Pirisi Rita, 2021, Sa Mandra, l' Agnello e le ricette della tradizione, La Nuova Sardegna
Porzio Stanislao, 2008, Cibi di Strada, Italia del Nord, Toscana, Umbria, Marche, Guido Tommasi Editore
Porzio Stanislao, 2017, Cibi di Strada, Il Sud. Italia, Lazio, Abruzzo, Isole, Guido Tommasi Editore
Provincia Regionale di Trapani, 2006, Piano di gestione del sito "Natura 2000" Saline di Trapani e Marsala
Rizzo Paolo, 2015, Street Food, Food District, Lit Edizioni Srl
Rossi Sergio, 2018, Focaccia genovese, SAGEP
Salento, 2018, Il Salentino Editore
Serao Matilde, 1884, (2019 edition) Ventre di Napoli. Diogene Edizioni.
Unione Ristoranti Buon Ricordo, 2021, I Ristoranti del Buon Ricordo
Valli Carlo G., 2014, Cibi di strada, C' erano una volta. Azzurra Publishing

Newspapers

Puricella Anna, 16 MAGGIO 2019, Il miglior panzerotto di Bari? Ecco quelli preferiti dai nostri lettori: (altri) 7 locali da non perdere, in La Repubblica

Online resources

www.agrodolce.it
www.britannica.com
www.buttalapasta.it
www.campania.info/napoli
www.dissapore.com/cucina/pomodori-campani-le-varieta-da-conoscere/
www.fondazioneslowfood.com
www.gamberorosso.it
www.giornaledipuglia.com
www.ilcomuneinforma.it/viaggi/16535/personaggi-famo-si-del-lazio/
www.ilgiornaledelcibo.it
www.ilpaninoitaliano.org/articolo/il-panino-secondo-di-gualtiero-marchesi.html
www.italia.it
www.italysfinestwines.it/vini-lazio
www.informacibo.it/cosa-e-pinsa-romana-ricetta
www.napolitoday.it
www.redacademy.it/cucina-romana-storia-e-piatti
www.regione.lombardia.it
www.repubblica.it
www.sardegnaturismo.it
www.siviaggia.it/idee-di-viaggio/ghetto-ebraico-roma-storia-cosa-vedere/251939/
www.strictlysardinia.com/sardinia-blue-zone/
www.taccuinistorici.it
www.tortellini.it
www.en.uniroma2.it/about/rome

PHOTO CREDITS

p. 2: Suzanne Simons
p. 6: Suzanne Simons
p. 7: (top): Tiziano Canu
p. 7 (bottom): Roberto Magli
p. 8: Suzanne Simons
p. 9: (top): Gio Canini
p. 9: (middle): Suzanne Simons
p. 9: (bottom): Kris Jacobs
p. 10: Dries Buytaert
p. 11: (top): Gio Canini
p. 11: (middle) Suzanne Simons
p. 11: (bottom): Annette Canini-Daems
p. 12: (top) Matteo Baldini
p. 12: (middle) Matteo Baldini
p. 12: (bottom) Dries Buytaert
p. 14: Gio Canini
p. 16: Suzanne Simons
p. 17: Gio Canini
p. 18-19: iStock/Radiokukka
p. 20: Suzanne Simons
p. 21: iStock/Filippo Ceccanibbi
p. 22: Suzanne Simons
p. 23 (top): Suzanne Simons
p. 23(bottom): iStock/S. Greg Panosian
p. 24: Suzanne Simons
p. 25: Suzanne Simons
p. 26: Suzanne Simons
p. 27: Suzanne Simons
p. 29: iStock/Photo Italia LLC
p. 30: Annette Canini-Daems
p. 31 iStock/Gabriele Paris
p. 32: Suzanne Simons
p. 33: Giada Paolucci
p. 34: Suzanne Simons
p. 35: iStock/e55evu
p. 36: iStock/Freeartist
p. 37: Gio Canini
p. 38: Suzanne Simons
p. 39: Gio Canini
p. 40: Gio Canini
p. 41: Gio Canini
p. 42: Gio Canini
p. 43: Gio Canini
p. 44: iStock/Marco_Piunti
p. 45: Suzanne Simons
p. 46: Suzanne Simons
p. 47: Suzanne Simons
p. 48: Suzanne Simons
p. 49: Suzanne Simons
p. 50: Suzanne Simons
p. 51: Suzanne Simons
p. 52: Suzanne Simons
p. 53: Suzanne Simons
p. 54: Annette Canini- Daems
p. 55: Suzanne Simons
p. 56: Annette Canini-Daems
p. 57: Suzanne Simons
p. 58: iStock/stocknshares
p. 59: iStock/Olga Tarasyuk
p. 60: Annette Canini-Daems
p. 61: Annette Canini-Daems
p. 62: iStock/EunikaSopotnicka
p. 63: Annette Canini-Daems
p. 64: iStock/StefanoZaccaria
p. 65: Annette Canini-Daems
p. 66: Suzanne Simons
p. 67: Suzanne Simons
p. 68: Suzanne Simons
p. 70: Suzanne Simons
p. 71: Suzanne Simons
p. 73: Suzanne Simons
p. 74: Suzanne Simons
p. 75: Suzanne Simons
p. 76: iStock/Antonel
p. 78: Suzanne Simons
p. 79: Suzanne Simons
p. 80: iStock/domeniconardozza
p. 81: Annette Canini-Daems
p. 82: Annette Canini-Daems
p. 83: Annette Canini-Daems
p. 84: Suzanne Simons
p. 85: Suzanne Simons
p. 86: iStock/giovanni1232
p. 87: Suzanne Simons
p. 88: Suzanne Simons
p. 89: iStock/eZeePics Studio
p. 90: Annette Canini-Daems
p. 91: Suzanne Simons
p. 92: Suzanne Simons
p. 94: Suzanne Simons
p. 95: Suzanne Simons
p. 96: iStock/GMVozd
p. 97: iStock/energyy
p. 98: kris Jacobs
p. 99: Suzanne Simons
p. 100: Suzanne Simons
p. 101: Suzanne Simons
p. 102: Annette Canini-Daems
p. 103: iStock/graemenicholson
p. 104: Gio Canini
p. 105: Gio Canini
p. 106: Gio Canini
p. 107: Gio Canini
p. 108: Gio Canini
p. 109: Gio Canini
p. 110: Gio Canini
p. 111: Gio Canini
p. 112: iStock/FilippoBacci
p. 113: Gio Canini
p. 114: Gio Canini
p. 115: Gio Canini
p. 116: Gio Canini
p. 117: Gio Canini
p. 118: Gio Canini
p. 119: Martinez
p. 120 (left): iStock/boblin
p. 120 (right): Gio Canini
p. 121: Gio Canini
p. 122: Gio Canini
p. 123: Gio Canini
p. 124: iStock/RomanBabakin
p. 125: iStock/Travel Wild
p. 126: iStock/Emiliano Pane
p. 127 (top): iStock/ivan canavera
p. 127 (bottom): iStock/Stormcab
p. 129: Tiziano Canu
p. 130: iStock/AlKane
p. 131: Annette Canini-Daems
p. 132 (top): iStock/pkazmierczak
p. 132 (bottom): Annette Canini-Daems
p. 133: Tiziano Canu
p. 134: iStock/marmo81
p. 135: Tiziano Canu
p. 136 (left): Annette Canini-Daems
p. 136 (right): iStock/alpaksoy
p. 137: Tiziano Canu
p. 138: iStock/kekko73
p. 139: Tiziano Canu
p. 140: iStock/kekko73
p. 141: Tiziano Canu
p. 142: iStock/encrier

ABOUT ANNET

I got married in a small, picturesque village in *bella Italia* and temporarily moved to Tuscany for my work with the Thomas More College as a guide for exchange students from the Journalism department. And so, in 2006, I became an honorary citizen of Sinalunga. My children, Ramona, Vittorio, and Lorena went to school with the 'suore', the sisters. I made a lot of friends in Tuscany. The 'amici della chianina' (Society of Friends of the Chianina cattle breed), my neighbour, who was an olive grower, and a few local chefs drew me into their culture and fascinating stories. After Thomas More, I took a post as a researcher at the Vrije Universiteit Brussels' SMIT (Studies in Media, Innovation and Technology) department. My curious nature drove me to keep searching for new challenges. I moved to Antwerp, where I dedicated my heart and soul to running Sette Piatti, an Italian catering and delicatessen shop that caters to Italophiles everywhere. All these experiences have come together in this book. Which goes to show, destiny always finds its way!

www.gustoeamore.com
www.instagram.com/annet.cibodistrada/
www.tiktok.com/@annet.cibodistrada

COLOPHON

www.lannoo.com
Sign up for our newsletter with news about new and forthcoming publications as well as exclusive offers and events.
If you have any questions or comments about this book, please do not hesitate to contact our editorial team: **info@lannoo.be**

Texts
Annette Canini-Daems

Translation
Textcase, Deventer

Photography
Annette Canini-Daems, with additional images taken from iStock

Cover & book design
Letterwerf, Klaartje De Buck

Typesetting
Rogier Stoel, rogierstoel.nl

Maps
Myrthe Van Rompaey

© Lannoo Publishers, Belgium, 2024

D/2024/45/273 – NUR 512 & 442
ISBN 978-94-014-9906-4

Street in Genova